MESTIZAJE

THE FEMINIST ART OF KATHY SOSA

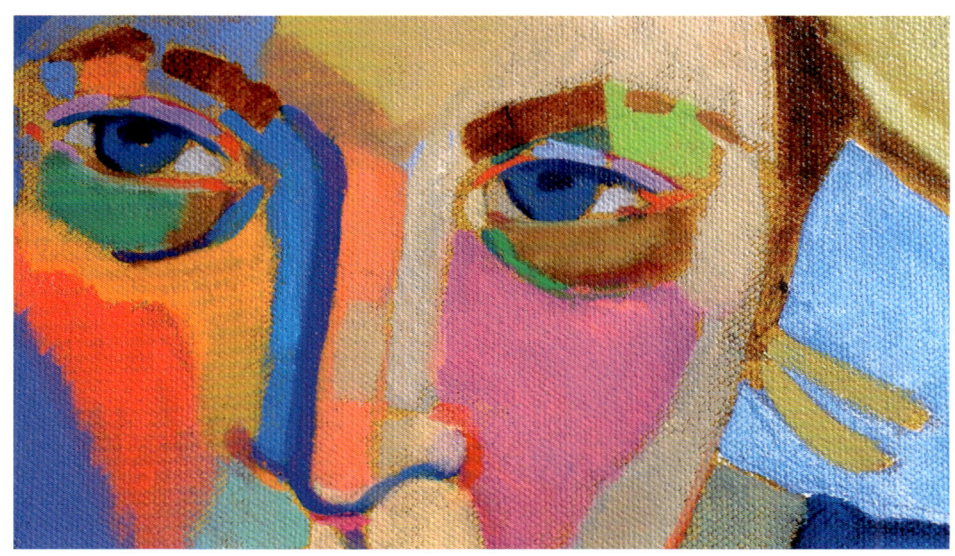

Foreword by Sandra Cisneros

Tinta Books / Trinity University Press
San Antonio

Tinta Books, an imprint of Trinity University Press
San Antonio, Texas 78212

Book design by Edgar Ortiz

Cover image: *Vamos al Flea Market—Portrait of Abuela as a Young Woman on My Mind,*
Kathy Sosa, 2020

Artist and essayist contributor notes and Tomás Ybarra-Frausto quotation translated by
Gabriela Gámez; Eleanor Heartney quotation translated by Tony Beckwith and Gabriela
Gámez

978-1-59534-315-4 hardcover

Trinity University Press strives to produce its books using methods and materials in an
environmentally sensitive manner. We favor working with manufacturers that practice
sustainable management of all natural resources, produce paper using recycled stock, and
manage forests with the best possible practices for people, biodiversity, and sustainability.
The press is a member of the Green Press Initiative, a nonprofit program dedicated to
supporting publishers in their efforts to reduce their impacts on endangered forests, climate
change, and forest-dependent communities.

The paper used in this publication meets the minimum requirements of the American
National Standard for Information Sciences—Permanence of Paper for Printed Library
Materials, ANSI 39.48-1992.

Printed in Canada

CIP data on file at the Library of Congress

28 27 26 25 | 5 4 3 2

For Lionel

The future is mestizo.

— *Virgilio Elizondo*

Contents

Foreword

Sandra Cisneros

Before Kathy Sosa became Kathy Sosa, she was once Mrs. Peña, Title I reading teacher at Washington Irving Middle School on San Antonio's West Side. "Miss" to her students or "Mama" to her two boys. And long before that, she was Kathy Chapman, teen transplant from Troy, Alabama.

From the border between girlhood and adulthood, Sosa came to live in San Antonio in 1968, when the city hosted the World's Fair and welcomed newcomers. San Antonio was an explosive big city for an adolescent looking to belong. Like most individuals launching into maturity, Sosa peered into the *nuevo mundo* laid out before her and resisted her past. She chose to cross borders, because she did not want to emulate the segregated life of her childhood. Comforted by the familiar and marveling at the new, she easily relinquished pork rinds for chicharrones, black-eyed peas for frijoles, buttermilk biscuits for breakfast tacos.

A brief foray at Incarnate Word High School inspired Sosa to abandon the austerity of her Protestant upbringing and acquire a genuine admiration for the rococo altars of Catholic saints and angels. She went through several more metamorphoses in her life, meeting remarkable situations and astonishing individuals, each inviting her to cross a border a step at a time until arriving at her current life.

This invitation to cross borders inspires Sosa's art to this day. Because the story the Alamo forgets to remember is that South Texas is particularly unique for former adversaries wedding each other. Die-hard Chicanos with gringo surnames abound, as do blond *blancas* honoring a long-ago *abuelita*, proving the universe is large enough to encompass contradictions.

Inducted twice into the Tex-Mex heritage by way of marriage and motherhood, Sosa has evolved an intriguing blend of cultures. The trees of life that figure predominantly in her paintings are ultimately portraying her own life tree, as observer and participant.

Her artwork is intensely woman centered. It's as joyous as discovering an armoire packed with precious vintage cloth. As a textile collector myself, I appreciate this. The polka dots in her art are as reminiscent of Alabama quilts as they are of Tehuantepec fabric. Turn any Oaxacan huipil inside out, and you will see the beloved dotted design. The brilliant embroidered flowers from the iconographic huipiles of the Mexican isthmus were co-opted from shawls delivered by Manila galleons that touched the shores of Acapulco after forays in China, their true source.

For the record, the beautiful lace headdresses the Tehuanas are famous for also arrived by way of colonial-era trade. They say they were originally Dutch christening gowns, until some Zapoteca trendsetter decided to wear one on her head. And how did the Bolivian Indigenous women acquire the European derby? Pull one thread, and the whole story connects one culture to another.

So it is no surprise that Sosa's art should weave new worlds to old, present to past. Are the inspirations for these angels and icons in her paintings from Saint Petersburg or Constantinople or Florence? Or perhaps from the gilded altar in Taxco? Or maybe from the Little Flower Basilica on San Antonio's West Side? It's hard to know.

What I do know is this. Sosa sees women as glorious beings. Trees of life gathered from Mexican folk art morph into crowns; ornate headdresses made of gardens raising their subjects to the status of goddesses and saints. She adds nimbi around their hair to remind us that these aren't just ordinary portraits of neighbors and friends but women distilled, women spirit filled. Maybe history ignored them, but here they are rightfully honored.

I am thinking of the late Señora María Luisa Camacho de López, a San Antonio *huipilista* who taught Sosa and me about Mexican culture. The subject of one of Sosa's paintings, our revered *maestra* shared her knowledge generously and altered our lives and art irrevocably. It is only proper that she should be exalted and remembered here. We thought her gorgeous and said so. "Ustedes me ven con ojos de amor," she would say. But that's what we do, isn't it? When we admire someone, something. See them with eyes of love.

For the art of Kathy Sosa is above all celebratory. Alive even when honoring death. Delivered with admiration. She is seeing her subjects with *ojos de amor*. There can be no higher praise than that.

Prefacio

Sandra Cisneros

Traducción por Liliana Valenzuela

Antes de que Kathy Sosa se convirtiera en Kathy Sosa, ella fue una vez la señora Peña, una maestra de lectura en la escuela intermedia Washington Irving en el West Side de San Antonio. La "miss" para sus estudiantes o "mamá" para sus dos chicos. Y mucho antes que eso, ella fue Kathy Chapman, una adolescente transplantada de Troy, Alabama.

En la frontera entre la infancia y la mayoría de edad, Sosa llegó a vivir a San Antonio en 1968, cuando la ciudad fue anfitriona de la Feria Mundial y daba la bienvenida a los recién llegados. San Antonio era una gran ciudad explosiva para una adolescente que buscaba pertenecer a algo. Como la mayoría de los individuos que se inician en la madurez, se asomó a un *new world* postrado ante ella y resistió su pasado. Sosa eligió cruzar fronteras, porque no quería emular la segregada vida de su niñez. Reconfortada por lo familiar y maravillada ante lo nuevo, renunció fácilmente a los *pork rinds* por los chicharrones, los chícharos salvajes por los frijoles y los *buttermilk biscuits* por tacos de desayuno.

Una breve incursión en la preparatoria Incarnate Word inspiró a Sosa a abandonar la austeridad de su crianza protestante y adquirir una genuina admiración por altares rococó de santos y ángeles católicos. Atravesó varias metamorfosis más en su vida, encontrando situaciones extraordinarias e individuos sorprendentes, cada uno invitándola a cruzar una frontera un paso a la vez hasta que llegó a su vida actual.

Esta invitación a cruzar fronteras inspira el arte de Sosa hasta el día de hoy. Porque la historia que El Álamo olvida recordar es que el sur de Texas es particularmente único para los antiguos adversarios que se casan entre ellos. Chicanos de hueso colorado con apellidos gringos abundan, así como blancas rubias que honran a una abuelita de hace mucho, comprobando que el universo es lo suficientemente grande como para abarcar contradicciones.

Inducida dos veces a la herencia Tex-Mex por la vía del matrimonio y la maternidad, Sosa ha evolucionado hacia una mezcla intrigante de culturas. Los árboles de la vida que figuran de manera prominente en sus pinturas retratan en última instancia su propio árbol de la vida, como observadora y participante.

El arte de Sosa se centra intensamente en las mujeres. Es gozoso como descubrir un armario repleto de preciosas telas de antaño. Como coleccionista de textiles, esto es algo que yo aprecio. Los lunares en su arte recuerdan tanto las colchas de retazos de Alabama como las telas de Tehuantepec. Voltea cualquier huipil oaxaqueño al revés y verás un diseño amorosamente punteado. Las brillantes flores bordadas de los iconográficos huipiles del itsmo mexicano fueron apropiadas de los chales que entregaban los galeones de Manila que tocaban las costas de Acapulco después de incursiones en China, su verdadera fuente.

Para que conste, los hermosos tocados de encaje de las tehuanas son famosos por también haber llegado mediante el comercio de la época colonial. Dicen que fueron originalmente ropones de bautizo holandeses, hasta que una zapoteca *trendsetter* decidió ponerse uno en la cabeza. ¿Y cómo adquirieron las indígenas bolivianas el sombrero de *derby* europeo? Tira de un hilo y toda la historia conecta a una cultura con otra.

Así que no es de sorprender que el arte de Sosa entreteja nuevos y viejos mundos, el presente con el pasado. ¿Se inspiran los ángeles e íconos de las pinturas de Sosa en San Petersburgo o Constantinopla o Florencia? ¿O tal vez en el altar dorado de Taxco? ¿O quizá en la basílica Little Flower del West Side de San Antonio? Quién sabe.

Lo que sí sé es esto. Sosa ve a las mujeres como seres gloriosos. Árboles de la vida recogidos del arte popular mexicano se trasforman en coronas; tocados ornamentados compuestos de jardines elevan a sus sujetos al rango de diosas y santos. Ella les añade aureolas alrededor del cabello para recordarnos que estos no son retratos comunes y corrientes de vecinos y amigos, sino mujeres destiladas, mujeres llenas de espíritu. Quizá ignoradas por la historia, pero aquí se les reconoce como merecen.

Me viene a la mente la difunta señora María Luisa Camacho de López, una huipilista de San Antonio que nos enseñó a Sosa y a mí sobre la cultura mexicana. El sujeto de una de las pinturas de Sosa, nuestra venerada maestra compartió generosamente sus conocimientos y alteró irrevocablemente nuestras vidas y arte. Es solo propio que ella sea aquí exaltada y recordada. Nos parecía espléndida y se lo decíamos. "Ustedes me ven con ojos de amor", nos respondía. Pero eso es lo que hacemos, ¿no es cierto? Cuando admiramos a alguien, a algo. Los vemos con ojos de amor.

Porque el arte de Kathy Sosa es sobre todo una

celebración. Vivo aun cuando honra la muerte. Entregado con admiración. Ella ve a sus sujetos con ojos de amor. No puede haber alabanza más grande que esa.

Kathy Sosa's women-centric exploration of the visual and cultural fusions and exchanges among and between world cultures is a magnum opus of the artistic imagination. Resistance and affirmation anchor diverse thematic clusters woven around the Tree of Life motif. They celebrate the tangible and intangible heritage of women anchored in transnational borderlands.

With wit and elegance, Sosa's dreamlike fantasies and meditations honor and respect the life and accomplishments of grand, larger-than-life personalities. The artist's luminous images and imaginaries remind us that traditions are simultaneously evanescent and eternal. In her paintings, installations, and works on paper, the artist documents how the marvelous is rooted in reality. Sosa's aesthetic ruminations are painted with vivid, bold, dazzling, jewellike, opulent colors.

Sosa's haunting and transformative portraits of women represent imagined worlds where nothing is so wonderful not to be true.

La exploración de Kathy Sosa concentrada en las mujeres y las fusiones e intercambios visuales y culturales entre las civilizaciones del mundo es una obra maestra de la imaginación artística. La resiliencia y la afirmación afianzan diversos grupos temáticos entretejidos en torno al motivo del árbol de la vida. Celebran el patrimonio tangible e intangible de las mujeres arraigadas en zonas fronterizas transnacionales.

Con ingenio y elegancia, las fantasías y meditaciones oníricas de Sosa honran y respetan la vida y los logros de personalidades grandiosas y extraordinarias. Las imágenes luminosas y los imaginarios de la artista nos recuerdan que las tradiciones son a la vez efímeras y eternas. En sus pinturas, instalaciones y obras sobre papel, la artista documenta cómo lo maravilloso tiene sus raíces en la realidad. Las reflexiones estéticas de Sosa están pintadas con colores vivos, atrevidos, deslumbrantes y opulentos, simulando joyas.

Los retratos inquietantes e innovadores de las mujeres de Sosa representan mundos imaginarios donde nada es tan maravilloso como para no ser una realidad.

— *Tomás Ybarra-Frausto*

Essays

A Mestizo Feminism: The Art of Kathy Sosa

Ricardo Romo

Kathy Sosa describes herself as an artist inspired by Mexican traditions, Henri Matisse, and borderland culture. She is all of that and more. Her book *Revolutionary Women of Texas and Mexico*, which she coedited, celebrates her feminist and storytelling interests. Her inquiry into Mexican huipil textiles led to an artistic collaboration with Sandra Cisneros, Ellen Riojas Clark, Liz Garza Williams, and Veronica Prida called *Huipiles: A Celebration*, an exhibition that debuted at the Mexican Cultural Institute in Washington, DC, as part of the Smithsonian Latino Center's 2007 summer season, "Mexico at the Smithsonian." She is credited with the conceptual impetus for the book *Children of the Revolución* and the documentary series based on the book. Not surprisingly, artists and writers who know Sosa describe her as creatively multitalented and highly versatile in all areas of visual communication.

Sosa came to San Antonio as a child and instantly fell in love with the language, food, traditions, and culture known as Tex-Mex. Her introduction to Mexican and Chicano art came in the early 1980s, when she was hired by an advertising firm to be the project manager for a traveling Latino art exhibition titled *¡Mira! The Canadian Club Hispanic Art Tour, 1983–1984.*

Sosa began painting in midlife. She is self-taught but readily acknowledges that her initial interest in painting was the result of watching her husband, Lionel, his brother Robert, and artistic friends gather on Sundays to paint in the Sosas' home studio. One day she asked if she could finish a farcical painting of the family dog that Lionel had grown bored with. Then she painted more dogs, and they sold. As her interest in painting grew, she joined Lionel in Philadelphia to participate in Studio Incamminati workshops with famed artist Nelson Shanks and a group of his student teachers that included Kerry Dunn. Dunn's main focus is on painting people and using "line, form, and color to communicate character, storytelling, and spirit." Studying with world-class artists and instructors can be intimidating, but the workshops proved illuminating and helped prepare Sosa for an artistic career. Dunn has since become the Sosas' lifelong friend and teacher.

Painters seek inspiration and summon conceptual ideas from many sources. Sosa found a life-changing opportunity for artistic expression when she traveled to Oaxaca in 2004. As Lionel and Kathy visited the Oaxacan villages and markets, she found herself drawn to the indigenous woven garments known as huipiles.

The huipil is a dress or top worn in indigenous regions of southern Mexico and Guatemala that predates the Spanish Conquest of 1521. Evidence of the ancient tradition of the huipil was preserved in the codices of the Maya and Aztecs. Hernán Cortés's translator, Doña Marina, also known as La Malinche, is pictured in the Florentine Codex wearing a huipil. The intricately woven huipiles triggered Sosa's artistic ambition, leading to a new artistry and expressiveness in her paintings.

Sosa's paintings are also influenced by the legendary French painter Henri Matisse. *Matisse: The Fabric of Dreams—His Art and His Textiles*, an exhibition exploring the artist's prodigious integration of fabrics into his paintings at New York's Metropolitan Museum of Art in 2005, was a turning point, profoundly validating her desire and intention to integrate Mexican textiles into her art. Also in 2005, as Sosa painted women with fabric or Mexican iconic backgrounds, she was struck by the powerful image of the *árbol de la vida*, the Tree of Life, which she first encountered in *Ceramic Trees of Life: Popular Art from Mexico* by Lenore Hoag Mulryan with contributions from Marta Turok and others. Sosa drank in the photographs and the text in this book and later, through folk art dealers Amy and Bob Niederhauser, the original sculptures of Mexican ceramic masters like Aurelio Flores, Herón Martinez, and Alfonso Castillo. She successfully converted these Tree of Life images to canvas, blending them with women's images in colorful portraits that she began to exhibit in 2009.

It was a career highlight when in 2016 Sosa was invited to meet and participate in a two-woman show with Verónica Castillo, master of the ceramic árbol de la vida and daughter of Alfonso Castillo.

For Sosa's most recent commissioned art project, a monumental work of public art for Bexar County, Texas, she joined her husband, Lionel, to create artistic mural panels on the concrete banks of San Pedro Creek in San Antonio near the famed Teatro Alameda. Unveiled in fall 2022, these works feature trees of life adorned with Latino cultural icons. The murals started as paintings and then were photographed and transferred to porcelain tile, which can withstand severe weather and periodic flooding and outlast traditional painted murals. There are five murals, each twenty-six feet wide and fifteen feet high, with large human figures at the bottom and a thought bubble behind the figures telling the stories of five themes: foundation, conquest, separation, inundation, and restoration.

Many of the women Sosa paints identify as mestiza, representing a blend of two worlds, generally Mexicans with Indian and European heritage. The concept of *mestizaje*, however, is more complex than biological identity.

A definition is offered by a team of scholars from the pedagogical website English Studies. They write: "[Mestizaje] represents the intricate blending of Indigenous, European, and African heritages, resulting in diverse racial identities and the fusion of cultural elements, including languages and customs."

John Philip Santos, professor of mestizo studies at the University of Texas at San Antonio, detailed his definition of *mestizaje* in a 2011 interview with Chuck Mejia of the UTSA publication *Spectrum*, noting his interest in "the extent to which *mestizaje* is a process and how *mestizo* identities, as a framework, applies to a whole series of cultural expressions in the era of globalization." Santos suggests that the idea of mestizaje "is proving to be, in fact, a kind of a fundamental process in not only shaping out what Mexico, Texas, and especially South Texas have become, but what America has always been."

Feminismo mestizo: El arte de Kathy Sosa

Ricardo Romo

Traducción por Gabriela Gámez

Kathy Sosa se describe a sí misma como una artista inspirada en las tradiciones mexicanas, Henri Matisse y la cultura fronteriza. Ella es todo eso y más. Su libro de reciente edición, *Revolutionary Women of Texas and Mexico*, que ella coeditó, celebra sus inquietudes feministas y narrativas. Su interés por los textiles de los huipiles mexicanos la llevó a una colaboración artística con Sandra Cisneros, Ellen Riojas Clark, Liz Garza Williams y Veronica Prida llamada *Huipiles: A Celebration*, una exhibición que debutó en el Instituto Cultural de México en Washington, DC, como parte de la temporada de verano 2007 del Centro Latino Smithsonian, "México en el Smithsonian". Se le atribuye el impulso conceptual del libro *Children of the Revolución* y la serie documental basada en el libro. No es de extrañar que los artistas y escritores que conocen a Sosa la describan como una creativa polifacética y versátil en todas las áreas de la comunicación visual.

Sosa llegó a San Antonio cuando era niña y al instante se enamoró del idioma, la comida, las tradiciones y la cultura conocida como Tex-Mex. Su introducción al arte mexicano y chicano se produjo a principios de la década de 1980, cuando una empresa de publicidad la contrató para ser la directora de proyectos de una exposición itinerante de arte latino titulada *¡Mira! The Canadian Club Hispanic Art Tour, 1983–1984*.

Sosa comenzó a pintar en la madurez. Es autodidacta, pero reconoce con facilidad que su interés inicial por la pintura fue el resultado de ver a su esposo, Lionel; al hermano de éste, Robert, y otros amigos artistas reunirse los domingos para pintar en el estudio de la casa de los Sosa. Un día, solicitó permiso para terminar un retrato farsesco del perro de la familia del que Lionel había perdido interés. Luego pintó más perros y los vendió. A medida que crecía su inclinación por la pintura, se unió a Lionel en Filadelfia para participar en los talleres de Studio Incamminati con el famoso artista Nelson Shanks y un grupo de sus profesores estudiantes que incluía a Kerry Dunn. El enfoque principal de Dunn es pintar personas y usar "líneas, formas y colores para comunicar carácter, narrativa y espíritu". Estudiar con artistas e instructores de talla mundial puede resultar intimidante, pero los talleres resultaron esclarecedores y la ayudaron a prepararse para una carrera artística. Desde entonces, Dunn se ha convertido en amigo de toda la vida y maestro de los Sosa.

Los pintores buscan inspiración y reúnen ideas conceptuales de muchas fuentes. Sosa encontró una oportunidad de expresión artística que le cambió la vida cuando viajó a Oaxaca en 2004. Mientras Lionel y Kathy visitaban los pueblos y mercados de Oaxaca, ella se sintió atraída por las prendas indígenas tejidas, conocidas como huipiles.

El huipil es una blusa o vestido usado en las regiones indígenas del sur de México y Guatemala que es anterior a la conquista española de 1521. La evidencia de la antigua tradición del huipil se conserva en los antiguos códices de los mayas y aztecas. La traductora de Hernán Cortés, doña Marina, también conocida como La Malinche, aparece representada en el Códice Florentino vistiendo un huipil. Los huipiles intrincadamente tejidos desencadenaron la ambición artística de Sosa, lo que la llevó a una nueva maestría y expresividad en sus pinturas.

Las pinturas de Sosa también están influenciadas por el legendario pintor francés Henri Matisse. *Matisse: The Fabric of Dreams—His Art and His Textiles*, una exposición que exploró la prodigiosa integración de las telas en sus pinturas en el Museo Metropolitano de Arte de Nueva York en 2005, fue un punto de inflexión, validando profundamente su deseo e intención de integrar los textiles mexicanos a su arte. Ocurrió también en 2005, mientras pintaba mujeres con telas o fondos emblemáticos de México, que Sosa quedó impactada por la poderosa imagen del árbol de la vida que encontró por primera vez en *Ceramic Trees of Life: Popular Art from Mexico* de Lenore Hoag Mulryan con contribuciones de Marta Turok y otros. Sosa se sumergió en las fotografías y el texto del libro y más tarde, a través de los comerciantes de arte popular Amy y Bob Niederhauser, las esculturas originales de los maestros ceramistas mexicanos como Aurelio Flores, Herón Martínez y Alfonso Castillo. Sosa convirtió con éxito estas imágenes del árbol de la vida en lienzos, combinándolas con coloridas imágenes de retratos de mujeres, que comenzó a exhibir en 2009.

Un punto culminante en su carrera ocurrió cuando en 2016 Sosa fue invitada a conocer y participar en una exhibición de dos mujeres con Verónica Castillo, maestra ceramista de árboles de la vida e hija de Alfonso Castillo.

El proyecto artístico más reciente de Kathy Sosa ha sido la comisión de una obra monumental de arte público para el condado de Bexar, Texas; en éste se unió a su esposo, Lionel, para crear murales artísticos en paneles sobre los muros de contención de concreto del arroyo San Pedro en San Antonio, cerca del famoso Teatro Alameda. Estas obras, develadas en el otoño de 2022, muestran árboles de la vida decorados con íconos de la cultura latina. Los murales comenzaron como pinturas, fueron fotografiados y luego transferidos a azulejo porcelanizado, diseñado para resistir condiciones climáticas adversas, inundaciones periódicas y para durar más que los murales pintados tradicionales. Hay cinco murales, cada uno de veintiséis pies de ancho y quince pies de altura, con grandes figuras humanas en la parte inferior y globos de diálogo detrás de las figuras que cuentan las historias de cinco temas: fundación, conquista, separación, inundación y restauración.

Muchas de las mujeres que pinta Sosa se identifican como mestizas, representando la mezcla de dos mundos, generalmente mexicanas con herencia indígena y europea. Sin embargo, el concepto de mestizaje es más complejo que la identidad biológica.

Un equipo de académicos del sitio web pedagógico English Studies ofreció una definición. Escribieron: "[Mestizaje] representa la intrincada mezcla de herencias indígenas, europeas y africanas, resultando en diversas identidades raciales y la fusión de elementos culturales, incluyendo idiomas y costumbres".

John Philip Santos, profesor de estudios mestizos en la Universidad de Tejas en San Antonio, detalló su definición de *mestizaje* en una entrevista en 2011 con Chuck Mejía de la publicación de la UTSA, *Spectrum*, señalando su interés en "hasta qué punto el mestizaje es un proceso y cómo las identidades mestizas, como marco, se aplican a toda una serie de expresiones culturales en la era de la globalización". Santos sugiere que la idea de mestizaje "está demostrando ser, de hecho, una especie de proceso fundamental no solo para dar forma a lo que México, Texas y especialmente el sur de Texas se han convertido, sino lo que Estados Unidos siempre ha sido".

Kathy Sosa: Cosmic Race Portraiture

Carla Stellweg

1. Reference to the 1925 book *La raza cósmica* by José Vasconcelos (1882–1959), who has been called the "cultural caudillo" of the Mexican Revolution. An important Mexican writer, philosopher, and politician, Vasconcelos is one of the most influential and controversial personalities in the development of modern Mexico. His philosophy of the "cosmic race" affected all aspects of Mexican sociocultural, political, and economic policies.

The paintings of Kathy Sosa present brilliantly colored figures that are tightly woven into their backgrounds, much as traditional folkloric patterns are loomed together into a single textile. The subjects of her artworks may be contemporary women, but the handling of the paint describes a vibrant patchwork of interlocking colors, forms, and planes that strengthen the image and create a solid, faceted unit. Equal value is given to the portrait likeness, as well as to the environment in which the model is posing, as if to indicate that all protagonists are inseparably woven into their respective environments and personal histories. Shadows are represented not by value as much as by hue, and the figure is supported in a solid surrounding space. This bold warp and weft of pigment, mark, and shape creates a glowing and robust representation that not only transcends likeness but makes manifest the inner spirit.

In fact, it is the spirit world that is the true subject of Sosa's work. With trees growing out of women's heads and whirlwinds of saturated color, this kaleidoscope of space evokes the magical realism of Latin American writers such as Gabriel García Márquez and Isabel Allende. Works in the *Trees of Life*, *52*, *Huipiles*, and *Árboles mariposa* series may be grounded in reality, yet they all share an undercurrent of authentic fantasy.

One of the stories told by Sosa's artwork is about social context. These contemporary portraits depict the America of our lifetime, an America that shifts as one travels from east to west or north to south. Her work does what all the best of portraiture does, presenting us with a specific moment of social history. In both her paintings and her collages there is alteration between a Mexican or Tejano-borderland inspiration understood through a contemporary Western filter. This melting pot, or *crisol*, of cultures is charged with historically conflicting assumptions about race, class, and personal identity. This combination of traits is prominently present in Sosa's portraits, like *Ángel del Árbol No. 2 on My Mind Night Sky Angel* or *Árbol Blanco No. 3 on My Mind Nopalitos Varios*, both from her *Trees of Life* series (2008–ongoing), the titles of which point to the rich and peculiar variety of US borderland visual and verbal *mestizaje*.[1]

In the series *52* (2018) and *Face Painting* (ongoing), Sosa presents a collection of female portraits. As we look beyond the surface of Sosa's *52*, in which the artist took on the challenge of painting one face per week for a year, the sitters boldly return our gaze and confront us with questions of how we see ourself in public: Does this differ from our idea of self in private? To what extent is the face we have a mask? And what is the true identity of a person? García

Márquez said that "all human beings have three lives: public, private, and secret." The ever-shifting shards of Sosa's pictorial space created by her use of color bring these three alternating characteristics to the fore within each painting. The choice of these women vacillates between the specific and the symbolic: specific in that each likeness is too uniquely detailed to be random and symbolic in that they represent a global survey of contemporary women holding their space.

In another series of women's portraits, the *Face Paintings*, the viewer will observe a multiplicity of identities. These women, fiercely painted with bold colors on equally vibrant backgrounds, are united in strength. Individual portraits are inspired by specific women, including Sosa herself, each with their unique distinguishing features. Identity is, and always has been, a suspect construction in which some traits are visible, others are hidden, and the rest is intuited. Varied mask traditions around the world, such as those in Mexico or in Japanese Noh theater, evoke these forthright character likenesses. These can be seen in Sosa's *No. 9* and *No. 25* paintings (2018) and in *Las Máscaras* (2005), artworks that explore to what extent we all wear masks and to what extent these masks can be seen through.

Magical realism also plays a strong role in Sosa's paintings. Trees, like thoughts made manifest, grow from women's heads, and elegant folkloric dress patterns and powerful background shapes seem to embody the personal history of each painted subject. The overall pictorial flatness in most of Sosa's imagery enables her figures to reside on surfaces that unite her work with contemporary painting. In several works from the *Huipiles* series (2005–2008), however, the background surfaces are a rich layer of allegory, such as those found on painted colonial wood-carved saints or patterns of indigenous loom weavings made by country women for the market. The symbols in Sosa's paintings and collages take us further back, to examples of Italian Renaissance Madonnas and the symbols of each item of clothing, gesture, and position that ultimately refer to a narra-

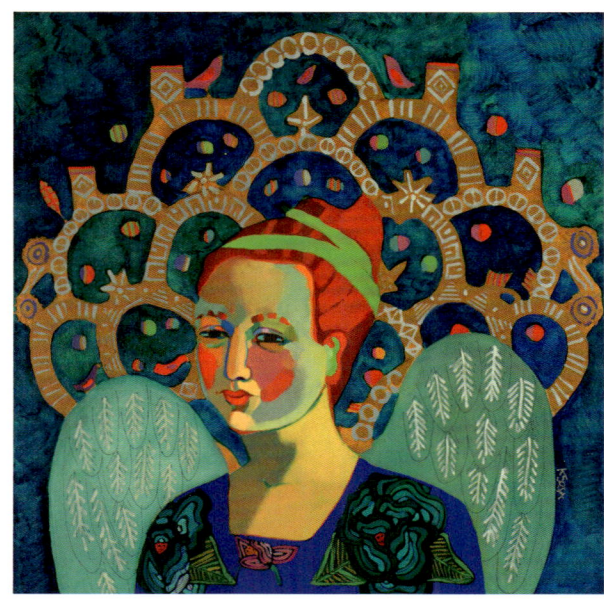

Ángel del Árbol No. 2 on My Mind Night Sky Angel

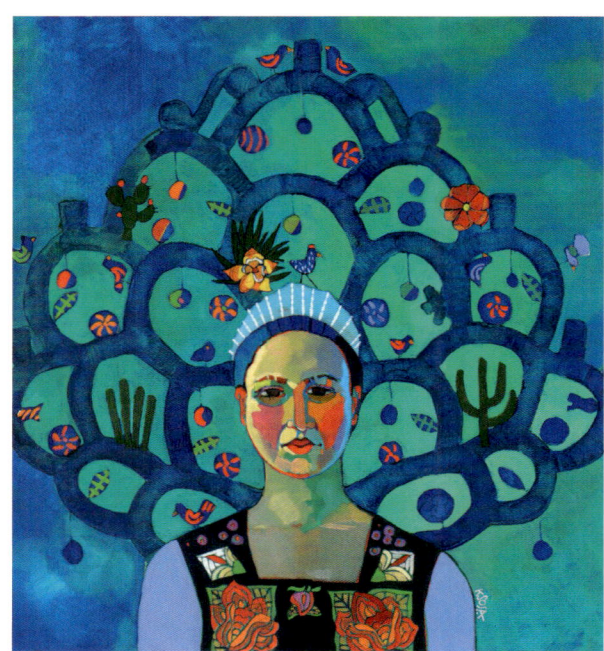

Árbol Blanco No. 3 on My Mind Nopalitos Varios

2. Originally used during the early colonial period, the Tree of Life iconography was intended to indoctrinate and teach the gospel to the Indigenous population of Mexico. The first Trees of Life illustrated biblical passages, such as the story of Adam and Eve. What began as a mechanism to evangelize the native population over the centuries became an often wild fusion of Spanish and indigenous techniques and designs.

tive that guides the painter and inspires the viewer.

Sosa's subjects are for the most part painted on backgrounds that reduce visual noise in order to focus the viewer's attention on their faces, which are topped by heavily adorned headdresses. What strikes the viewer is that they all stare right back at us, heightening our consciousness of looking and being looked at. This is Sosa's method: she has portrayed a distinct body of individuals for years, and as we look more deeply we realize that their idiosyncrasies elicit backstories we as viewers can only guess at. As such, Sosa's art becomes a kind of narrative quiz, anchored in storytelling, that we, her viewers, are left trying to complete by ourselves, as though she is presenting us with unfinished scripts.

Fashion and portrait photography also play a role and clearly influence Sosa's compositions, starting with the clothing her figures are wearing. Rarely drab, they feature dazzling patterns in bright colors that contrast and add fascinating oscillations between flatness and illusions of form, as in *Señora López, Somos Huipilistas*, and *Olivia's Offering* (2005). This hovering between the literal realism of the observed world and the introduction of the fantastic captures the oneiric experience of straddling both dimensions at once: the perceived and the intuited.

In her *Trees of Life* series, Sosa has clearly let her imagination run loose, traveling far and in distinctly varied directions while bringing to life a dreamlike narrative, much like that created by the original árbol de la vida artisan ceramists of Metepec, Mexico, whose fantasy and detailed figures weave together surrealism with utility. Sosa's titles point to those connections, as in *Archangel Contemplating Creation on My Mind* and *Corazón on My Sleeve on My Mind* (2020) or *Ángel del Árbol No. 2 on My Mind Night Sky Angel* (2015).[2]

Visual art is almost always a translation of impressions of the physical world, on a continuum that ranges from the most realistic of figurative practices, such as Sosa's artwork, through the most abstract or nonrepresentational concepts. These two endpoints are often portrayed as being in opposition. Prior to

the emergence of abstract art, however, the illusion of visible reality had been at the core of Western art-making practices, with artists getting ever more accurate in depicting real things or people in real spaces. Modernism unharnessed this obligation to make realistic depictions of the physical world. The conventional modern art narrative presents a contentious shift from figuration into nonobjective abstract art, creating a gap between the two. Only in the last part of the twentieth century would this intellectual wound separating abstraction and figuration begin to mend as artists such as Sosa emerged who embraced both. Today we can appreciate how the historical conflicts between the languages of figuration and abstraction ultimately enabled artists of the present moment to be "bilingual" and work in either abstract or figurative art—a consideration particularly relevant in Sosa's case, as she bridges this gap and resolves the paradox.

Sosa's art is about storytelling: each color, brush-

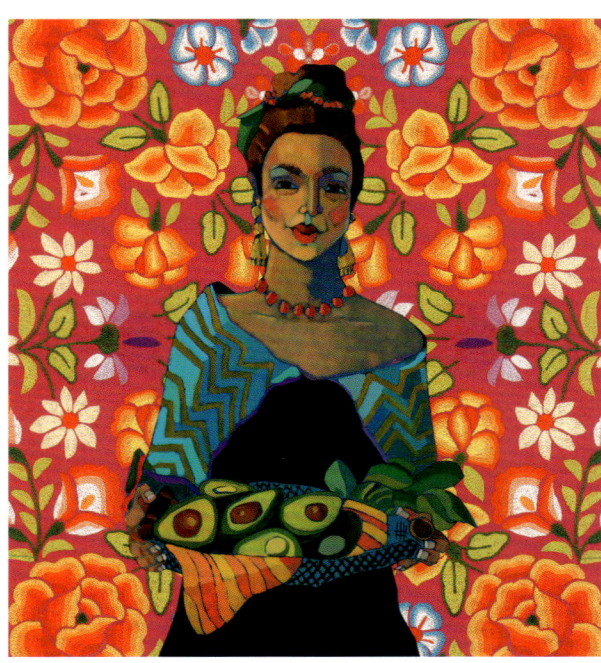

Olivia's Offering

stroke, and texture serves to construct the character and the real material presence of the subject. Equal value is given to the portrait likeness and the environment where the sitter is posing, as if to indicate that all protagonists are inseparably woven into their respective environments and personal histories. Taken in their entirety, Sosa's paintings and collages present us with a dazzling and uplifting opportunity to participate in this magical world of color, share her borderland portrait stories, and see the origins of contemporary women, all of whom echo García Márquez's sentiment: "It's enough for me to be sure that you and I exist at this moment."

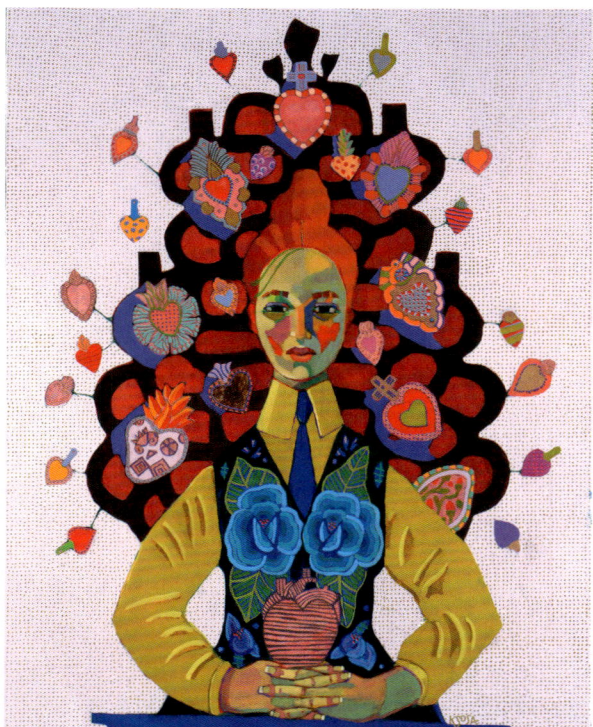

Corazón on My Sleeve on My Mind

Kathy Sosa: Retratos de la raza cósmica

Carla Stellweg

Traducción por Tony Beckwith y Gabriela Gámez

1. Referencia al libro de 1925 *La raza cósmica* de José Vasconcelos (1882–1959), conocido como el "caudillo cultural" de la Revolución Mexicana, un escritor, filósofo y político mexicano de gran importancia. Es una de las figuras más influyentes y polémicas en el desarrollo del México moderno. Su filosofía respecto a la "raza cósmica" tuvo un impacto generalizado en México a nivel sociocultural, político y económico.

Las pinturas de Kathy Sosa presentan figuras de colores brillantes firmemente entrelazadas con el fondo, tal como los tejidos populares tradicionales se plasman en una trama determinada. Si bien los temas de sus obras son mujeres contemporáneas, su manejo de la pintura describe un laborioso y vibrante mosaico de colores, formas y planos entretejidos que intensifican la imagen para crear una unidad sólida y facetada. Se le concede igual valor al retrato que al entorno en el cual está posada la modelo, como para indicar que todas las protagonistas viven entrelazadas en sus respectivos ambientes e historias personales. Las sombras se presentan, no por trascendencia, pero por matiz, y la figura descansa sobre un espacio sólido que la rodea. Esta maniobra audaz y entramada de pigmento, traza y forma crea una representación resplandeciente y robusta que no solo trasciende el parecido, sino que manifiesta el espíritu interior del personaje.

De hecho, el mundo de los espíritus es el tema real de la obra de Sosa. Entre mujeres con árboles creciéndoles en la cabeza y torbellinos saturados de colores, este caleidoscopio espacial evoca el realismo mágico de escritores latinoamericanos como Gabriel García Márquez e Isabel Allende. Aunque obras en las series *Trees of Life, Faces, Huipiles* y *Árboles mariposa* son fundamentadas en la realidad, todas comparten un trasfondo de auténtica fantasía.

Uno de los relatos contados por las pinturas de Sosa se centra en el contexto social. Estos retratos contemporáneos representan la América de nuestra vida, una que cambia al recorrerla del este al oeste o del norte al sur. La obra de Sosa alcanza lo que consiguen los mejores retratos: presentarnos ante un momento específico de la historia social. En sus pinturas, como en sus collages, es notorio el cambio entre la inspiración mexicana y la de la zona fronteriza texana, leídas a través de un filtro occidental contemporáneo. Este crisol cultural, o *melting pot*, está cargado de suposiciones históricamente contradictorias en cuanto a raza, clase e identidad individual. Esta combinación de características destaca en los retratos de Sosa, como *Ángel del Árbol No. 2 on My Mind Night Sky Angel* o en *Árbol Blanco No. 3 on My Mind Nopalitos Varios*, ambos de la serie *Trees of Life* (2008–a la fecha), cuyos títulos reflejan la rica y peculiar variedad de mestizaje[1] visual y verbal propia de la zona fronteriza de Texas.

En las series *52* (2018) y *Face Painting* (en curso), Sosa presenta una colección de retratos de mujeres. Cuando observamos más allá de la superficie de *52*, en la que el artista asumió el reto de pintar una cara por semana durante un año, las modelos nos devuelven audazmente la mirada, animándonos a explicar cómo es que nos vemos en público: ¿Es distinto a cómo nos vemos en privado? La cara que tenemos, ¿hasta qué punto es una máscara? Y ¿cuál es la verdadera identidad de una persona determinada? García Márquez decía: "Todos los seres humanos tenemos tres vidas: la pública, la privada y la secreta". Los fragmentos en movimiento constante del espacio pictórico de Sosa, creados por su empleo del color, logran destacar estas tres características alternas en cada cuadro. La selección de estas mujeres oscila entre lo específico y lo simbólico: específico, porque cada semejanza está trabajada de manera tan singular que no podría ser aleatoria, y simbólico, en el sentido de que representan un estudio global de mujeres contemporáneas que mantienen su espacio.

En otra serie de retratos de mujeres, los *Face Paintings*, el espectador nota una gran diversidad de identidades. Estas mujeres, extraordinariamente pintadas con colores llamativos sobre fondos igualmente vibrantes, encuentran su unidad en la fuerza. Estos retratos individuales fueron inspirados en mujeres determinadas, incluida la artista, cada una con sus rasgos únicos. La identidad es, y siempre ha sido, una interpretación muy sospechosa en la cual hay rasgos visibles y ocultos, y lo demás es intuitivo. Estos parecidos semejantes de los personajes se inspiran de las distintas tradiciones en torno a las máscaras en todo el mundo, como las de México o el teatro nō japonés que aparecen en sus pinturas *No. 9* y *No. 25* (2018) o en *Las máscaras* (2005). Estas obras nos muestran hasta qué punto todos usamos máscaras y hasta qué punto esas máscaras resultan transparentes.

El realismo mágico también desempeña un papel importante en las pinturas de Sosa. Árboles crecen en las cabezas de las mujeres como manifestaciones de sus pensamientos, y tanto los elegantes estampados artesanales de los vestidos como las impactantes figuras en el fondo parecen encarnar la historia íntima de cada modelo. El efecto plano que destaca en casi todas las imágenes que pinta Sosa da lugar a que sus figuras descansen sobre superficies que aúnan su obra con la pintura contemporánea. Sin embargo, en varias obras de la serie *Huipiles* (2005–2008), las superficies del fondo consisten en una rica capa alegórica, similar a las que se ven en los estofados novohispanos de santos o en los diseños tejidos en telares artesanales indígenas por campesinas para vender en los mercados y plazas. La simbología en las pinturas y los collages de Sosa nos remontan aún más al pasado, a ejemplos de las madonas del Renacimiento italiano y al simbolismo de cada prenda, gesto y postura que, a fin de cuentas, remiten a una narrativa que orienta a la pintora e inspira al espectador.

La mayoría de los retratos de Sosa están pintados sobre fondos que reducen el ruido visual con el fin de concentrar la atención del espectador en los rostros, coronados con tocados abundantemente decorados. Lo que llama la atención del espectador es que todas ellas nos miran fijamente, intensificando nuestra consciencia de ver y ser vistos. Este es el método de Sosa: desde hace años esta artista ha representado un conjunto definido de personajes y, al ampliar nuestra mirada, nos damos cuenta de que sus idiosincrasias sugieren antecedentes que, como espectadores, apenas logramos adivinar. En este sentido, el arte de Sosa se convierte en una especie de juego de preguntas y respuestas, anclado en la narrativa de cuentos, que a nosotros, los espectadores, nos toca completar, como si nos hubieran presentado unos guiones sin terminar.

La moda y el retrato fotográfico también son factores determinantes en las composiciones de Sosa, empezando por el vestuario que llevan sus modelos. Estas prendas, raramente monótonas, se distinguen por sus diseños deslumbrantes en colores vivos que contrastan con y oscilan de manera fascinante entre lo plano y la forma, como en *Señora López*, *Somos huipilistas* y *Olivia's Offering* (2005). Esta fluctuación entre el realismo literal del mundo observado y la introducción de lo fantástico refleja la experiencia onírica de manipular ambas dimensiones a la vez: lo percibido y lo intuido.

En su serie titulada *Trees of Life*, queda claro que Sosa ha dado rienda suelta a su imaginación, dejándola volar muy lejos en distintas direcciones para animar una narrativa de ensueño que recuerda la tradición original característica de los artesanos ceramistas del árbol de la vida de Metepec, México, cuya

2. Empleado originalmente durante el período colonial temprano, el árbol de la vida sirvió para adoctrinar y enseñar el evangelio a la población indígena de México. Los primeros árboles de la vida ilustraron pasajes bíblicos, así como la historia de Adán y Eva. Al correr de los siglos este mecanismo destinado a evangelizar a la población se transformó a menudo en una fusión alocada de técnicas y diseños españoles e indígenas.

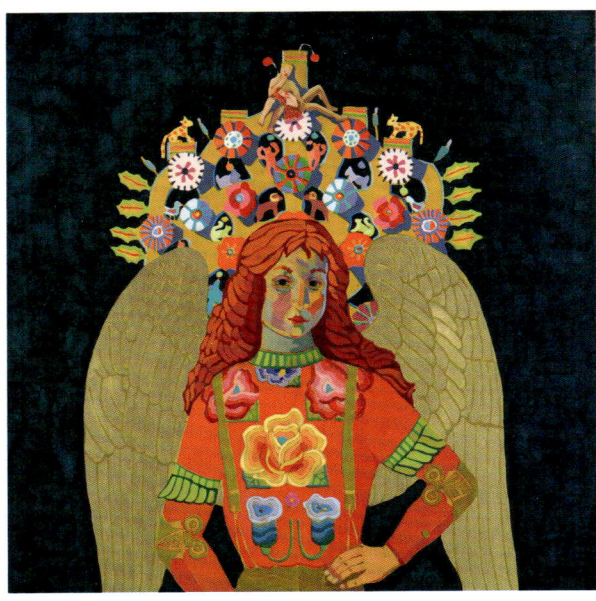

Archangel Contemplating Creation on My Mind

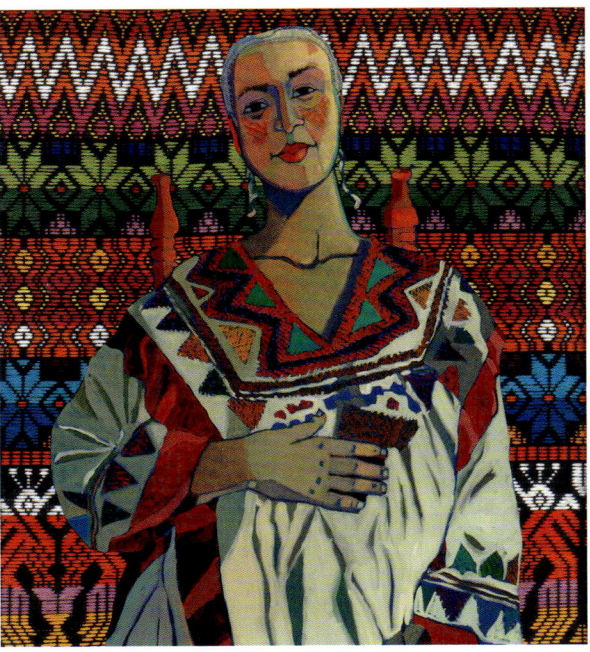

Señora López

fantasía y figuras detalladas entretejen el surrealismo con lo utilitario. Los títulos de Sosa apuntan hacia esos vínculos, como en *Archangel Contemplating Creation on My Mind* y *Corazón on My Sleeve on My Mind* (2020) o *Ángel del Árbol No. 2 on My Mind Night Sky Angel* (2015).[2]

El arte plástico casi siempre implica una rotación de impresiones del mundo físico en una continuidad que se extiende desde las prácticas más realistas o figurativas, como en el arte de Sosa, hasta los conceptos más abstractos. Estos dos extremos a menudo se consideran polos opuestos. Sin embargo, antes de que existiera el arte abstracto, la ilusión de la realidad visible existía a nivel medular en las prácticas artísticas occidentales, cuando los artistas lograban representar objetos o personas reales en espacios reales cada vez con una mayor exactitud. El modernismo desencadenó la obligación de representar el mundo físico de manera realista. La narrativa convencional del arte moderno plantea un desplazamiento polémico de la figuración hacia el arte abstracto, creando así una separación entre los dos movimientos. Esta herida intelectual que separa la abstracción de la figuración no empezó a sanar sino hasta finales del siglo XX, con la llegada de artistas como Sosa que se expresan en ambos estilos. Hoy podemos entender cómo aquellos conflictos históricos entre los lenguajes figurativo y abstracto consiguieron por fin que los artistas en la actualidad sean "bilingües", capaces de trabajar tanto el arte abstracto como el figurativo —siendo esta una consideración de relevancia especial en el caso de Sosa, ya que esta artista supera la escisión y resuelve la paradoja—.

El arte de Sosa es una narrativa: cada color, pincelada y textura sirve para construir el carácter y la presencia material auténtica de la retratada. Tanto la semejanza del retrato como el ambiente en el que la modelo está posando son valorados equitativamente, como para indicar que toda protagonista vive indisolublemente entrelazada a sus respectivos ambientes e historias personales. Vistos en conjunto, las pinturas y los collages de Sosa nos ofrecen la oportunidad deslumbrante y animadora de participar en este mundo mágico del color, compartir sus historias fronterizas retratadas y apreciar los orígenes de la mujer contemporánea. Todo esto nos recuerda lo que decían García Márquez: "Es suficiente para mí estar seguro de que tú y yo existimos en este momento".

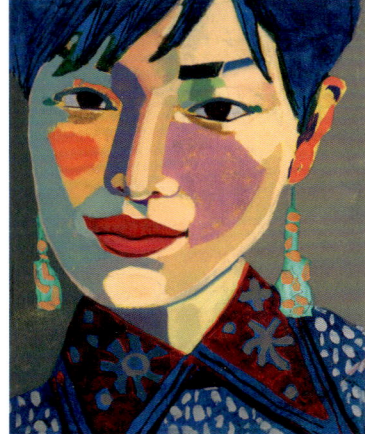

No. 9

Past and Present: Reflections on the Tree of Life

Jennifer Speed

1. Simo Parpola, "The Assyrian Tree of Life: Tracing the Origins of Jewish Monotheism and Greek Philosophy," *Journal of Near Eastern Studies* 52 (1993): 161–208, esp. 170–71.

The Tree of Life is a religious icon—of the cosmos, of creation, of life and death, of redemption and re-birth—as ancient as it is universal. In some way or another, distinctive versions of Tree of Life reveal a culture's understanding of the universe, namely that the divine or cosmic order reflects human society and the natural world. Moreover, the Tree of Life often serves as an axis connecting the divine and human worlds (of both the living and dead). Its par-ticularities, then, tell us of the contours and rhythms of life that matter most.

That so many cultures and communities the world over have utilized a Tree of Life to express ideas about life and the divine speaks not to its meaninglessness as a symbol but instead to its or-ganic appeal. The Tree of Life has its origins in the earth and draws its strength from things unseen, from somewhere below or sometimes above. It is on account of this unknown world with its unknown mechanisms that human imagination is put to the test. Human beings try to apprehend: what must there be *there* that shapes life *here*? At the same time, the visible parts of trees are unmistakable in their importance for life: trunks anchor and sustain the entire tree; canopies shade and give shelter; fruits and seeds nourish both people and animals; branch-es, whether shed or removed, can be burned for warmth or stacked and layered for protection. And the leaves! That is where each species of tree most emphatically proves itself different from the next. Finally, in order to survive, each and every living tree needs to be balanced in its form and suited to its physical environment.

In the Indian epic, the *Baghavad Gita*, Lord Krishna teaches that the universe is an eternal tree whose origins are divine and whose branches stretch over the cosmos. The Buddha achieved Enlighten-ment after meditating under a Sacred Fig tree, thus the name of the tree itself is now the Bodhi (or En-lightenment) Tree. It has come to represent the po-tential of Enlightenment for anyone, not only for the Buddha.

In the Norse traditions of Scandinavia, the great Tree of Life is the Yggdrasil, spanning both time and space. The Semitic and Assyrian cultural traditions of the Near East transmitted to Judaism and Christianity an image of the Tree of Life both mystical and allegorical. The Torah itself is the Tree of Life for those who embrace it, and in the Kabbal-istic tradition, God's wisdom is represented as a Tree of Life.[1] When Adam and Eve ate the forbidden fruit in the Garden of Eden, they took it from the Tree of Wisdom. For their defiance, God cast them from Eden, then set cherubim to guard the Tree of Life, lest Adam and Eve eat from it as well and live forever.[2] In the Christian tradition, humankind finds redemption as described in the Book of Revelations. On both sides of the river that flows from God stands the Tree of Life; it provides a dozen kinds of fruit and its leaves will serve to heal the nations.[3]

In the centuries following the Spanish and Portuguese conquests of Latin America, Christian imagery came to dominate religious expressions there. In some areas, however, pre-Colombian traditions either persisted after European conquest or blended with elements of the new religion. Mesoamerica, for example, has a rich Tree of Life iconography that predates the introduction of Christianity. At a complex of Maya temples at Palenque, in Chiapas, Mexico, dating to the late seventh century, the Temple of the Cross is dominated by a funerary carving of the Tree of Life. This sacred Ceiba (Cottonsilk) tree is a manifestation of the resurrected maize god, who stands at the center of the world and supports the heavens.[4] Farther south, at Izapa near the Mexican border with Guatemala, there survive a series of carved stelae (created no later than 250 BCE) bearing images of dragon trees. On Izapa Stela 5, the tree-dragon becomes a Tree of Life; it gives life-giving water and provides fruit or berries for both people and animals.[5]

In southwestern Mexico near the Pacific Coast, ceramic funerary objects found in shaft burial sites are noteworthy because they are symbols and images crafted from clay, rather than carved into stone. Such composition makes them at once more flexible and fluid in their imagery, but very fragile. Regrettably, grave robbers have looted or destroyed the contents of nearly all of the shafts. Among the exceptional artifacts that have survived is a World Tree, or Tree of Life, now in the American Museum of Natural History in New York and which dates from between 300 BCE and 300 CE. From the village of Narayit, it remains the oldest known ceramic Tree of Life from Mexico, if not the world.[6] Though a number of southern Mexican communities claim to originate the tradition of the now popular ceramic Tree of Life (known as candelabras and given as wedding gifts), any such claim would be hard to substantiate. We might properly say that communities in southern Mexico and northern Guatemala share a cultural heritage that includes both their Tree of Life religious imagery and their ceramic craftsmanship. Certainly the Nayarit exemplar was neither the only, nor the last, example of a traditional Tree of Life.

While we as yet have no clear explanation for the renewed popularity of the ceramic Tree of Life beginning in the early twentieth century, the popularity of the idea of the Tree of Life may owe something to both the Mexican Revolution and the painters Frida Kahlo and Diego Rivera. As to the first, the Mexican Revolution initiated a flood of interest in indigenous culture, to include pre-Columbian religiosity and traditional handcrafts. Given the extent of foreign or modernizing influences that dominated northern Mexico (not to mention the destruction or relocation of northern villages by President Porfirio Díaz), the south of Mexico drew those who wished to embrace or recover Mexico's authentic heritage. Mexicans first—and foreigners later—flocked to southern Mexico in search of clothing and music and art. Among the items of folk art that became high art were traditional ceramics, the crafting of which drew on traditions and a religious sensibility nearly two thousand years old. No doubt the Tree of Life ceramics were tremendously appealing, for they were native, open to diverse interpretation, and came to be varied in style and subject from town to town.

As to Frida Kahlo's and Diego Rivera's influence, they embraced indigenous culture in their art. Diego made frequent use of the imagery of the Tree of Life, not for its cosmology but instead for its fecundity. Importantly, the public nature of his murals gave extraordinary visibility not only to his work but also to his rendering of traditional religious imagery. For the nation, Frida reached back to Mexico's past, before violence and conquest had ruptured it, hoping to bring Mexico into a more hopeful post revolutionary era. Woman herself was to be the Tree of Life for

2. Genesis 3.

3. Revelations 22:1–2.

4. Robert J. Sharer and Loa P. Traxler, *The Ancient Maya*, 6th ed. (Stanford, Calif.: Stanford University Press, 2006), 454.

5. Virginia Grady Smith, *Izapa Relief Carving: Form, Content, Rules for Design, and Role in Mesoamerican Art and Archaeology* (Washington, D.C.: Dumbarton Oaks, 1984), 29.

6. It is known in the museum's collection as the Village Model. American Museum of Natural History, Anthropology Division, New York, catalog no. 30.3/2461, acq. 1988.

7. Dina Comisarenco, "Frida Kahlo, Diego Rivera, and Tlazolteotl," *Woman's Art Journal* 17 (1996): 15–21, esp. 17–18 and n. 26.

a new Mexico. Also, Frida, who suffered extraordinarily from a childhood disease and a traumatic accident, sought spiritual refuge in everything that was available to her. Thus, she blended Catholic and Aztec religious imagery as means of expressing the pain of a second miscarriage. In her 1947 painting *Sun and Life*, Frida included an aspect of the Aztec and Mesoamerican Tree of Life, one in which the souls of babies draw nourishment from the Tree of Life until such time as they are reborn.[7]

Pasado y presente: Reflexiones sobre el árbol de la vida

Jennifer Speed
Traducción por Gabriela Gámez

El árbol de la vida es un ícono religioso —del cosmos, de la creación, de la vida y la muerte, de la redención y el renacimiento— tan antiguo como universal. De una forma u otra, las versiones distintivas del árbol de la vida revelan la comprensión del universo por parte de una cultura, es decir, que el orden divino o cósmico refleja la sociedad humana y el mundo natural. Además, el árbol de la vida a menudo sirve como eje que conecta los mundos divino y humano (tanto de los vivos como de los muertos). Sus particularidades, entonces, nos hablan de los contornos y ritmos de vida que más importan.

El hecho de que tantas culturas y comunidades en todo el mundo hayan utilizado un árbol de la vida para expresar ideas sobre la vida y lo divino no habla de su falta de significado como símbolo, sino de su atractivo orgánico. El árbol de la vida tiene su origen en la tierra y obtiene su fuerza de cosas invisibles, de algún lugar abajo o, a veces, arriba. Es a causa de este mundo desconocido, con sus mecanismos desconocidos, que la imaginación humana se pone a prueba. Los seres humanos intentan aprender: ¿qué debe haber allí que da forma a la vida aquí? Al mismo tiempo, las partes visibles de los árboles son inconfundibles por su importancia para la vida: los troncos anclan y sostienen todo el árbol; los follajes dan sombra y refugio; los frutos y las semillas nutren tanto a las personas como a los animales; las ramas, ya sean caídas o removidas, pueden quemarse para calentarse o apilarse y colocarse en capas para protegerse. ¡Y las hojas! Ahí es donde cada especie de árbol se muestra más enfáticamente diferente de las demás. Finalmente, para sobrevivir, todos y cada uno de los árboles vivos deben tener una forma equilibrada y adaptarse a su entorno físico.

En la epopeya india el *Baghavad Gita*, el Señor Krishna enseña que el universo es un árbol eterno cuyos orígenes son divinos y cuyas ramas se extienden sobre el cosmos. El Buda alcanzó la iluminación después de meditar bajo una higuera sagrada, por lo que el nombre del árbol en sí es ahora árbol bodhi (o iluminación). Ha llegado a representar el potencial de la iluminación para cualquiera, no solo para el Buda.

En las tradiciones nórdicas de Escandinavia, el gran árbol de la vida es el Yggdrasil, que abarca tanto el tiempo como el espacio. Las tradiciones culturales semíticas y asirias del Cercano Oriente transmitieron al judaísmo y al cristianismo una imagen del árbol de la vida tanto mística como alegórica. La Torá misma es el árbol de la vida para quienes la abrazan, y en la tradición cabalística, la sabiduría de Dios se representa como un árbol de la vida.[1] Cuando Adán y Eva comieron el fruto prohibido en el Jardín del Edén,

1. Simo Parpola, "The Assyrian Tree of Life: Tracing the Origins of Jewish Monotheism and Greek Philosophy," *Journal of Near Eastern Studies* 52 (1993): 161–208, esp. 170–71.

2. Génesis 3.

3. Apocalipsis 22:1–2.

4. Robert J. Sharer and Loa P. Traxler, *The Ancient Maya*, 6. ed. (Stanford, Calif.: Stanford University Press, 2006), 454.

5. Virginia Grady Smith, *Izapa Relief Carving: Form, Content, Rules for Design, and Role in Mesoamerican Art and Archaeology* (Washington, D.C.: Dumbarton Oaks, 1984), 29.

6. Se conoce en la colección del museo como el Village Model. American Museum of Natural History, Anthropology Division, New York, catalog no. 30.3/2461, acq. 1988.

lo tomaron del árbol del conocimiento del bien y del mal. Por su desafío, Dios los expulsó del Edén y luego puso querubines para proteger el árbol de la vida, para que Adán y Eva no comieran de él también y vivieran eternamente.[2] En la tradición cristiana, la humanidad encuentra la redención como se describe en el Libro del Apocalipsis. A ambos lados del río que fluye de Dios se encuentra el árbol de la vida; proporciona una docena de clases de frutos y sus hojas servirán para sanar a las naciones.[3]

En los siglos posteriores a las conquistas española y portuguesa de América Latina, la imaginería cristiana llegó allí a dominar las expresiones religiosas. En algunas zonas, sin embargo, las tradiciones precolombinas persistieron después de la conquista europea o se mezclaron con elementos de la nueva religión. Mesoamérica, por ejemplo, tiene una rica iconografía del árbol de la vida que es anterior a la introducción del cristianismo. En un complejo de templos mayas en Palenque, Chiapas, México, que data de finales del siglo VII, el Templo de la Cruz está dominado por una talla funeraria del árbol de la vida. Este árbol sagrado de ceiba es una manifestación del dios del maíz resucitado, que se encuentra en el centro del mundo y sostiene los cielos.[4] Más al sur, en Izapa, cerca de la frontera de México con Guatemala, sobreviven una serie de estelas talladas (creadas a más tardar en el año 250 aC) con imágenes de árboles de dragón. En la estela 5 de Izapa, el árbol de dragón se convierte en árbol de la vida; da agua que da vida y proporciona frutas o bayas tanto para las personas como para los animales.[5]

En el suroeste de México, cerca de la costa del Pacífico, los objetos funerarios de cerámica encontrados en sitios de entierro en pozos son dignos de mención porque son símbolos e imágenes elaborados en arcilla, en lugar de tallados en piedra. Tal composición los hace al mismo tiempo más flexibles y fluidos en su imaginería pero muy frágiles. Lamentablemente, los ladrones de tumbas saquearon o destruyeron el contenido de casi todos los pozos. Entre los artefactos excepcionales que han sobrevivido se encuentra un árbol del mundo, o árbol de la vida, ahora en el Museo Americano de Historia Natural de Nueva York y que data de entre el 300 aC y el 300 dC. Proveniente del pueblo de Nayarit, sigue siendo el árbol de la vida de cerámica más antiguo conocido de México, si no del mundo.[6] Aunque varias comunidades del sur de México afirman ser originarias de la tradición del ahora popular árbol de la vida de cerámica (conocido como candelabro y obsequiado como regalo de bodas), tal afirmación sería difícil de fundamentar. Podríamos decir correctamente que las comunidades del sur de México y el norte de Guatemala comparten una herencia cultural que incluye tanto su imaginería religiosa del árbol de la vida como su artesanía en cerámica. Ciertamente el ejemplar de Nayarit no fue ni el único ni el último ejemplo de un árbol de la vida tradicional.

Si bien todavía no tenemos una explicación clara para la renovada popularidad de la cerámica del árbol de la vida a partir de principios del siglo XX, la popularidad de la idea del árbol de la vida puede deber algo tanto a la Revolución Mexicana como a los pintores Frida Kahlo y Diego Rivera. En cuanto al primero, la Revolución Mexicana inició una avalancha de interés en la cultura indígena, que incluyó la religiosidad precolombina y las artesanías tradicionales. Dada la magnitud de las influencias extranjeras o modernizadoras que dominaron el norte de México (sin mencionar la destrucción o reubicación de pueblos del norte por el presidente Porfirio Díaz), el sur de México atrajo a quienes deseaban abrazar o recuperar la auténtica herencia de México. Los mexicanos primero, y los extranjeros después, acudieron en masa al sur de México en busca de ropa, música y arte. Entre los objetos de arte popular que se convirtieron en arte elevado se encontraba la cerámica tradicional, cuya elaboración se basaba en tradiciones y una sensibilidad religiosa de casi dos mil años de antigüedad. Sin duda, las cerámicas del árbol de la vida eran tremendamente atractivas, porque eran nativas, abiertas a diversas interpretaciones y variaban en estilo y tema de una ciudad a otra.

En cuanto a la influencia de Kahlo y Rivera, abrazaron la cultura indígena en su arte. Rivera hizo uso frecuente de la imaginería del árbol de la vida, no por su cosmología sino por su fecundidad. Es importante destacar que el carácter público de sus murales dio una visibilidad extraordinaria no solo a su obra sino también a su interpretación de la imaginería religiosa tradicional. Para la nación, Kahlo se remonta al pasado de México, antes de que la violencia y la conquista lo rompieran, con la esperanza de llevar a México a una era posrevolucionaria más esperanzadora. La propia mujer iba a ser el árbol de la vida de un nuevo México. Además, Kahlo, que sufrió extraordinariamente una enfermedad infantil y un accidente traumático, buscó refugio espiritual en todo lo que estaba a su alcance. Así, por ejemplo, combinó imágenes religiosas católicas y aztecas como medio para expresar el dolor de un segundo aborto espontáneo. En su pintura *Sol y vida* de 1947, Kahlo incluyó un aspecto del árbol de la vida mesoamericano, uno en el que las almas de los bebés se nutren del árbol de la vida hasta el momento en que renacen.[7]

7. Dina Comisarenco, "Frida Kahlo, Diego Rivera, and Tlazolteotl," *Woman's Art Journal* 17 (1996): 15–21, esp. 17–18 y n. 26.

Day of the Dead Gentleman Callers and Their Muse on My Mind: Homage to Mom

Kathy Sosa

In Tennessee Williams's play *The Glass Menagerie*, a widow and her daughter while away their time, the mother growing more and more desperate, waiting for gentleman callers who never come.

Gentleman caller is a Southern term, and my mother, who died last year at eighty-seven, was a Southern girl. But there the comparison ends, as my mother never lacked for gentleman callers. In fact, being a pretty woman with a vivacious personality, she was something of a gentleman caller magnet. Married five times, twice to my father, she was very popular, both in Alabama, where she and I were born, and in Texas, where my first stepfather brought her and, coincidentally, me in 1968. My childhood memories are populated with the comings and goings of my mother and her various husbands, boyfriends, suitors, and hopefuls, which I observed from the vantage point of a fly on the wall, a knickknack on the coffee table, or a kid on a bike in the driveway. Sometimes I heard stories of her youth straight from the horse's mouth.

From the time I was nine or so until the age of thirteen, one of my mother's favorite parlor tricks when having friends over (her friends, my friends, it didn't matter) was to have several cocktails and then stand on her head. "Who here can stand on their head?" she would say. My heart would drop. "Who

doesn't believe I can still stand on my head?" I was sure I might be sick. "I was a cheerleader, you know." And suddenly there she would go. Her legs would go up, her skirt would come down, and the gasps, cheers, and applause would begin.

I didn't think about it at the time, as I was way too busy being mortified, but no doubt this kind of stunt was gangbusters in the gentleman caller department. It is funny to think how long ago this was. The last time my mother stood on her head at a cocktail party, she was fifteen years younger than I am now.

My mother was not a floozy. But she was a behaviorally liberated, incorrigible flirt who loved to drive men mad and didn't give a flip what anybody thought. Especially me. Perhaps she was just ahead of her time.

Mom and her gentleman callers are gone now, but their memories remain. This painting is a tribute to them all.

Some of the gentleman callers pictured here are based on actual people; others are symbolic of general categories of males who found her irresistible. Here is a legend to some of the figures:

- Top center, large skeleton: this is Mom. Her skeleton is drawn upside down for reasons aforementioned (1).

- Heavy-set local entrepreneur pictured with money coming out of his ears but hands firmly planted in his pockets (2).

- Immediately to Mom's left (or right, if you are upside down) is my father. Dad is holding a light bulb, signifying that he was very bright—and also signifying my mother's opinion that he couldn't change a light bulb with both hands (3).

- The fellows who promised her the world on a platter. These guys generally didn't have two centavos to rub together (4).

- Swarmy, lecherous creeps (there were plenty of these, some of whom were uncles or distant cousins) (5).

- The tall, dark, handsome, and sweet state trooper. This guy looked like a movie star—I am not kidding. I suspect he was married. His son William was in my seventh grade class. William was lanky, dorky, and awkward. I've often wondered whether he took after his mother or matured into an Adonis, like his father (6).

- Gordon Hathaway (not his real name) thought waiting on my mother hand and foot would win her favor. He came by every week for years to do her laundry. As far as I know, all it ever got him was more errands (7).

- Two of Mom's husbands were in the army. First, my handsome brother's handsome father, whom neither my brother nor I ever met. He met my mother during World War II, when she was eighteen and he was stationed at Fort Rucker, Alabama. He was Polish and a Yankee. The marriage was doomed from the start. Twenty-something years later, my first stepfather was a helicopter pilot who served several tours in Vietnam. He was insanely jealous, apparently for good reason. He was also a Yankee. Some people never learn (8).

- Tightly wound, hypocritical Elmer Gantry types with short-sleeved dress shirts and sweaty armpits (9).

- Good dancers. My mother loved to dance. She was a sucker for a good dancer (10).

- Musicians, especially if they were also good dancers (11).

- My mother's fourth husband was a roofing supply salesman from Mississippi. He was a good-natured chain smoker who made her laugh for several years, until he died of lung cancer sometime during the Reagan administration (12).

Here's to you, Mom. *¡Vivan los muertos!* Long live the dead!

Pensando en los caballeros pretendientes y su musa en el Día de los Muertos: Homenaje a mi mamá

Kathy Sosa
Traducción por Tony Beckwith y Gabriela Gámez

En la obra de teatro *The Glass Menagerie*, de Tennessee Williams, una viuda y su hija pasan el rato mientras la madre se desespera cada vez más esperando a los "caballeros pretendientes" que nunca llegan.

Caballero pretendiente es un término que tuvo su origen en el sur de los Estados Unidos; mi madre, quien falleciera el año pasado a los ochenta y siete años, era una chica sureña. Pero hasta ahí llega la comparación con esa obra de Williams, ya que a mi madre jamás le faltaron caballeros pretendientes. De hecho, siendo una mujer guapa con una personalidad arrolladora, era algo así como un imán para aquellos caballeros. Casada cinco veces, dos de ellas con mi padre, era tan popular en Alabama —donde nacimos las dos— como en Texas, a donde en 1968 mi primer padrastro nos trajo a ella y, casualmente, a mí. Mis recuerdos de la infancia están poblados de idas y venidas de mi madre con sus distintos maridos, novios, pretendientes y candidatos, un desfile que pude observar desde la perspectiva de una mosca parada en la pared, una chuchería en la mesa de centro o una niña en su bicicleta en la entrada de la casa. Algunas veces llegué a oír anécdotas de su juventud narradas por ella misma.

Desde que tenía nueve años más o menos hasta los trece años, cuando teníamos visita (amigos suyos o míos, daba igual), después de haber tomado varios cócteles, uno de los trucos de salón favoritos de mi madre consistía en pararse de cabeza.

—¿Quién puede pararse de cabeza? —ella decía—.
El corazón se me caía al suelo.

— ¿Quién duda que aún soy capaz de pararme de cabeza?
Me daban ganas de vomitar.

—Que fui porrista, para que lo sepan.
Y de pronto, lo hacía. Con las piernas al aire y la falda caída, los amigos gritaban, aclamaban y aplaudían.

En aquel momento no se me ocurrió, puesto que me moría de la vergüenza, pero seguramente, ese truco les caía muy bien a los caballeros pretendientes. Resulta curioso recordar hace cuánto tiempo que se portaba así. Si mal no recuerdo, mi madre se paró de cabeza por última vez en un cóctel con amigos cuando tenía quince años menos de los que tengo yo ahora.

Mi madre no era una cualquiera. Pero si era una coquetona incorregible muy liberada que le encantaba enloquecer a los hombres y le importaba un pepino lo que pensaran los demás. Yo en particular. Quizás es que simplemente estaba adelantada a su tiempo.

Mamá y sus caballeros pretendientes ya se han ido, pero sus recuerdos permanecen vivos. Este cuadro es un homenaje a todos ellos.

Entre los caballeros pretendientes aquí retratados, algunos fueron inspirados en personas reales; otros simbolizan los distintos tipos de hombre para los cuales mi madre resultaba irresistible. A continuación se presentan las leyendas correspondientes a algunas de estas figuras:

- El esqueleto grande que aparece al centro en la parte superior es mi mamá. Está retratada al revés por los motivos antes mencionados (1).

- El empresario local corpulento retratado con dinero saliéndole de los oídos pero con las manos plantadas firmemente en sus bolsillos (2).

- Justo a la izquierda de mi mamá (o a la derecha, si usted está de cabeza) está mi papá. Papá sostiene un foco, simbolizando lo brillante que era. También simboliza la opinión de mi mamá de que era incapaz de cambiar un foco con las dos manos (3).

- Los individuos que le prometieron darle el mundo en bandeja de plata. Estos hombres, por lo general, no tenían ni un centavo (4).

- Los moscones canallas y libidinosos (de estos abundaban, algunos eran tíos o primos lejanos) (5).

- El policía estatal; alto, moreno, guapo y tierno. Este tipo parecía una estrella de cine y NO estoy bromeando. Sospecho que estaba casado. Su hijo William estaba en mi clase en séptimo grado. Era larguirucho, tonto y torpe. A veces me he pregun-

tado si William salió a su mamá o si se convirtió en un Adonis, como su papá (6).

- Gordon Hathaway (no es su verdadero nombre) pensaba que desviviéndose por mi mamá se la ganaría. Durante años estuvo yendo todas las semanas para lavarle la ropa. Hasta donde yo sé, lo único que consiguió fue que le dieran más labores (7).

- Dos de los esposos de mi mamá estuvieron en el ejército: Primero, el padre guapo de mi hermano guapo, al que ni mi hermano ni yo conocimos. Él conoció a mi mamá durante la Segunda Guerra Mundial, cuando ella tenía dieciocho años y él estaba prestando servicio en Fort Rucker, Alabama. Era polaco y yanqui. Desde el principio el matrimonio estaba condenado al fracaso. Veintitantos años después, mi primer padrastro fue un piloto de helicópteros que cubrió varios períodos de servicio en Vietnam. Era increíblemente celoso, aparentemente por una buena razón. También era yanqui. Hay gente que nunca aprenden (8).

- Los predicadores apáticos e hipócritas, tipos como Elmer Gantry, con camisas de vestir de manga corta y las axilas sudorosas (9).

- Los buenos bailarines. A mi mamá le encantaba bailar. Los buenos bailarines eran su debilidad (10).

- Los músicos, especialmente si también eran buenos bailarines (11).

- El cuarto esposo de mi mamá era un vendedor de materiales para techar de Mississippi. Era un fumador empedernido bondadoso que la hizo reír por varios años, hasta que falleció de cáncer de pulmón durante la administración de Reagan (12).

¡Brindo por ti, Mamá! ¡Vivan los muertos! *Long live the dead!*

*Day of the Dead Gentleman
Callers and Their Muse on My
Mind: Homage to Mom* (detail)
2018
Oil on canvas
60 x 60 in.

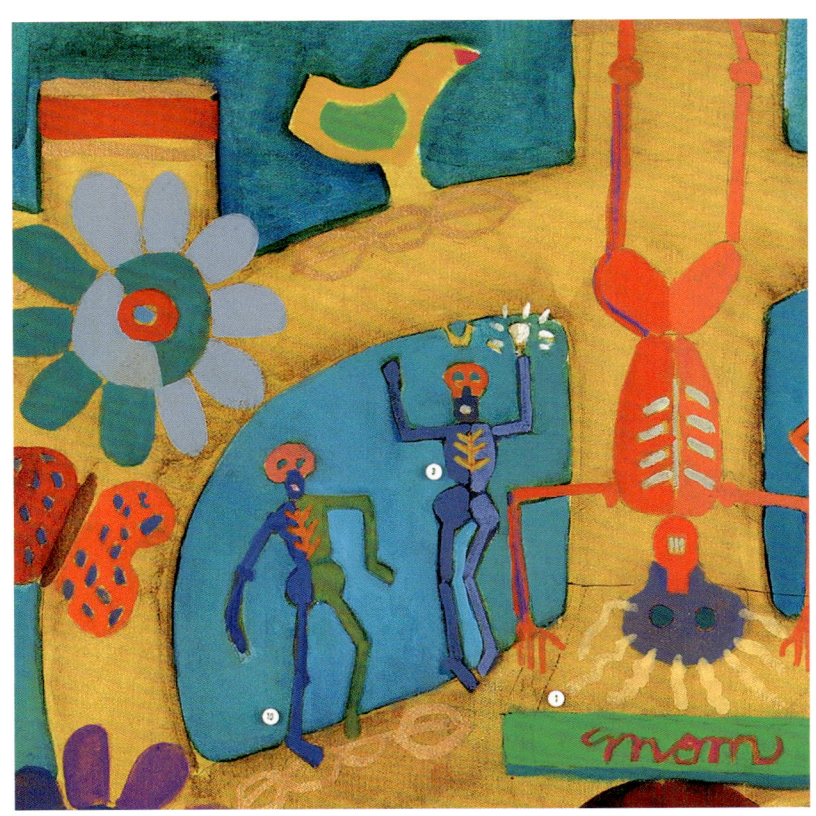

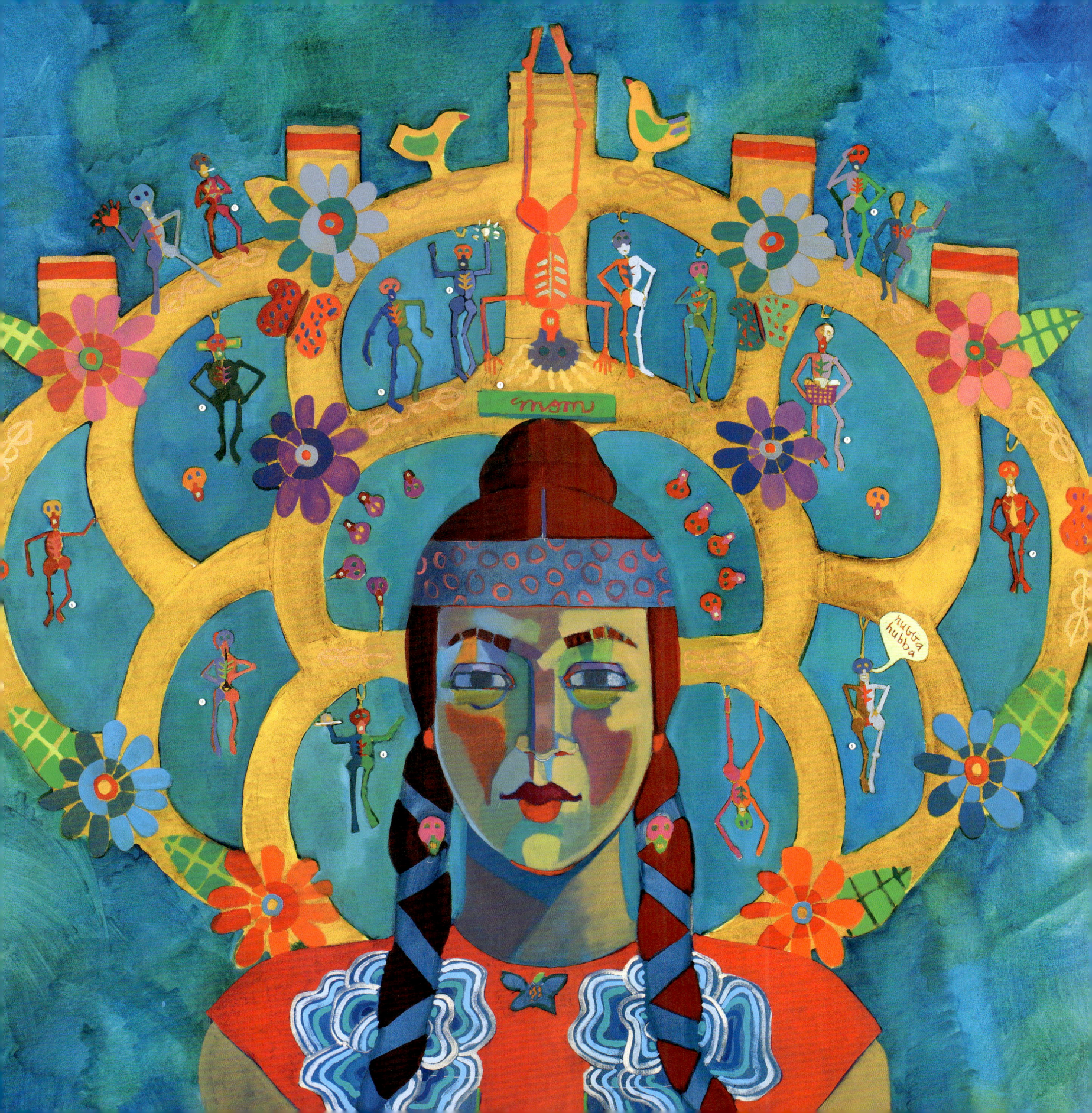

Fine Art Meets Street Art: In Defense of Borderland Culture

Kathy Sosa

On the borders of countries, where peoples meet and blend, something distinct and new emerges. A new language. A new cuisine. A new culture. A distinct identity. This is true in the Texas–Mexico borderland just as it is in other places around the world. People's crossing of borders back and forth, to and from family, friends, work, shopping, entertainment; the acceptance of the other as ourself; the intermarriage; and the *mestizaje* all feed the new culture and keep it vibrant.

Throughout history, immigrants have been our allies in change, innovation, and growth. In most cases they have done so in the face of meanness and mistreatment. Without them we are stale, inbred, and growing old. My artivism (art + activism) as a practice uses street art and social media to spread messages of encouragement where the welcoming of immigrants and the celebration of blended cultures are concerned.

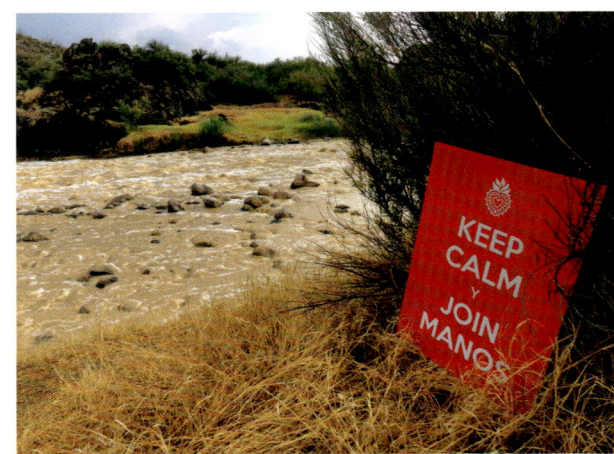

Photo by Kathy Sosa

Las bellas artes se encuentran con el arte de la calle: En defensa de la cultura fronteriza

Kathy Sosa

Traducción por Tony Beckwith y Gabriela Gámez

En las fronteras nacionales, donde los pueblos se juntan y se mezclan, surge algo distinto y nuevo. Un idioma nuevo. Una cocina nueva. Una cultura nueva. Una identidad distinta. Esto es cierto tanto en la zona fronteriza entre Texas y México como en otras partes del mundo. El cruce de las fronteras de la gente ida y vuelta, por motivos de familia, amigos, trabajo, compras o entretenimiento, la aceptación del otro como uno mismo, los matrimonios mixtos y el mestizaje, todos ellos nutren la nueva cultura y la mantienen viva.

A lo largo de la historia los inmigrantes han sido nuestros aliados en lo que se refiere al cambio, la innovación y el crecimiento. En la mayoría de los casos lo han sido a pesar de la maldad y los malos tratos. Sin ellos estamos anquilosados, endogámicos y envejecidos. La práctica de mi artivismo (arte + activismo) aprovecha el arte de la calle y las redes sociales para difundir mensajes de ánimo en cuanto a la acogida de inmigrantes y la aceptación de las culturas mezcladas.

The paintings of San Antonio–based Kathy Sosa reach across cultures to express a sense of female solidarity. She draws on the Mexican tradition of the Tree of Life as it appears in colorful, intricate clay sculptures that combine floral, figurative, and other motifs. Originally created to teach biblical stories to native people, Tree of Life sculptures have morphed into elaborate storytelling works that express all manner of personal and social concerns. In Sosa's hands they become elaborate headdresses that serve as portraits of sorts and provide vehicles for the exploration of the dreams, hopes, and fears of the women whom they ornament.

Las pinturas de Kathy Sosa, residente en San Antonio, Texas, se extienden a través de las culturas para expresar un sentido de solidaridad femenina. La artista se basa en la tradición mexicana del árbol de la vida tal y como aparece en las coloridas e intrincadas esculturas de barro que combinan motivos florales, figurativos y otra imaginería. Creadas originalmente para explicar los pasajes bíblicos a los indígenas, las esculturas del árbol de la vida se han transformado en elaboradas obras narrativas que expresan todo tipo de inquietudes personales y sociales. En las manos de Sosa, se convierten en elaborados tocados que ejercen como una especie de retratos y brindan una serie de conductos para la exploración de los sueños, esperanzas y temores de las mujereres a la que adornan.

— *Eleanor Heartney*

Artworks

Face Painting + 52

MESTIZAJE

No. 11
2018
Oil on canvas
10 x 8 in.

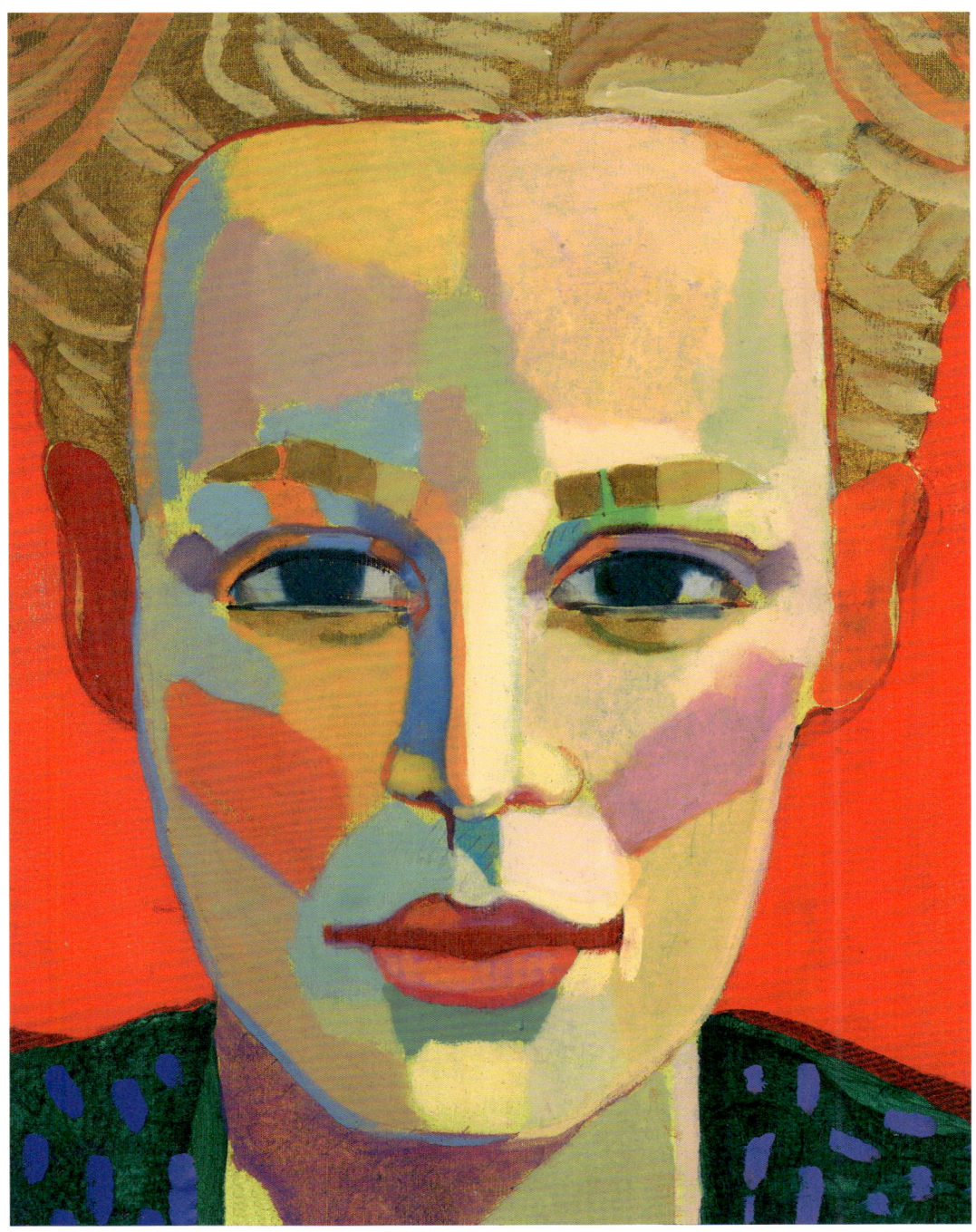

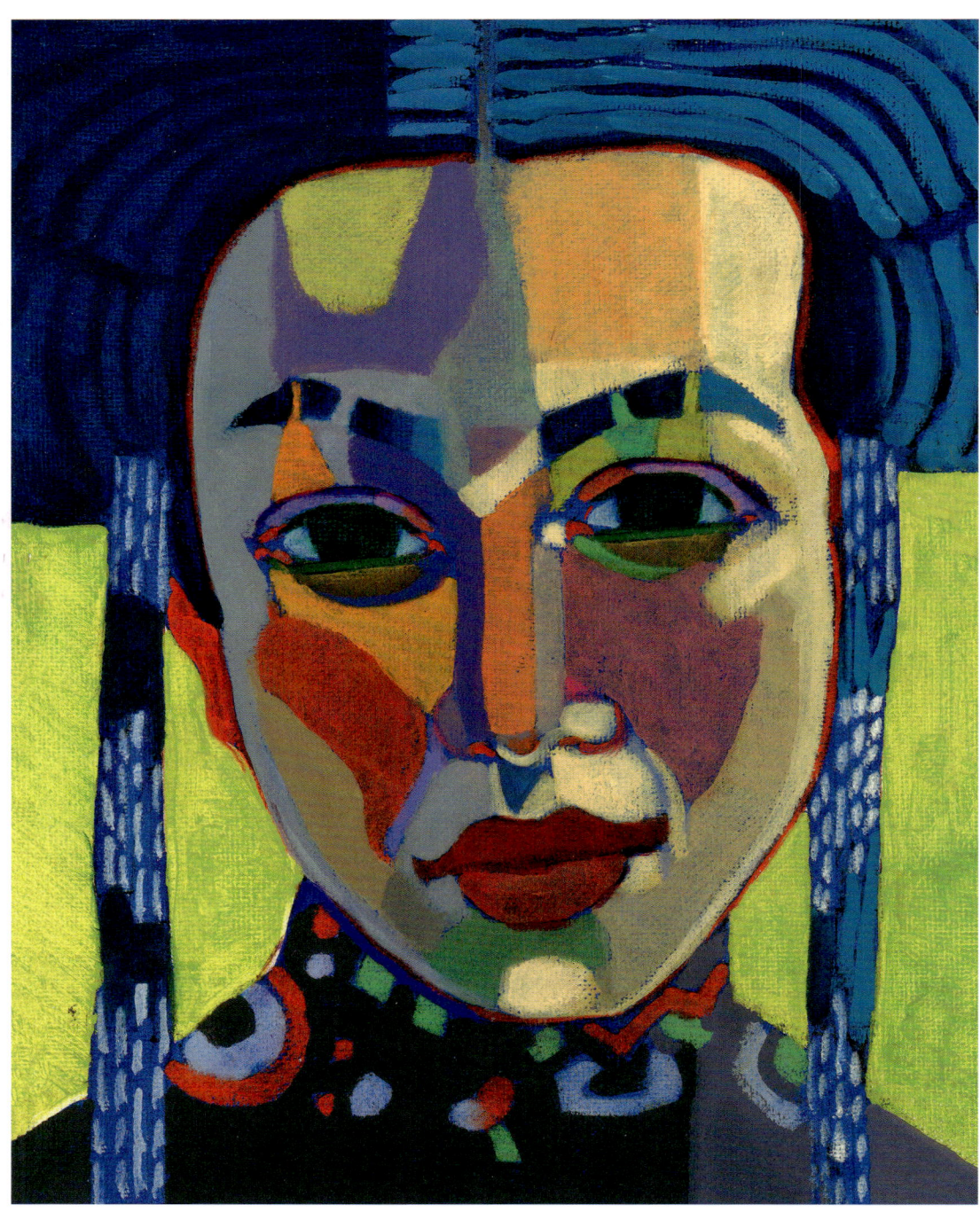

No. 2
2018
Oil on canvas
10 x 8 in.

No. 52
2018
Oil on canvas
10 x 8 in.

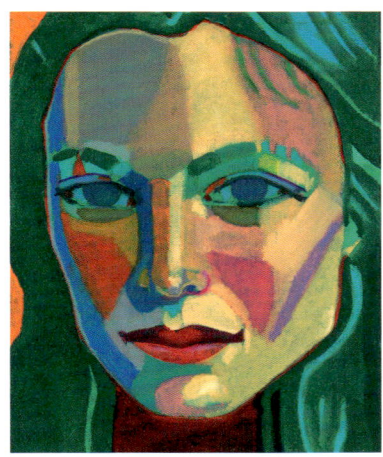

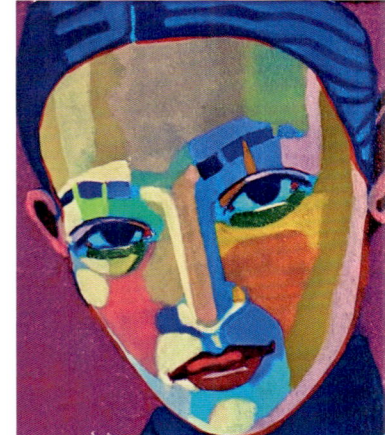

Sinceramente Sarah
2018
Oil on canvas
10 x 8 in.

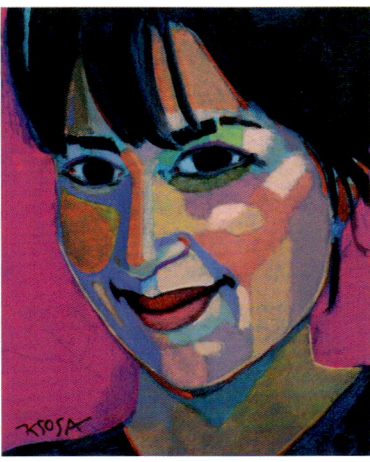

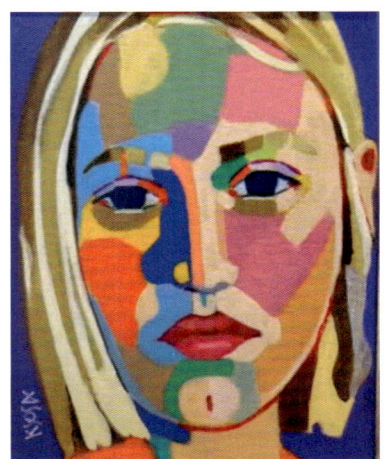

No. 43
2018
Oil on canvas
10 x 8 in.

Sincerely
2018
Oil on canvas
10 x 8 in.

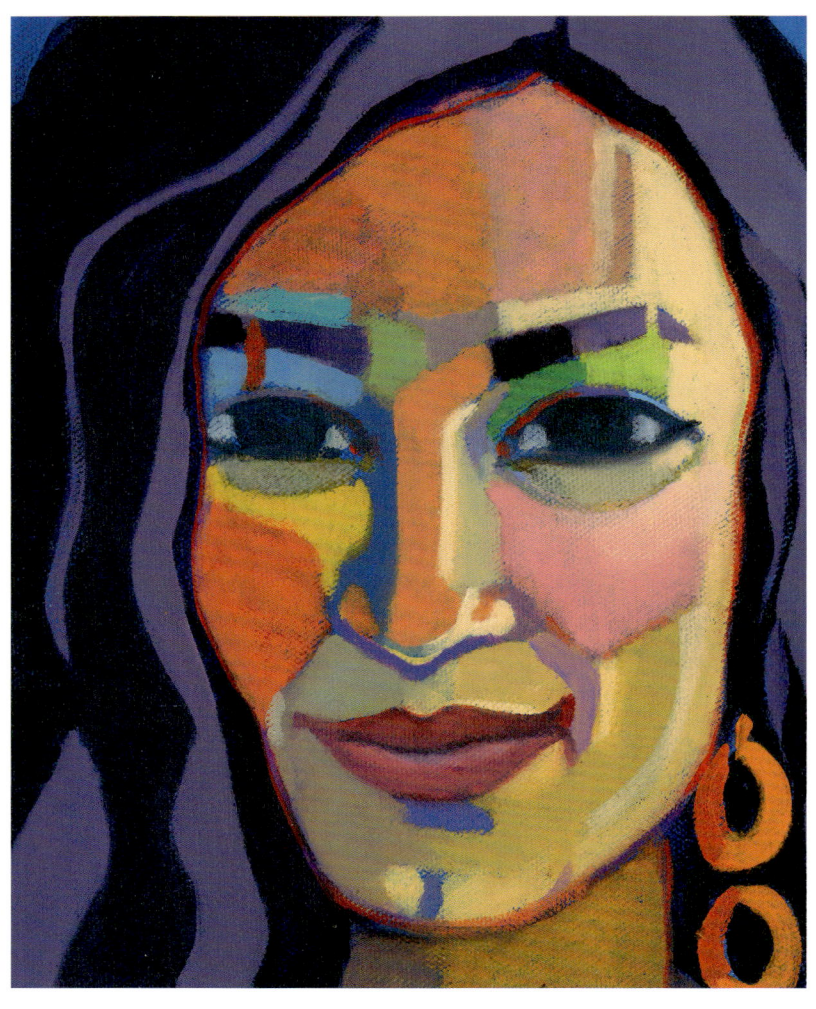

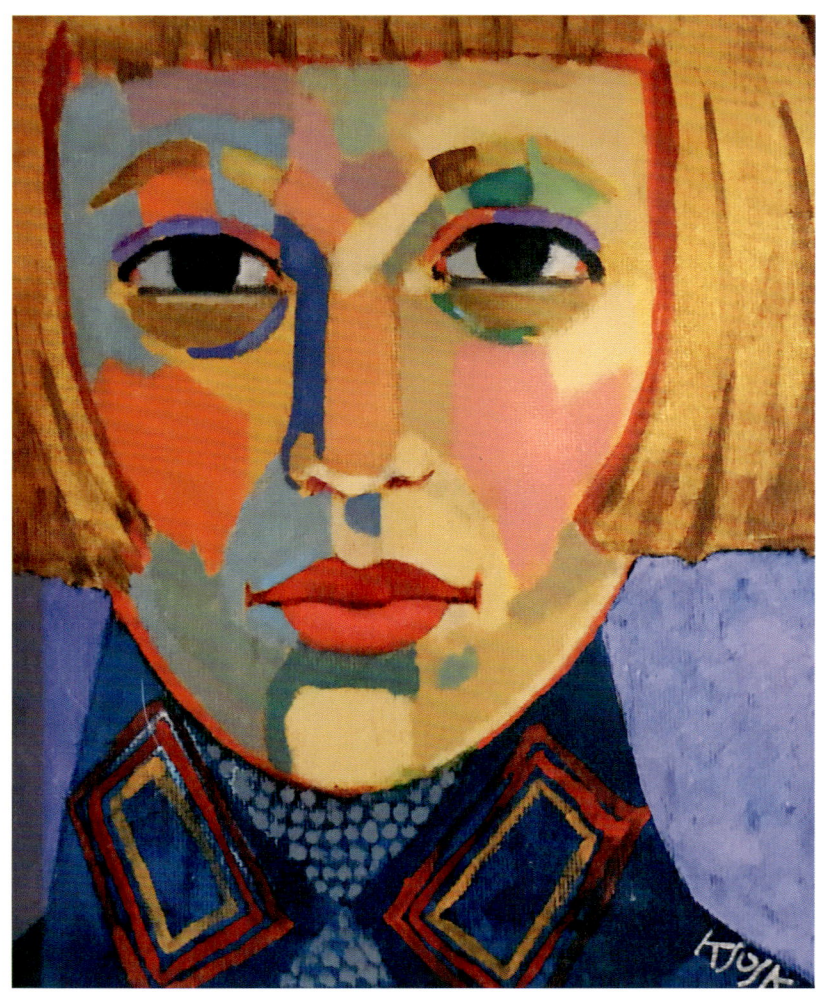

No. 42
2018
Oil on canvas
10 x 8 in.

Miranda Meets Mrs. Martinez 1
2018
Oil on canvas
10 x 8 in.

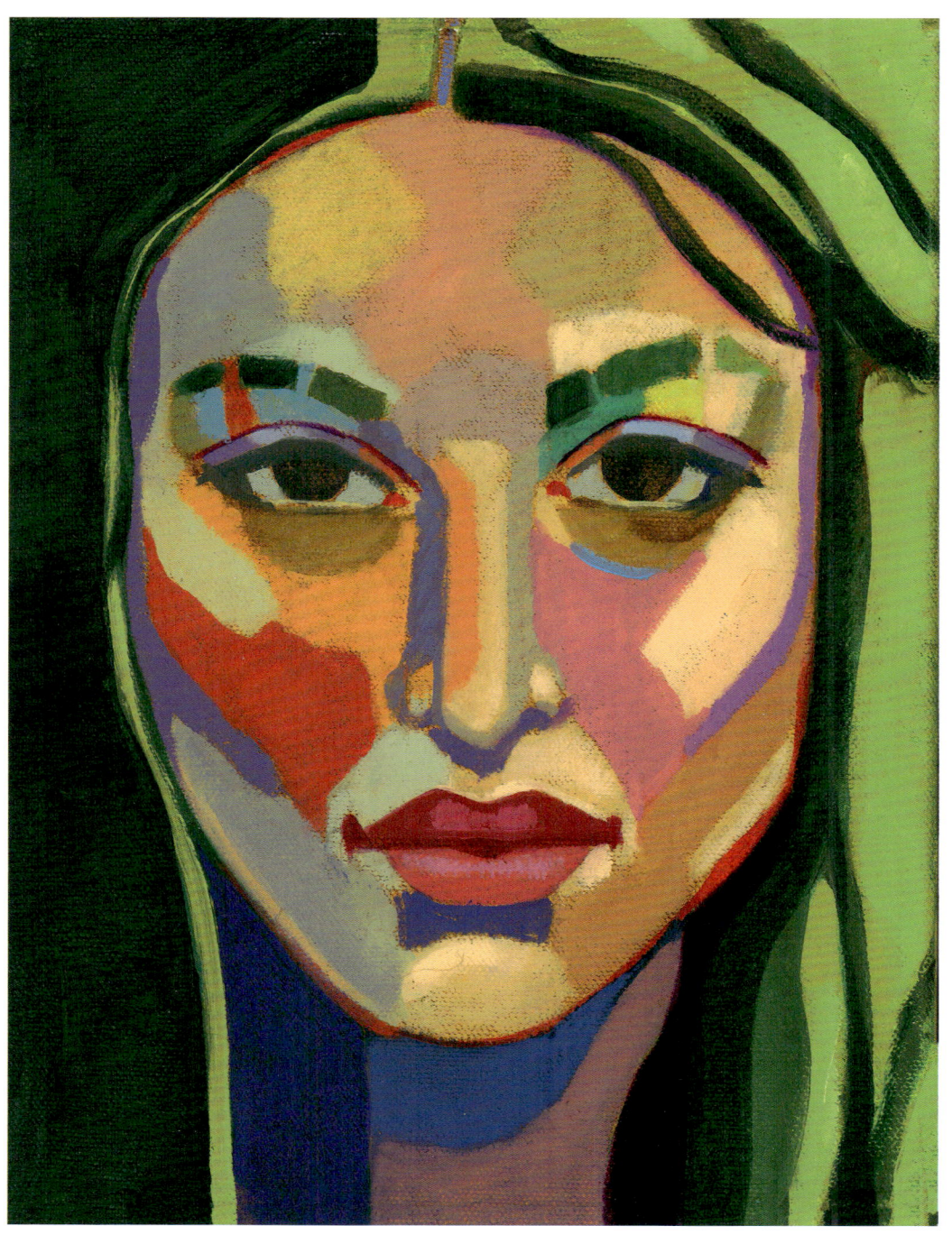

No. 43
2018
Oil on canvas
10 x 8 in.

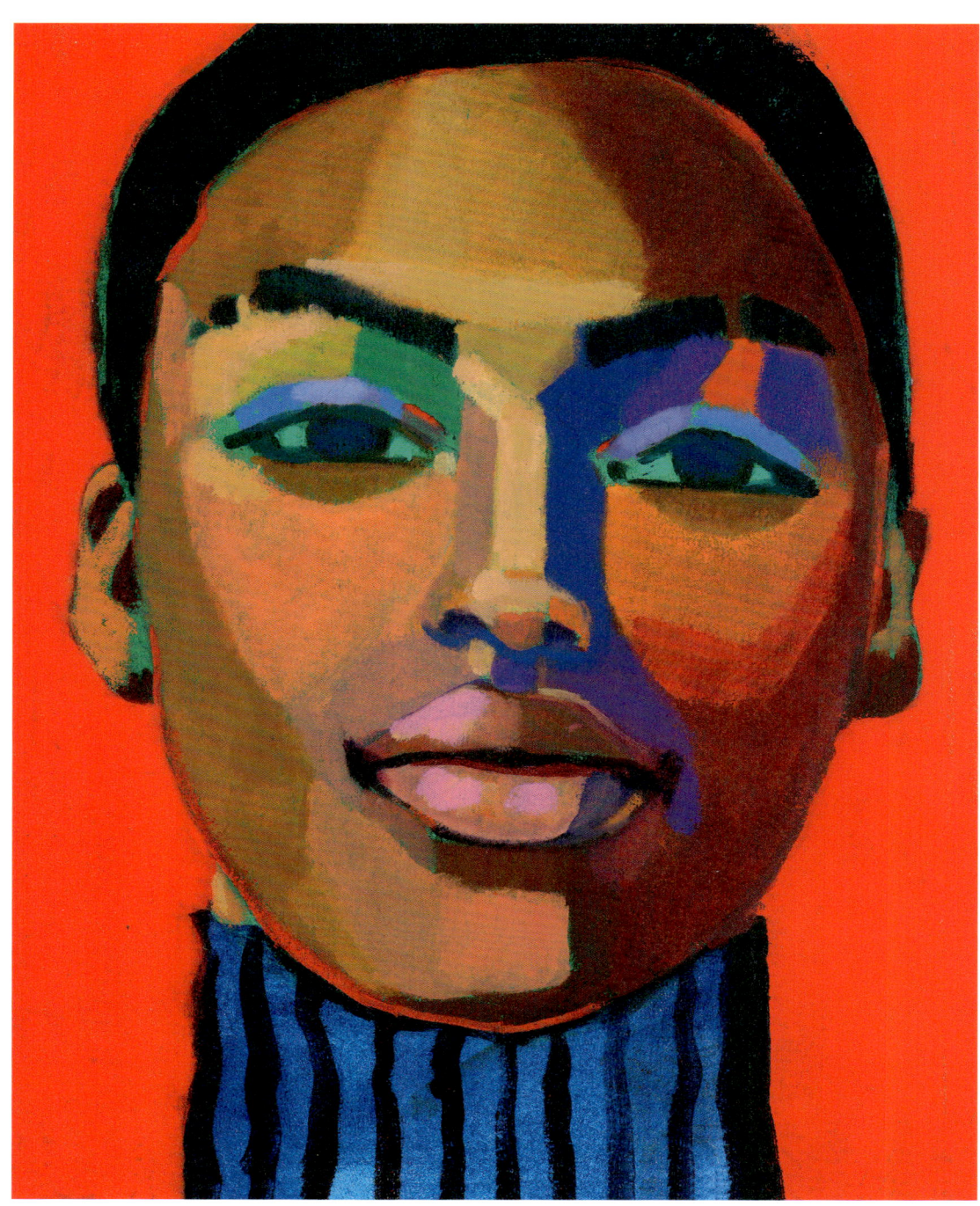

No. 41
2018
Oil on canvas
10 x 8 in.

No. 49
2018
Oil on canvas
10 x 8 in.

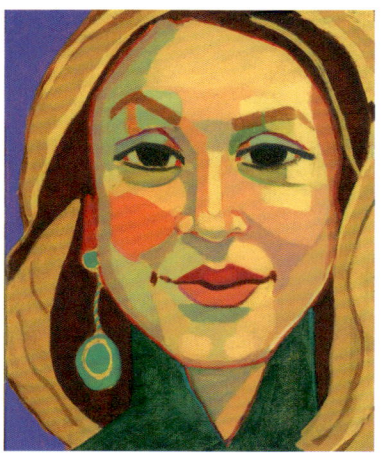

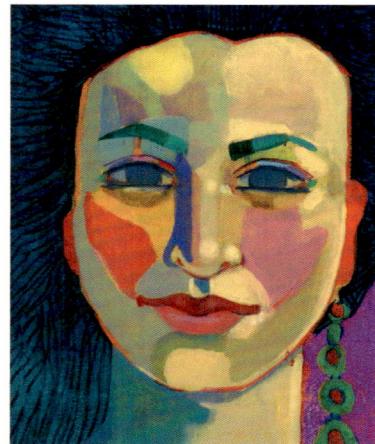

No. 19
2018
Oil on canvas
10 x 8 in.

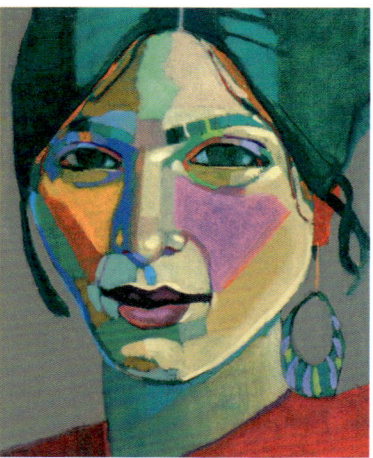

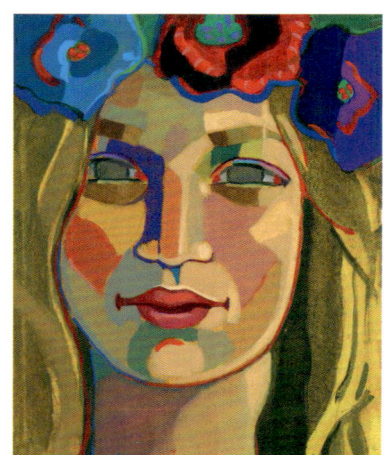

No. 17
2018
Oil on canvas
10 x 8 in.

No. 18
2018
Oil on canvas
10 x 8 in.

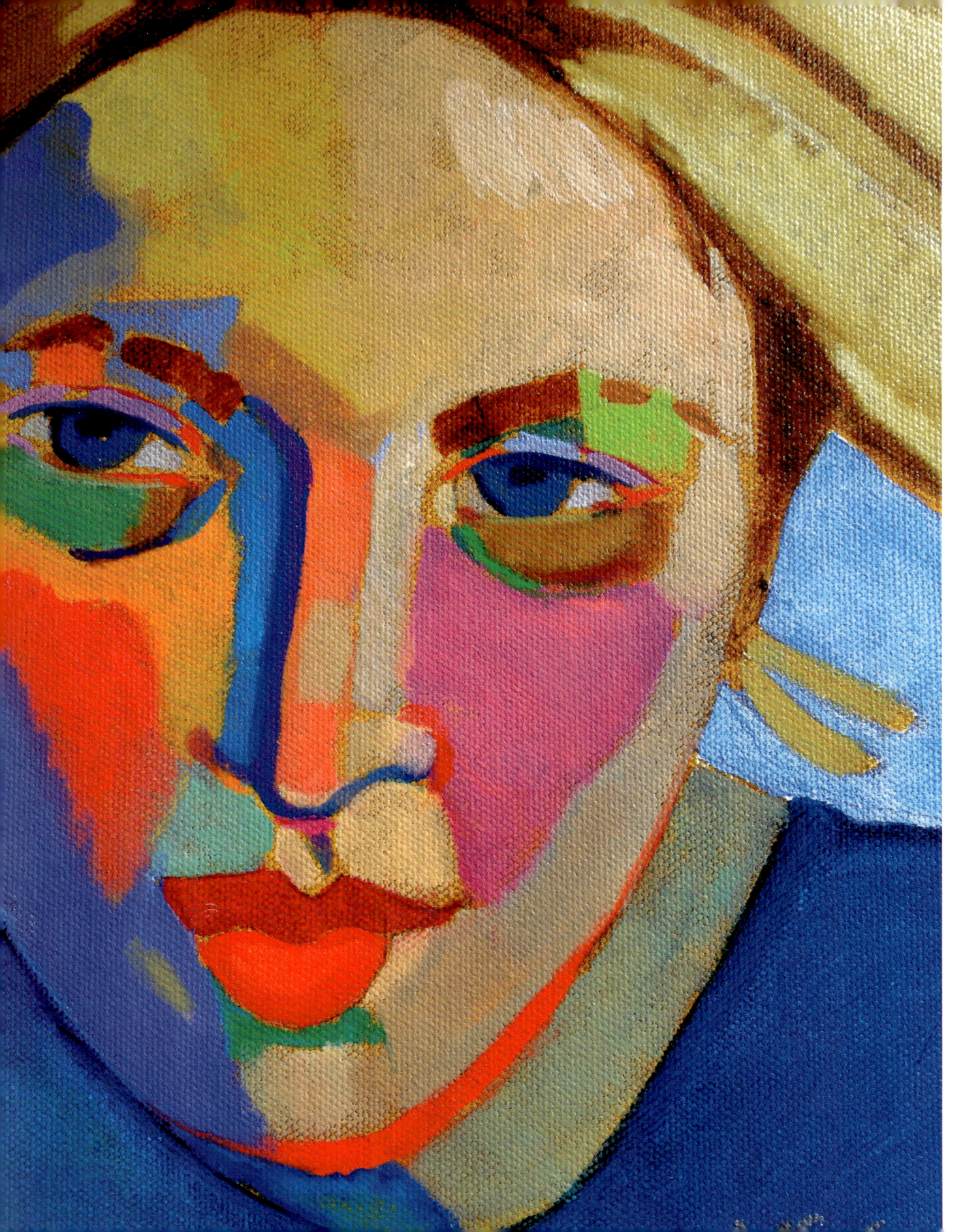

Bangs on the Run
2016
Oil on canvas
10 x 8 in.

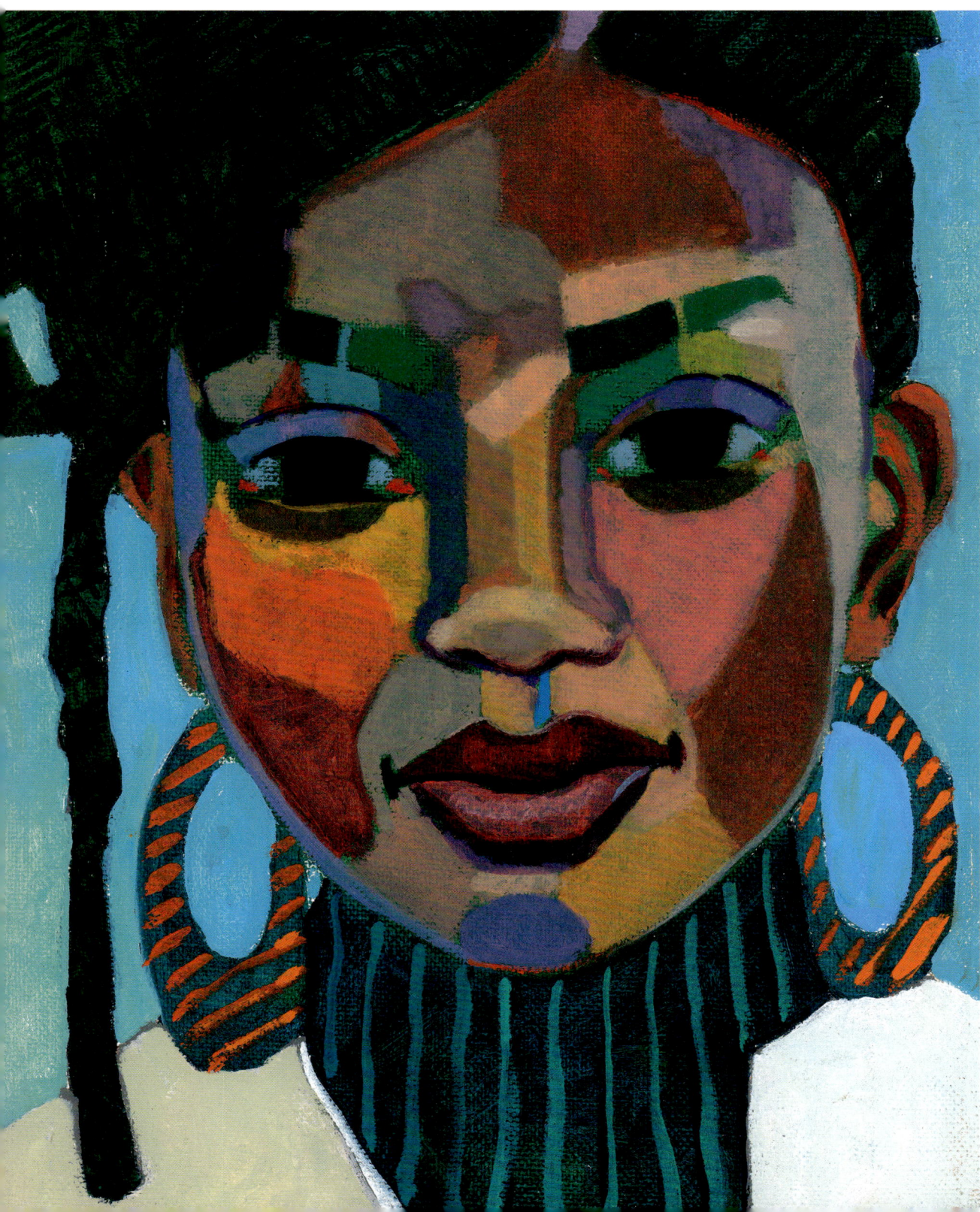

No. 32
2018
Oil on canvas
10 x 8 in.

No. 10
2018
Oil on canvas
10 x 8 in.

No. 9
2018
Oil on canvas
10 x 8 in.

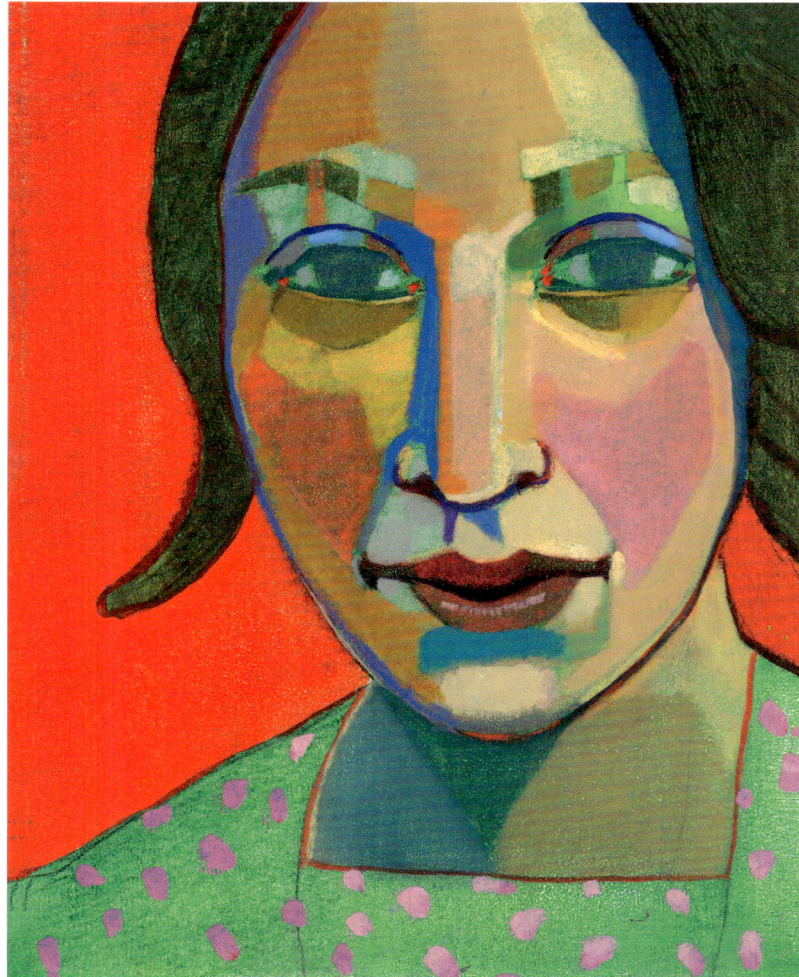

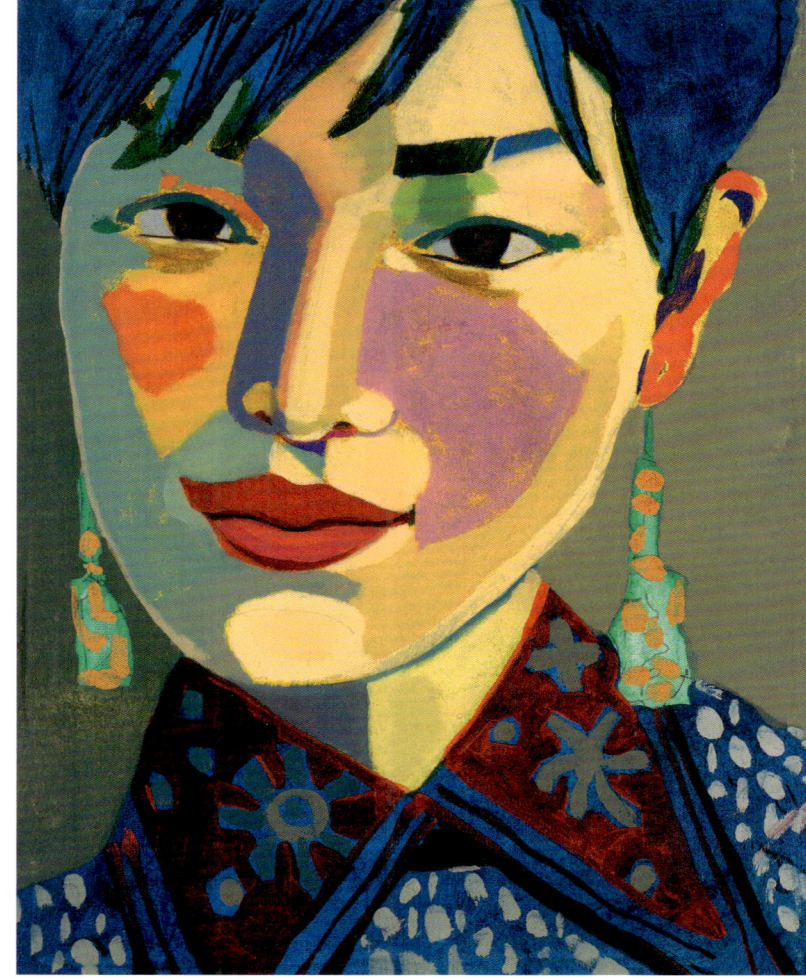

No. 46
2018
Oil on canvas
10 x 8 in.

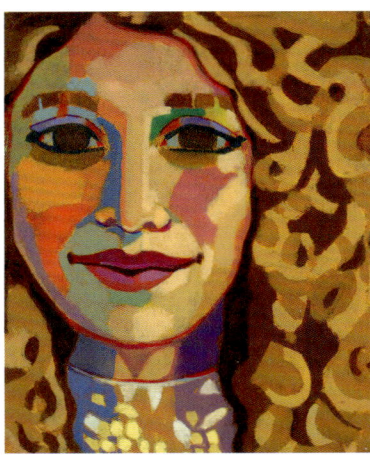

Nola
2021
Oil on canvas
10 x 8 in.

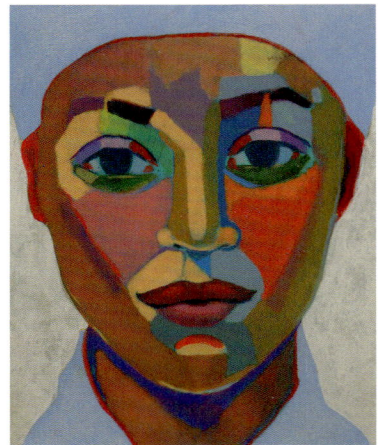

No. 28
2018
Oil on canvas
10 x 8 in.

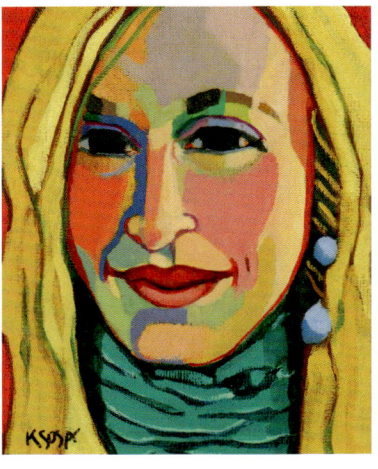

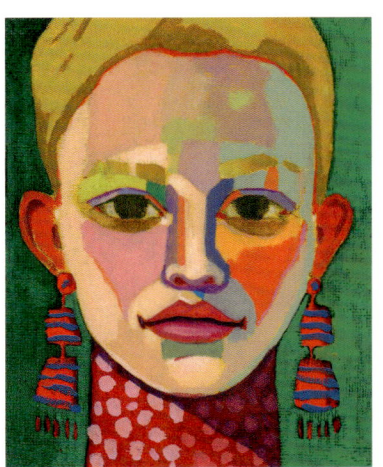

No. 33
2018
Oil on canvas
10 x 8 in.

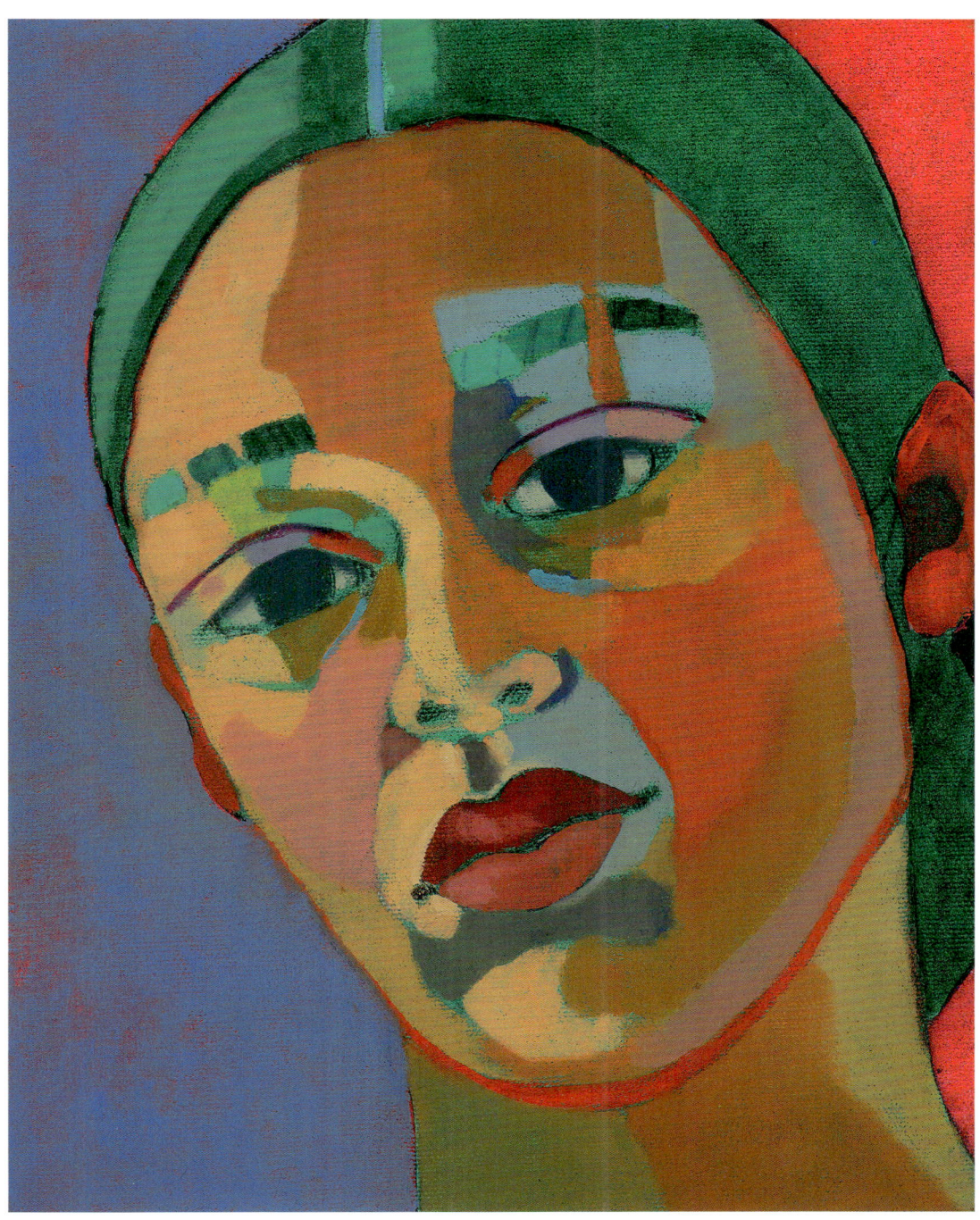

Tender Mercies
2021
Oil on canvas
10 x 8 in.

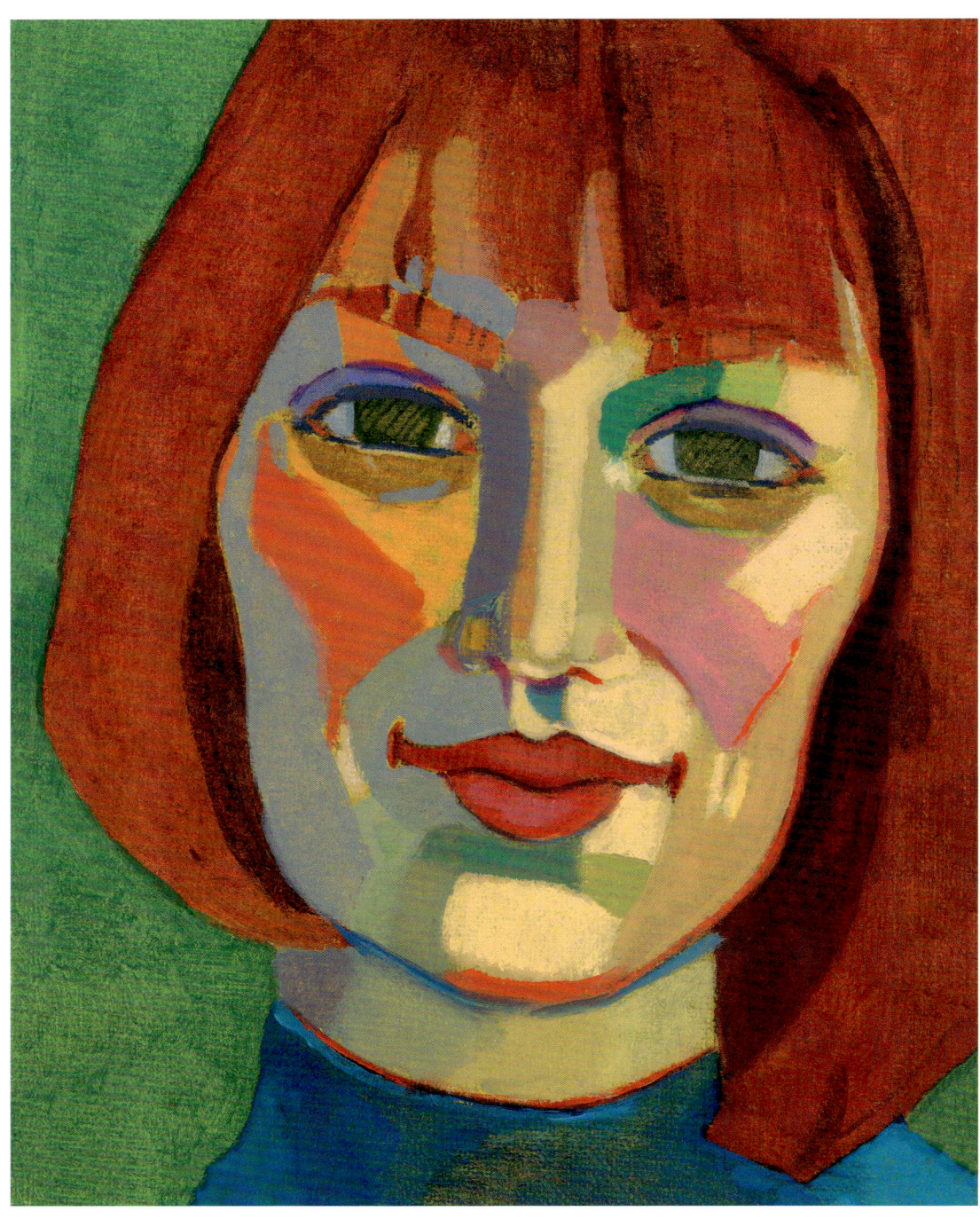

No. 12
2018
Oil on canvas
10 x 8 in.

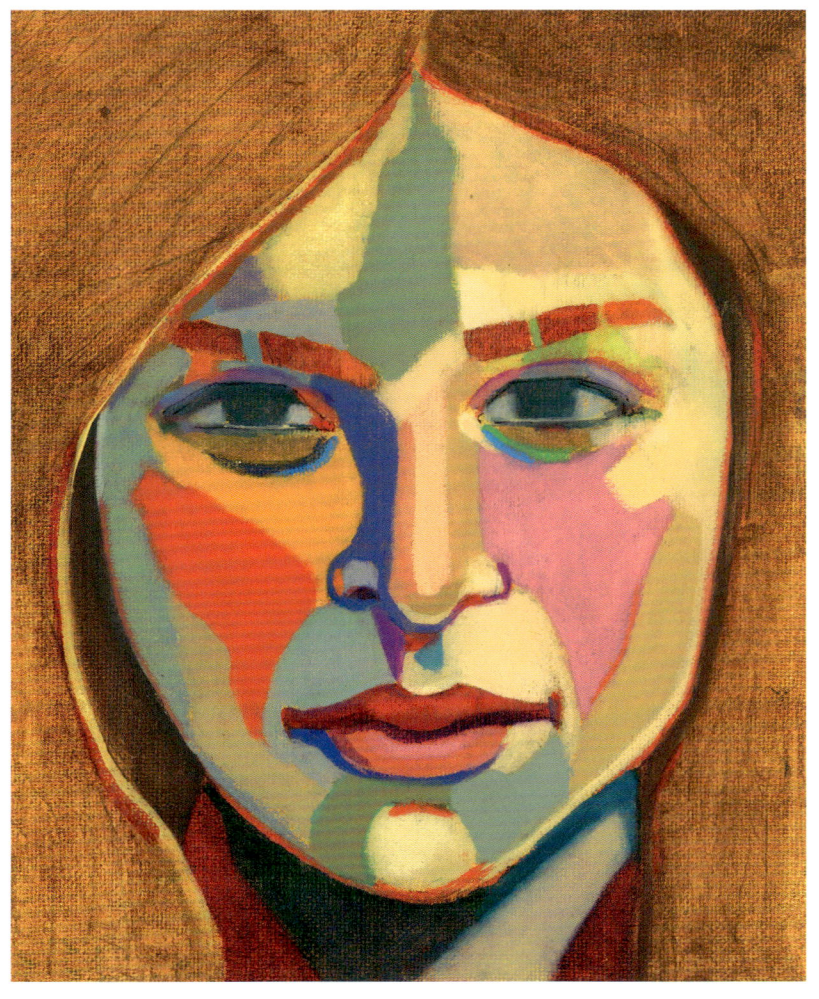

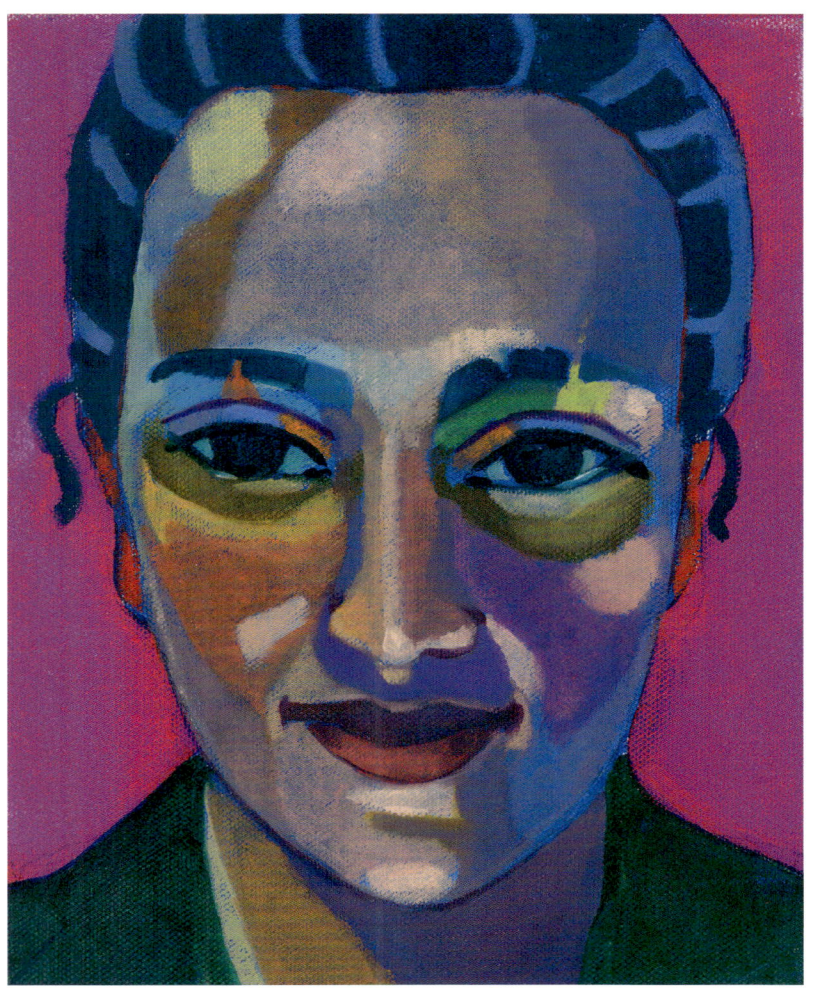

No. 7
2018
Oil on canvas
10 x 8 in.

No. 47
2018
Oil on canvas
10 x 8 in.

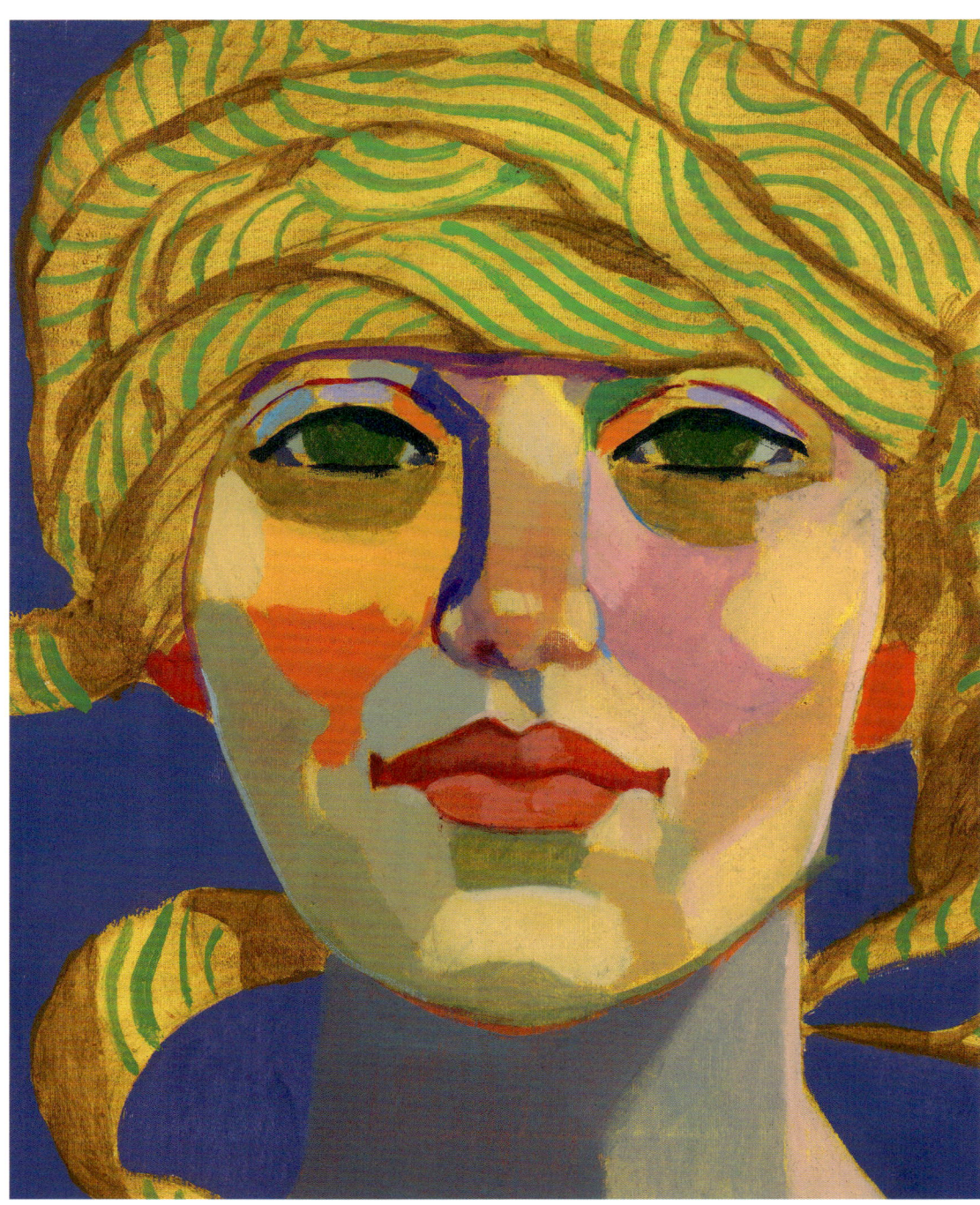

No. 21
2018
Oil on canvas
10 x 8 in.

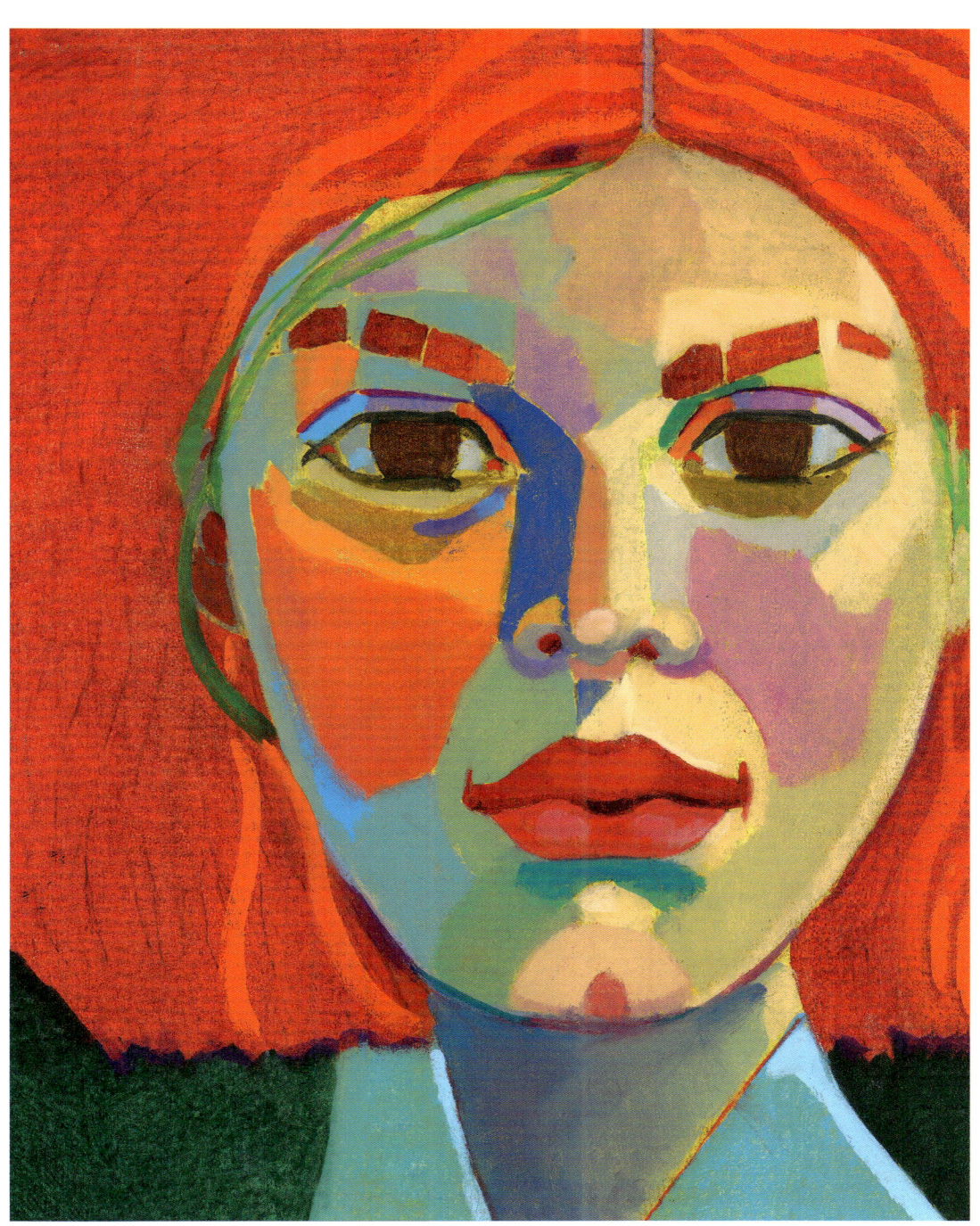

No. 37
2018
Oil on canvas
10 x 8 in.

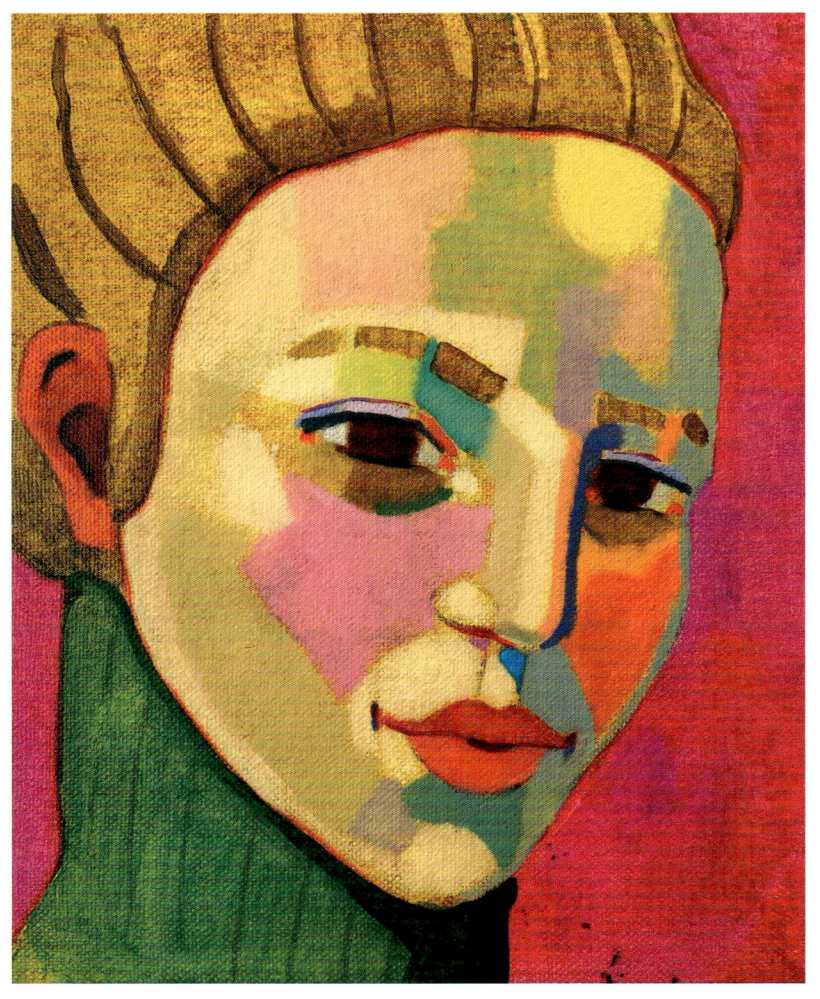

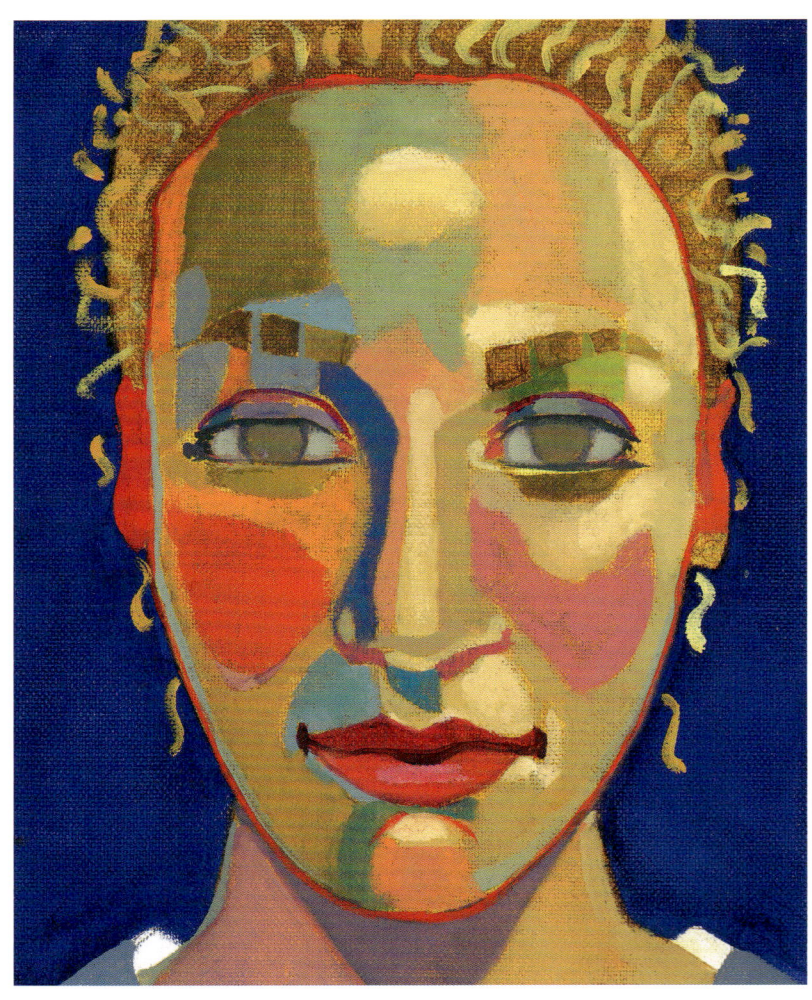

What's My Number?
2021
Oil on canvas
10 x 8 in.

No. 6
2018
Oil on canvas
10 x 8 in.

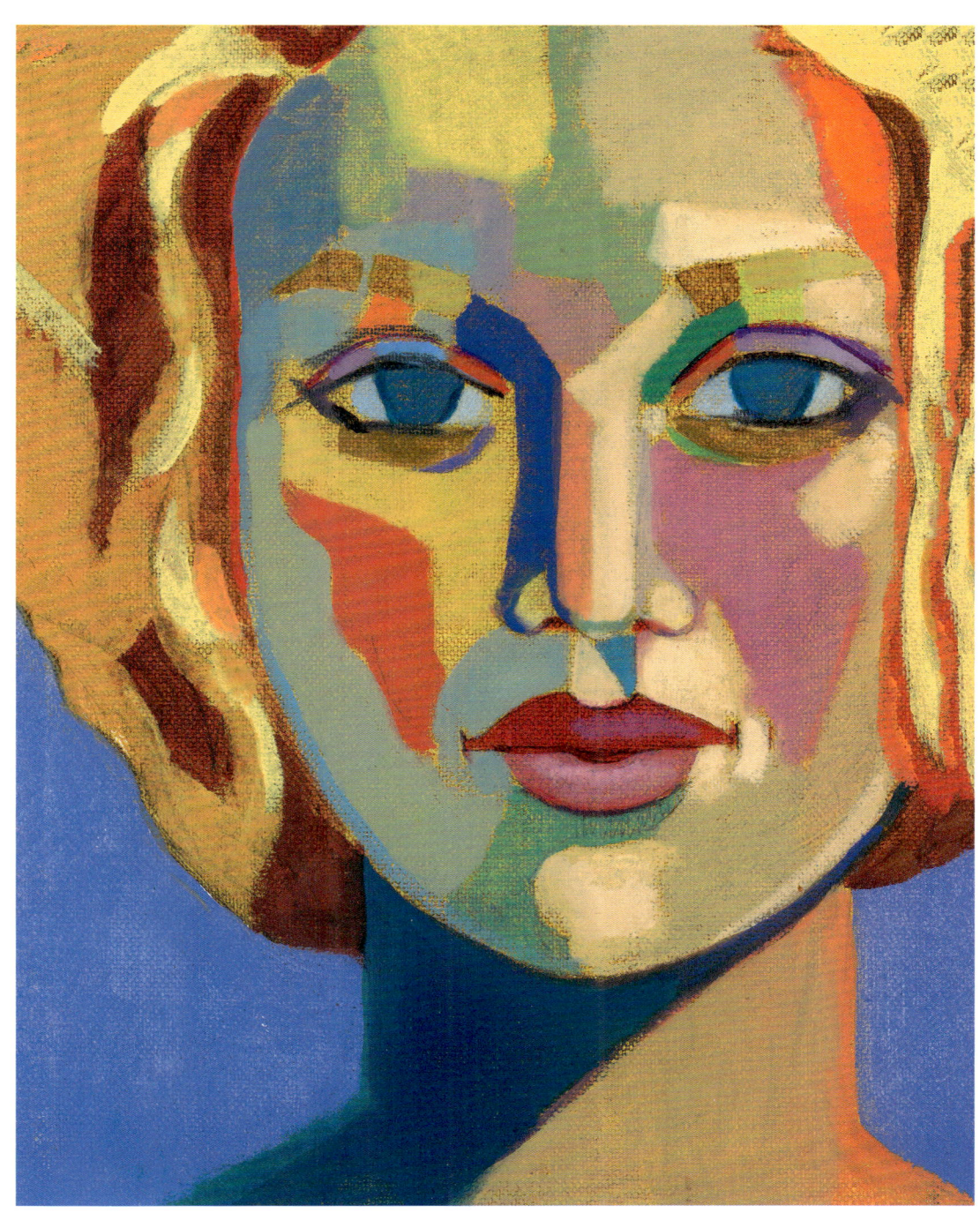

No. 14
2018
Oil on canvas
10 x 8 in.

Trees of Life

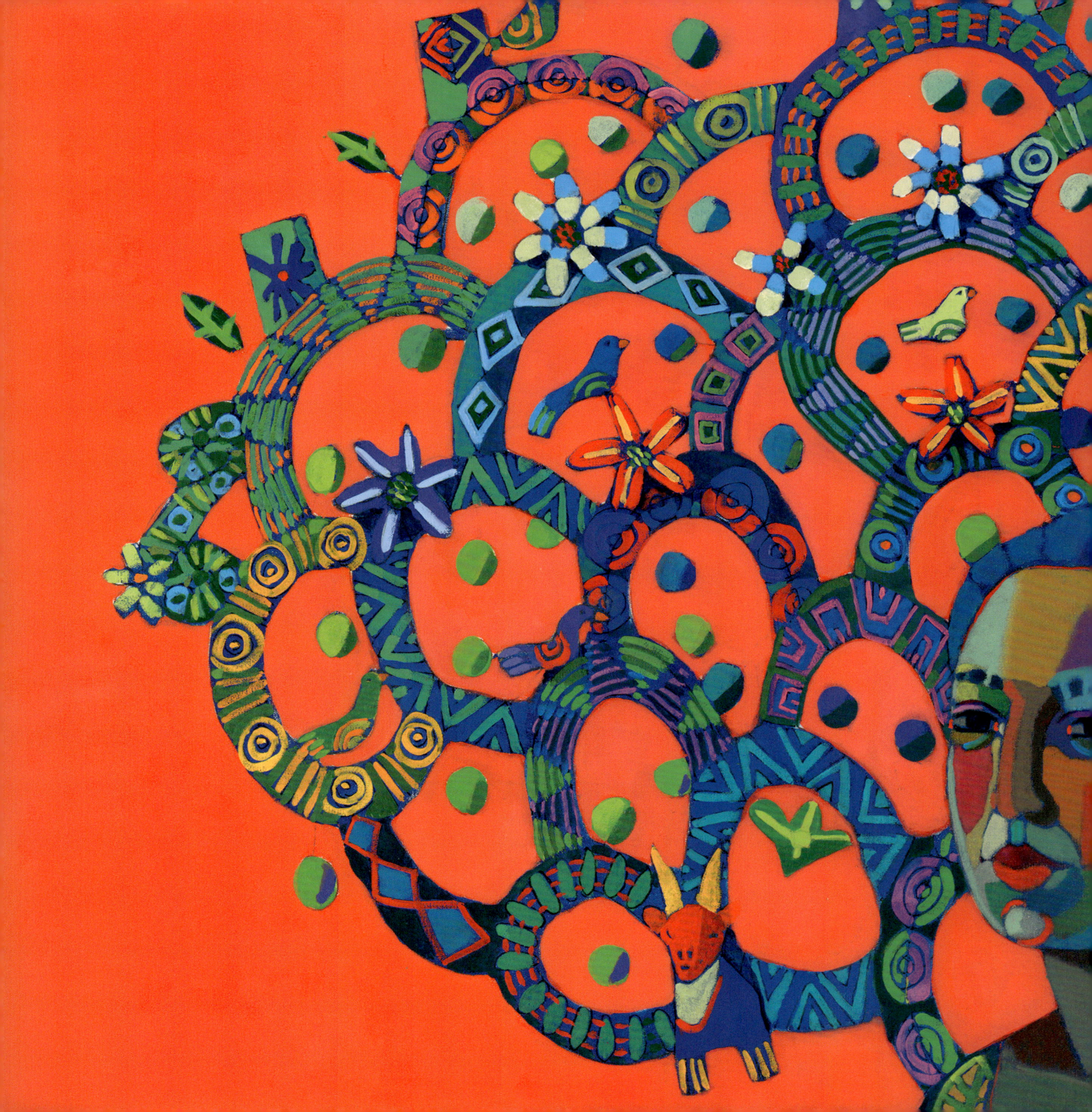

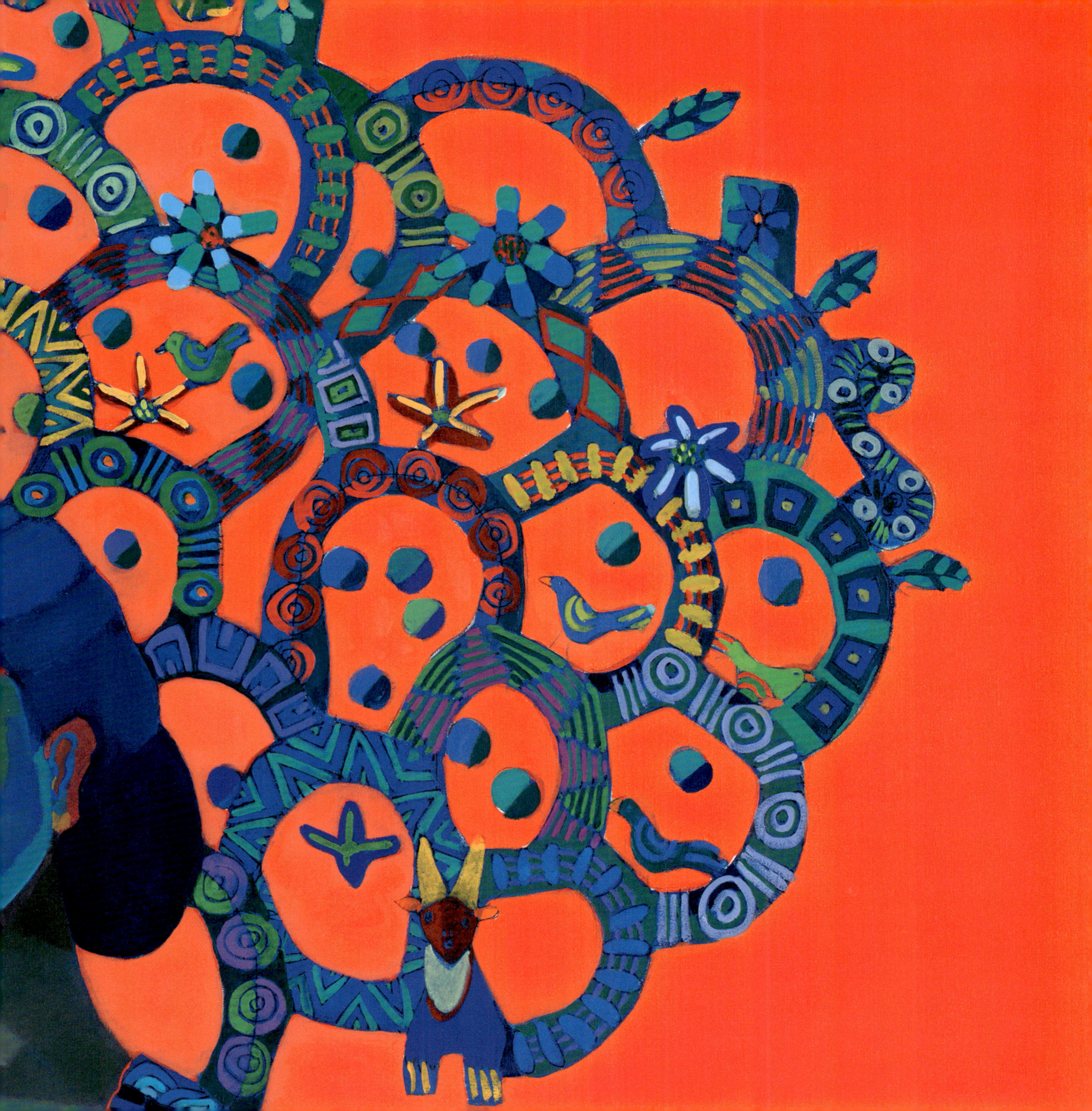

MESTIZAJE

Garden Aviary Rosa on My Mind
2012
Oil on canvas
40 x 60 in.

Mariachis on My Mind
2008
Oil on canvas
36 x 36 in.

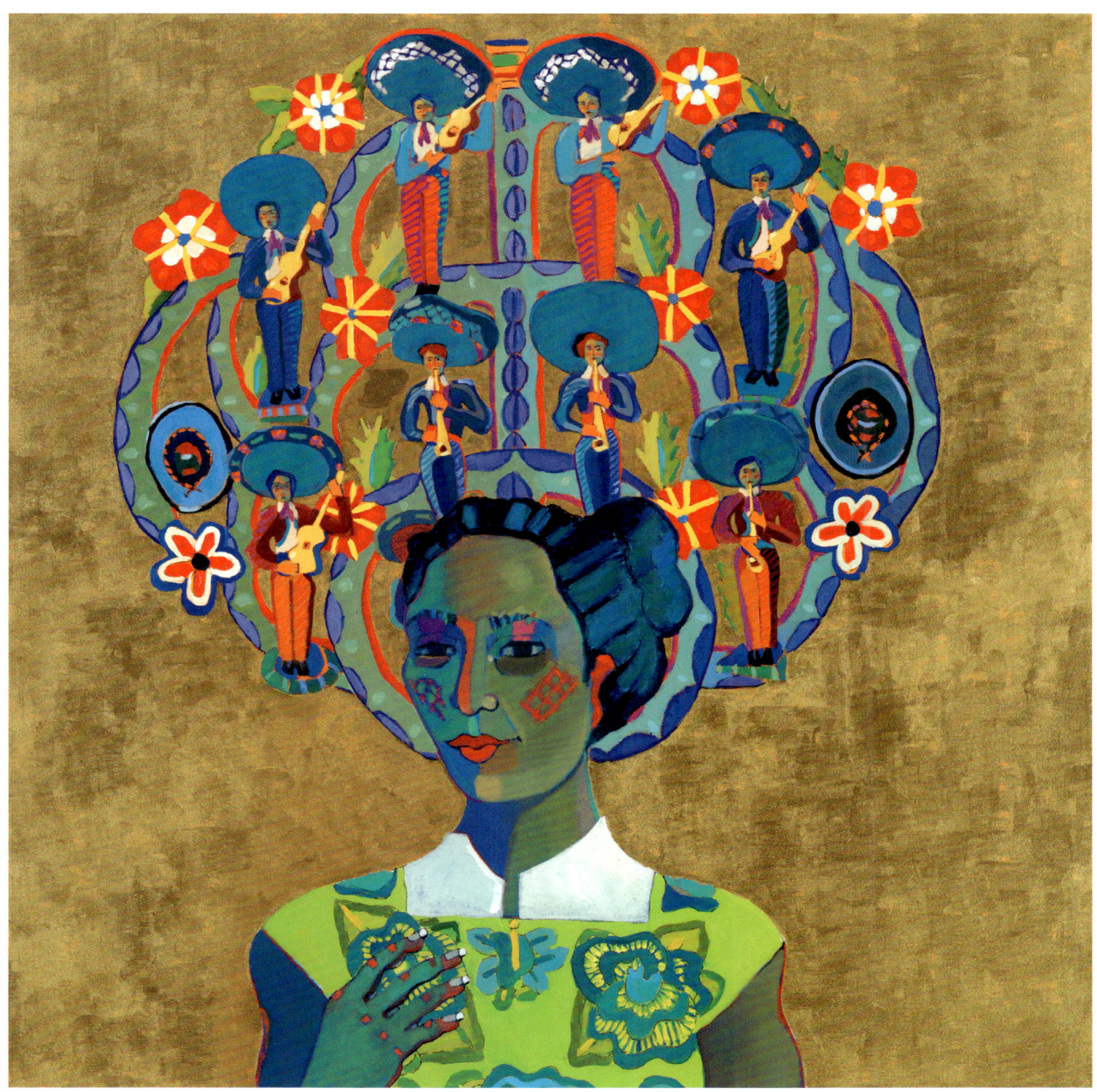

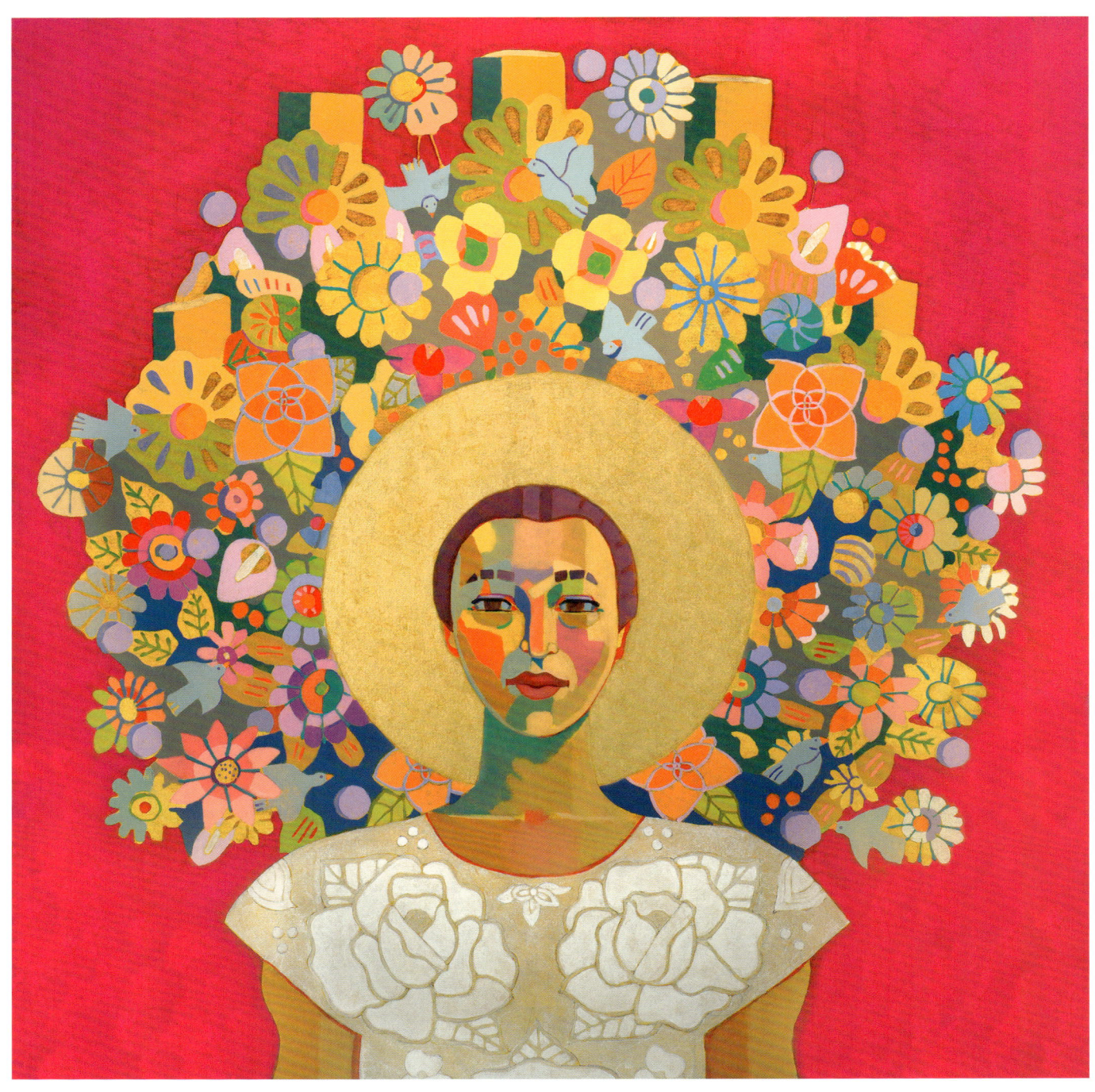

Reina de las Flores 6 on My Mind: Para Sandra
2023
Oil on canvas
48 x 48 in.

*Reina de las Flores 4
on My Mind*
2015
Oil on canvas
48 x 48 in.

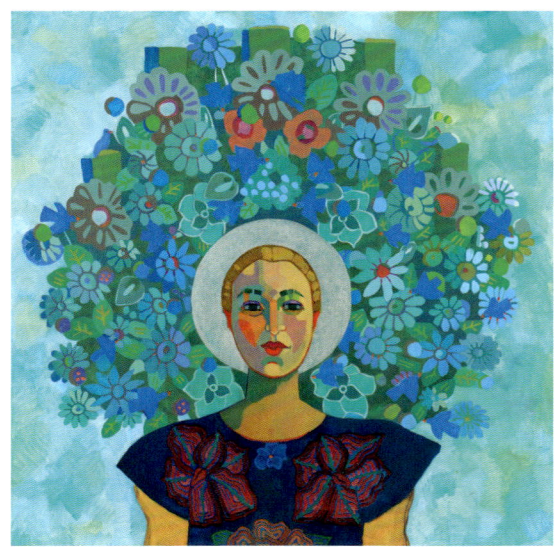

*Reina de las Flores 1
on My Mind*
2009
Oil on canvas
48 x 48 in.

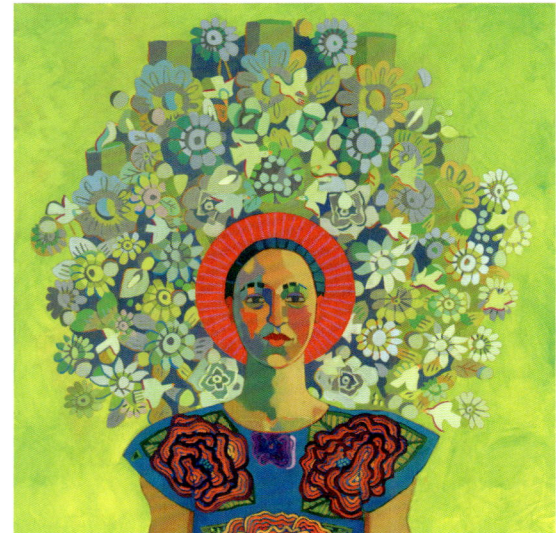

*Reina de las Flores 3
on My Mind*
2014
Oil on canvas
48 x 48 in.

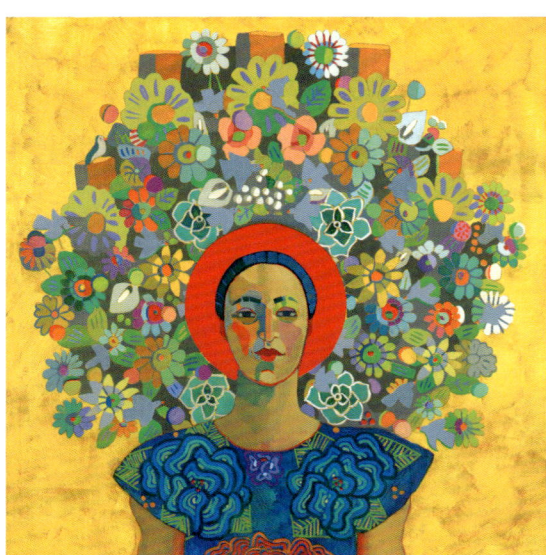

*Reina de las Flores 2
on My Mind*
2010
Oil on canvas
48 x 48 in.

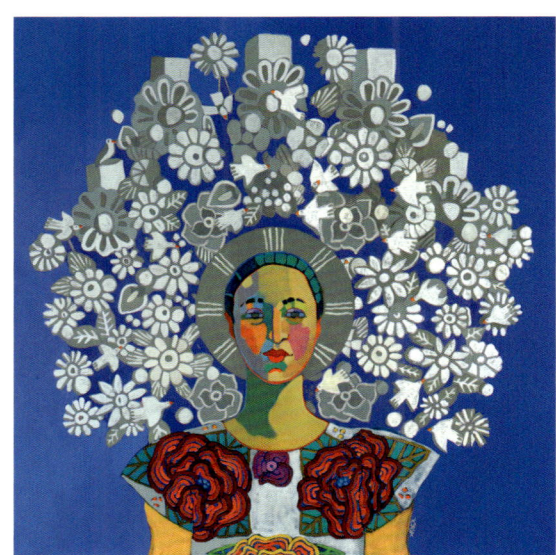

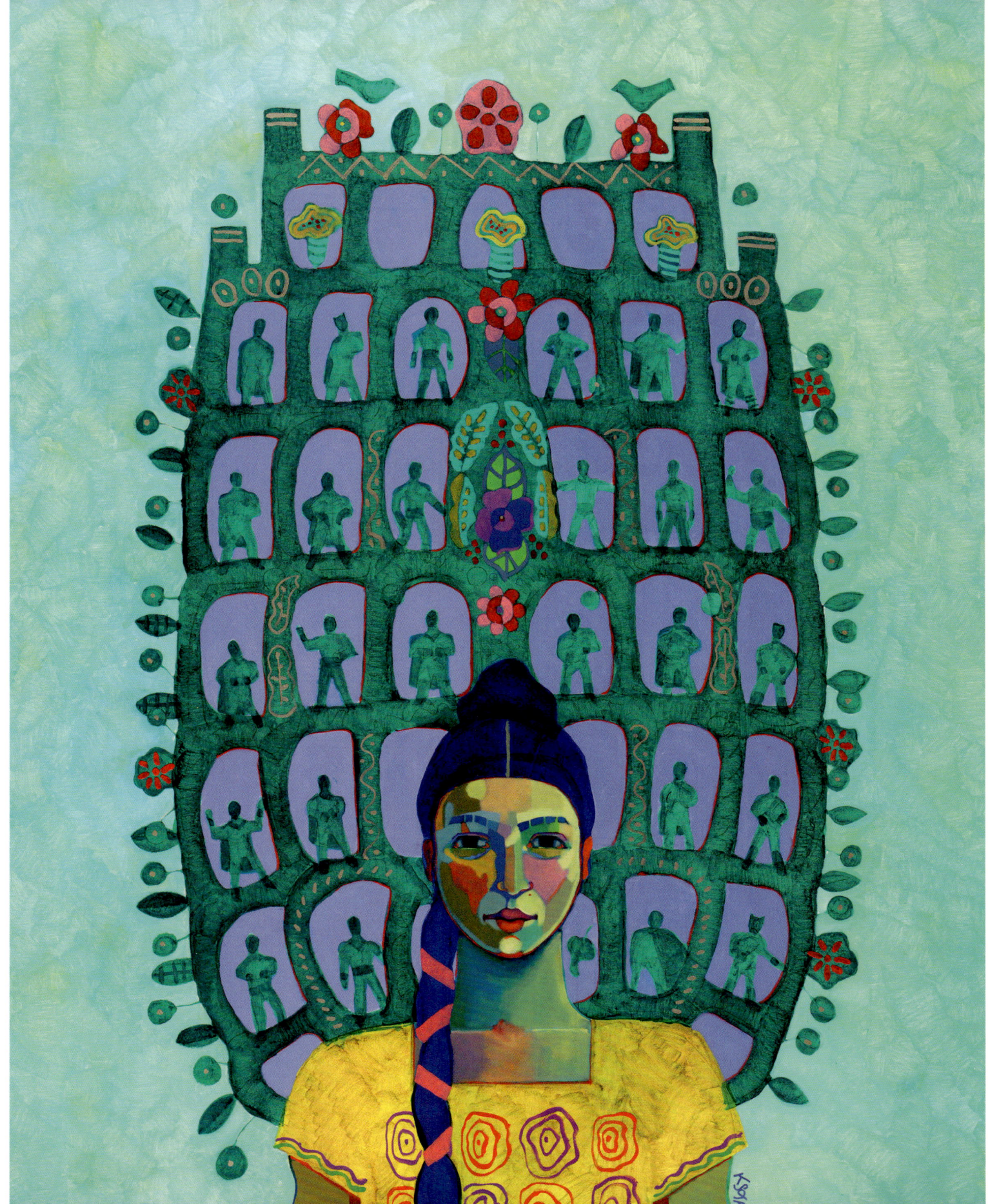

Luchadores Betty Ward
Gave Me on My Mind
2019
Oil on canvas
60 x 48 in.

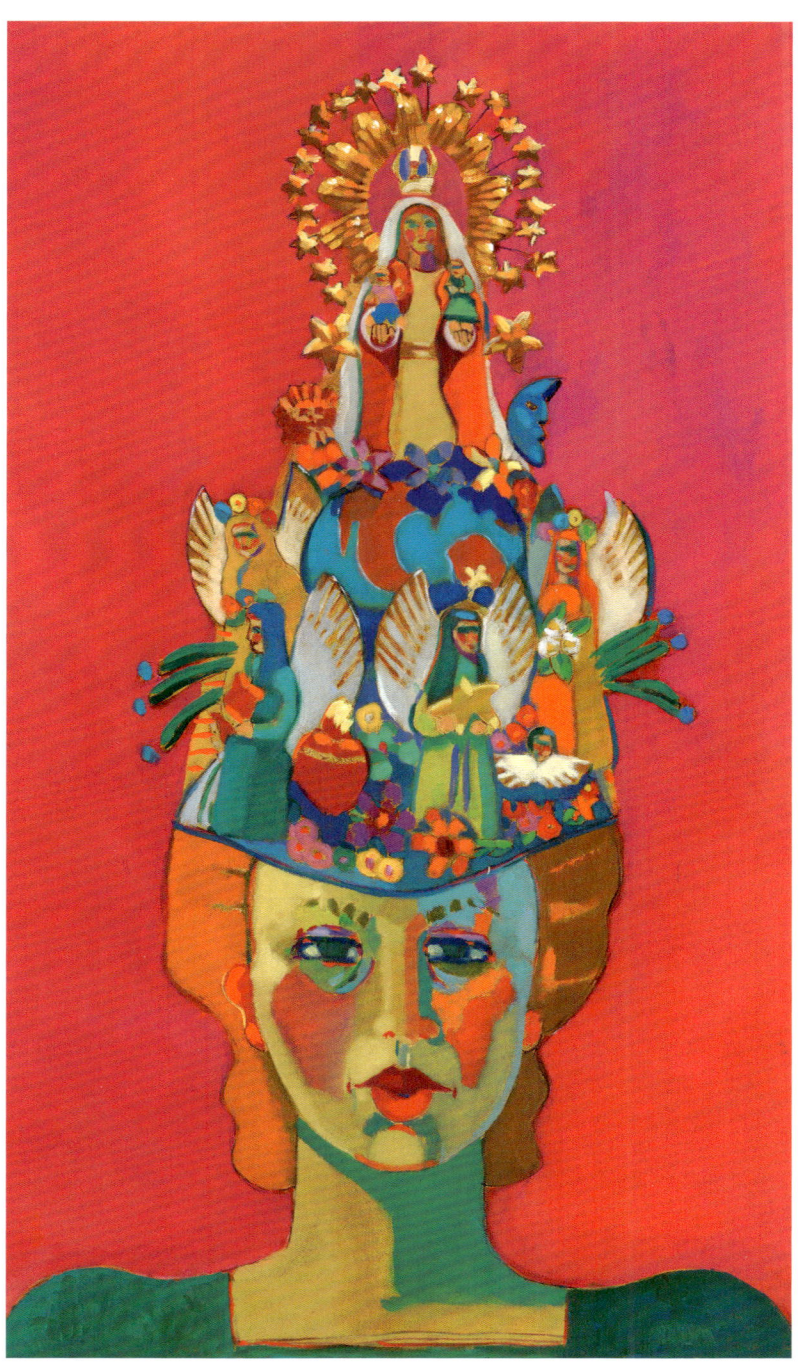

María Antonieta
on My Mind
2014
Oil on canvas
24 x 20 in.

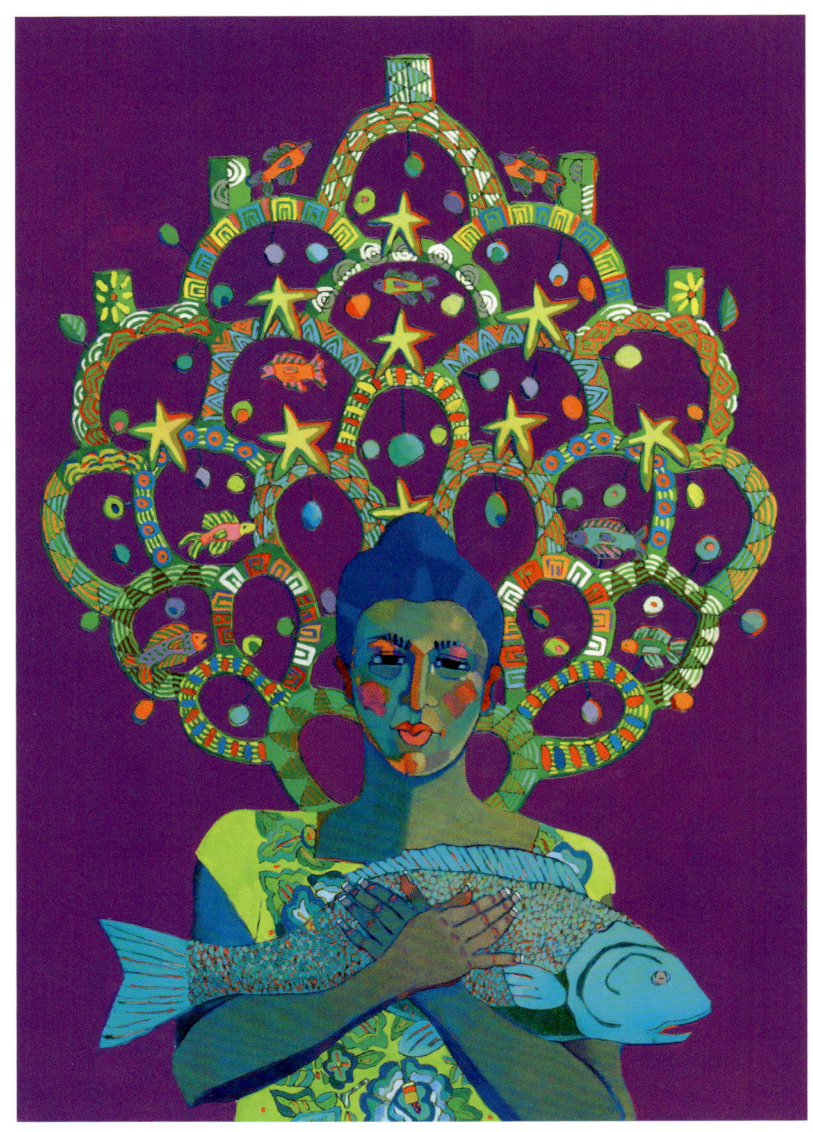

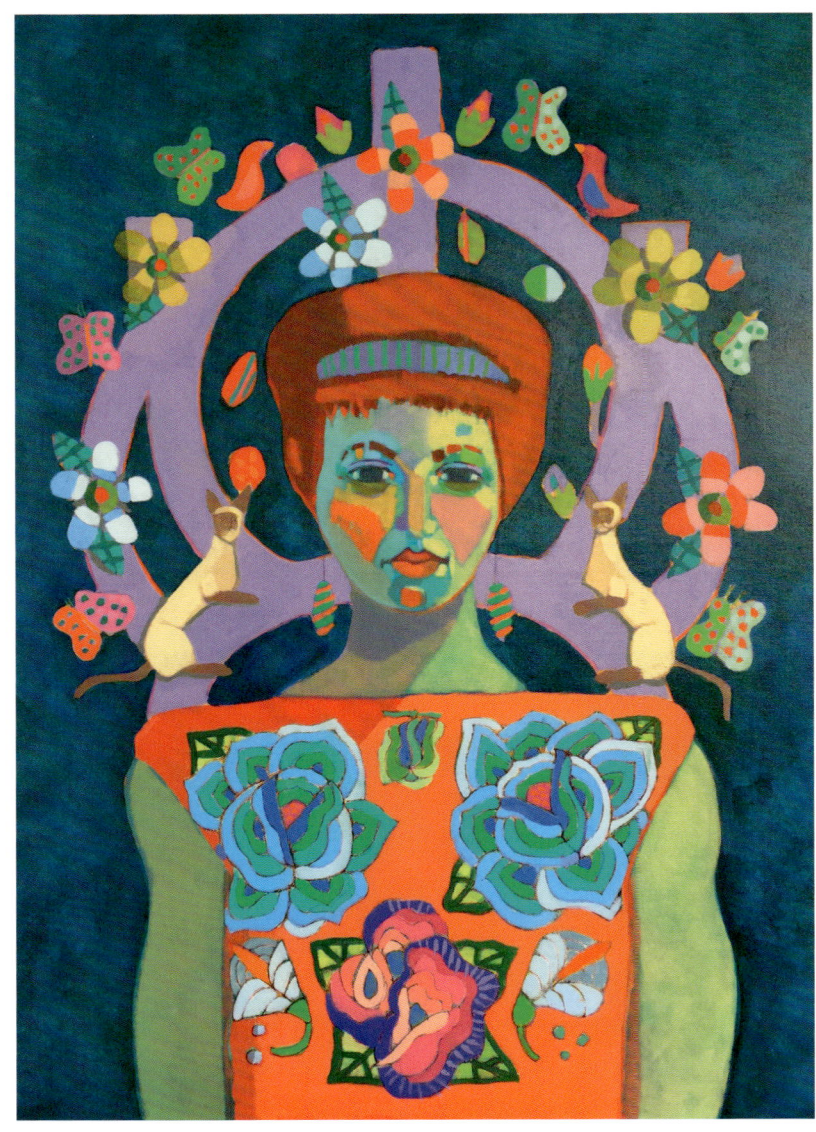

Mariscos on My Mind
2010
Oil on canvas
40 x 30 in.

Siamese Twins on My Mind
2016
Oil on canvas
30 x 24 in.

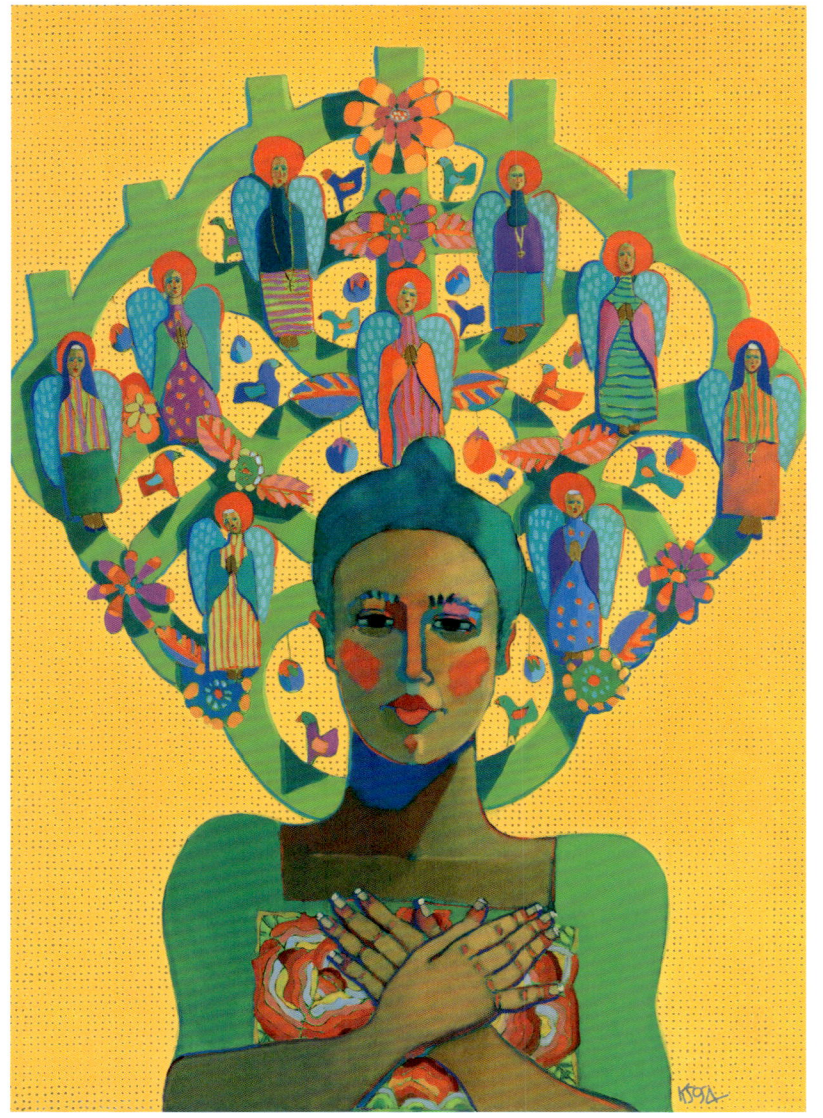

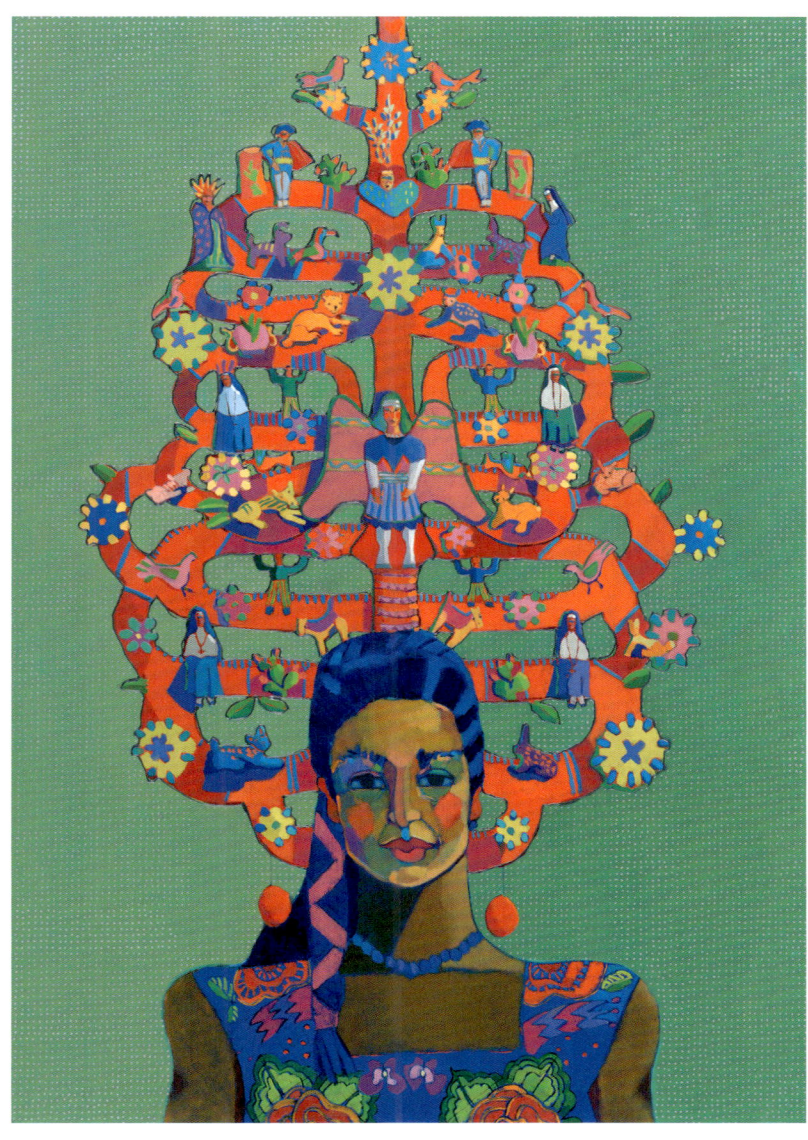

Angelitos on My Mind
2009
Oil on canvas
40 x 30 in.

Animalitos on My Mind
2009
Oil on canvas
48 x 36 in.

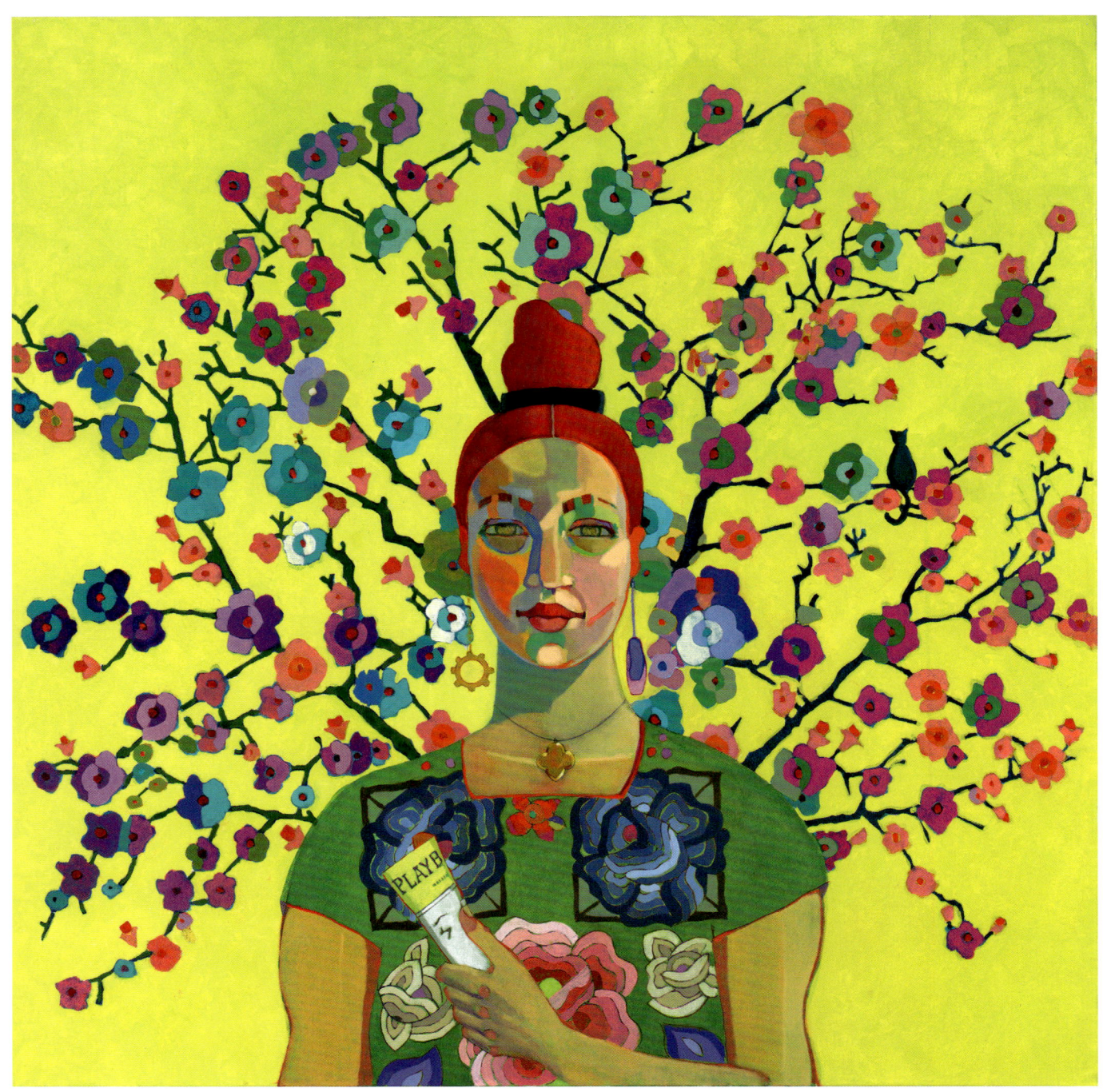

*Cherry Tree of Life:
Olivia's Memories
on My Mind*
2019
Oil on canvas
36 x 36 in.

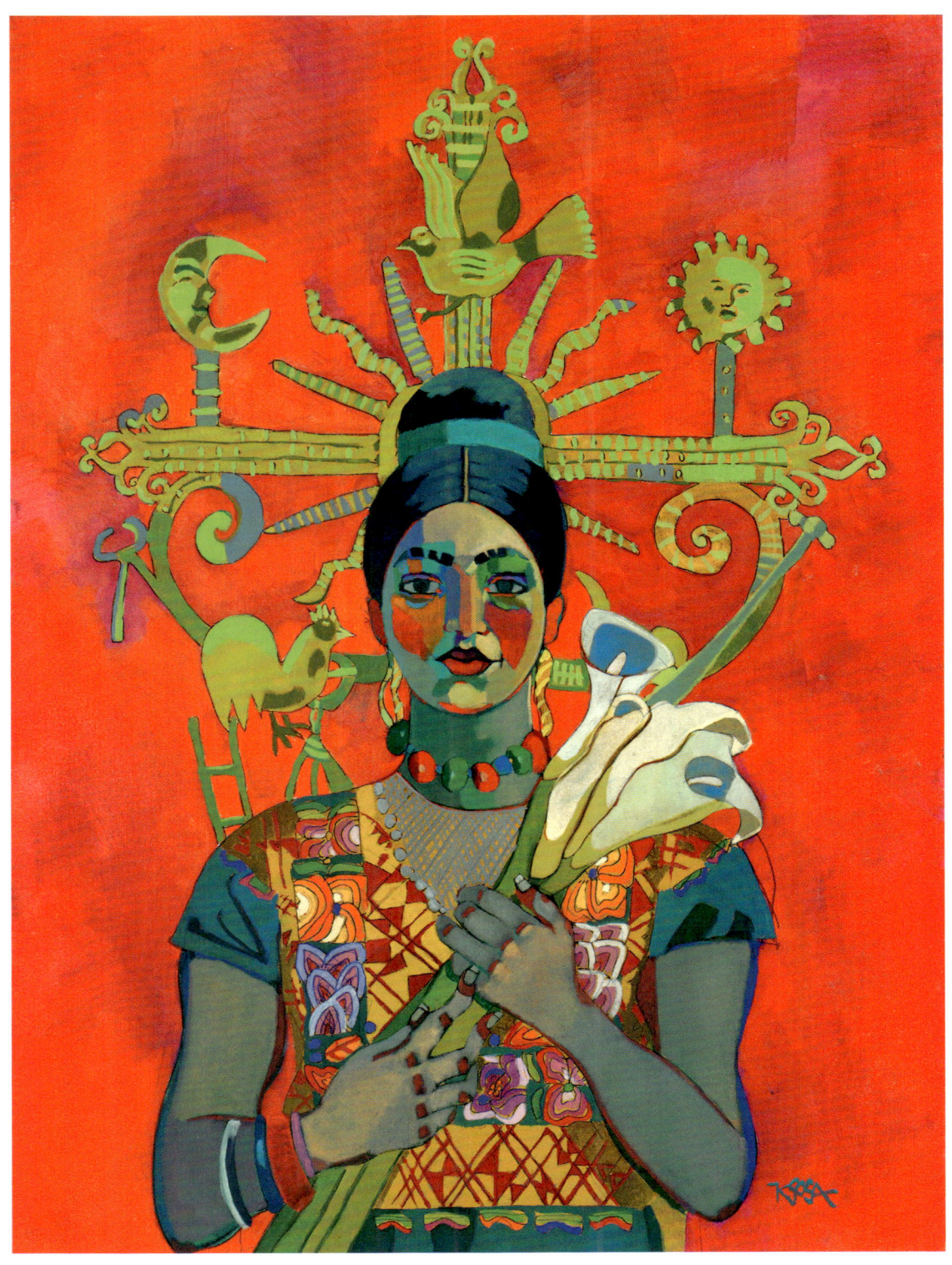

Árbol Metálico
on My Mind No. 1
2012
Oil on canvas
40 x 30 in.

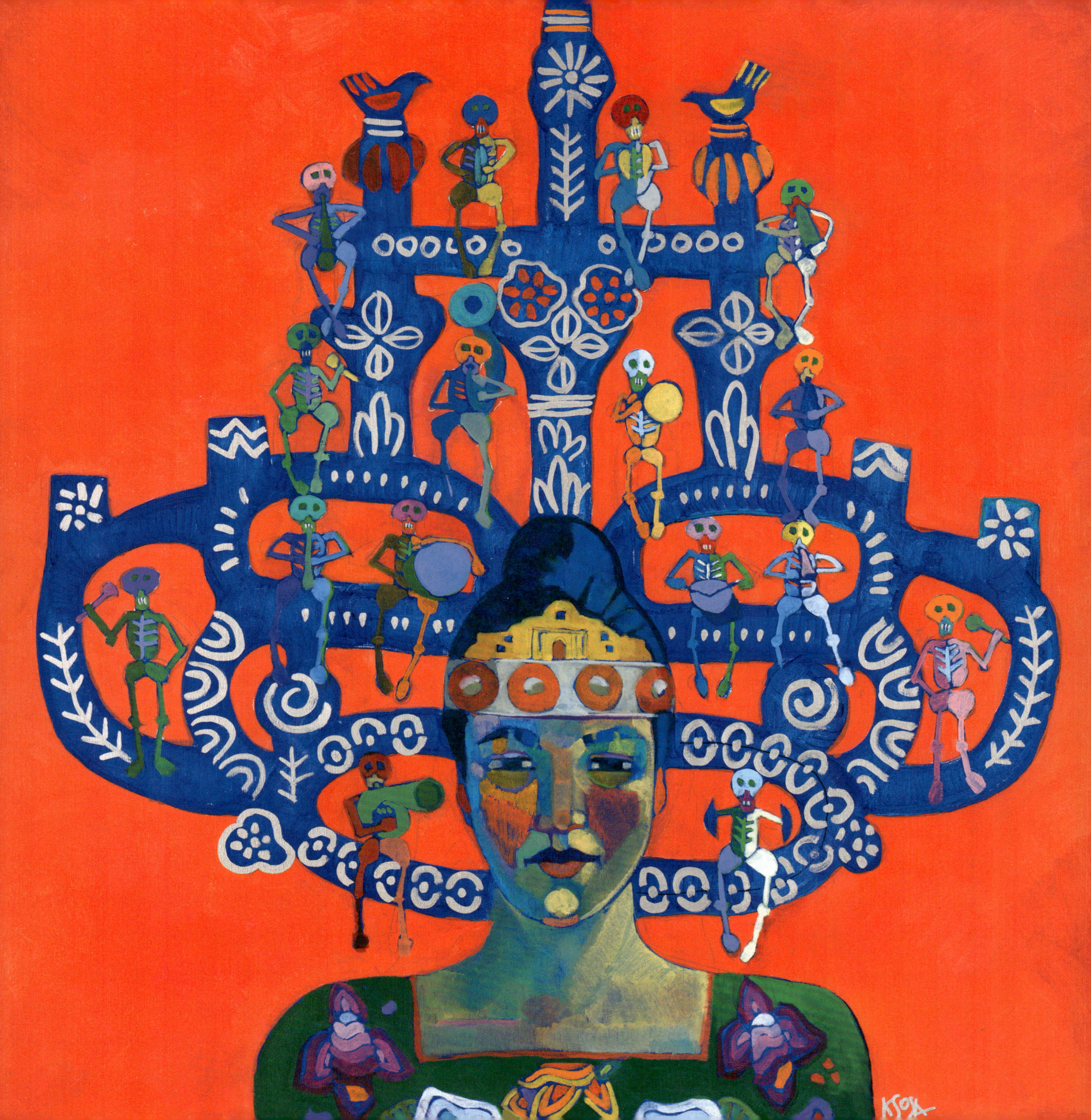

Alamo City Skeleton
Band on My Mind
2016
Oil on canvas
36 x 36 in.

*Mestiza de Felipe: Do I Ever
Cross Your Mind?* (detail)
2018
Oil on canvas
40 x 40 in.

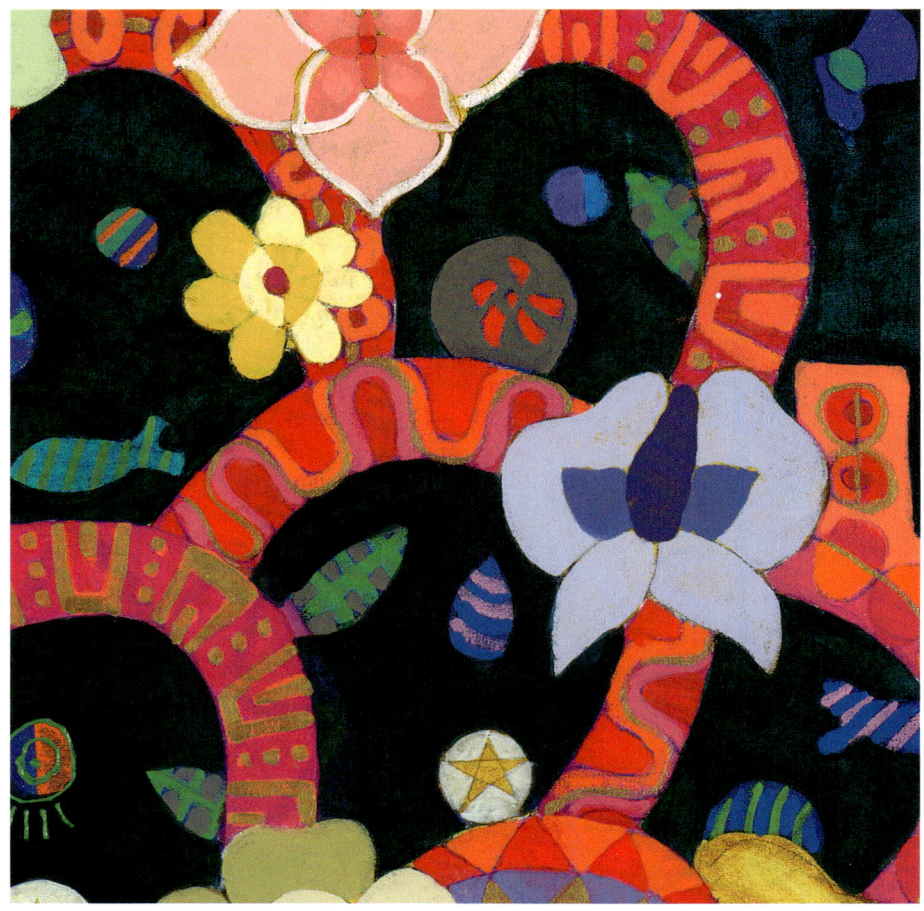

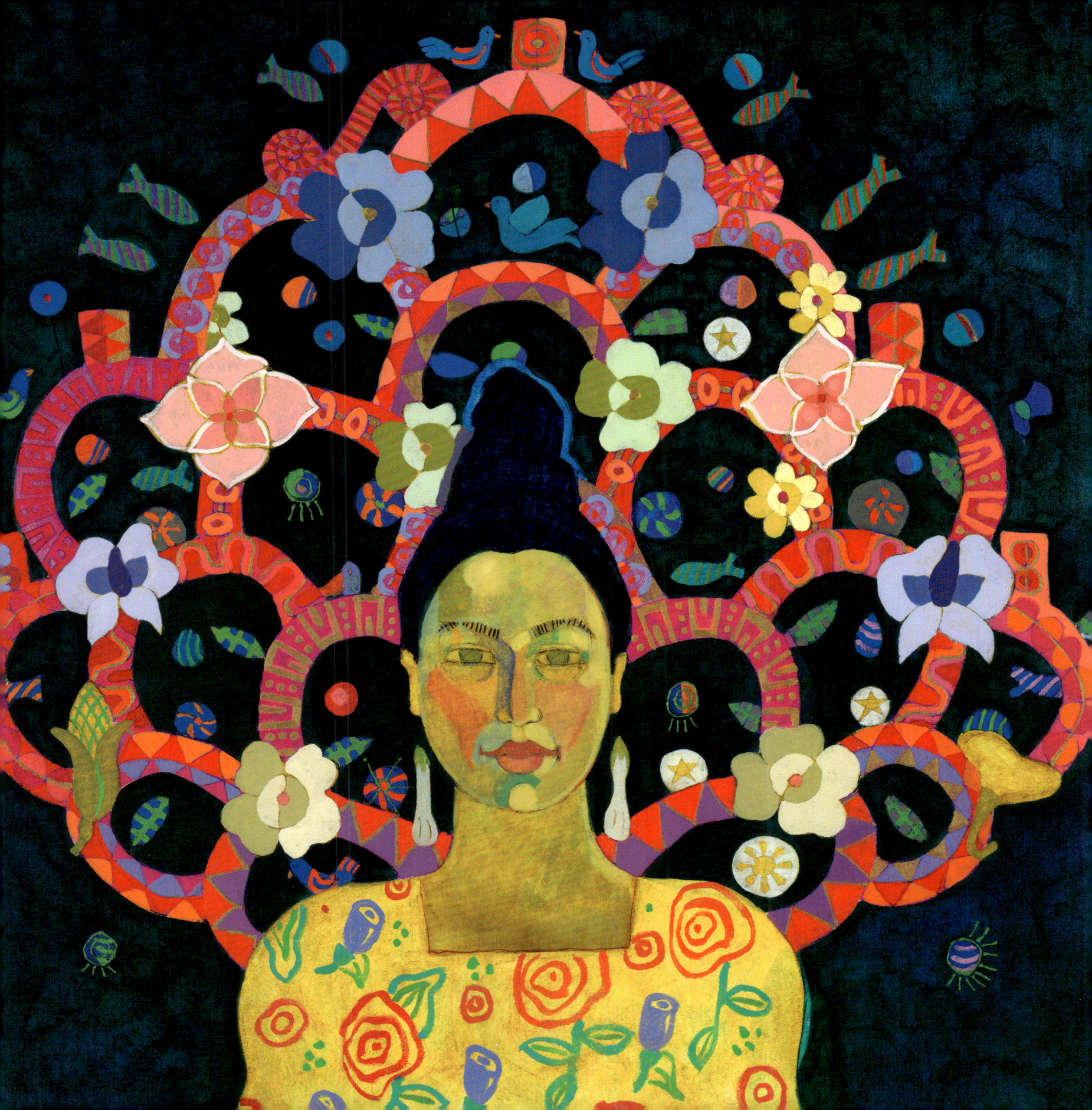

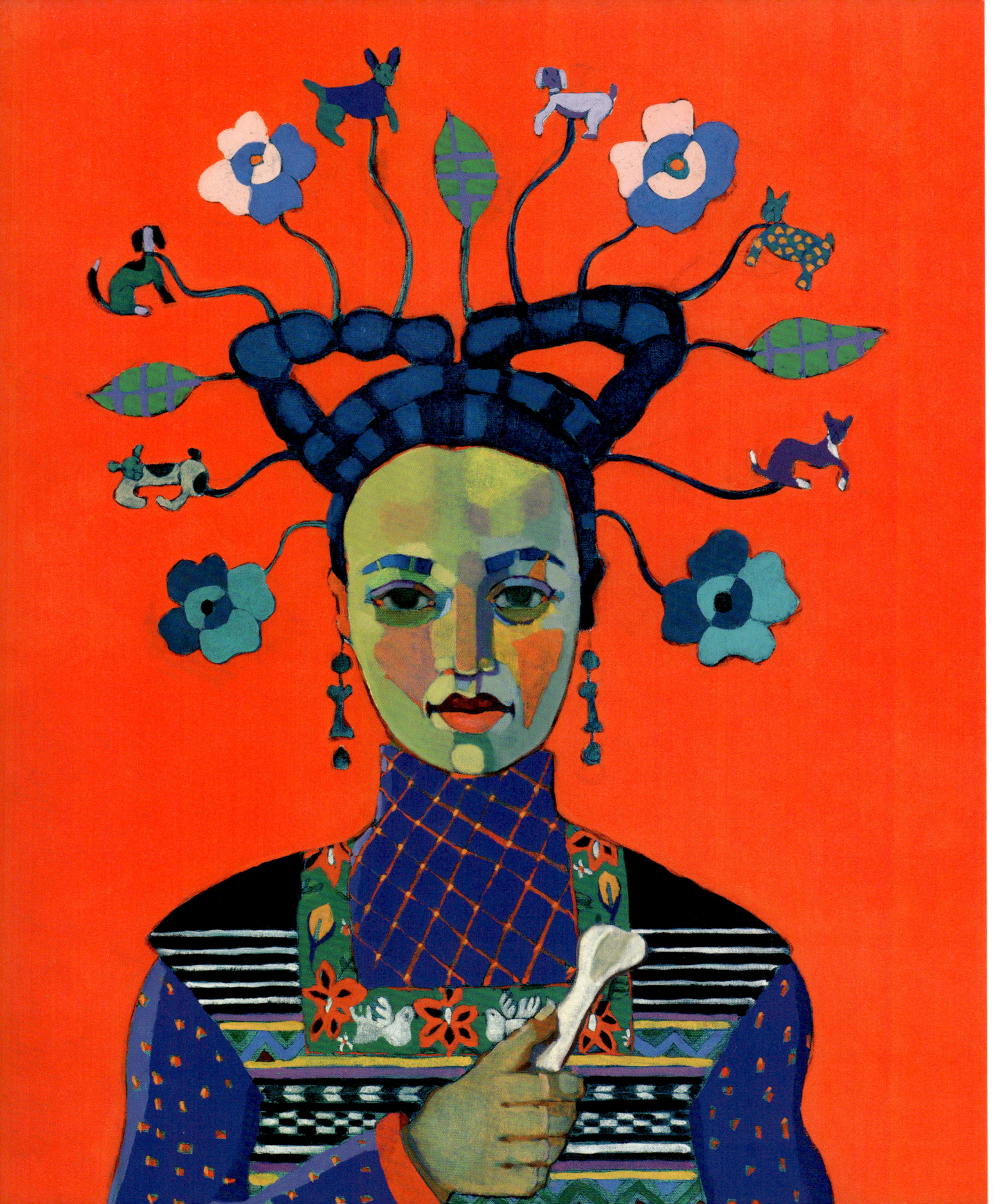

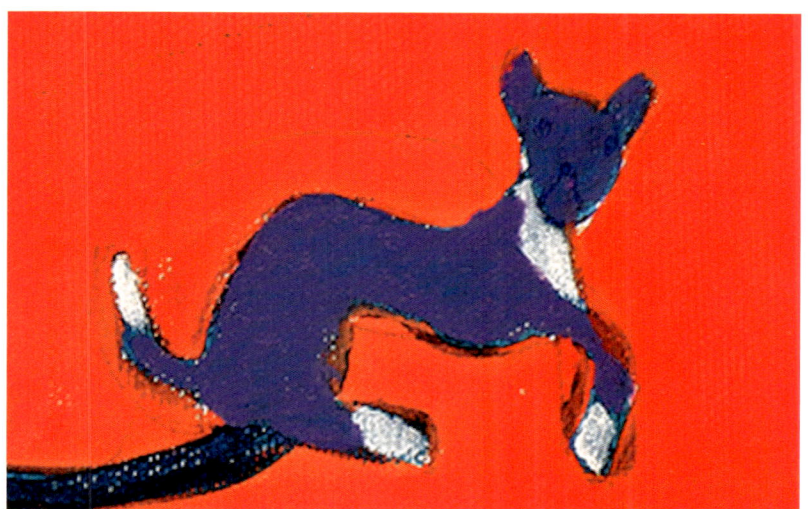

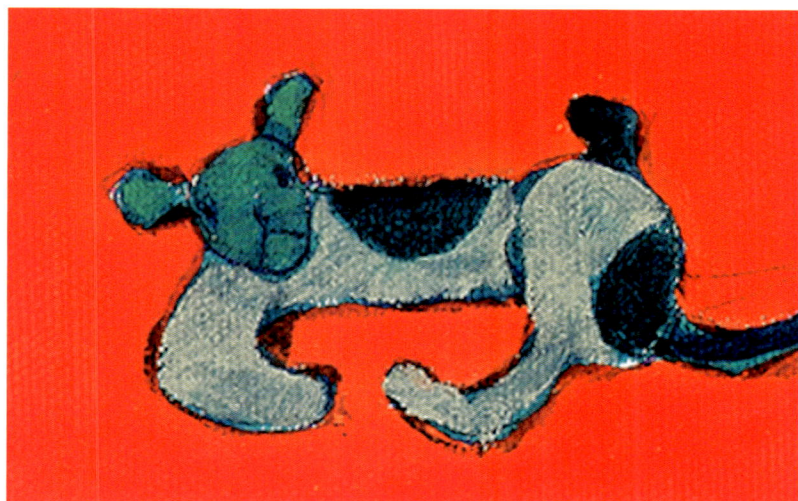

*Huipilista Dog Whisperer
on My Mind*
2016
Oil on canvas
30 x 24 in.

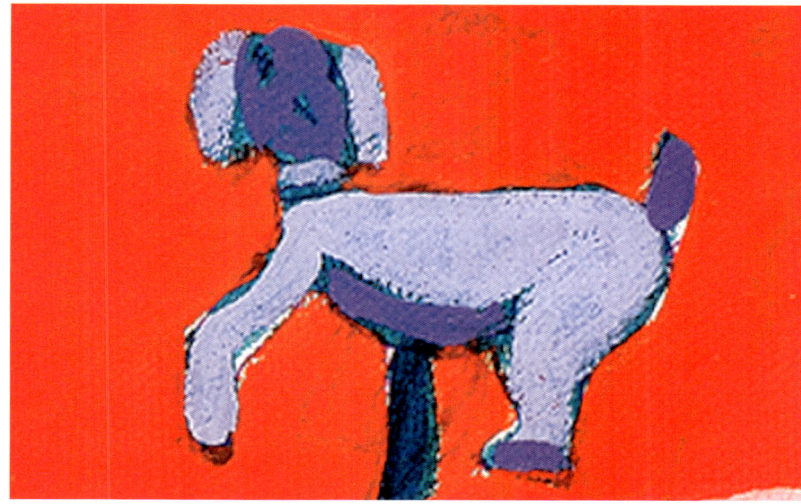

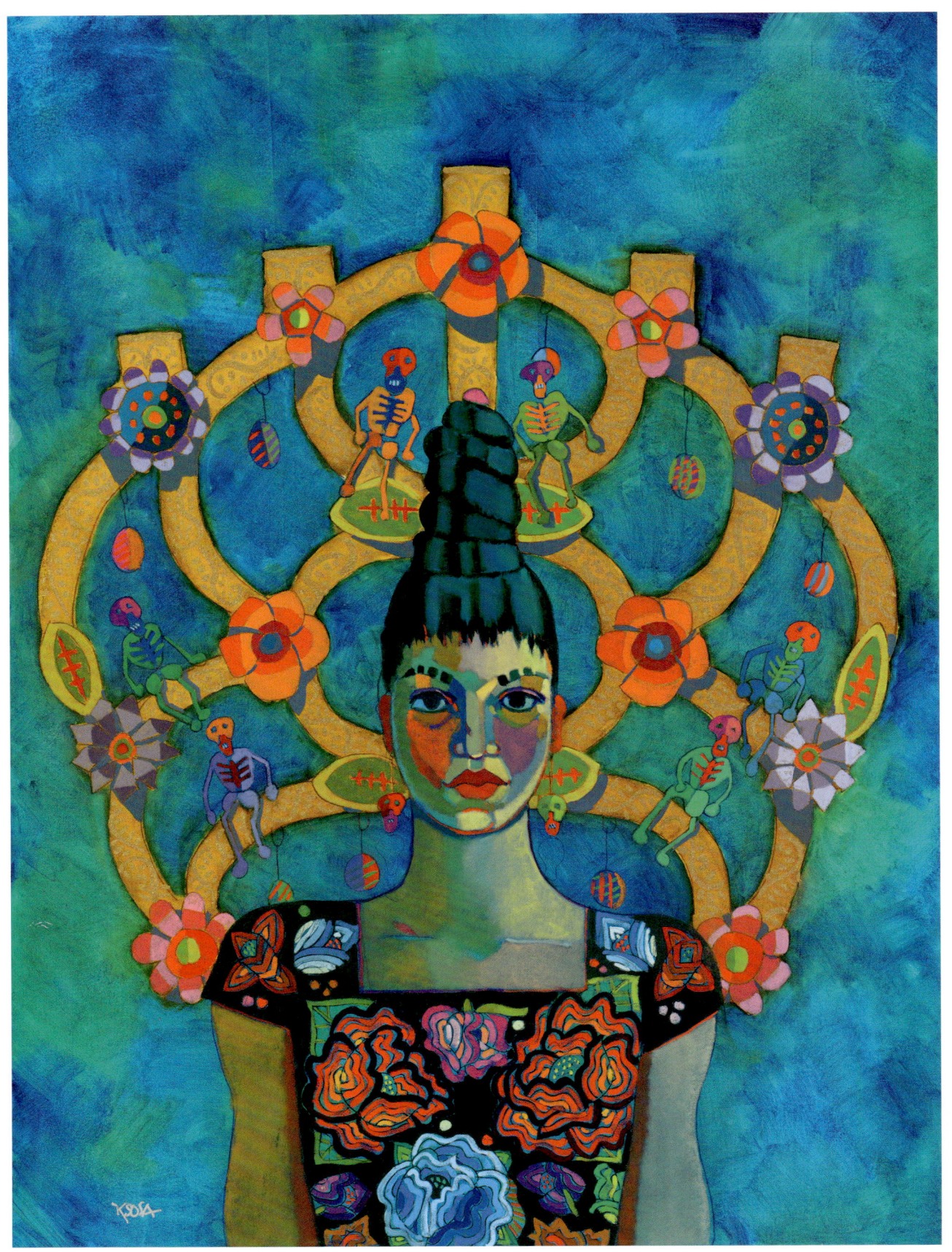

*Los Muertitos on
My Mind No. 1*
2012
Oil on canvas
48 x 36 in.

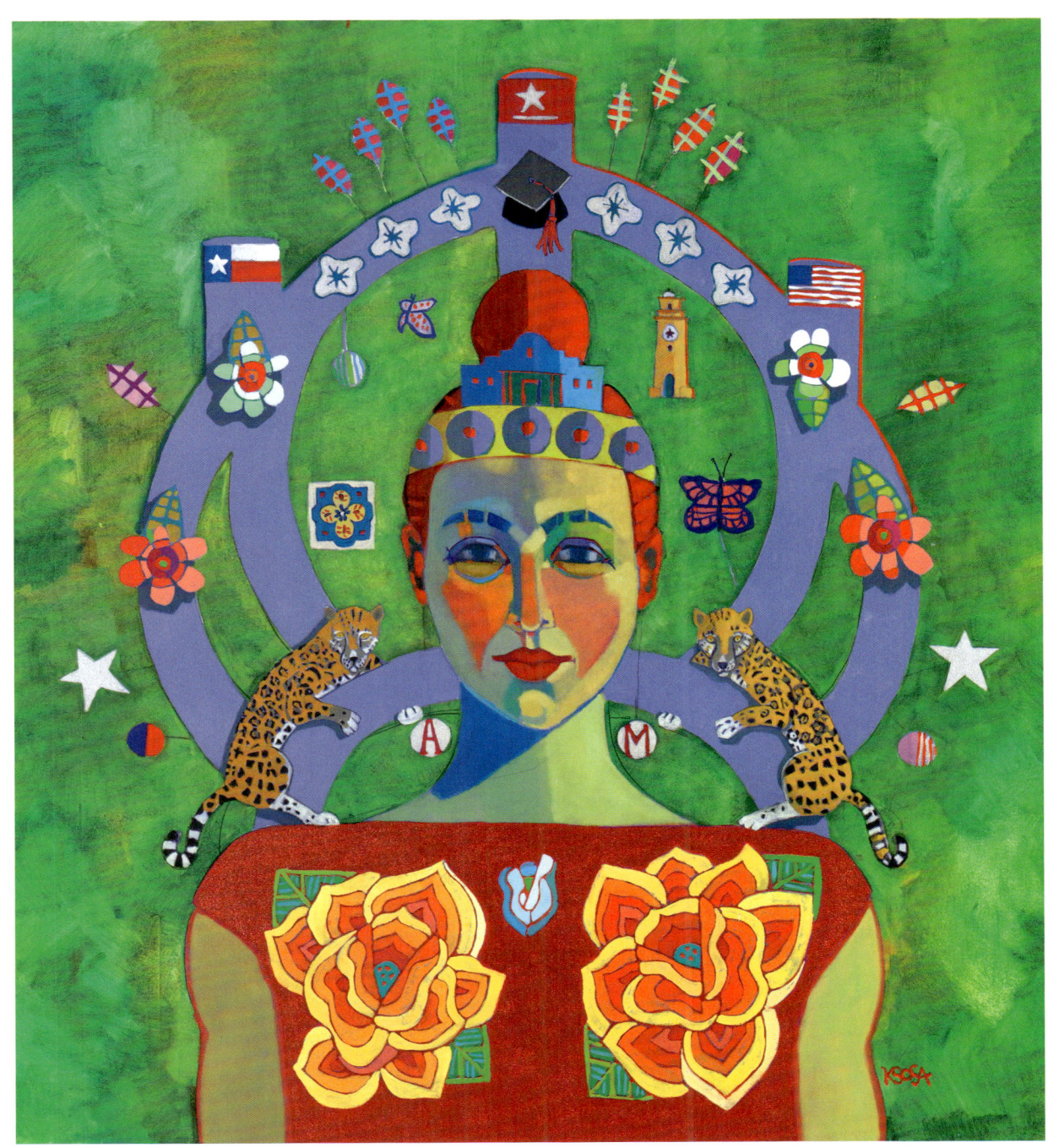

Jaguar on My Shoulder:
Texas A&M–San Antonio
on My Mind
2010
Oil on canvas
60 x 60 in.

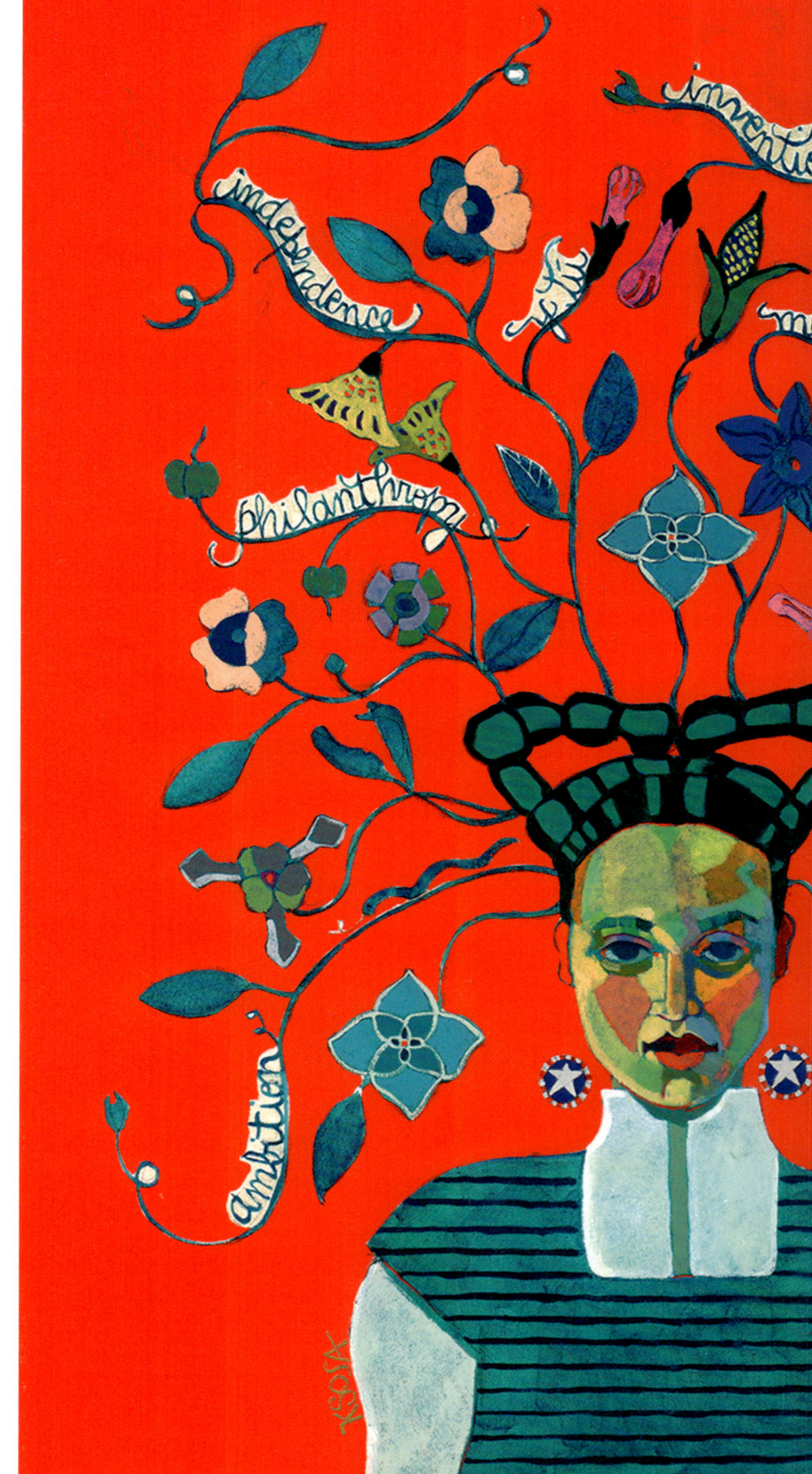

*Goddesses Contemplating
la Cultura on My Mind*
2016
Oil on canvas
42 x 78 in.

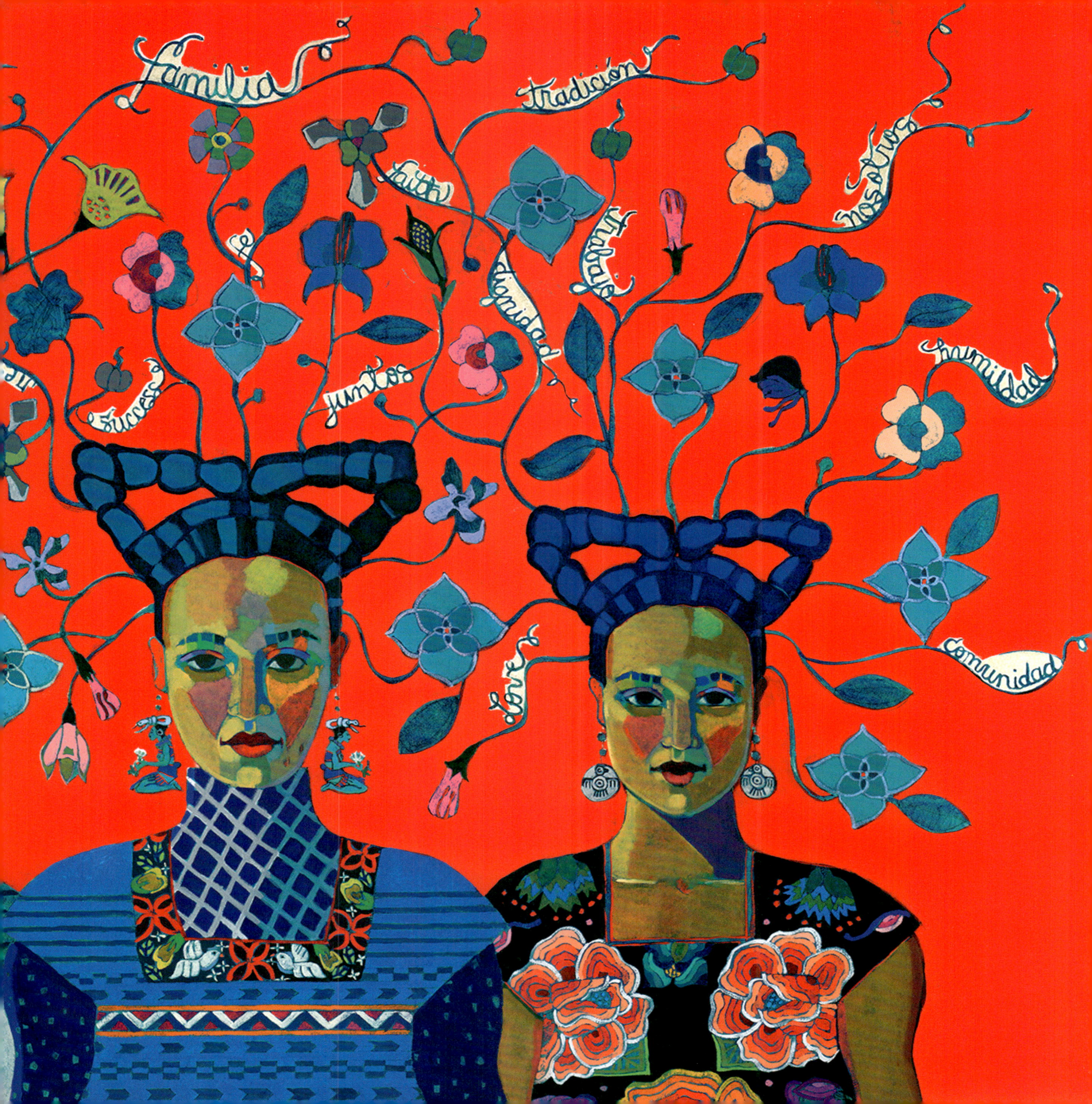

Legacy of Love on My Mind:
Homage to Deborah (detail)
2014
Oil on canvas
48 x 30 in.

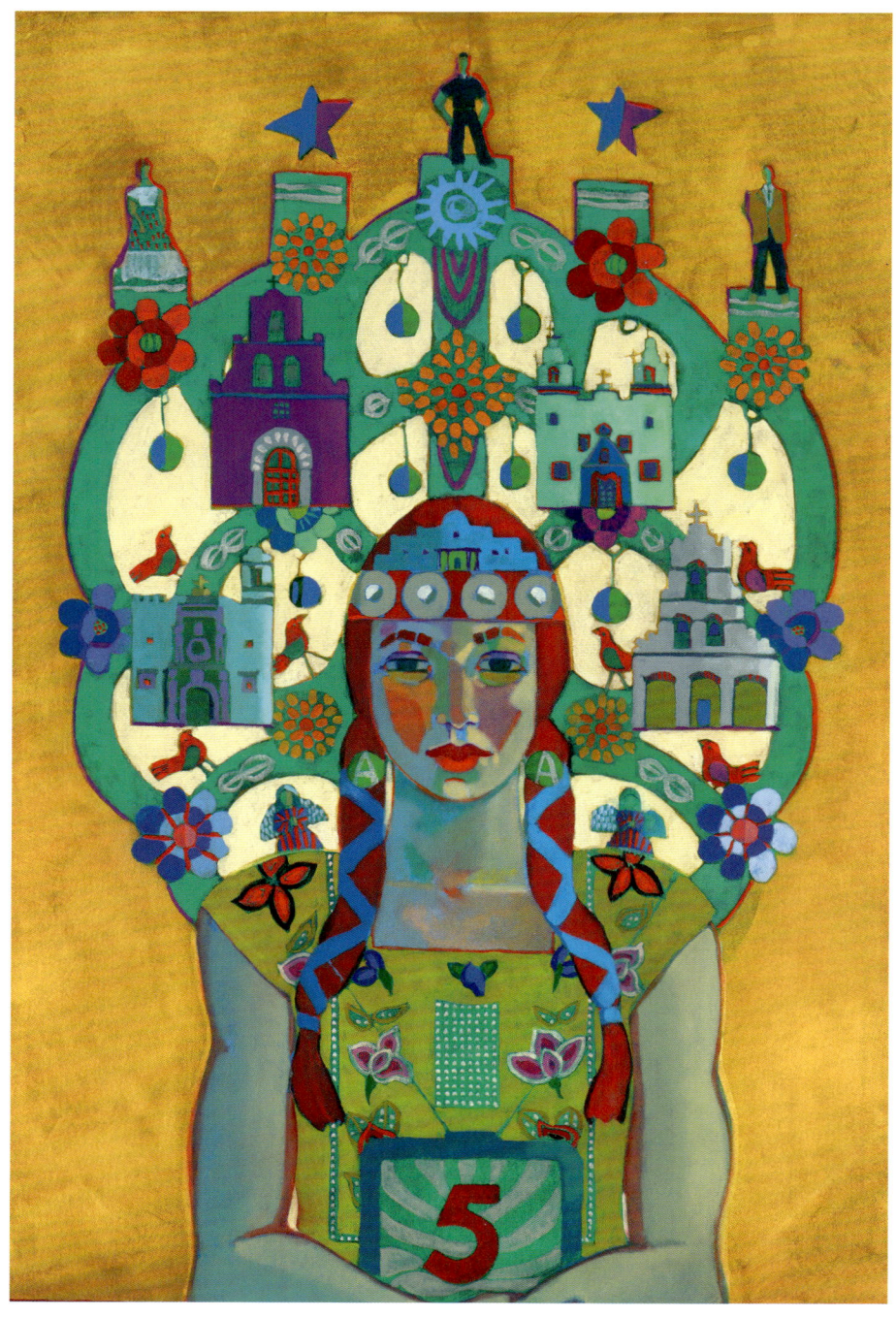

Los Niños on My Mind
2011
Oil on canvas
28 x 22 in.

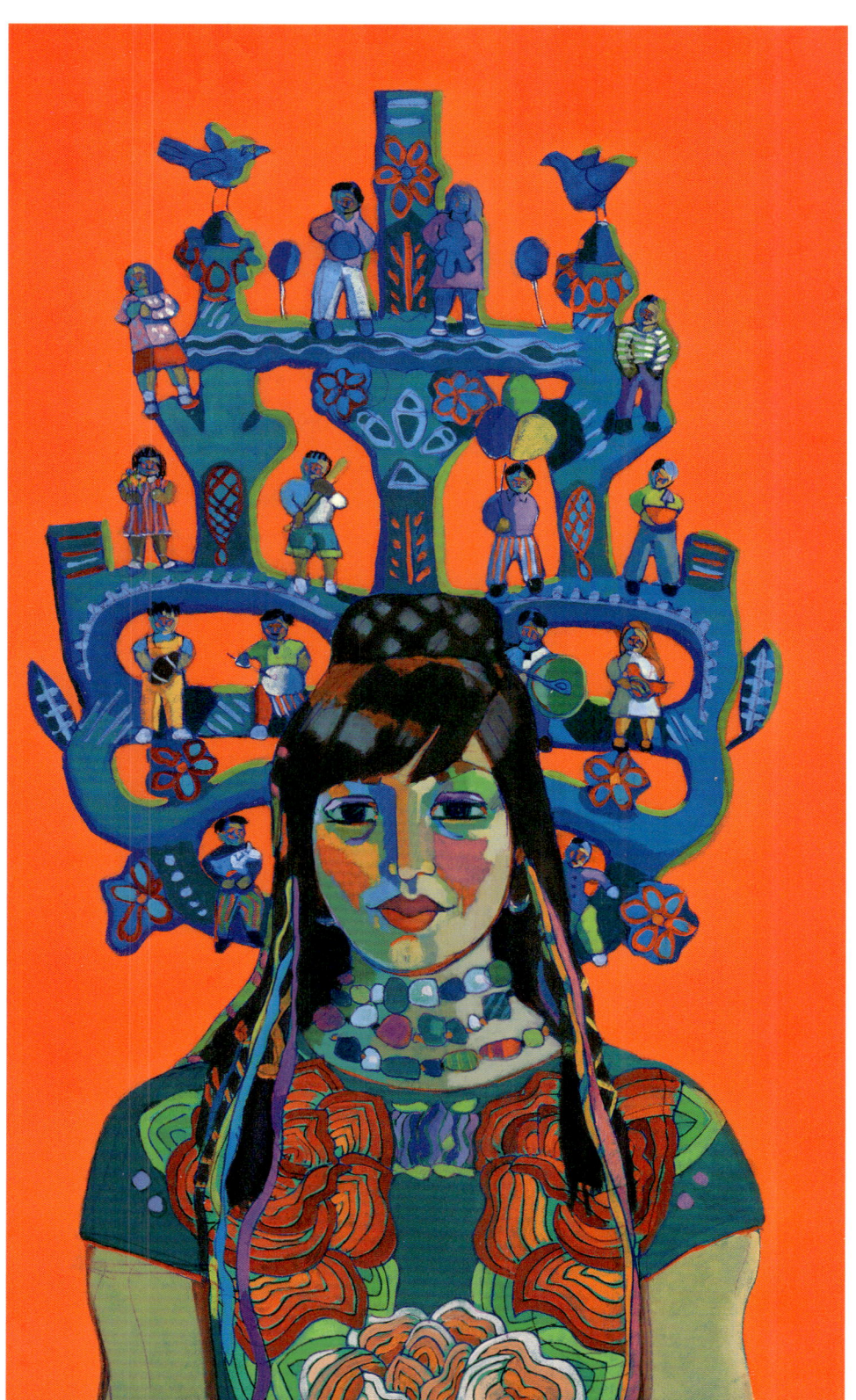

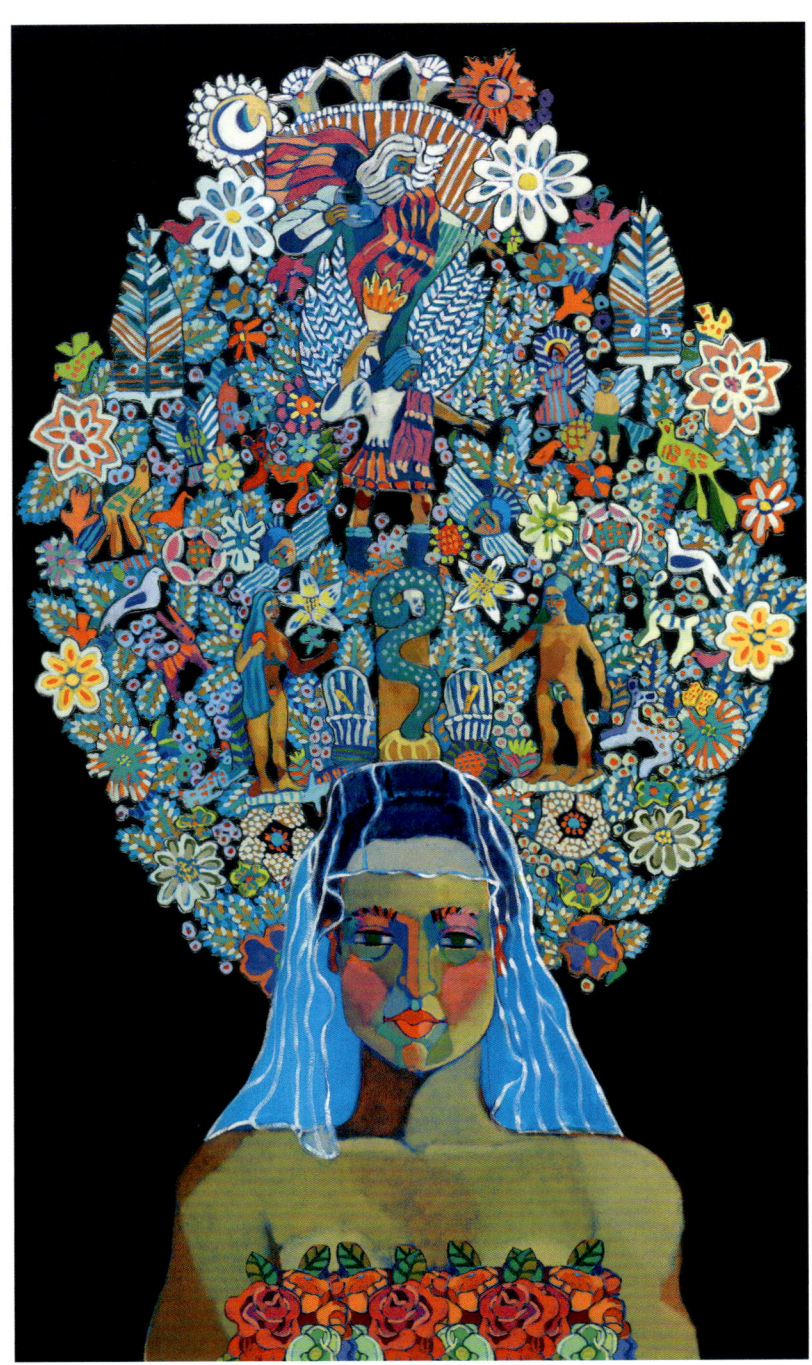

Matrimonio on My Mind
2009
Oil on canvas
48 x 36 in.

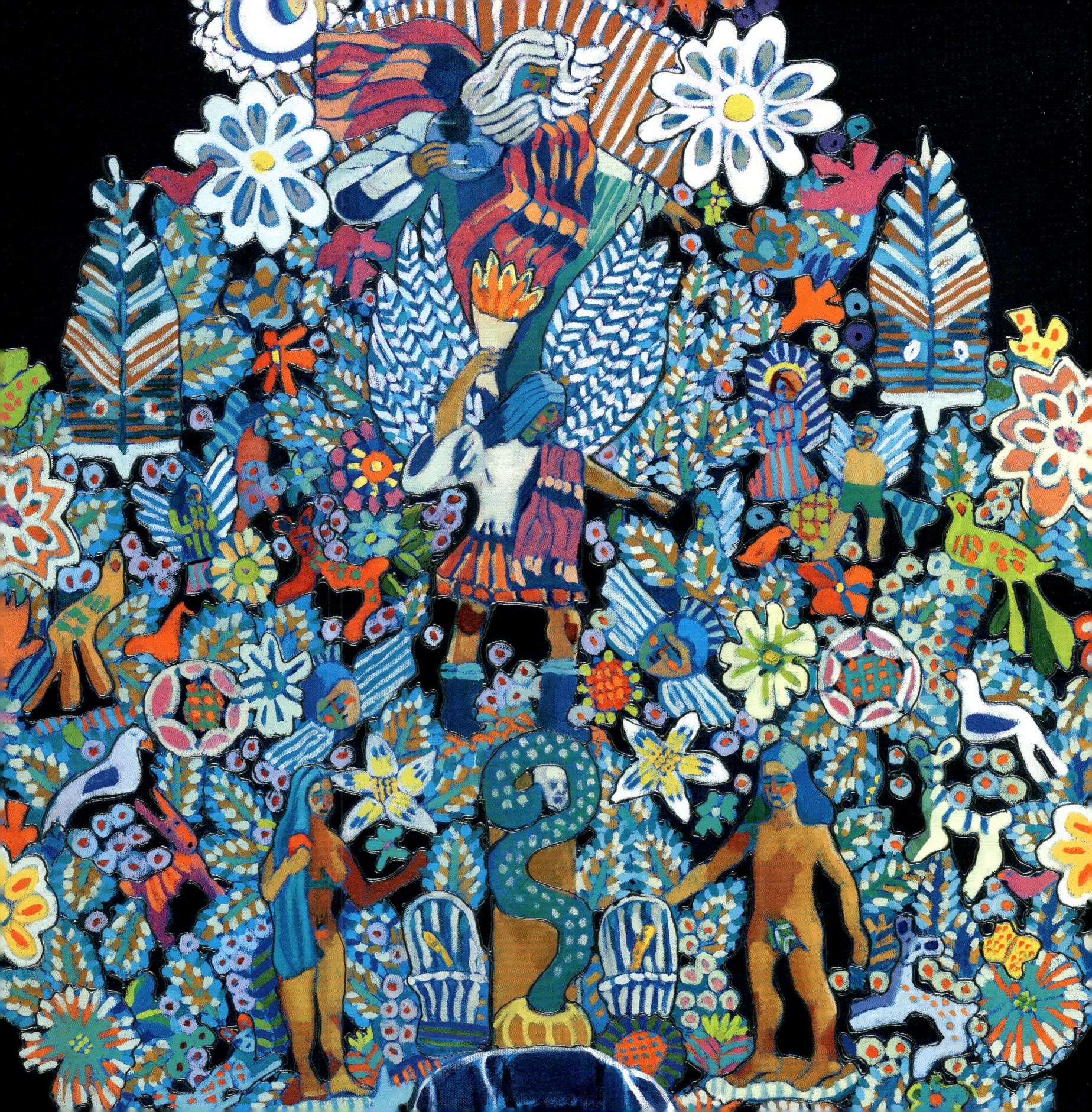

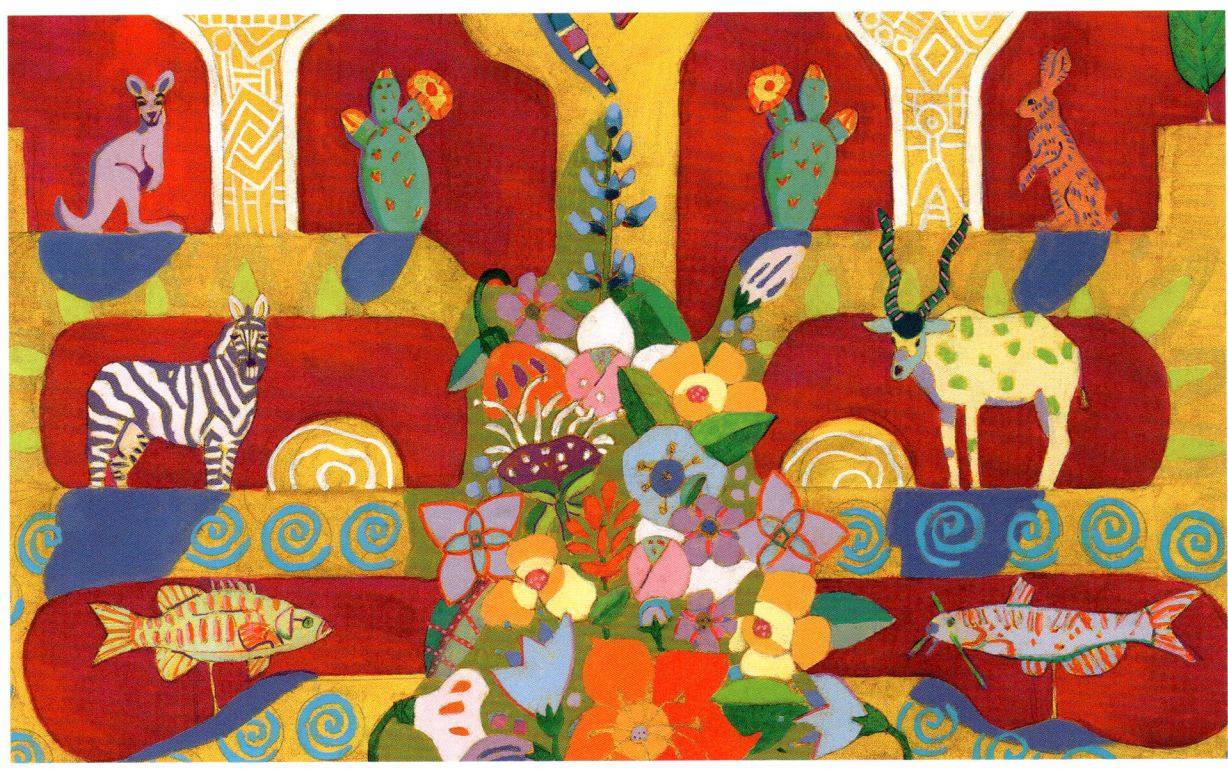

Piebald Ranch Live Oak County
Texas on My Mind (detail)
2023
Oil on canvas
72 x 48 in.

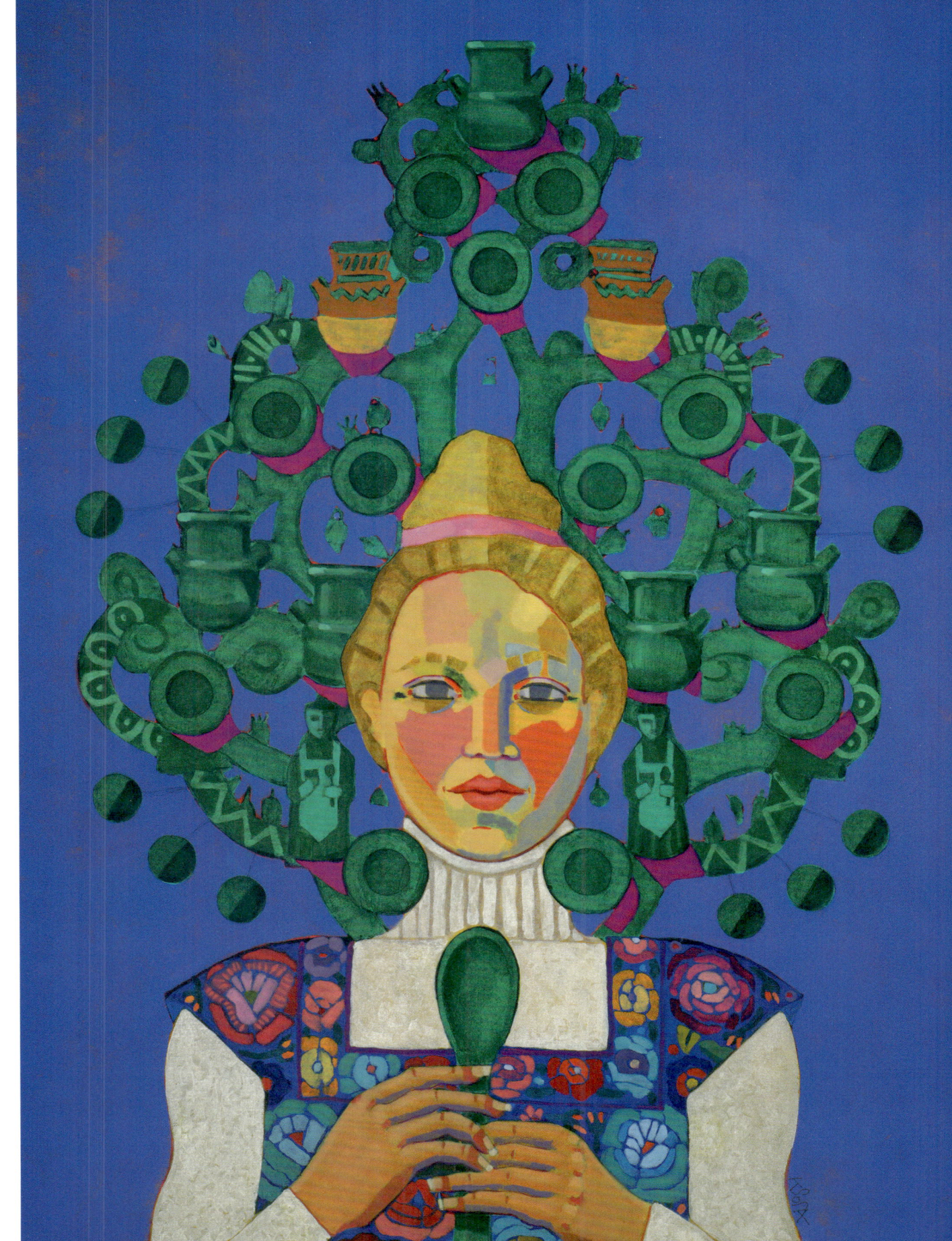

La Cocinera on My Mind
2021
Oil on canvas
40 x 30 in.

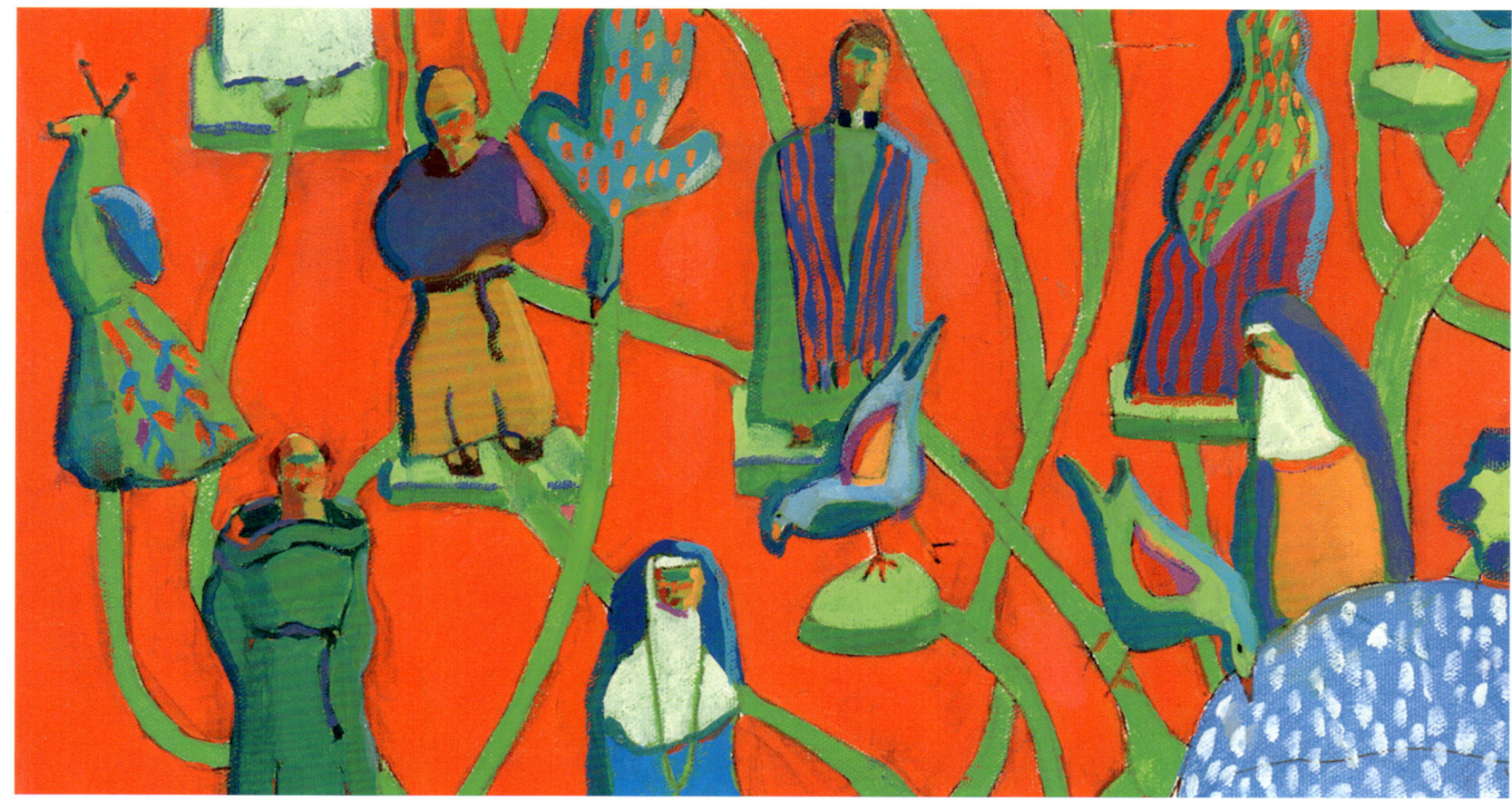

*Los Religiosos on
My Mind* (detail)
2009
Oil on canvas
40 x 20 in.

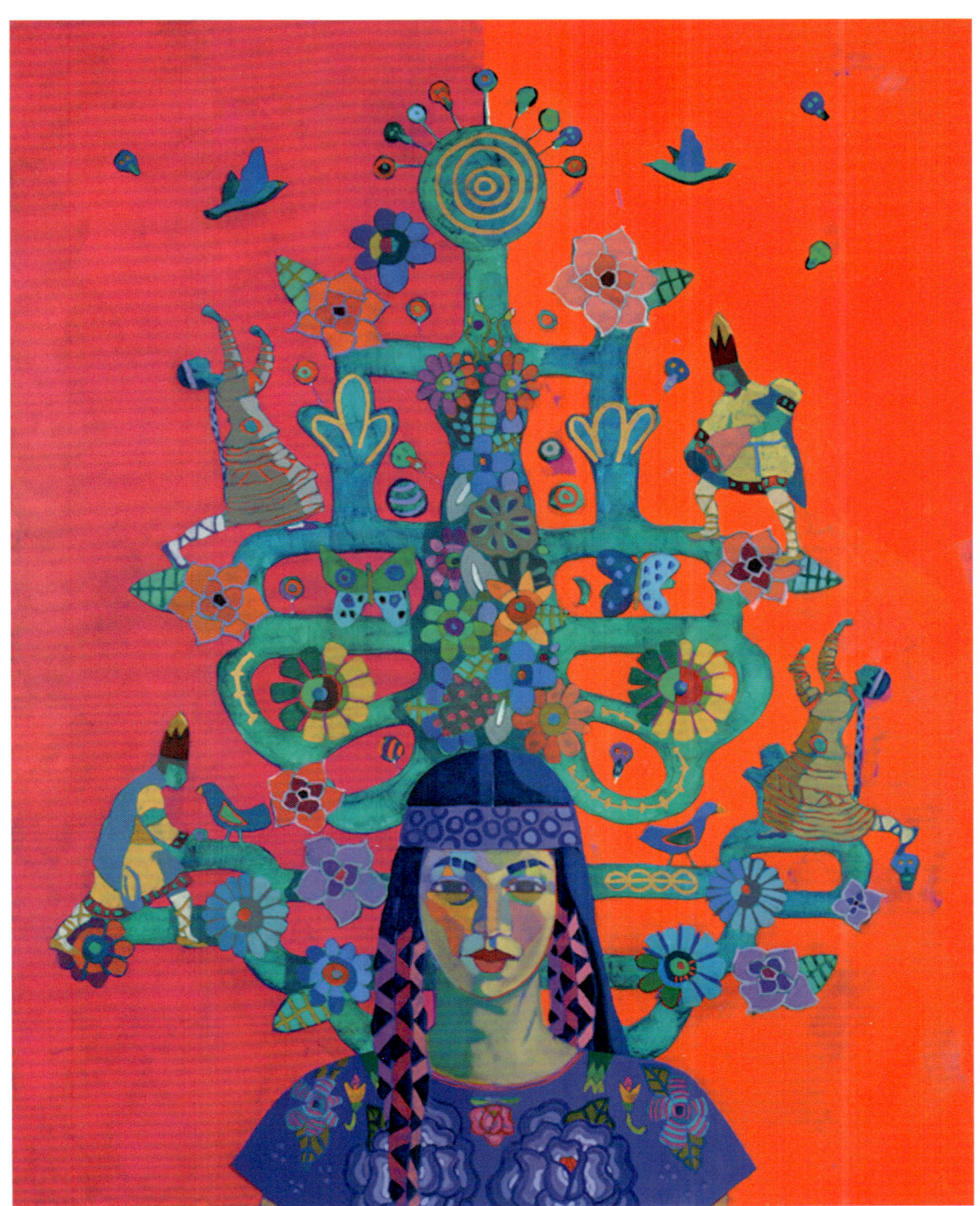

*Dance of Life and
Death on My Mind*
2015
Oil on canvas
60 x 48 in.

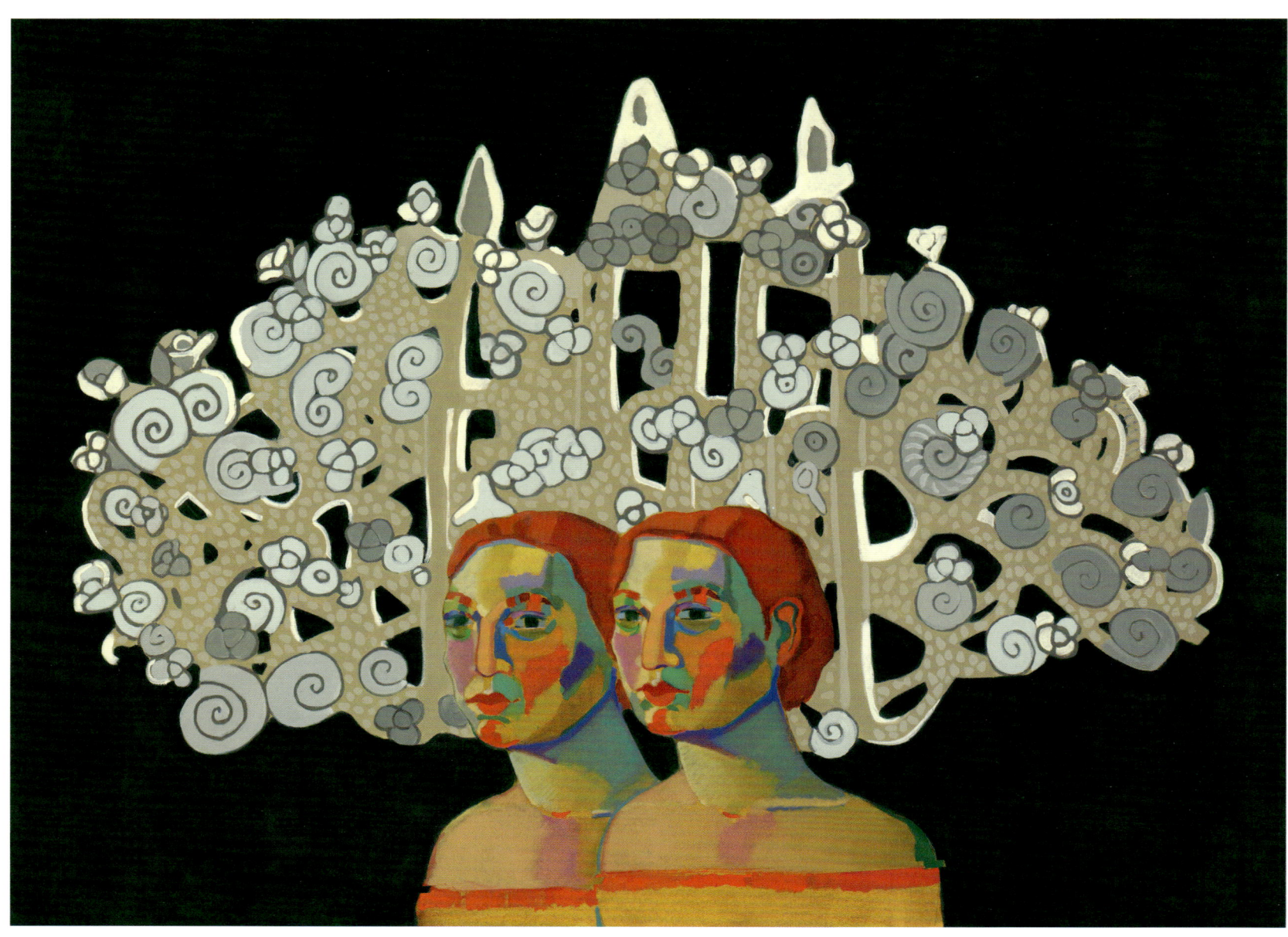

Seeing Double on My Mind
2012
Oil on canvas
36 x 48 in.

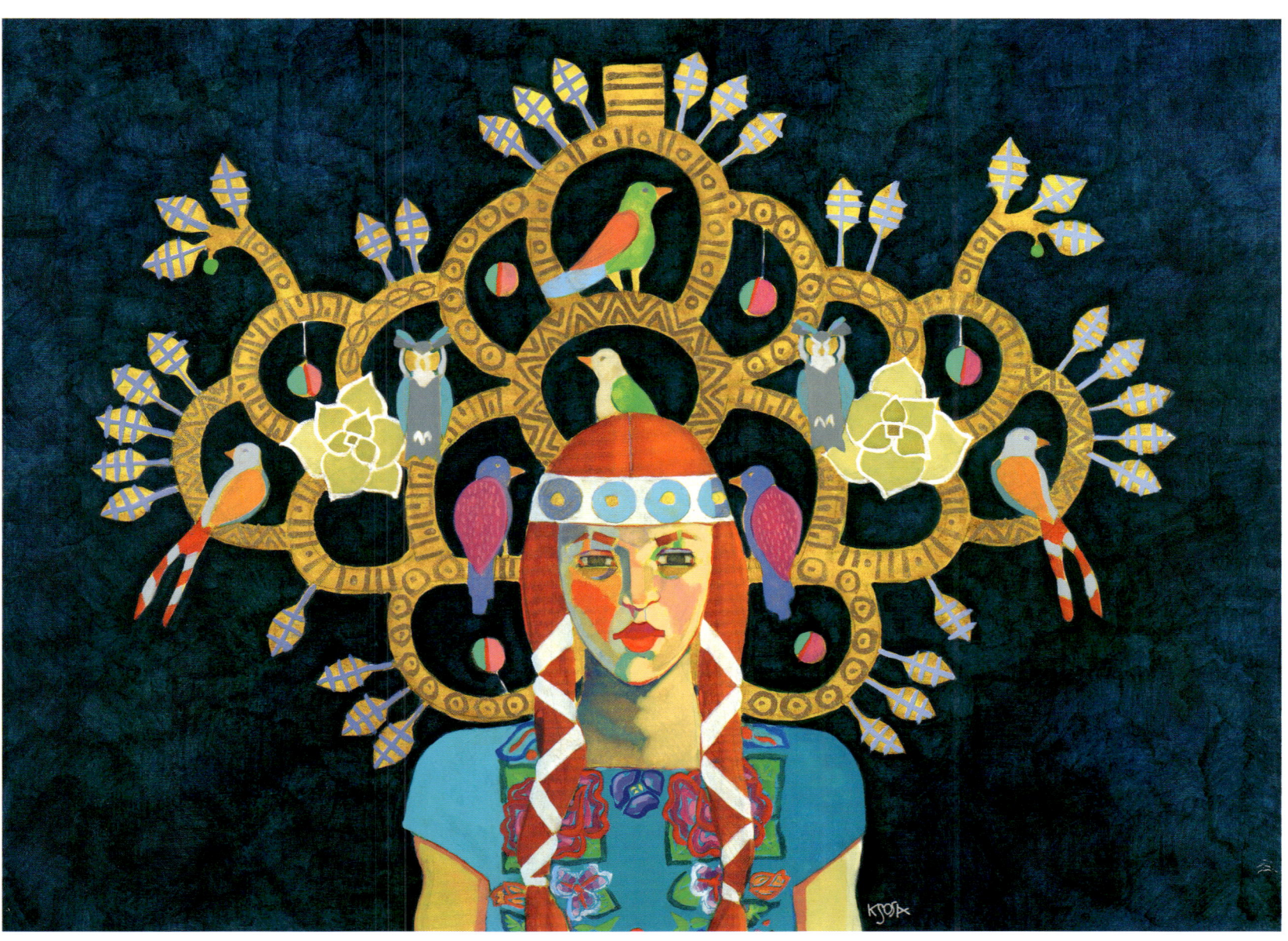

Veronica's Aviary on My Mind
2016
Oil on canvas
36 x 48 in.

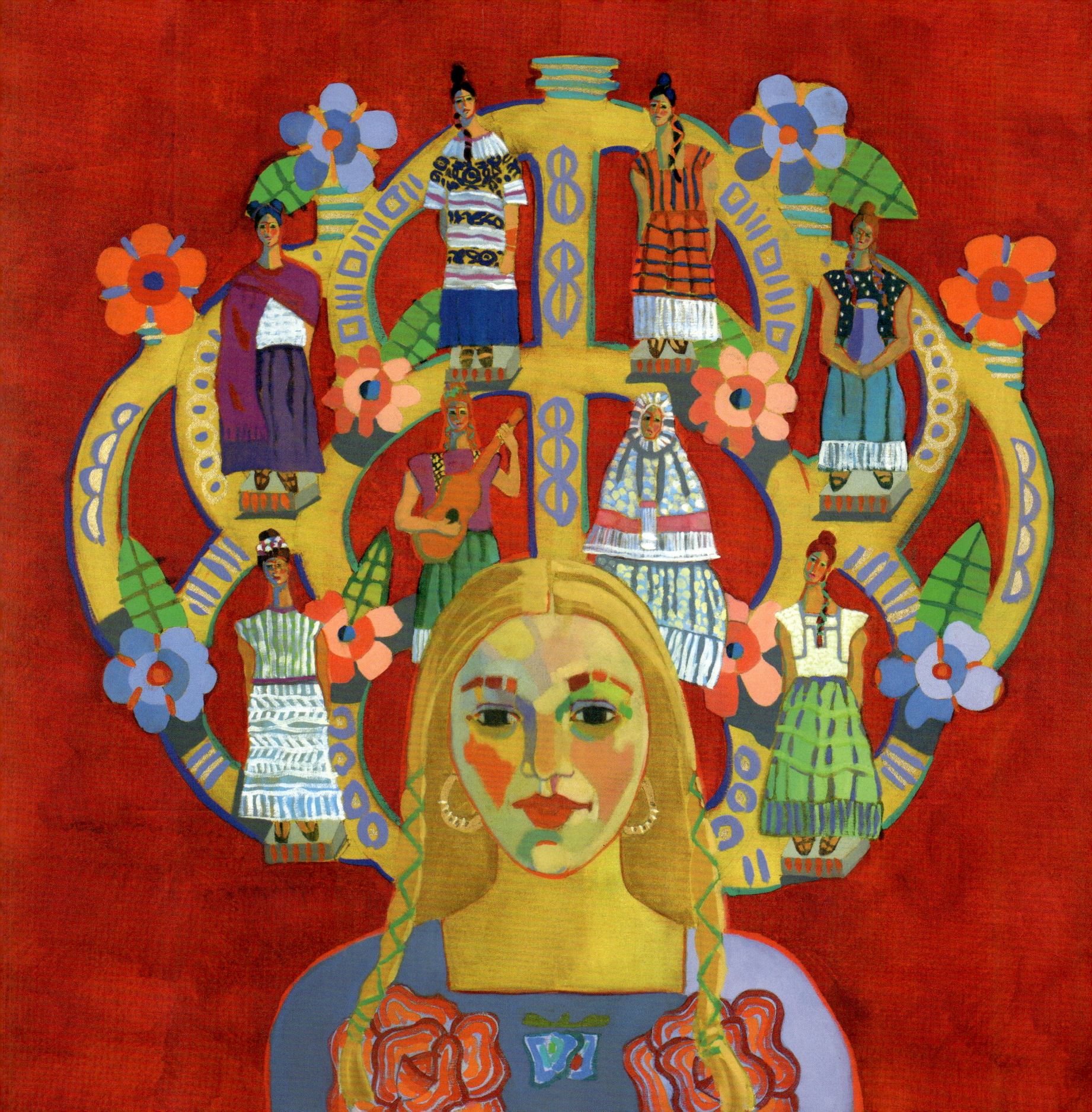

Self-Portrait in a Velvet Dress:
Frida's Wardrobe on My Mind
2015
Oil on canvas
36 x 36 in.

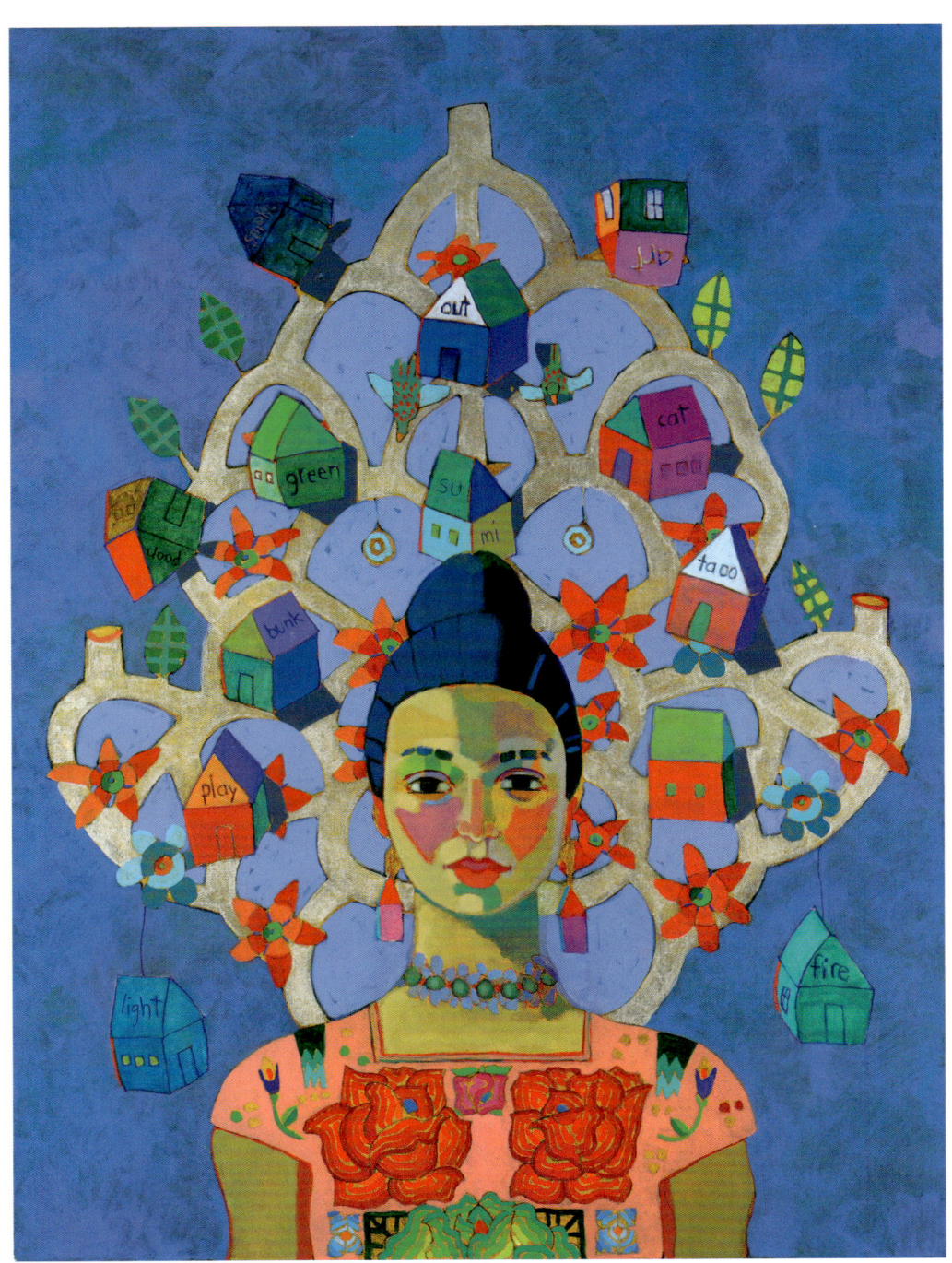

Tree Houses on My Mind
2009
Oil on canvas
48 x 36 in.

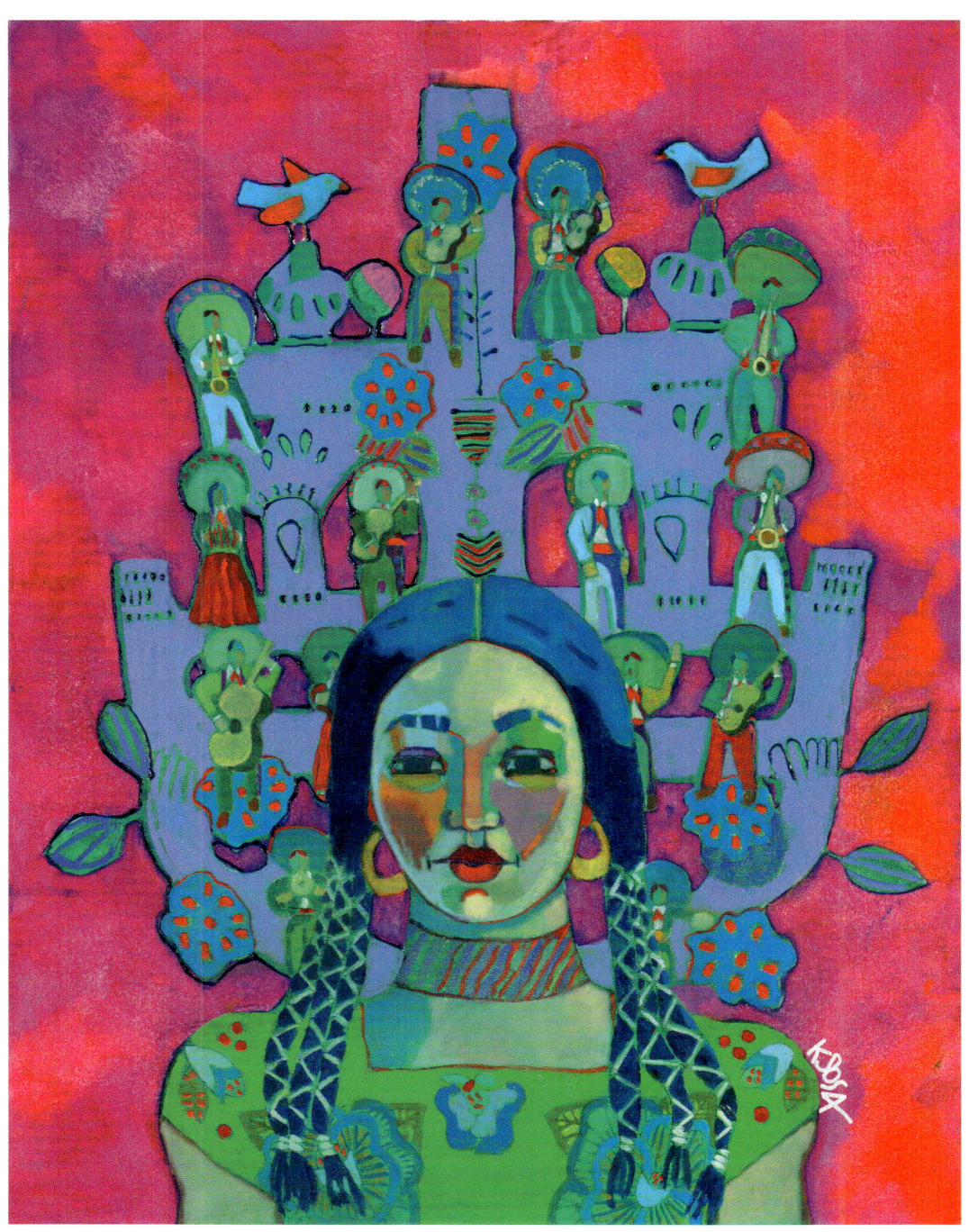

*La Banda Mariachi
on My Mind*
2014
Oil on canvas
28 x 22 in.

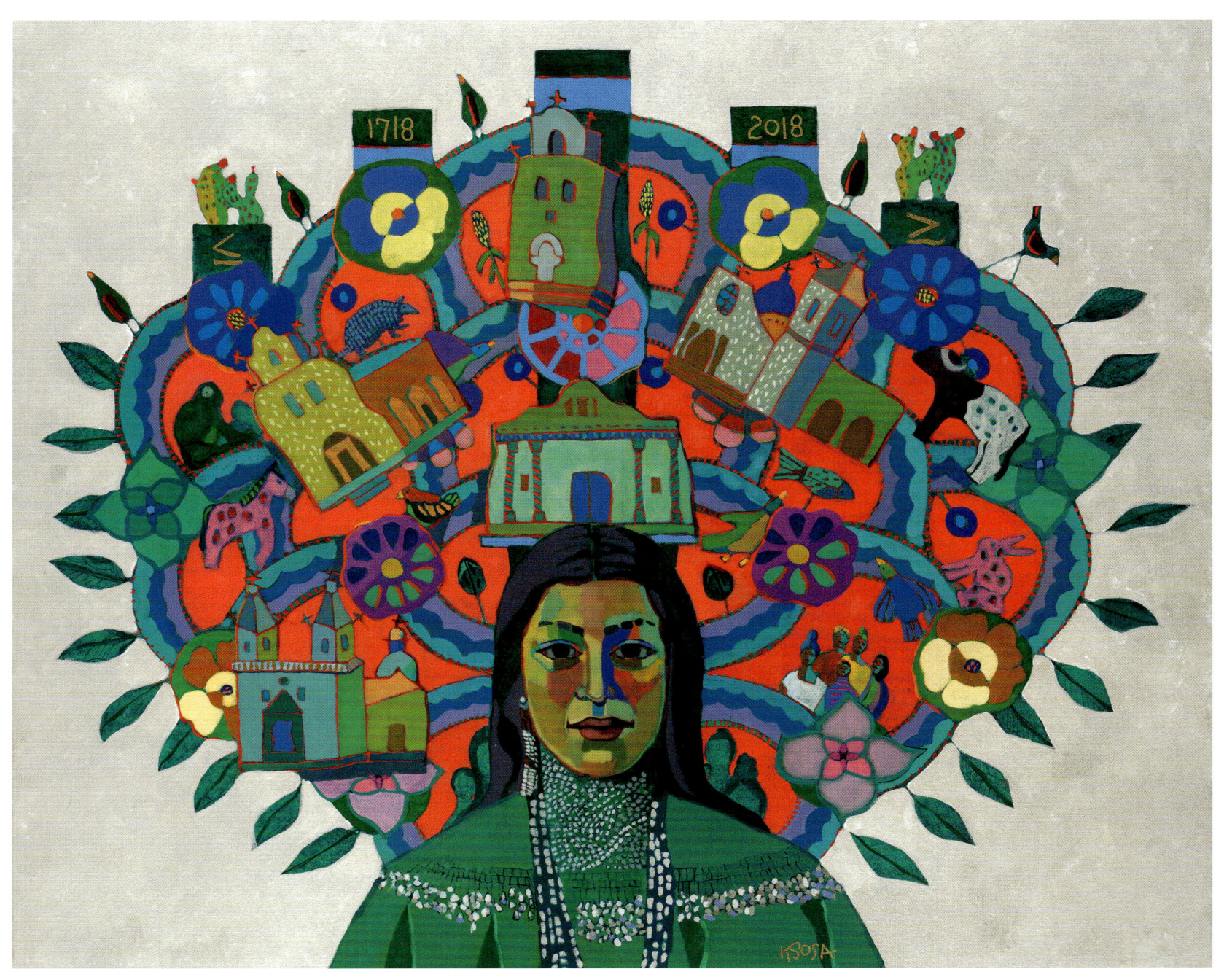

300 Years of Cultura
on My Mind
2018
Oil on canvas
36 x 48

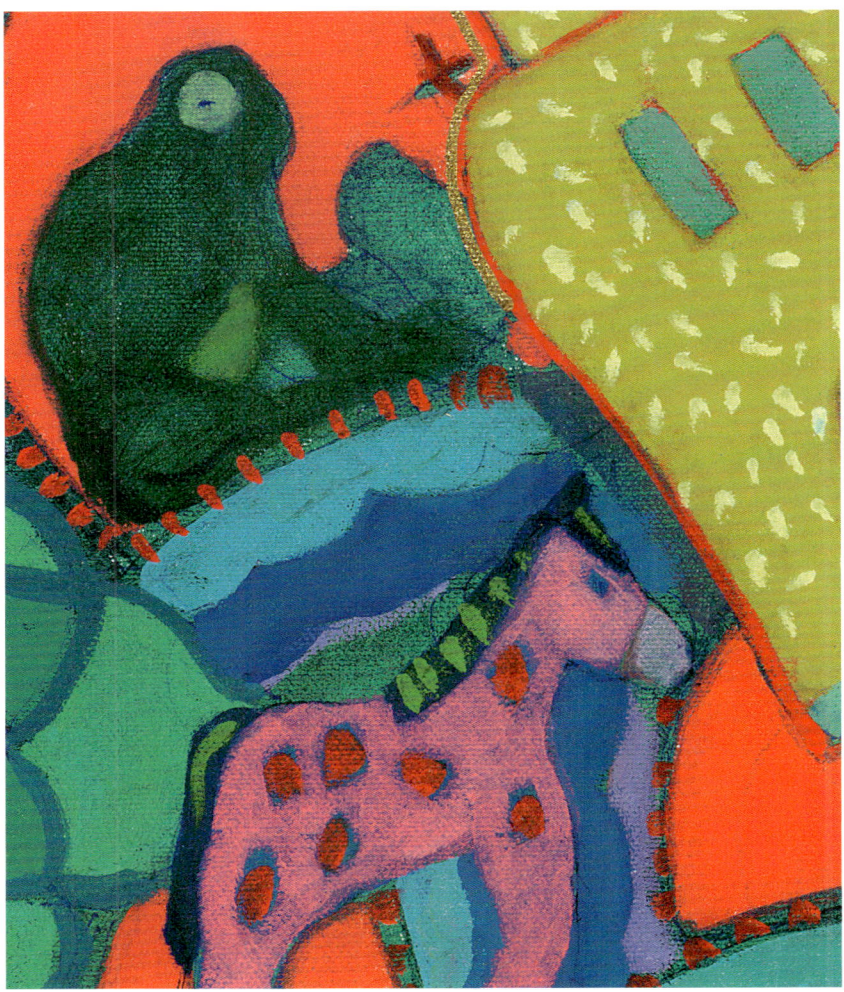

The Incredible Ligthness of
Being an Artist on My Mind
2015
Oil on canvas
36 x 36 in.

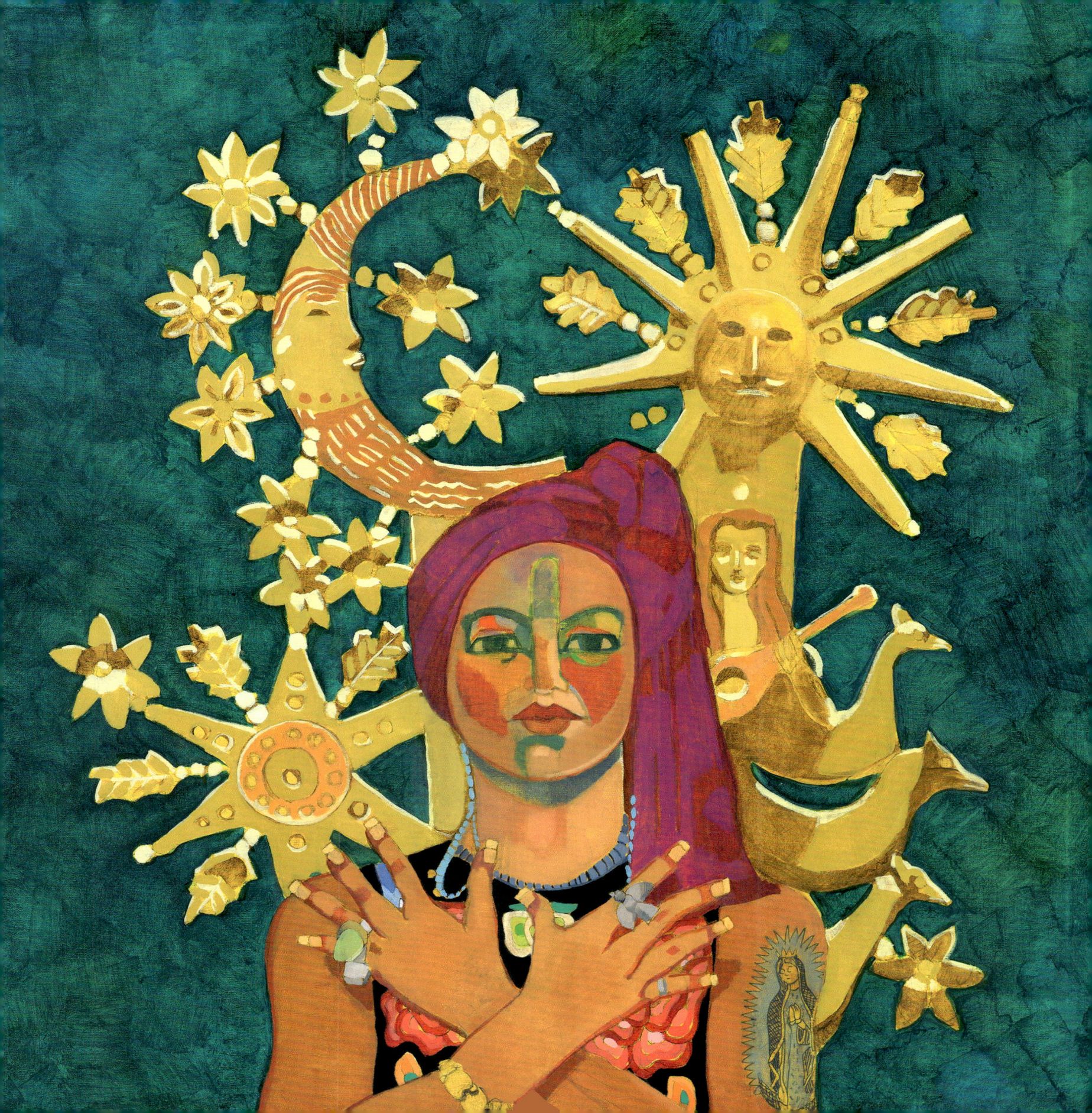

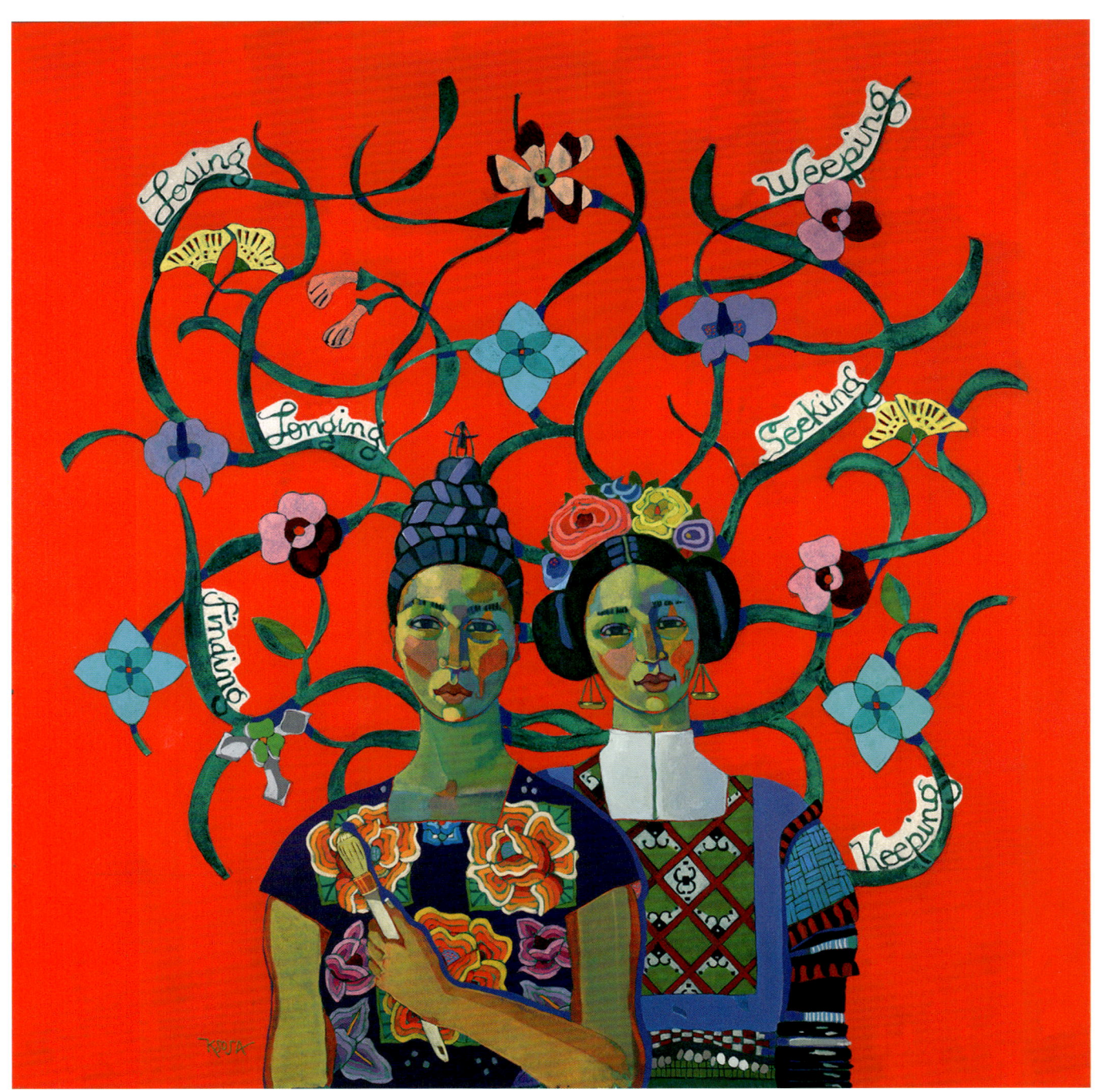

*Carolyn and Kristen
on My Mind*
2018
Oil on canvas
60 x 60 in.

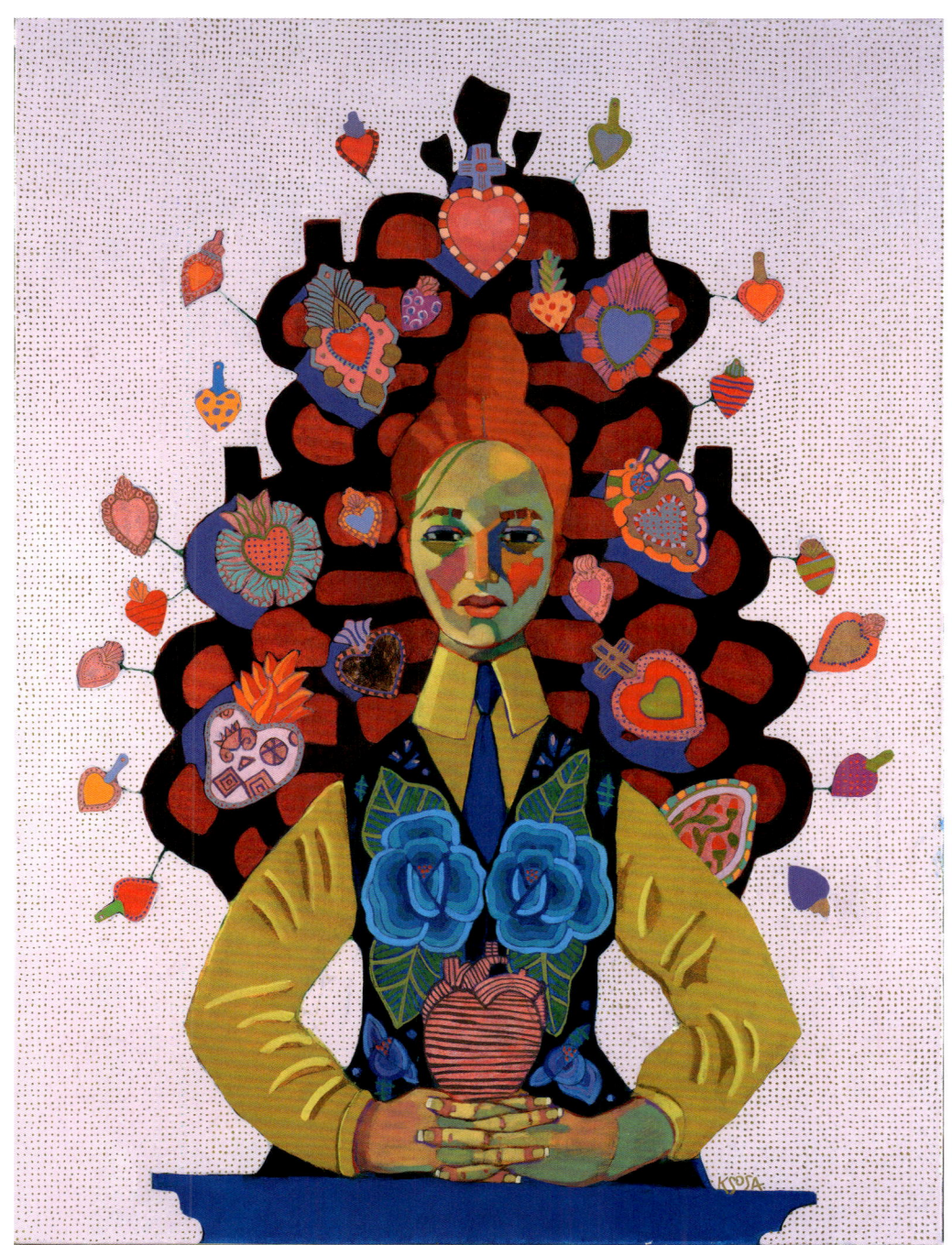

*Corazón on My
Sleeve on My Mind*
2017
Oil on canvas
48 x 36 in.

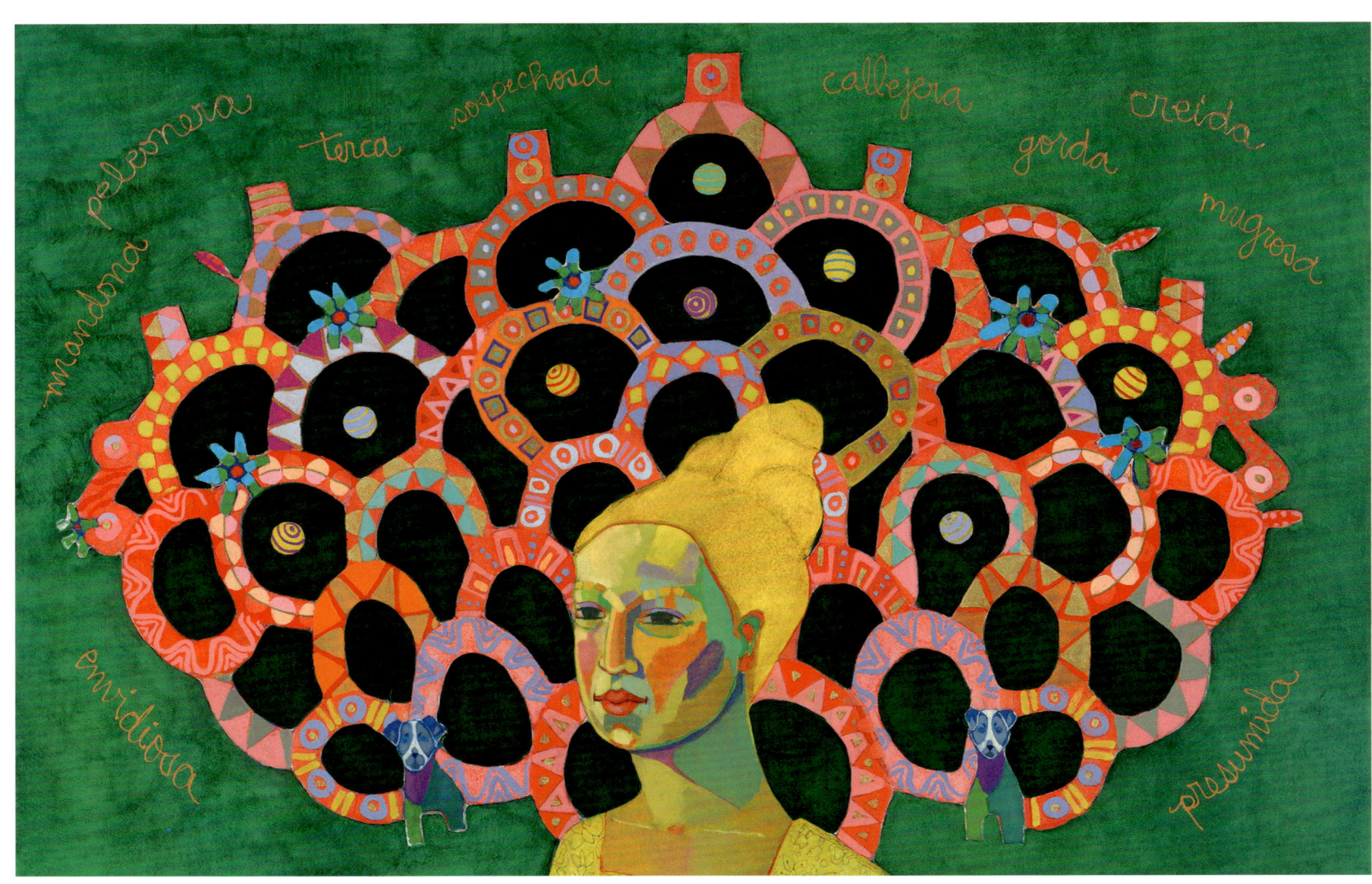

*The Ballad of Guadalupe y
Rosalinda on My Mind*
2018
Oil on canvas
40 x 60 in.

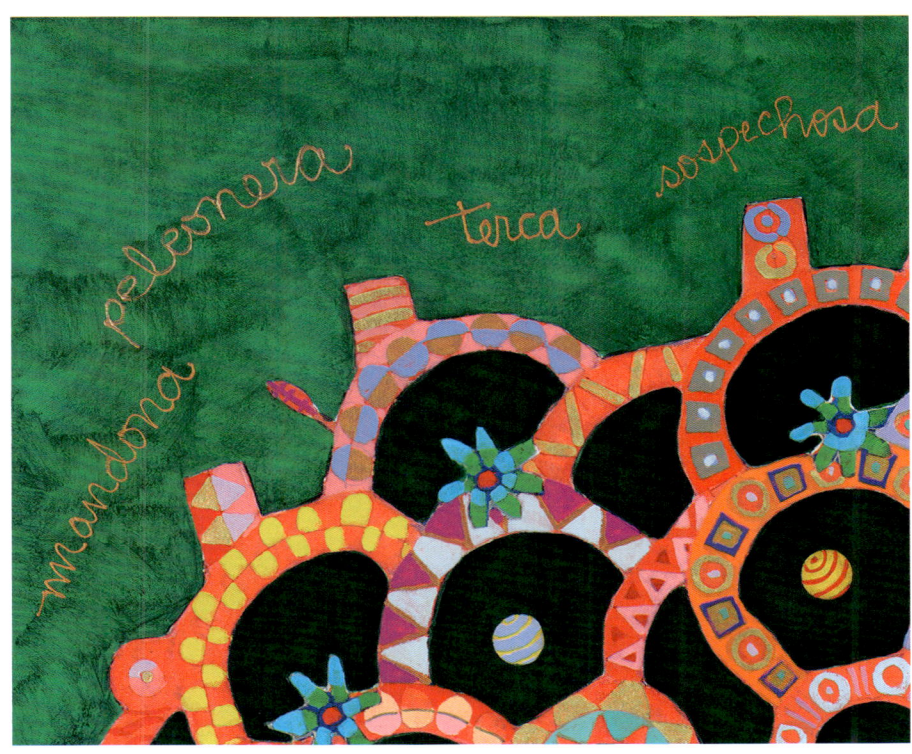

Amelia on My Mind
2019
Acrylic and oil on canvas
30 x 30 in.

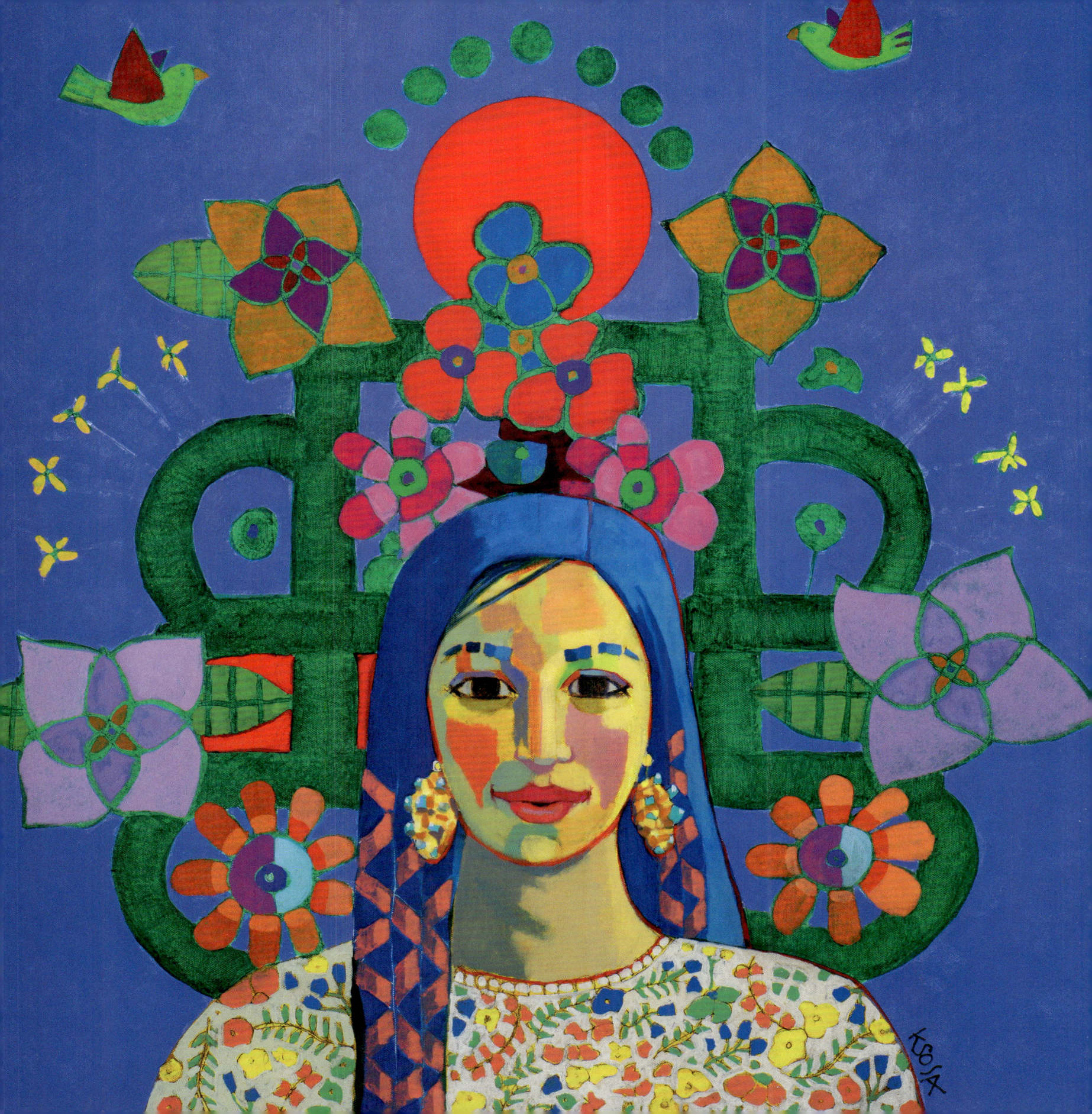

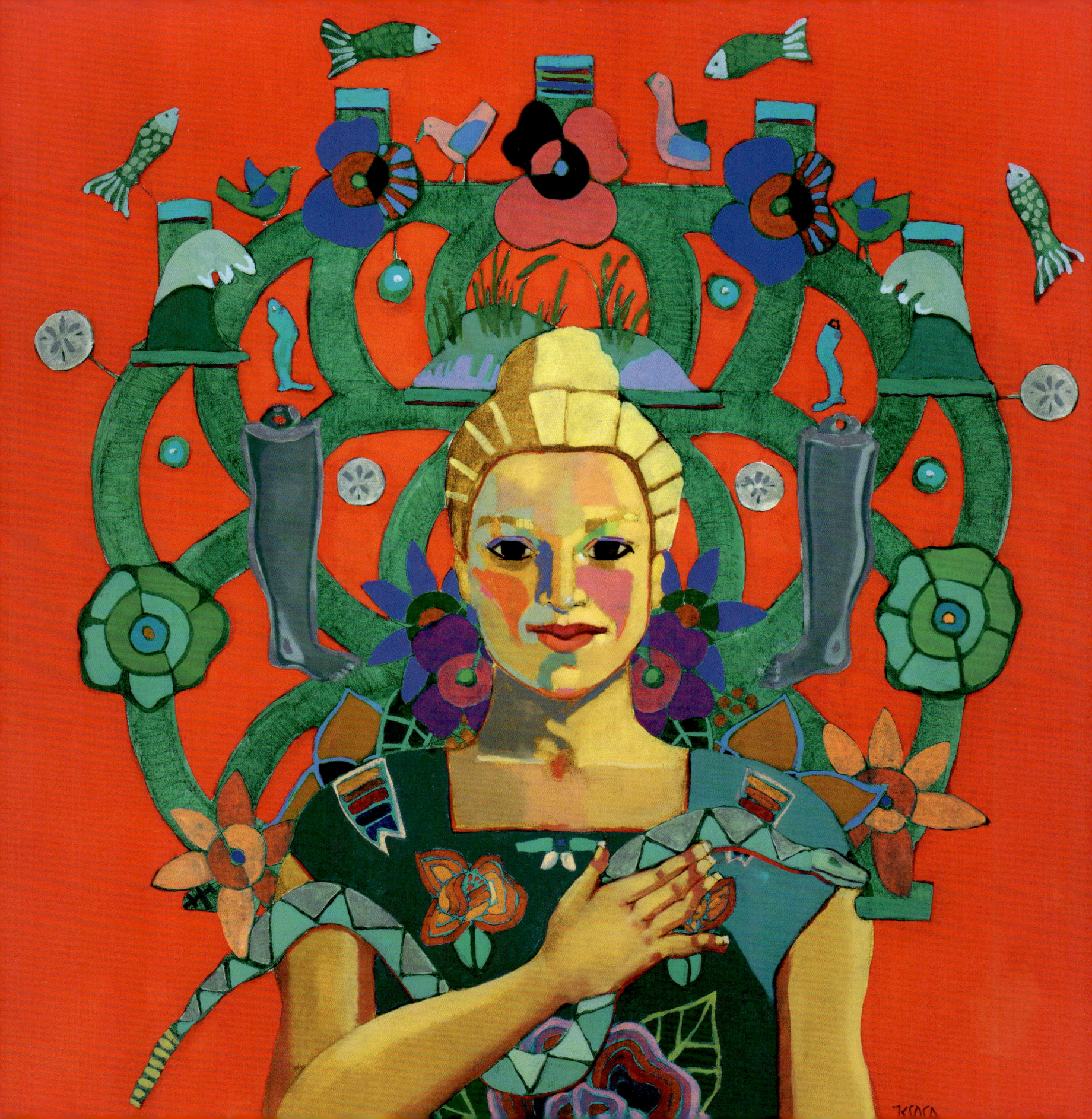

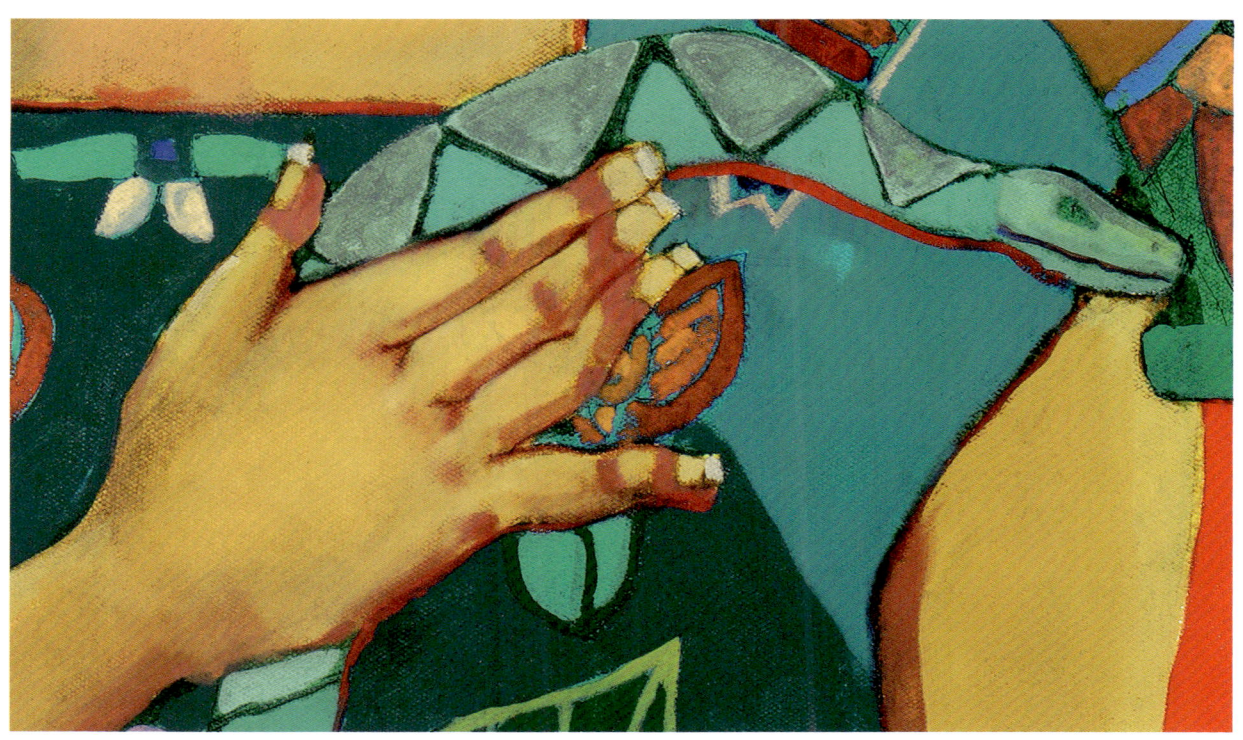

*Snake in the Grass
on My Mind*
2018
Oil on canvas
36 x 36 in.

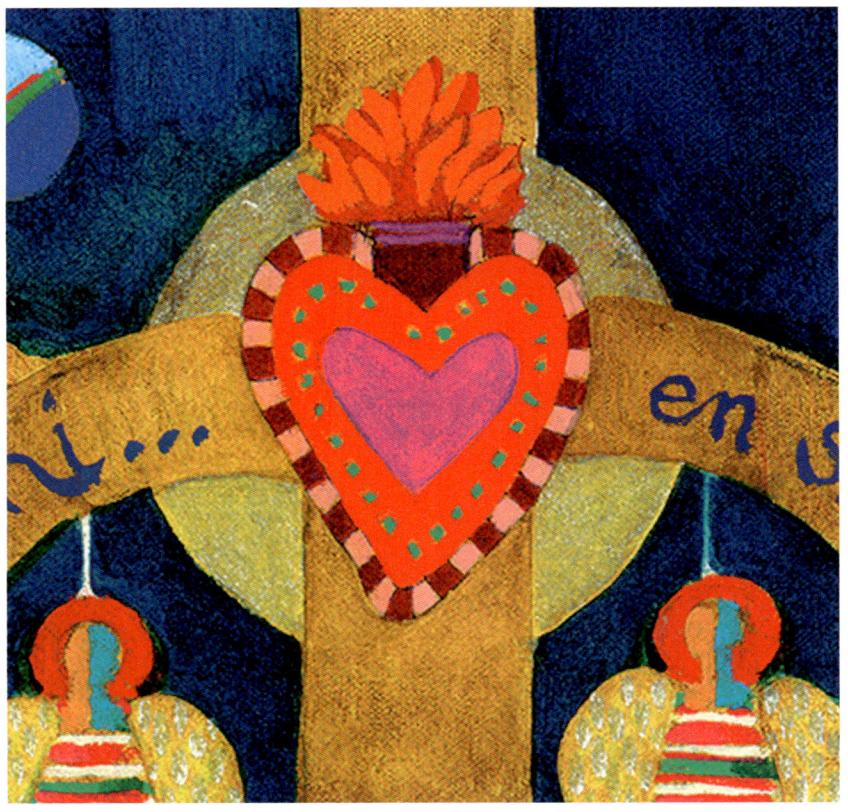

*I Found My Heart in San
Antonio on My Mind* (detail)
2018
Oil on canvas
40 x 40 in.

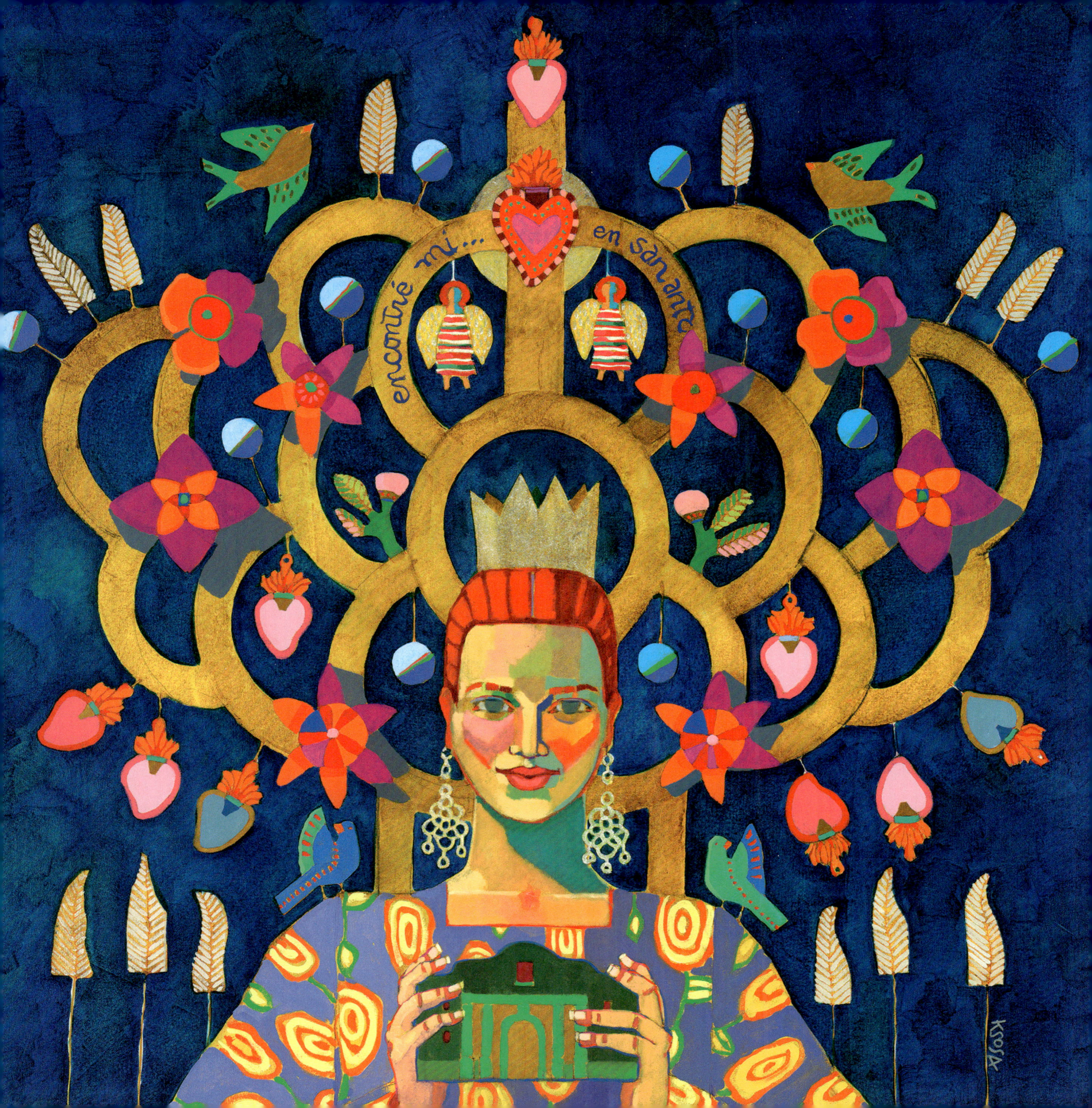

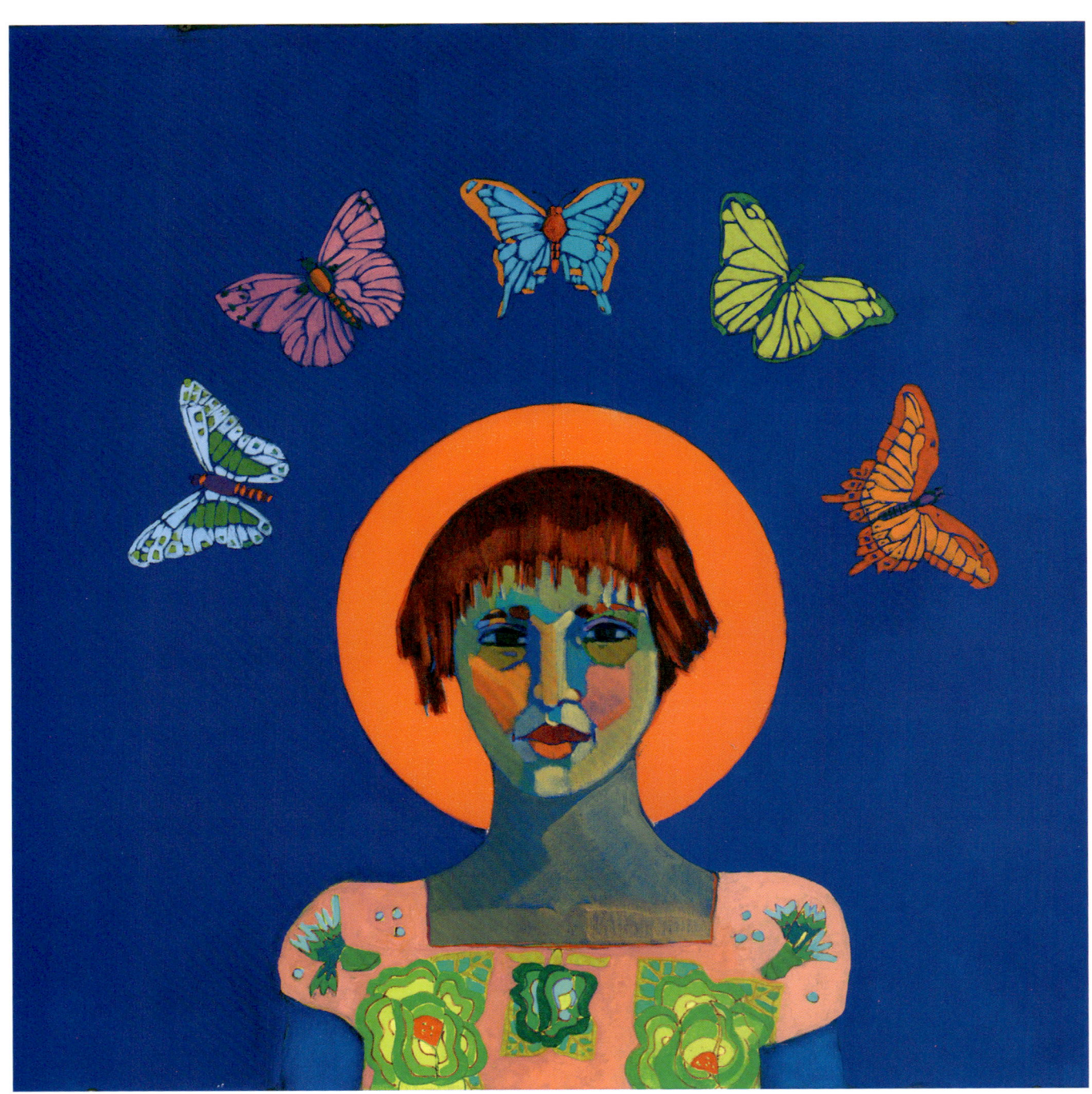

Nahui Olin Santa Mariposas
2013
Oil on canvas
36 x 36 in.

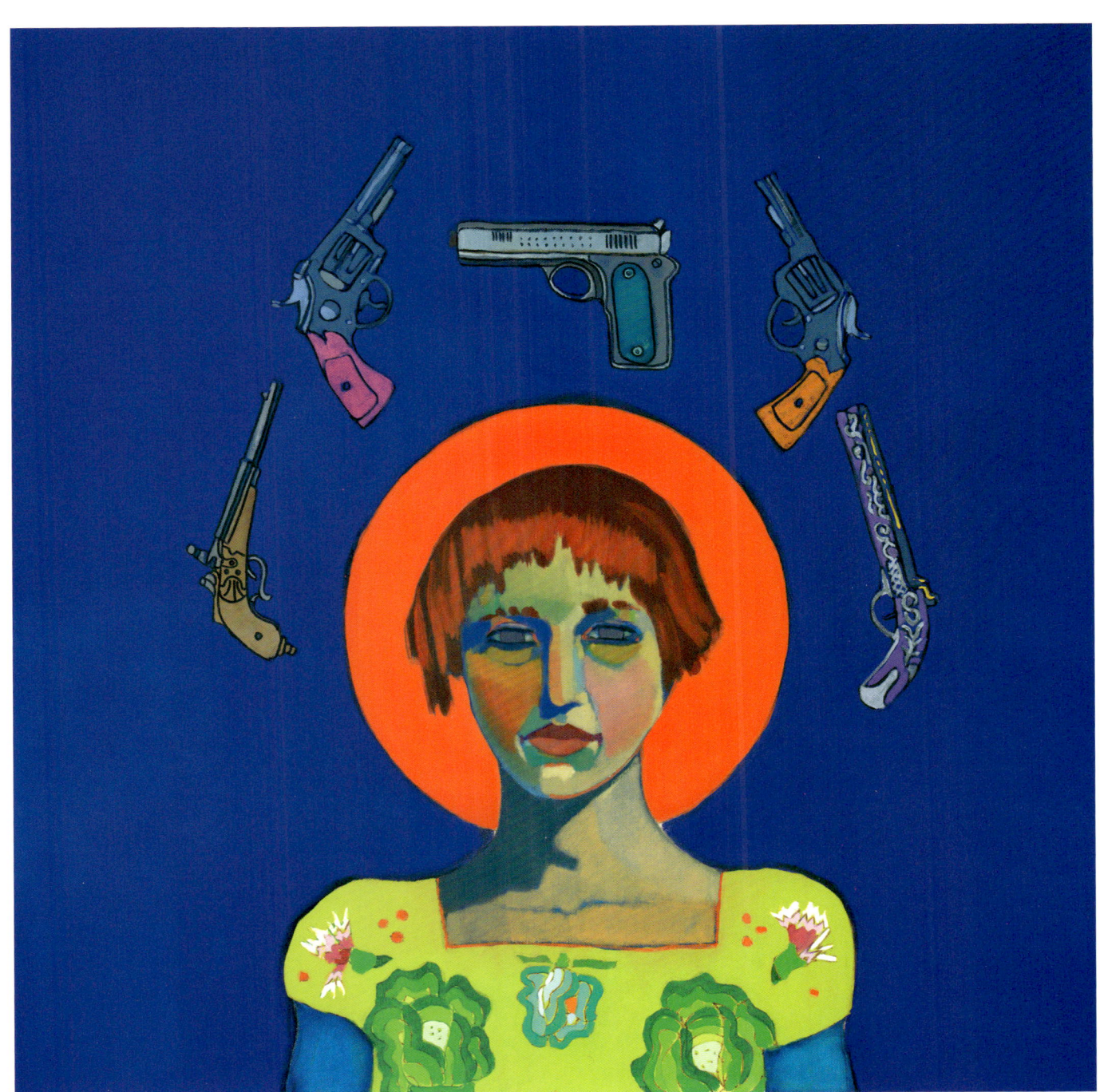

Nahui Olin Santa Pistolas
2013
Oil on canvas
36 x 36 in.

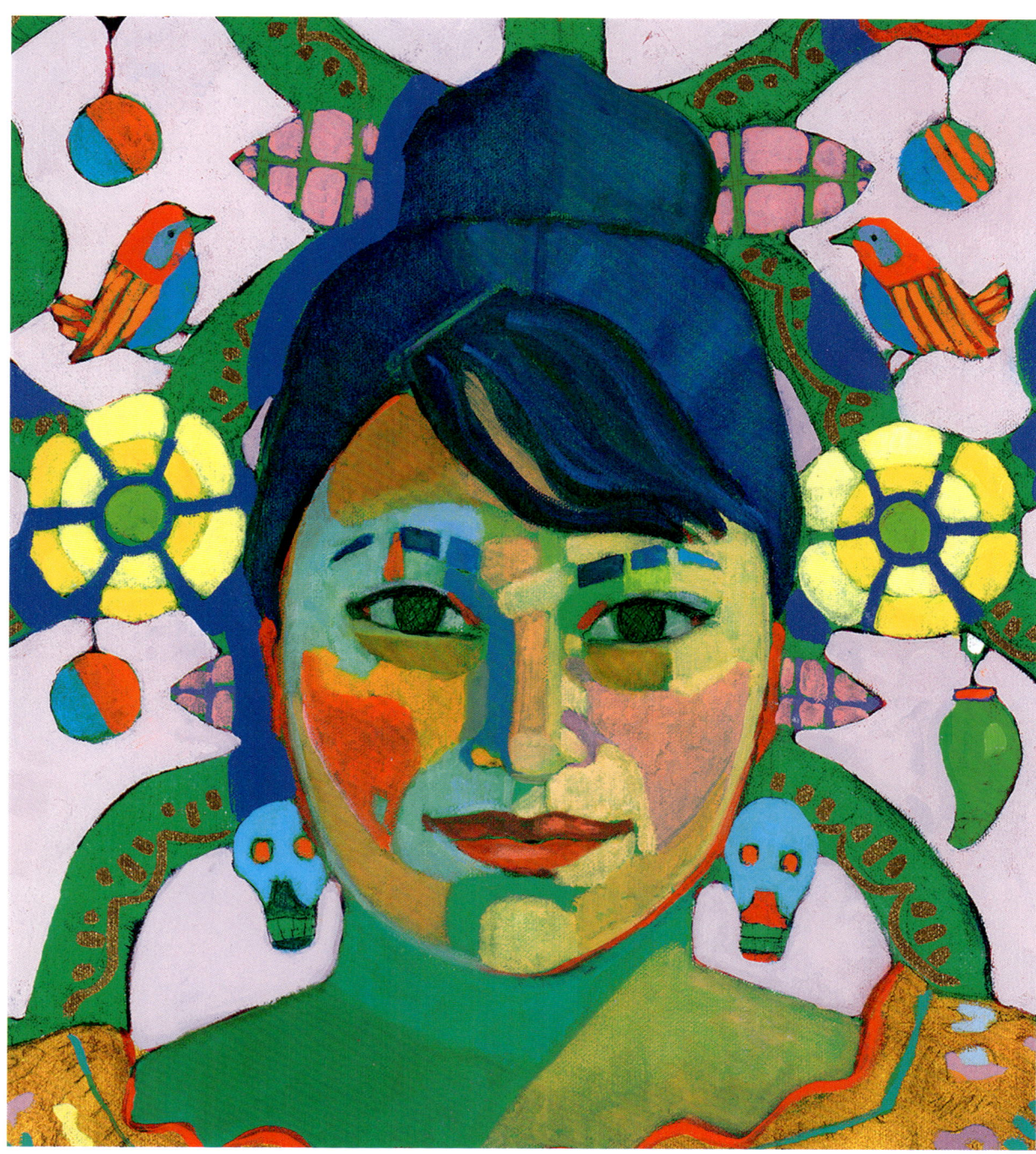

Alamo City Heart and Home on My Mind: Portrait of Erika Prosper (detail)
2023
Oil on canvas
48 x 36 in.

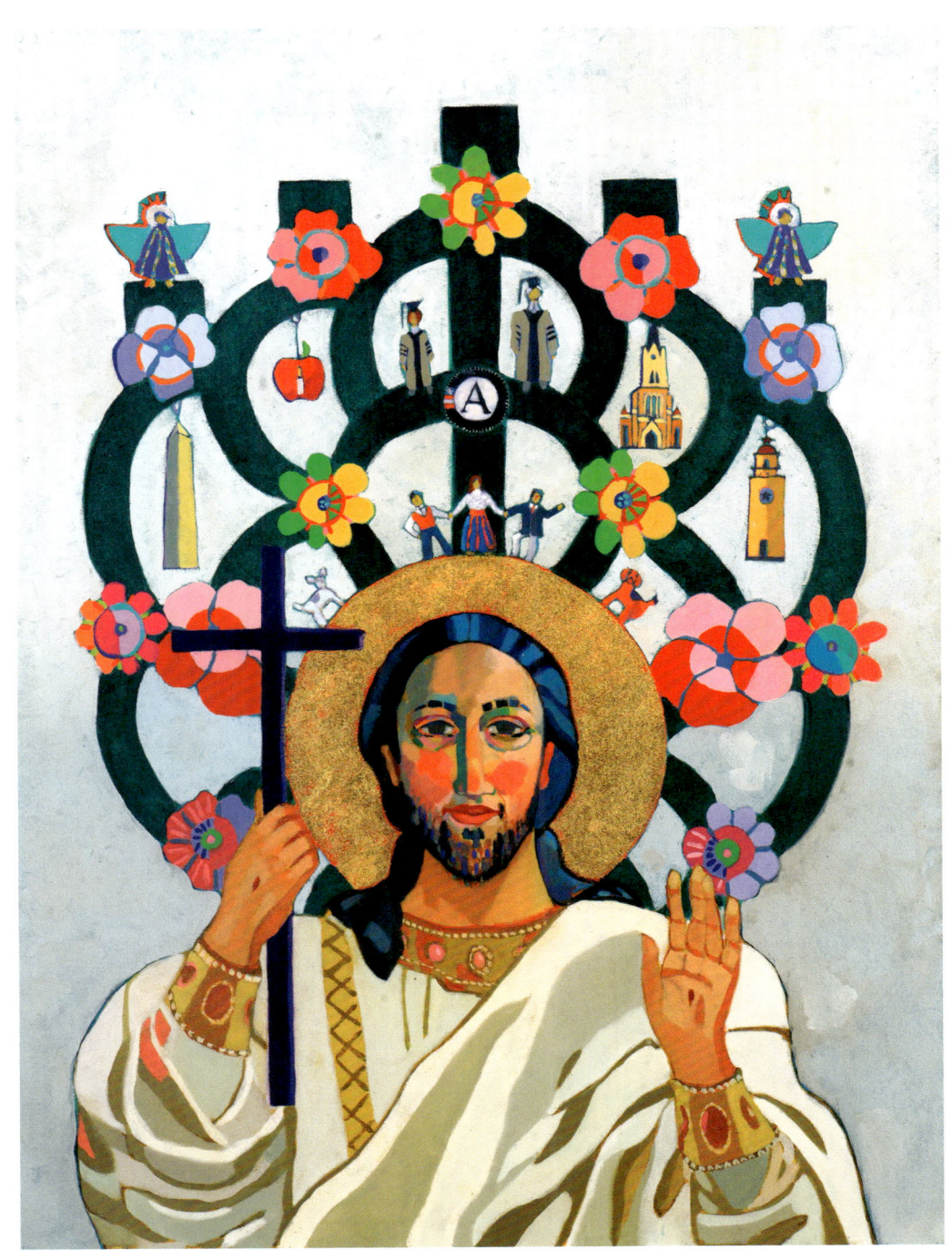

Jesus Loves Her This I Know:
Homage to Maria Ferrier on My Mind
2016
Oil on canvas
40 x 30 in.

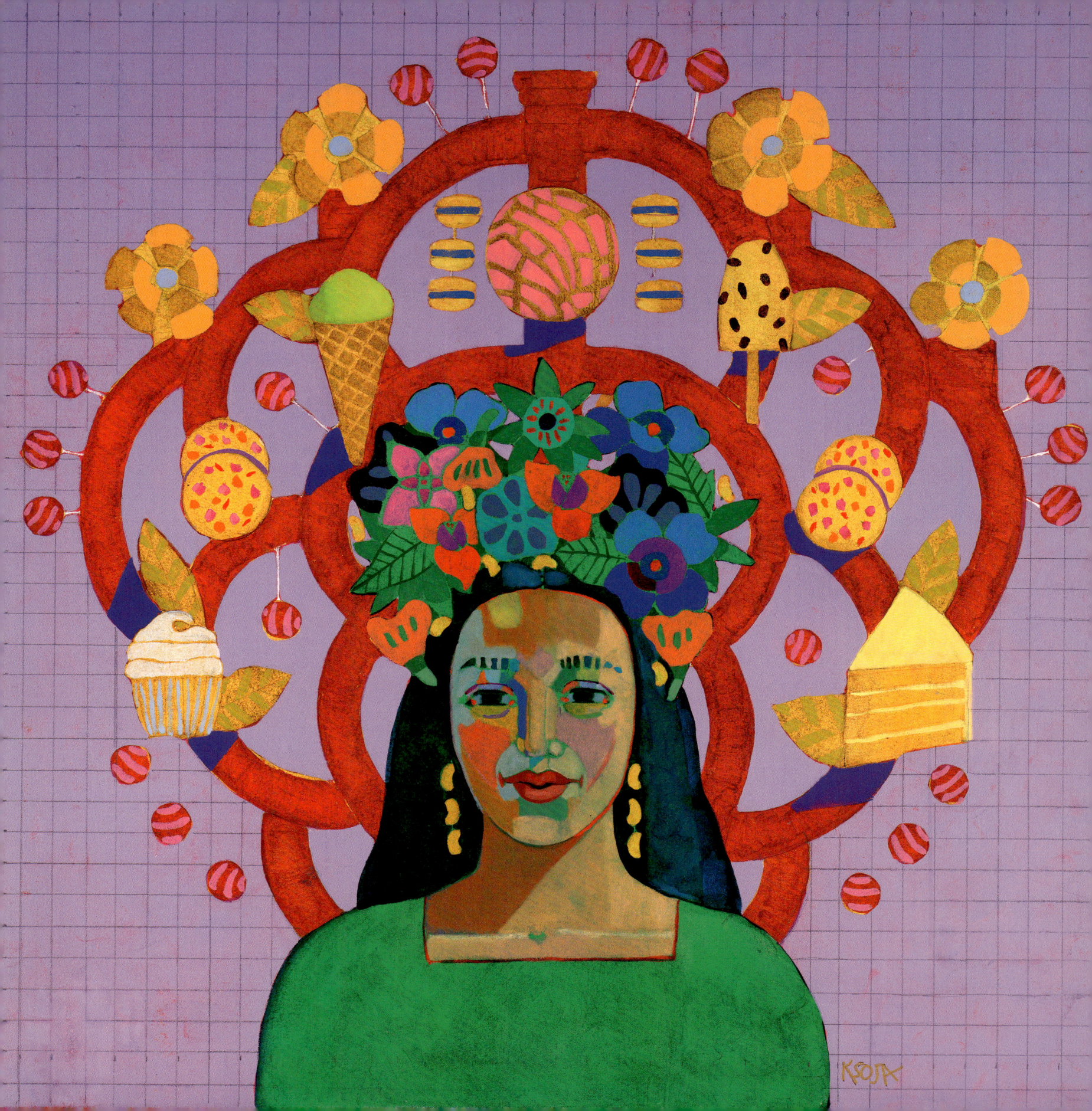

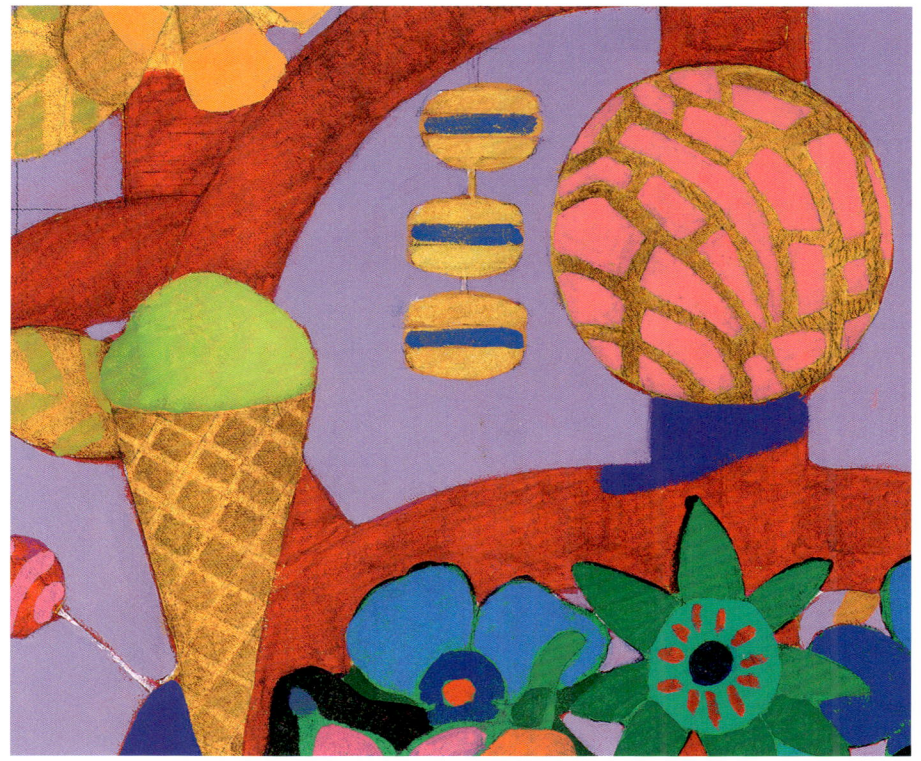

Damn This Low Carb
Diet on My Mind
2021
Oil on canvas
36 x 36 in.

Personalidades grandes

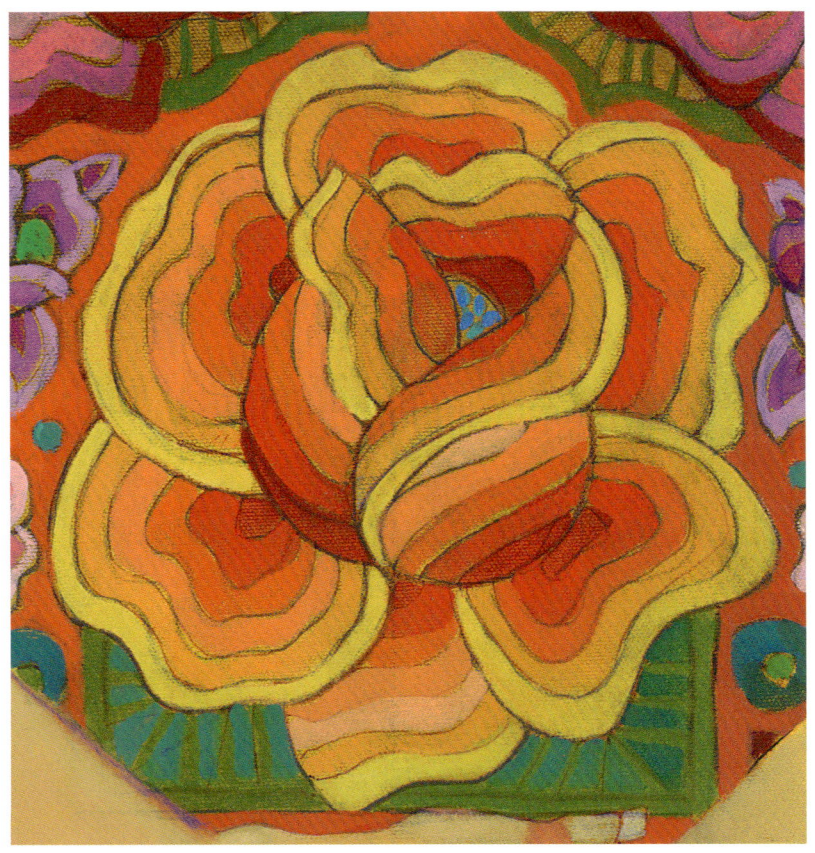

La Contessa de
San Antonio (detail)
2016
Oil on canvas
60 x 48 in.

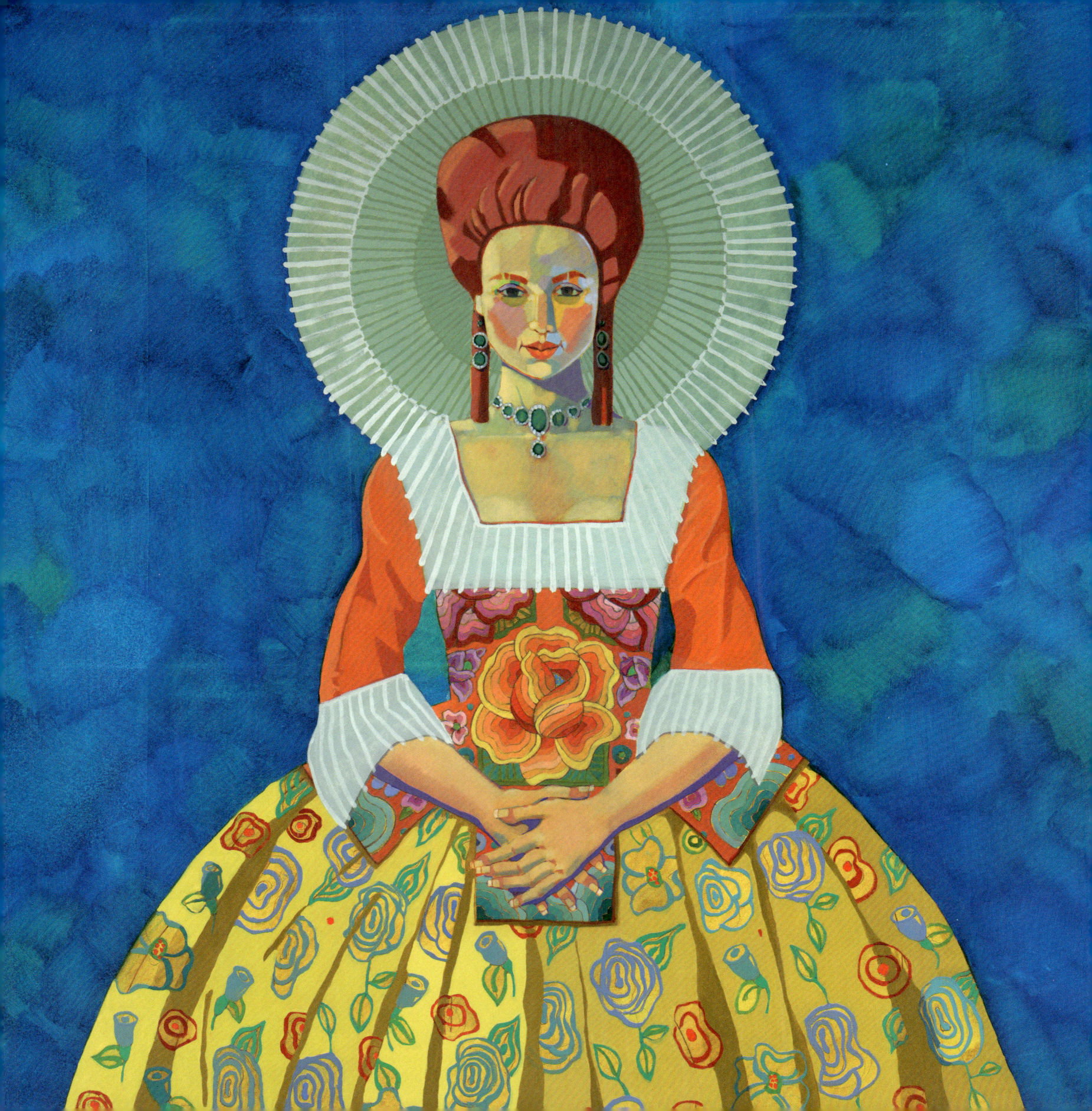

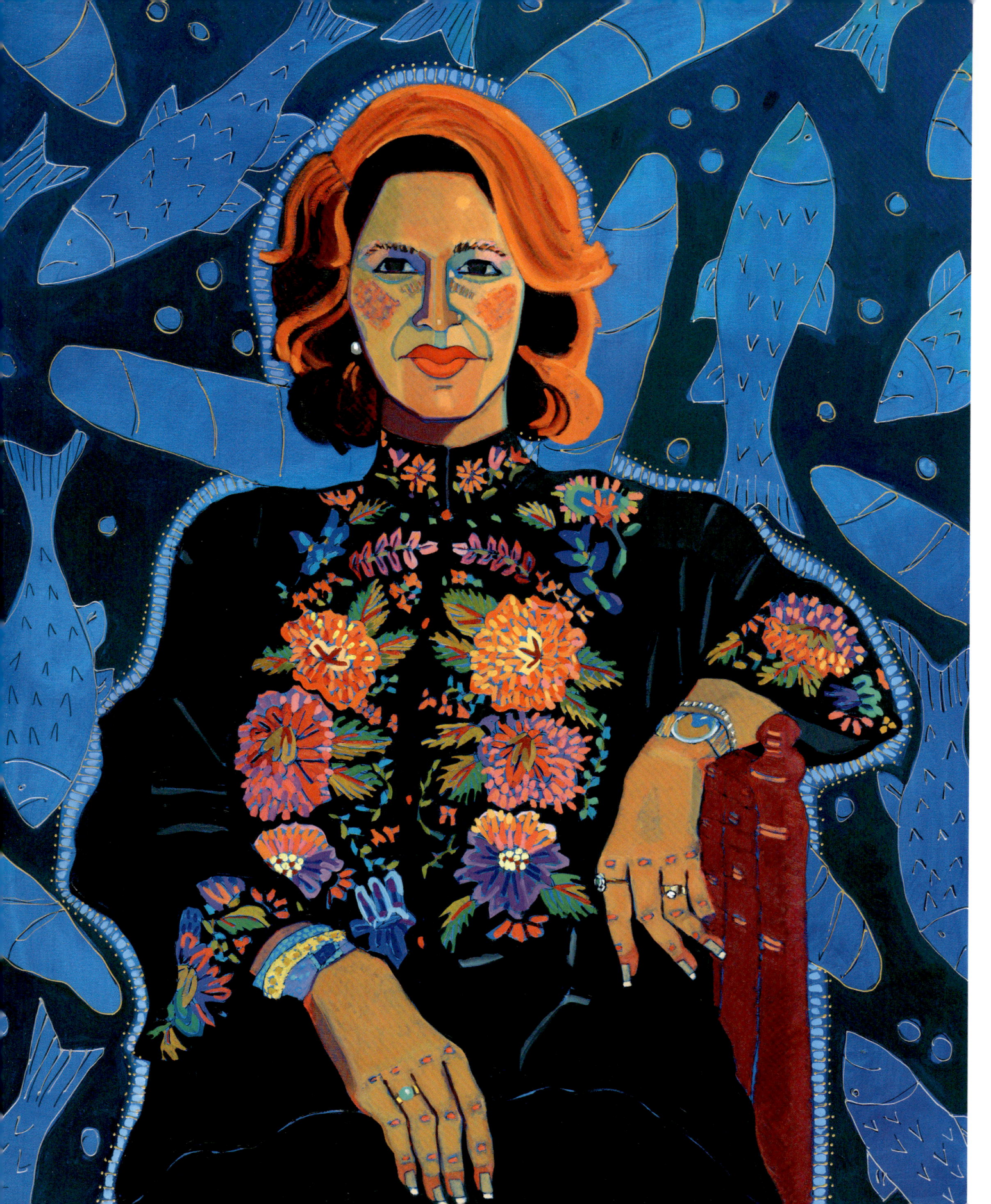

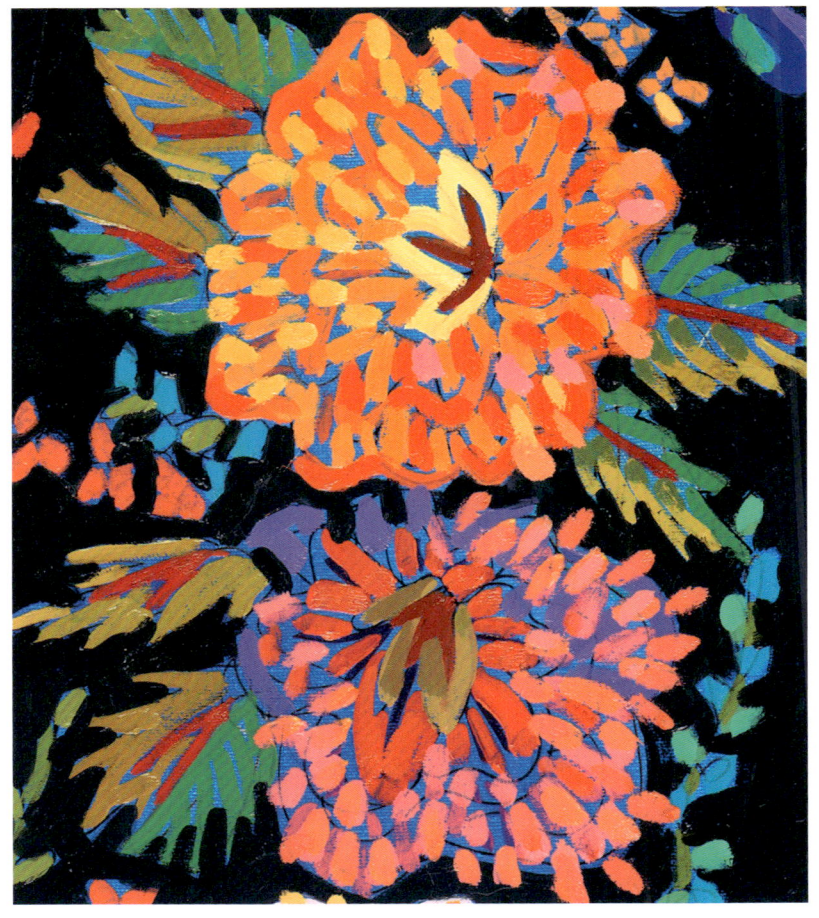

*Loaves and Fishes: Portrait
of Viola Barrios*
2008
Oil on canvas
60 x 48 in.

MESTIZAJE

The One That Got Away (detail)
2018
Oil on canvas
20 x 16 in.

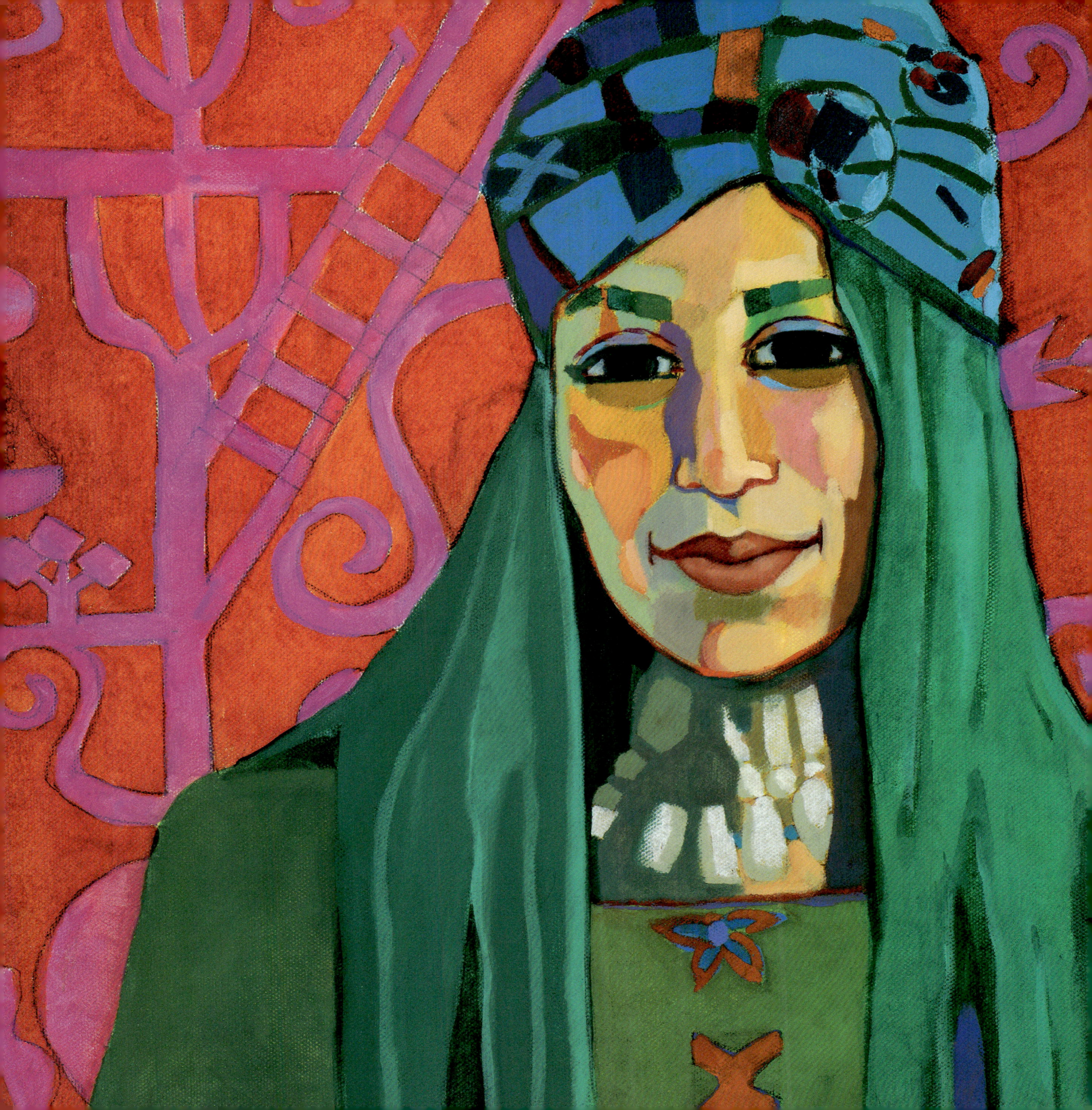

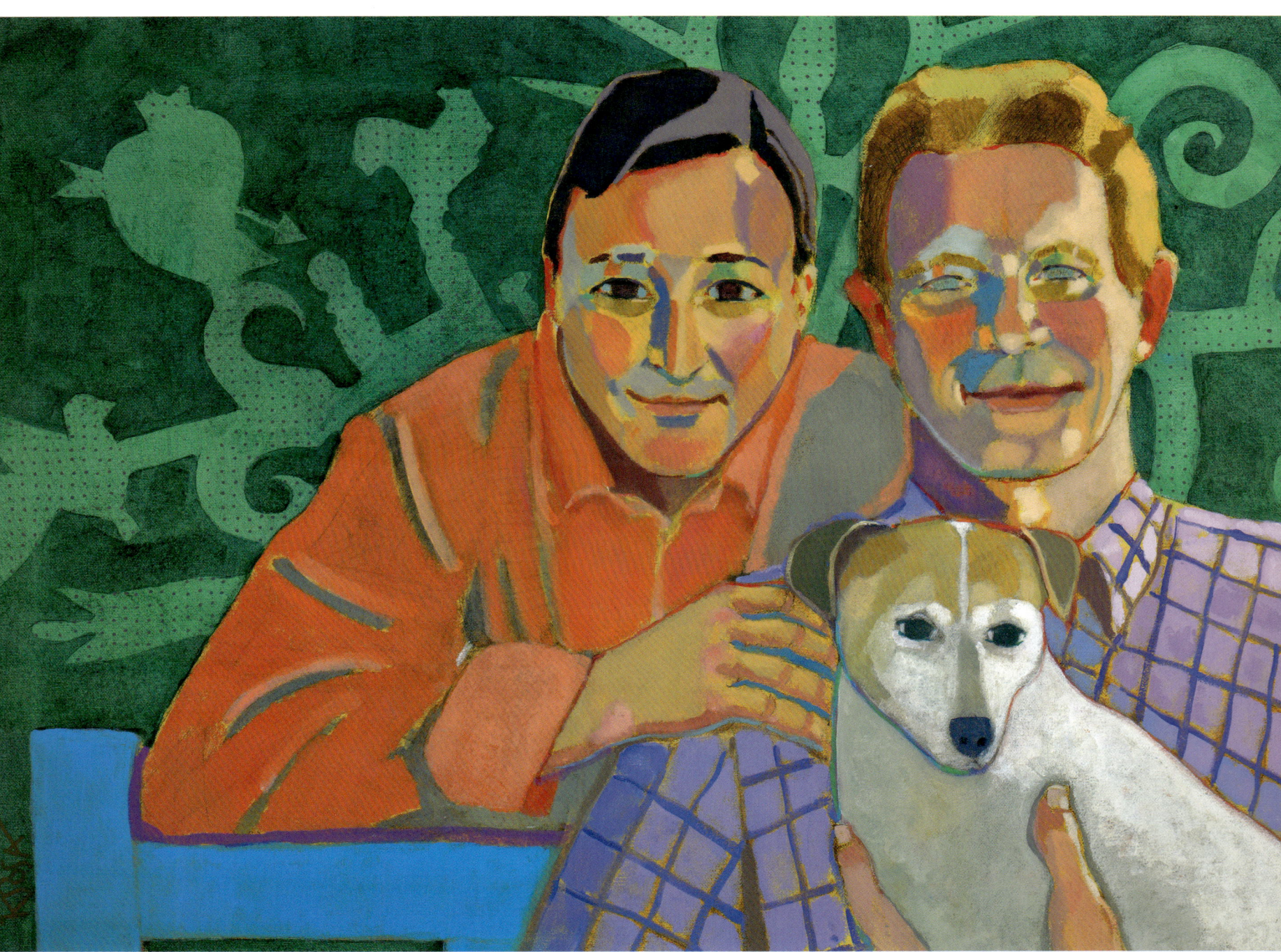

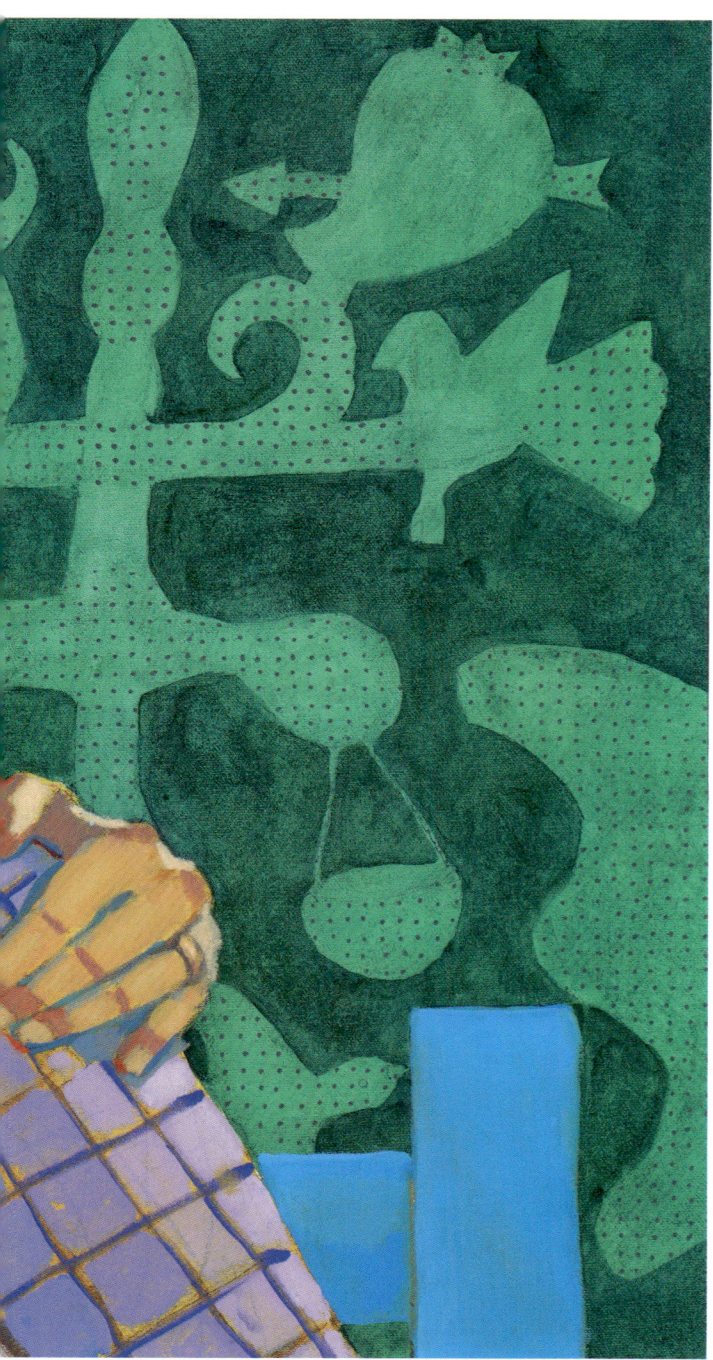

Robert, Dennis, and Betty
2018
Oil on canvas
20 x 40 in.

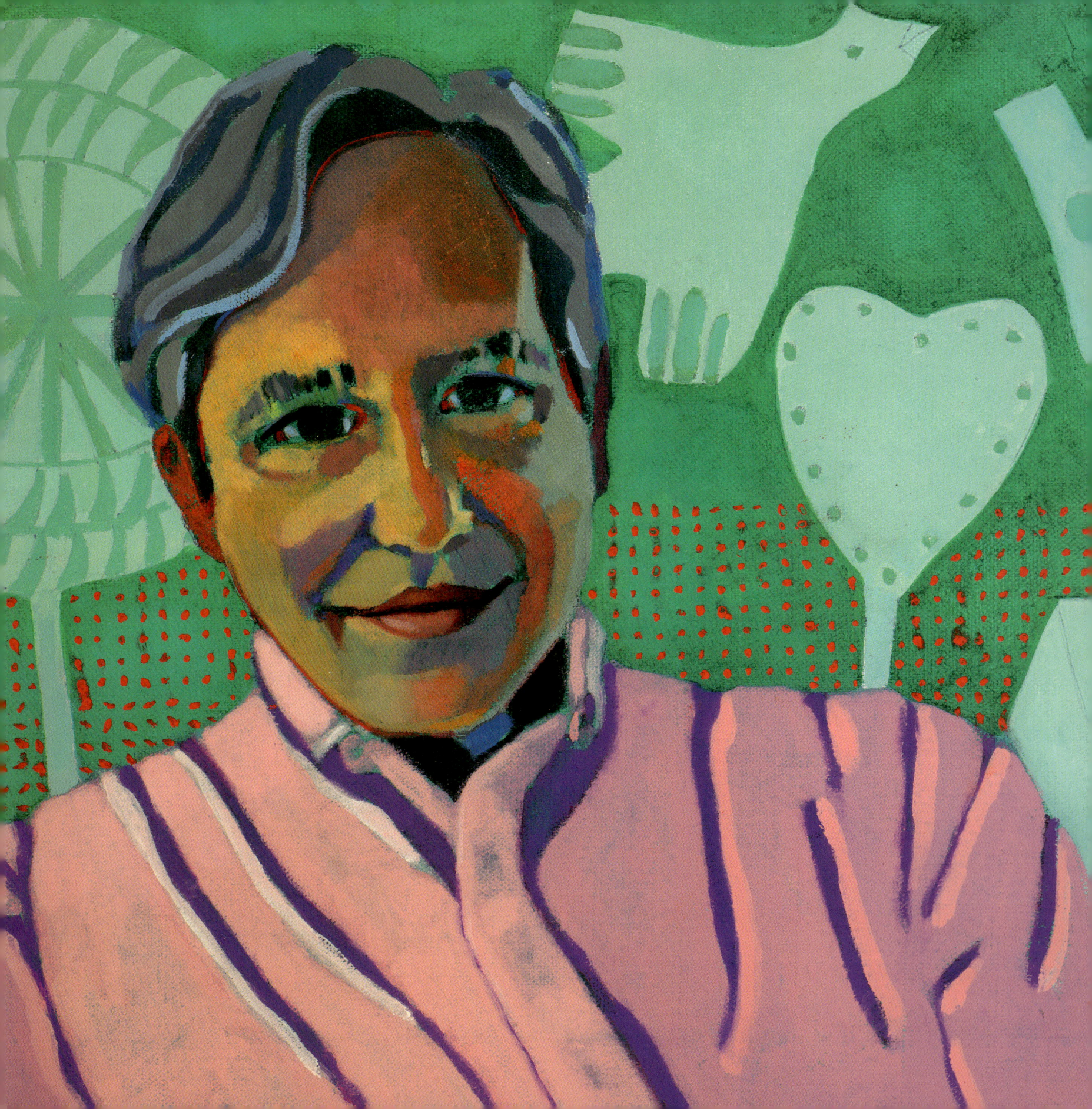

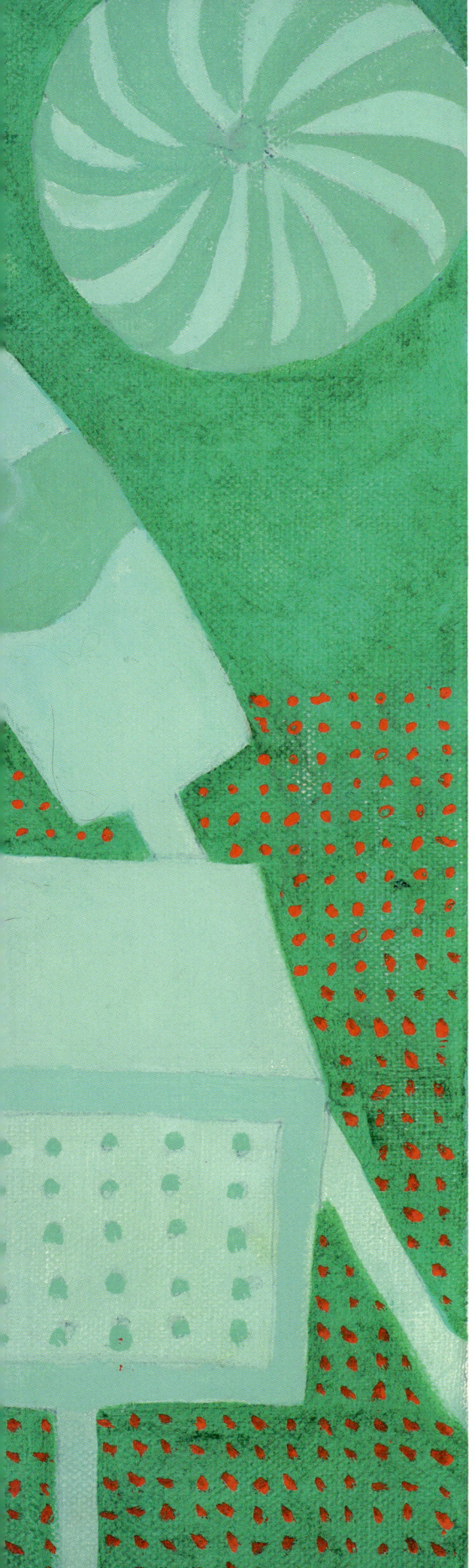

Scavenger Hunt @ Willow Way
aka Still Cute James
2020
Oil on canvas
20 x 24 in.

MESTIZAJE

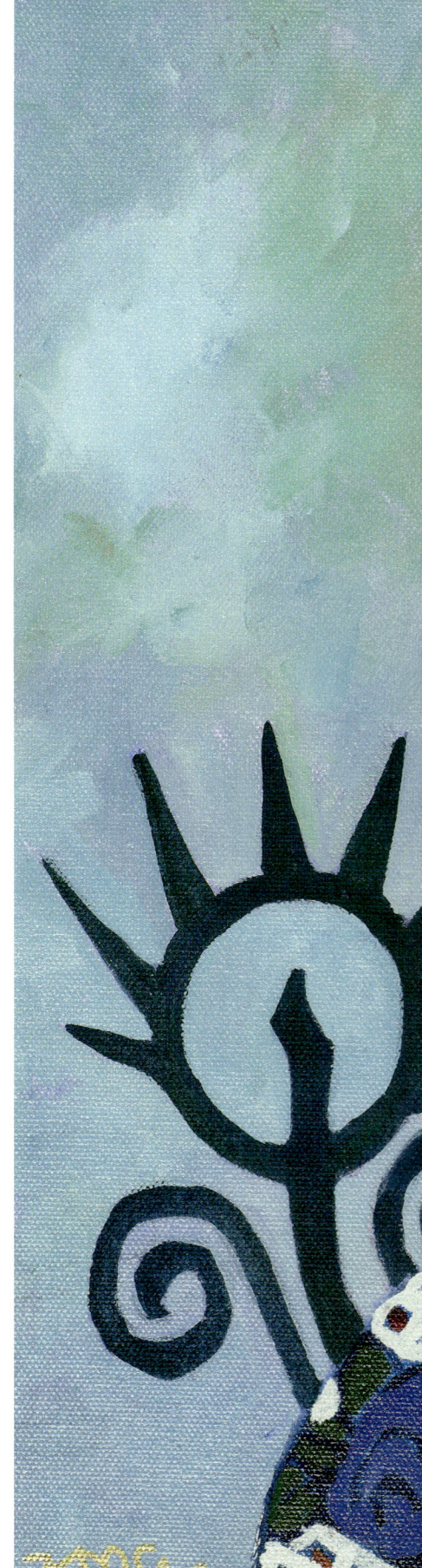

Gayna Dupont
2018
Oil on canvas
20 x 24 in.

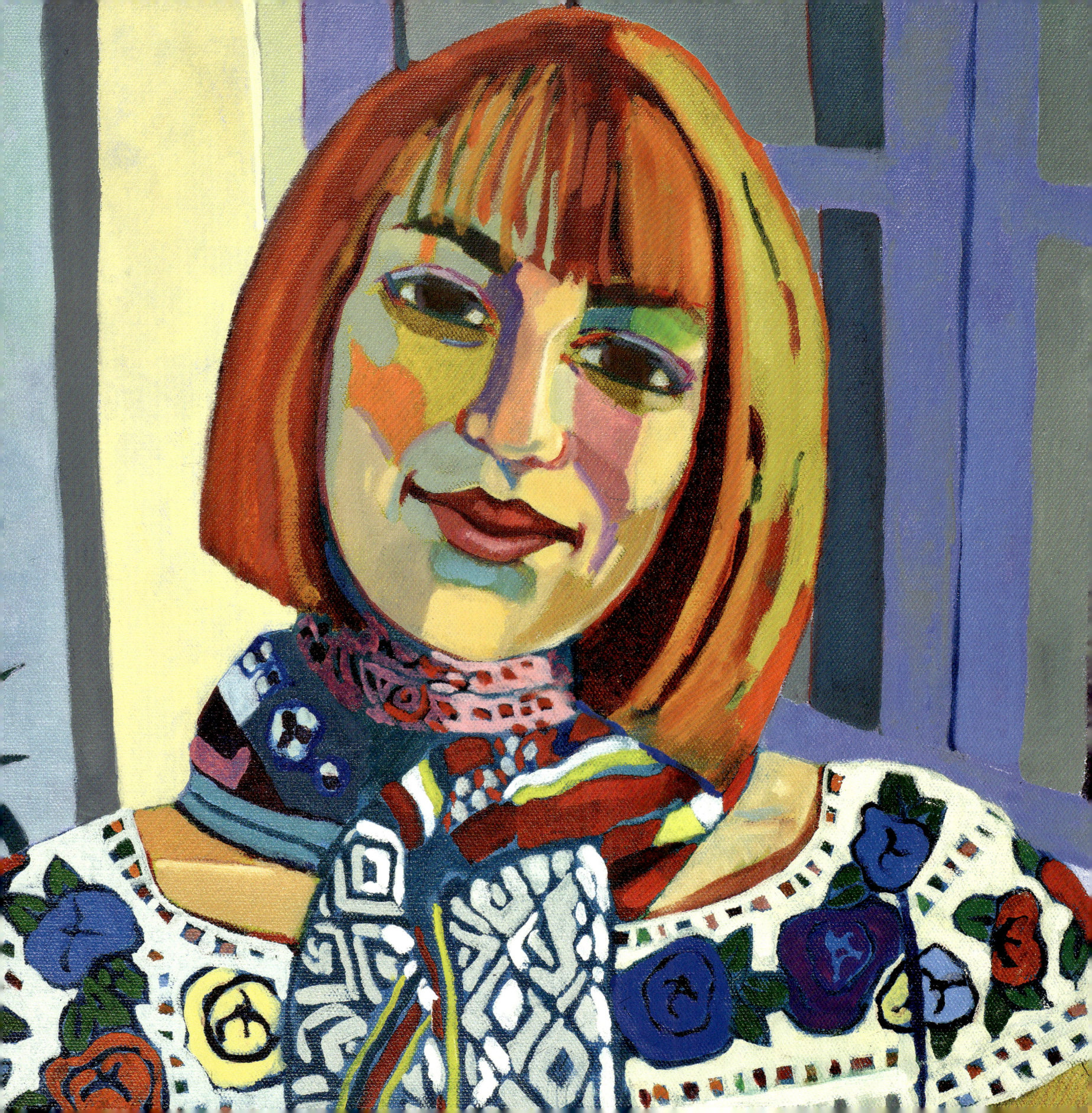

Winged Creatures

*Blessing of the Animals
on My Mind*
2016
Oil on canvas
36 x 36 in.

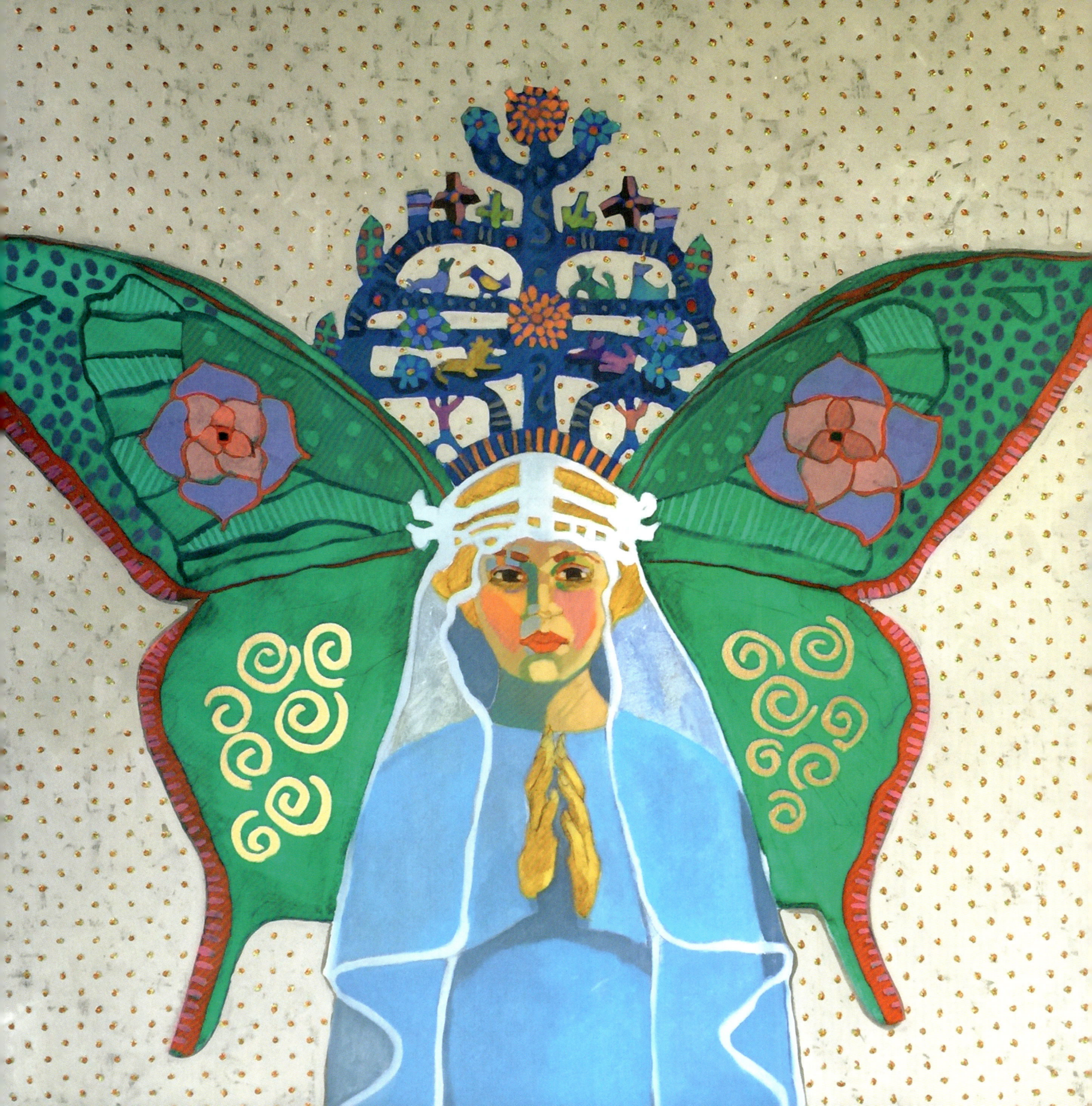

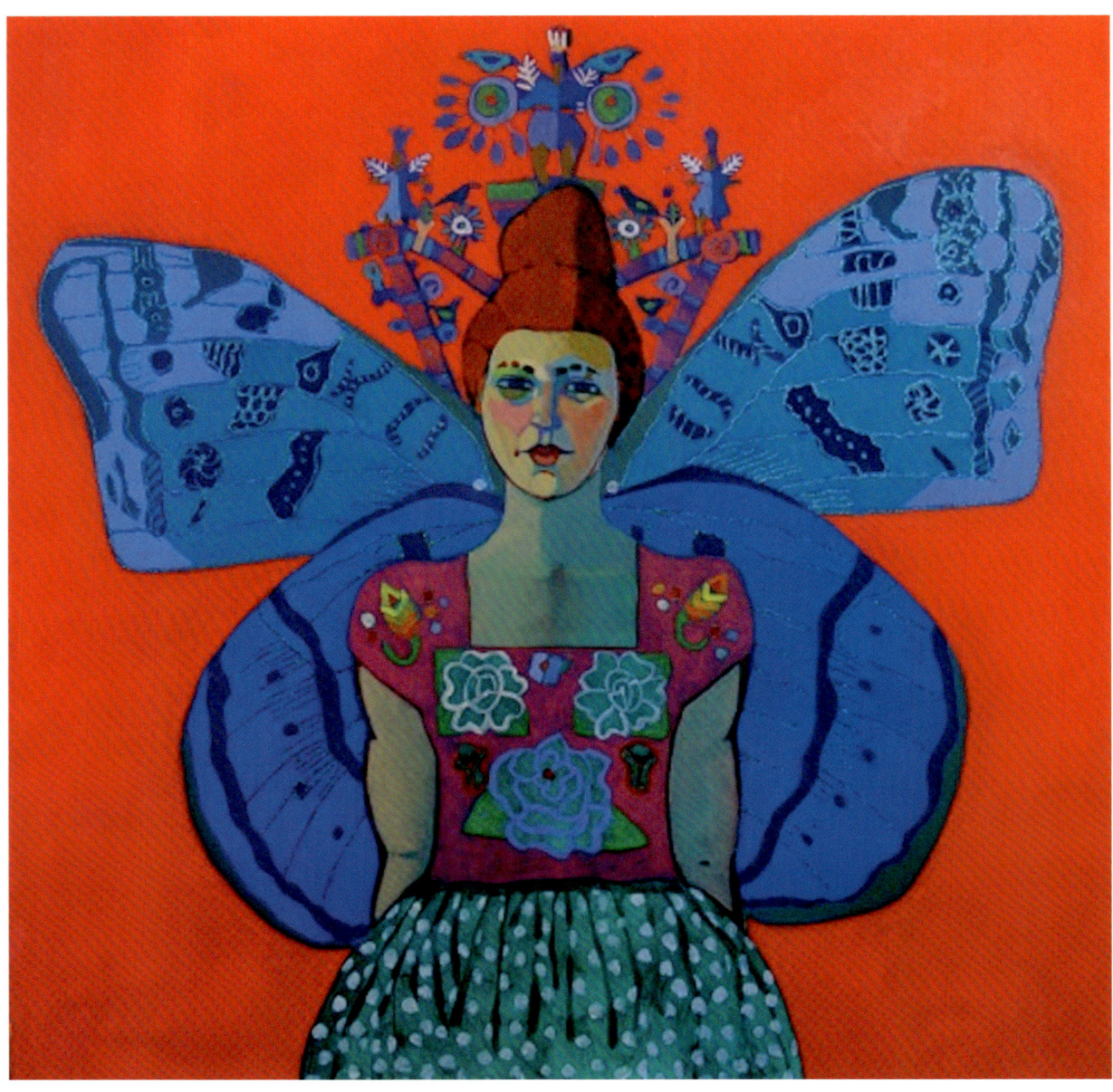

Primera Mariposa on My Mind
2017
Oil and mixed media on canvas
36 x 36 in.

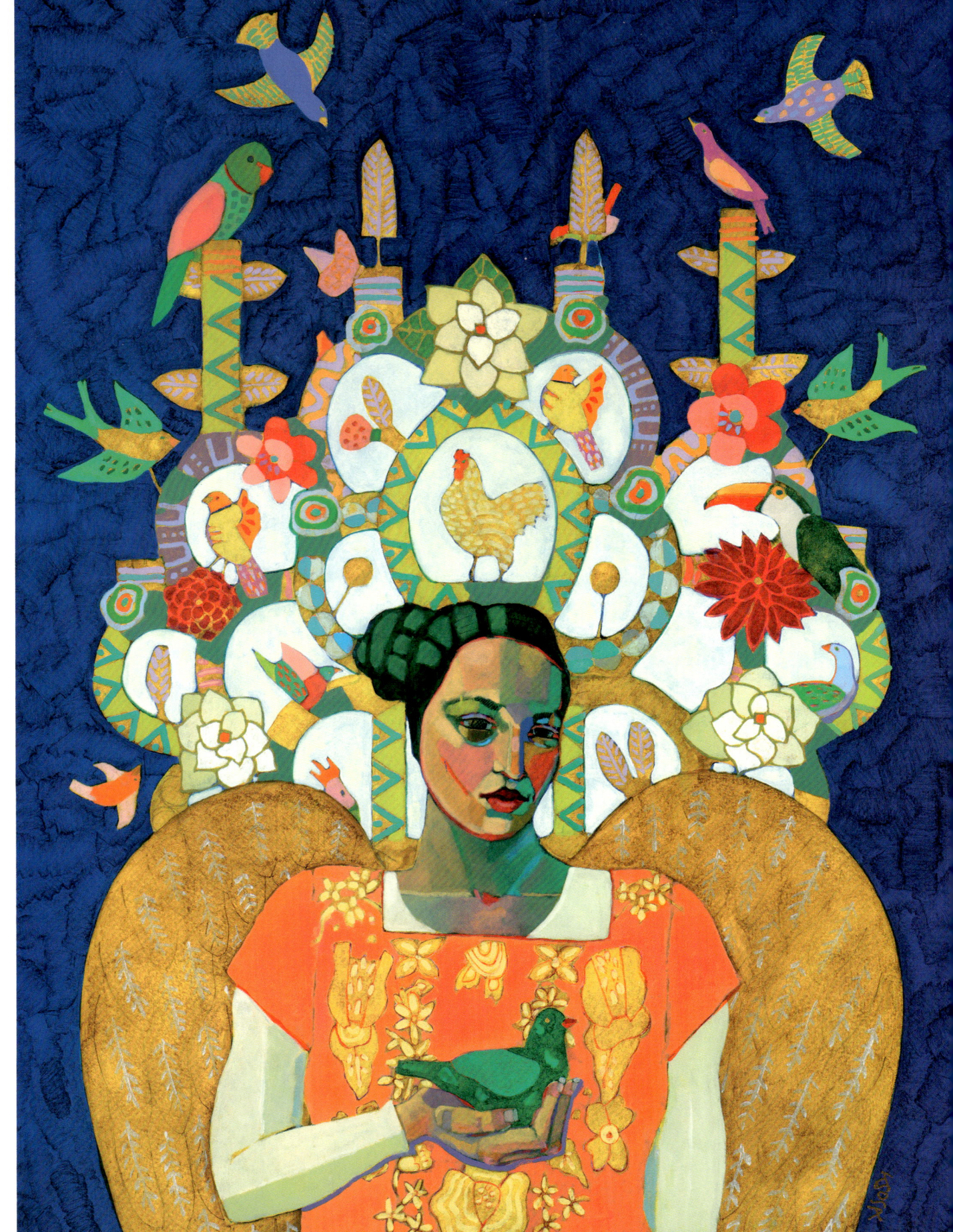

Bird in the Hand Worth Ten
in the Tree on My Mind
2021
Oil on canvas
36 x 48 in.

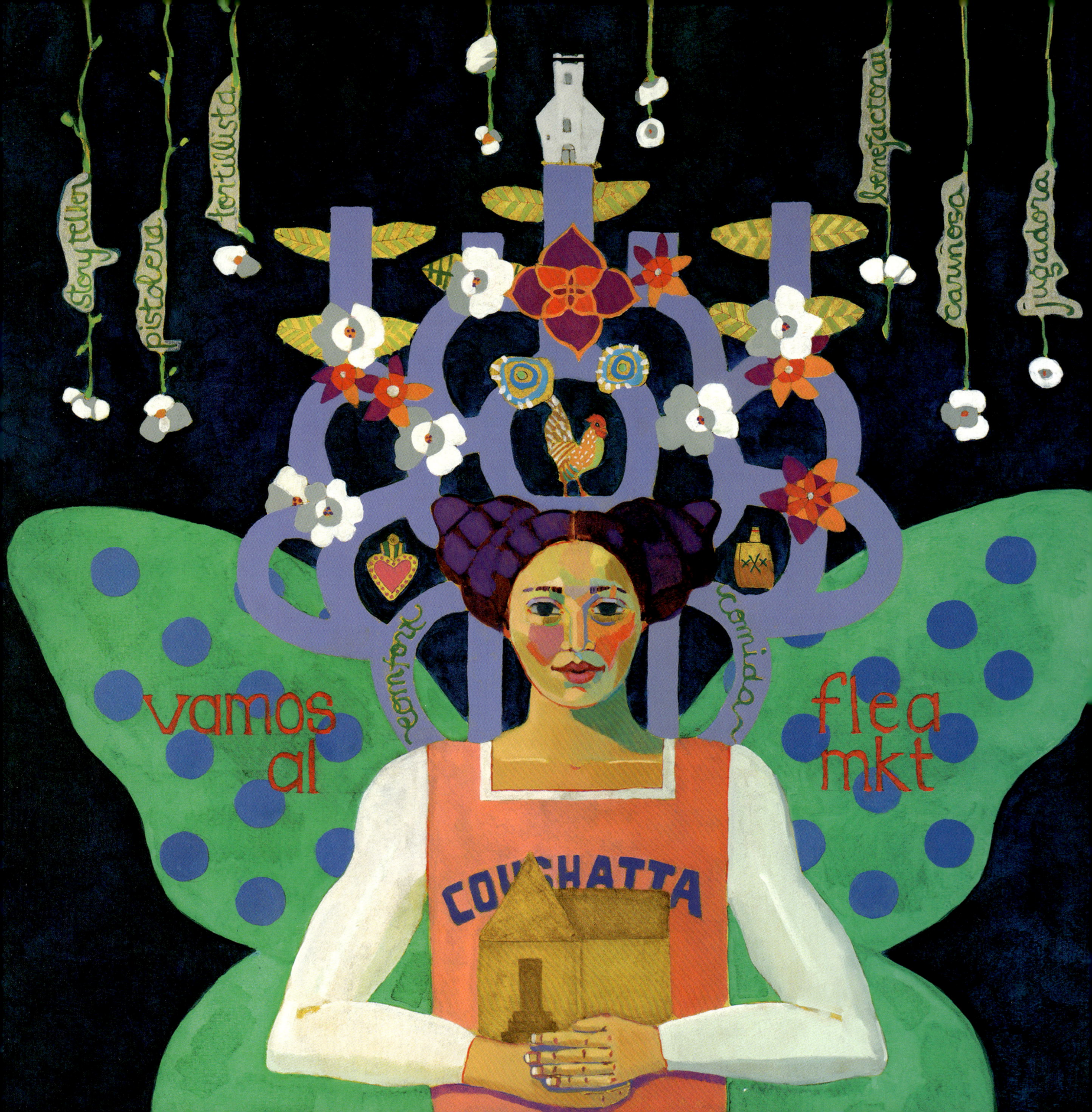

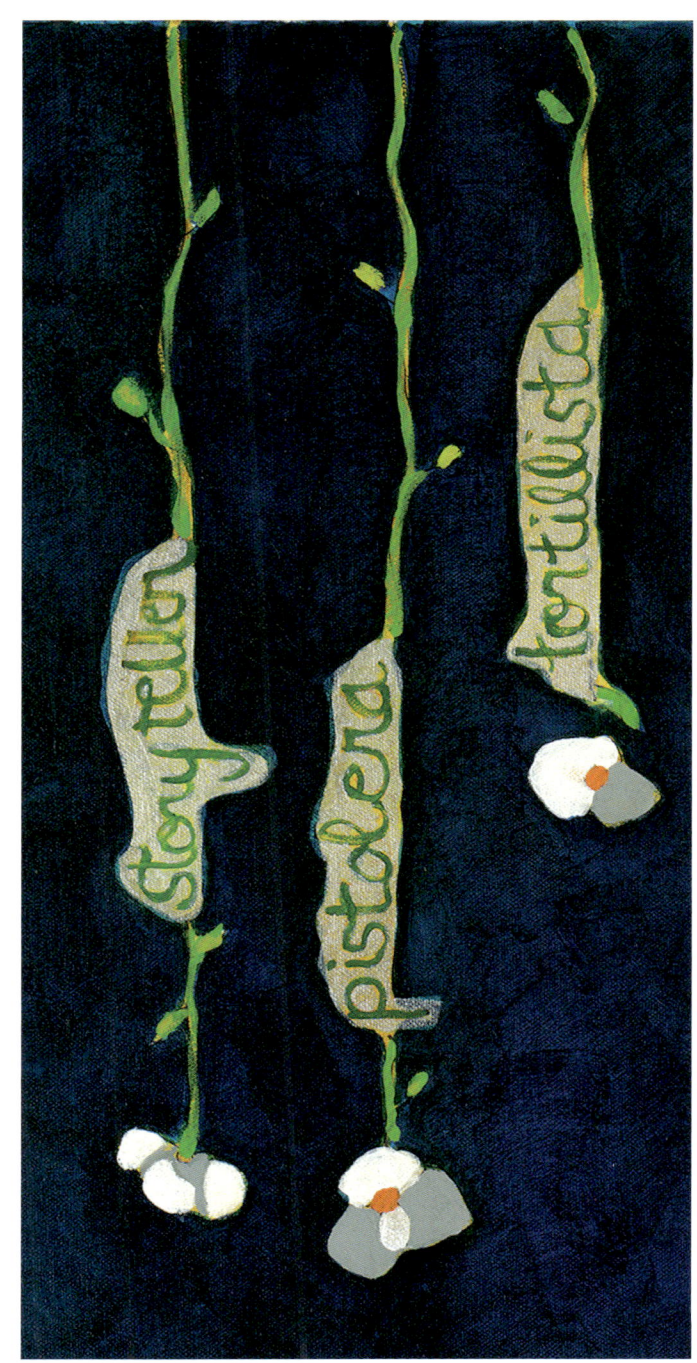

Vamos al Flea Market—
Portrait of Abuela as a Young
Woman on My Mind
2020
Oil on canvas
40 x 40 in.

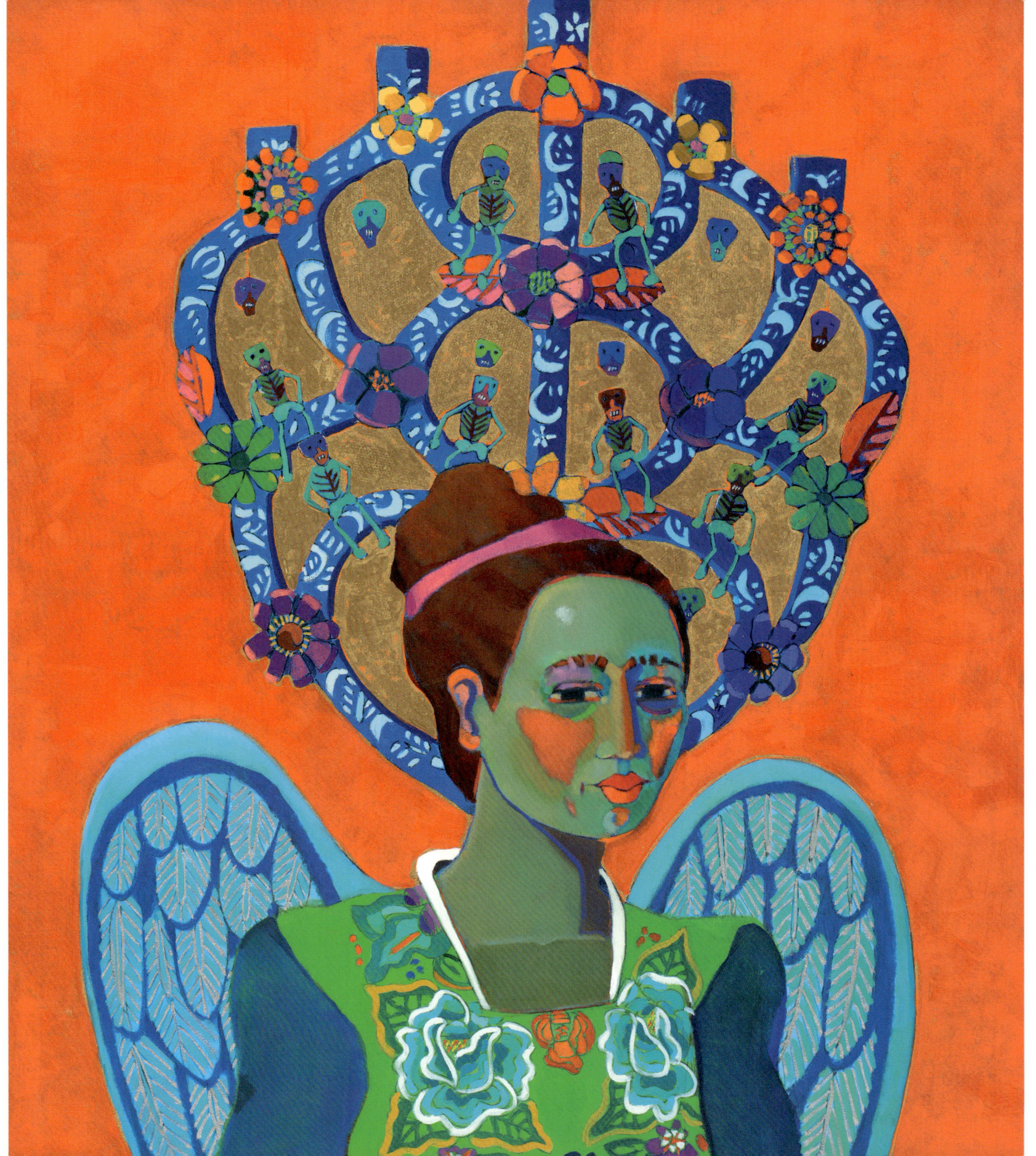

Ángel de los Muertos
on My Mind
2009
Oil on canvas
36 x 30 in.

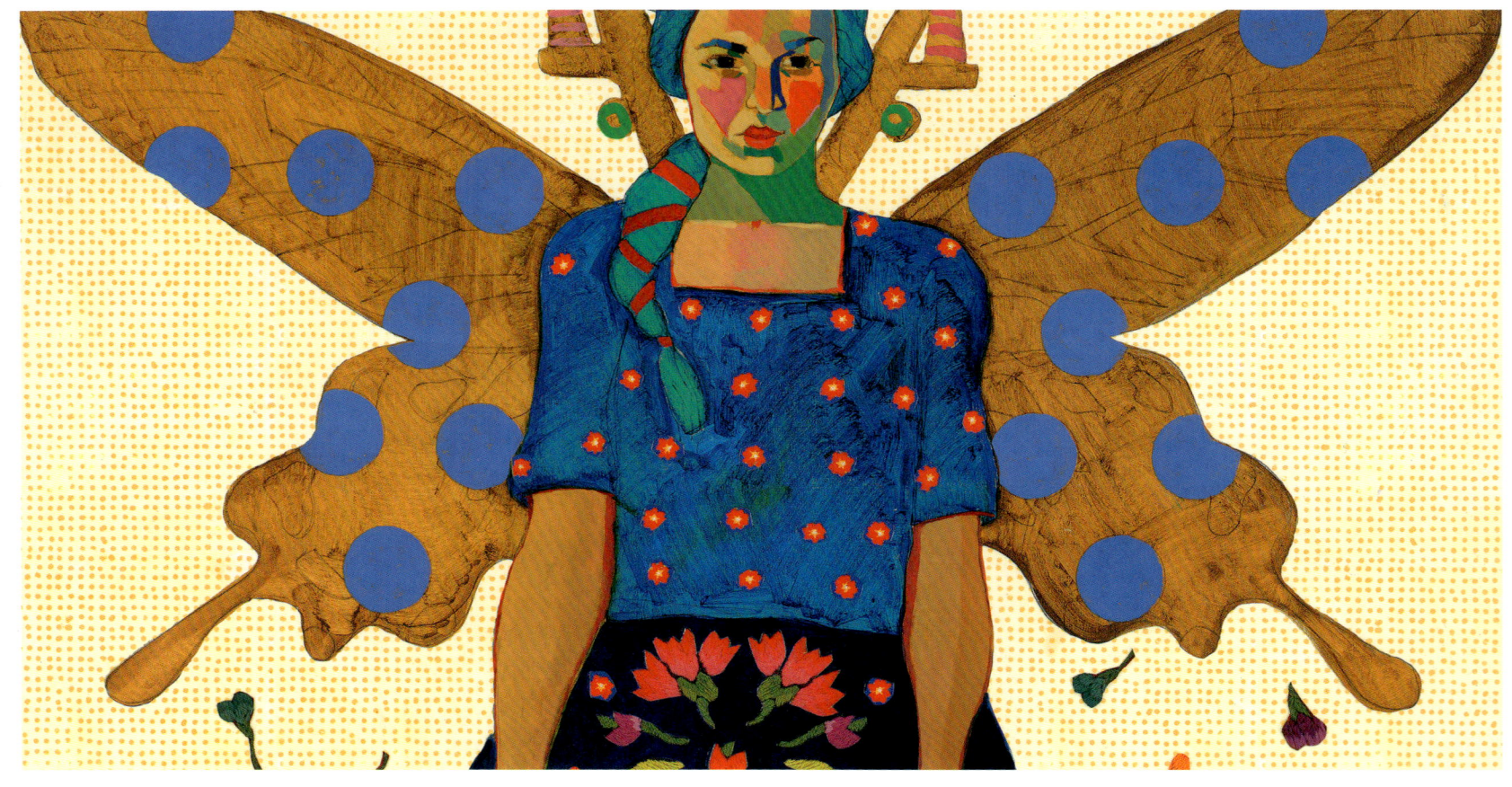

Mariposa Muñeca de Papel No. 2:
Dots over Mi Falda (detail)
2019
Oil portrait collage
36 x 36 in.

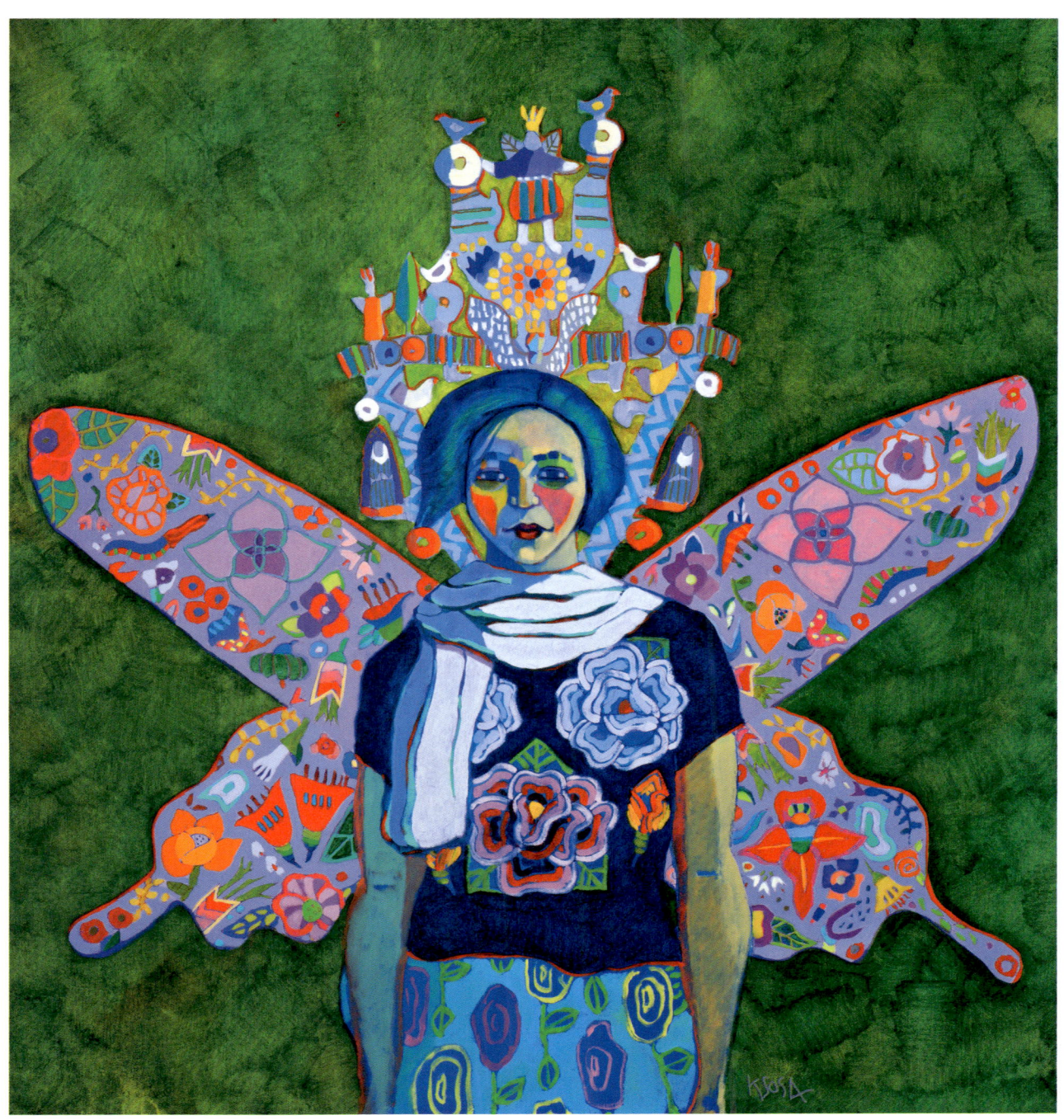

Mariposa Rosa on My Mind
2019
Oil on canvas
36 x 36 in.

Ángel del Árbol No. 2 on My
Mind: Night Sky Angel
2014
Oil on canvas
30 x 30 in.

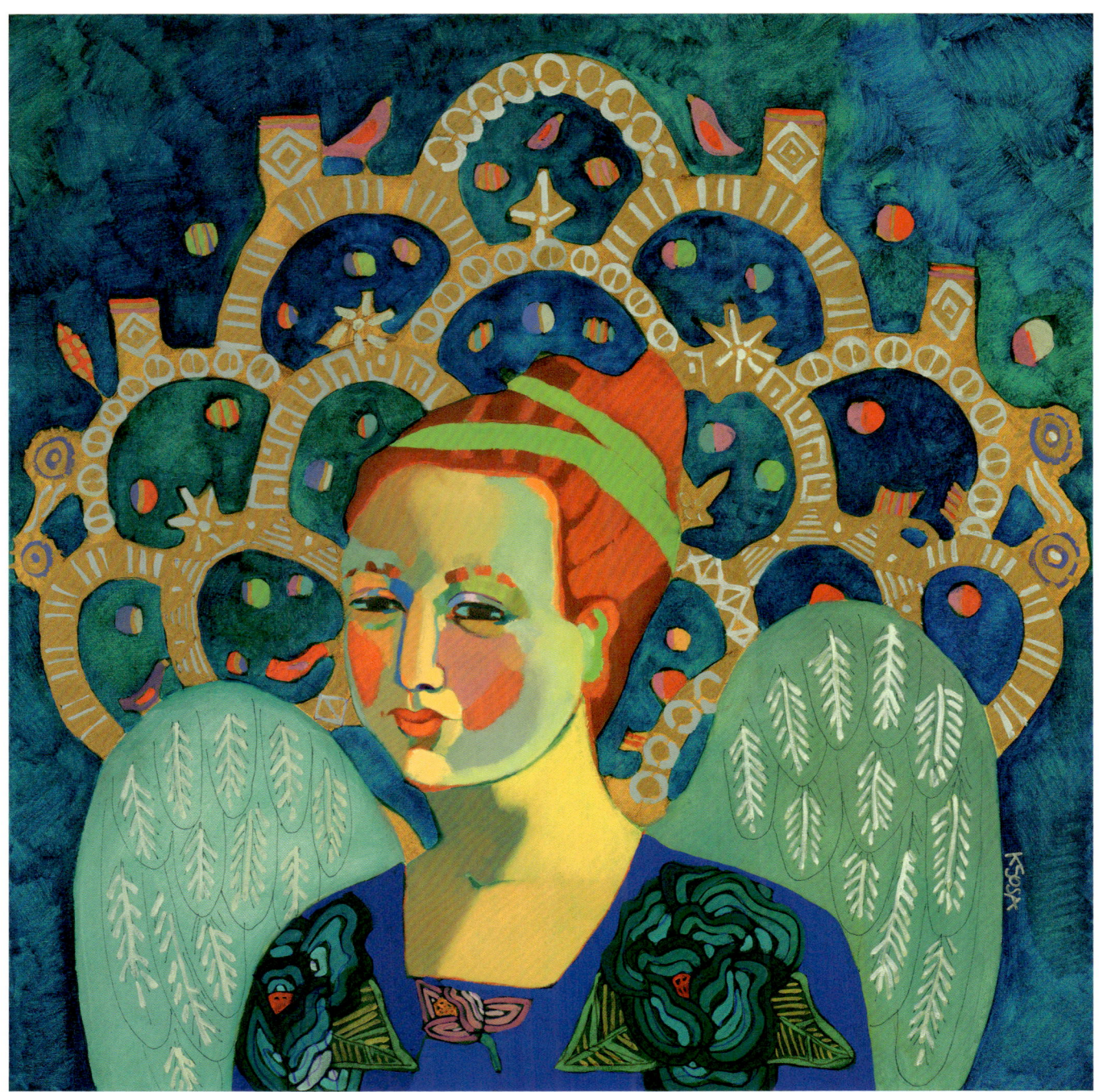

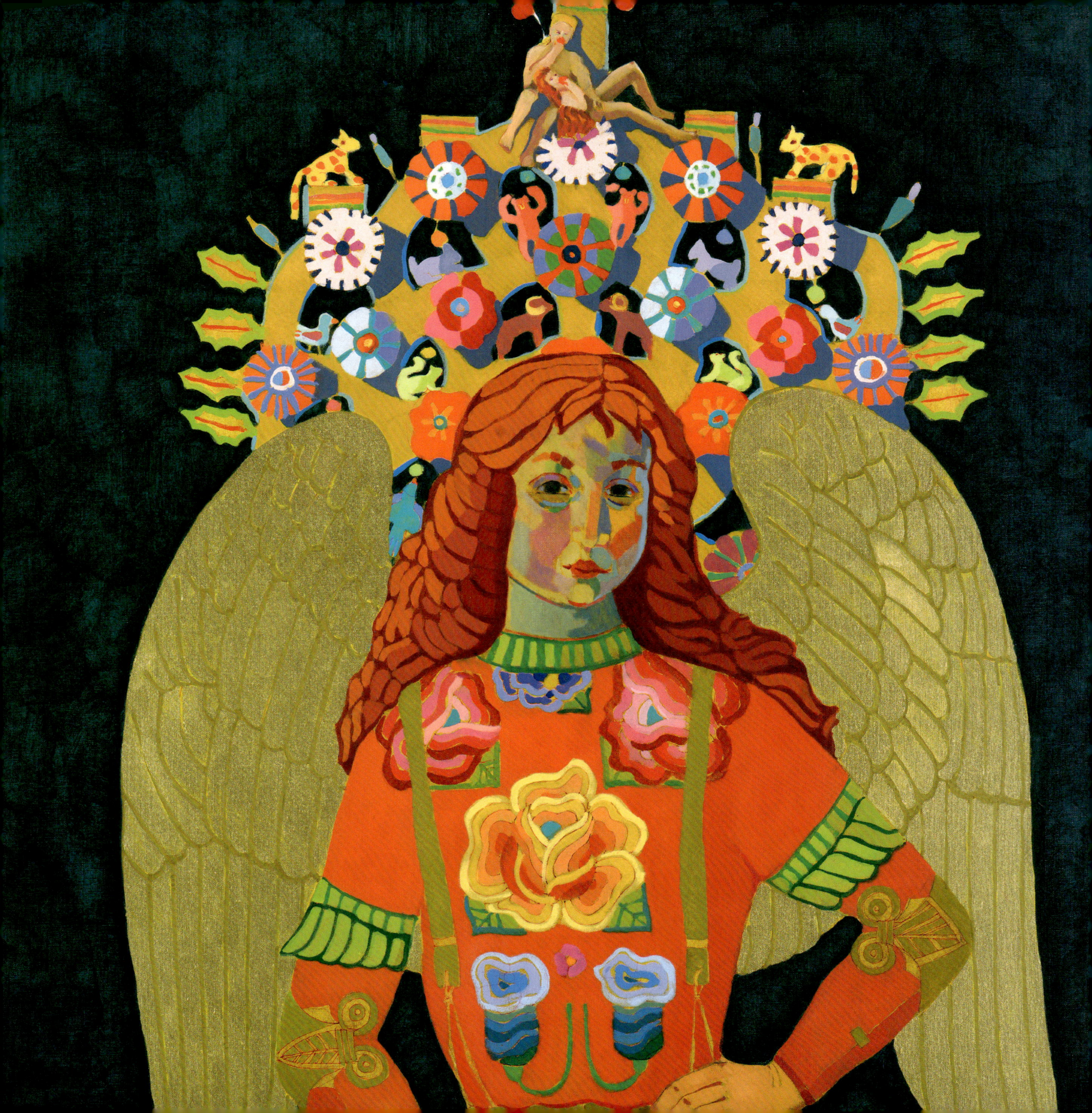

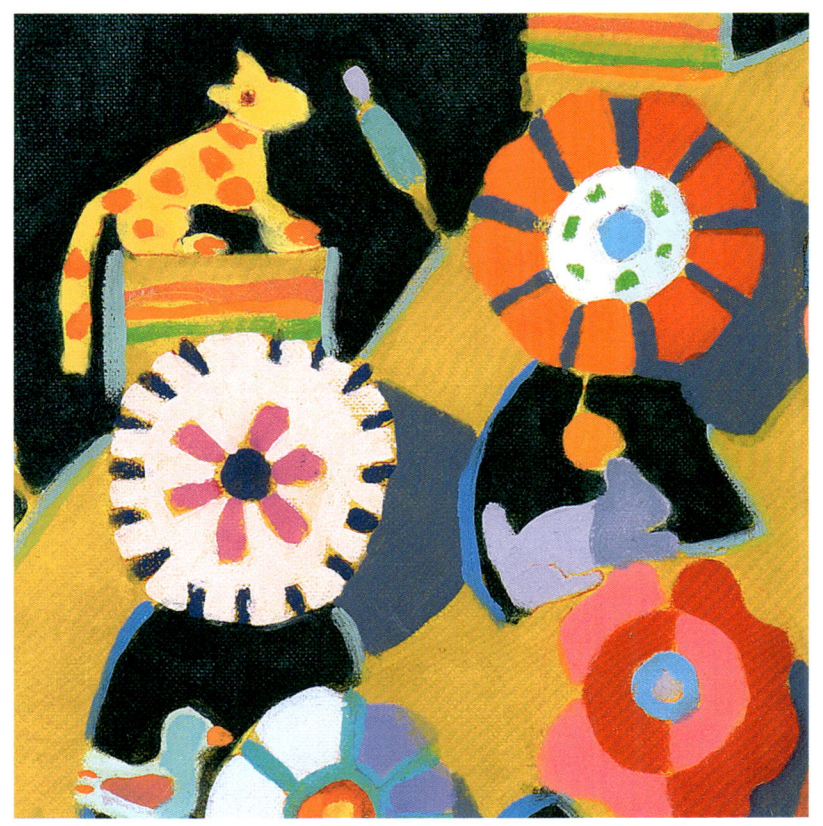

Archangel Contemplating
Creation on My Mind
2011
Oil on canvas
36 x 36 in.

MESTIZAJE

Viva la Revolución
on My Mind
2018
Oil portrait collage
36 x 36 in.

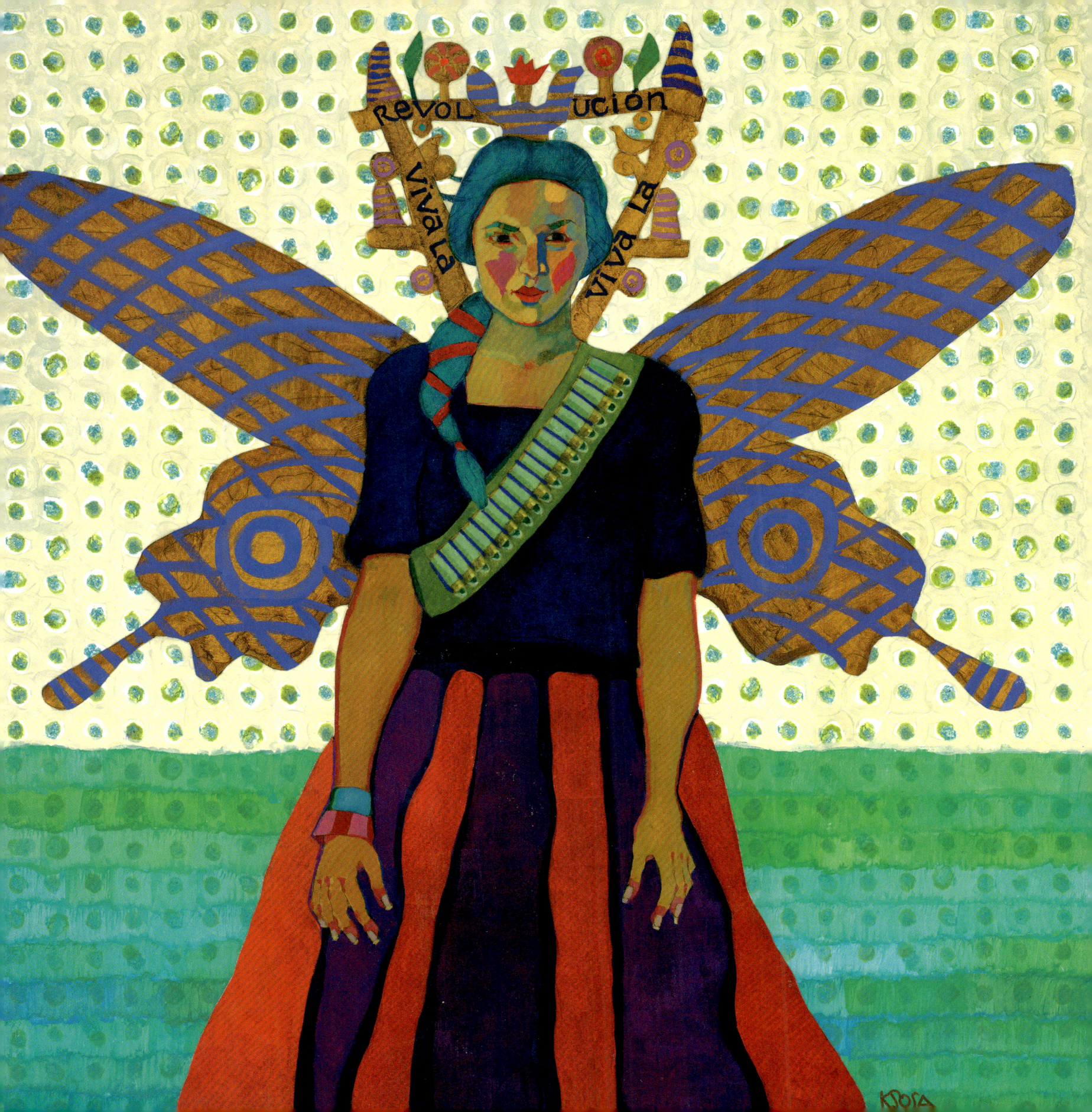

Paperwork

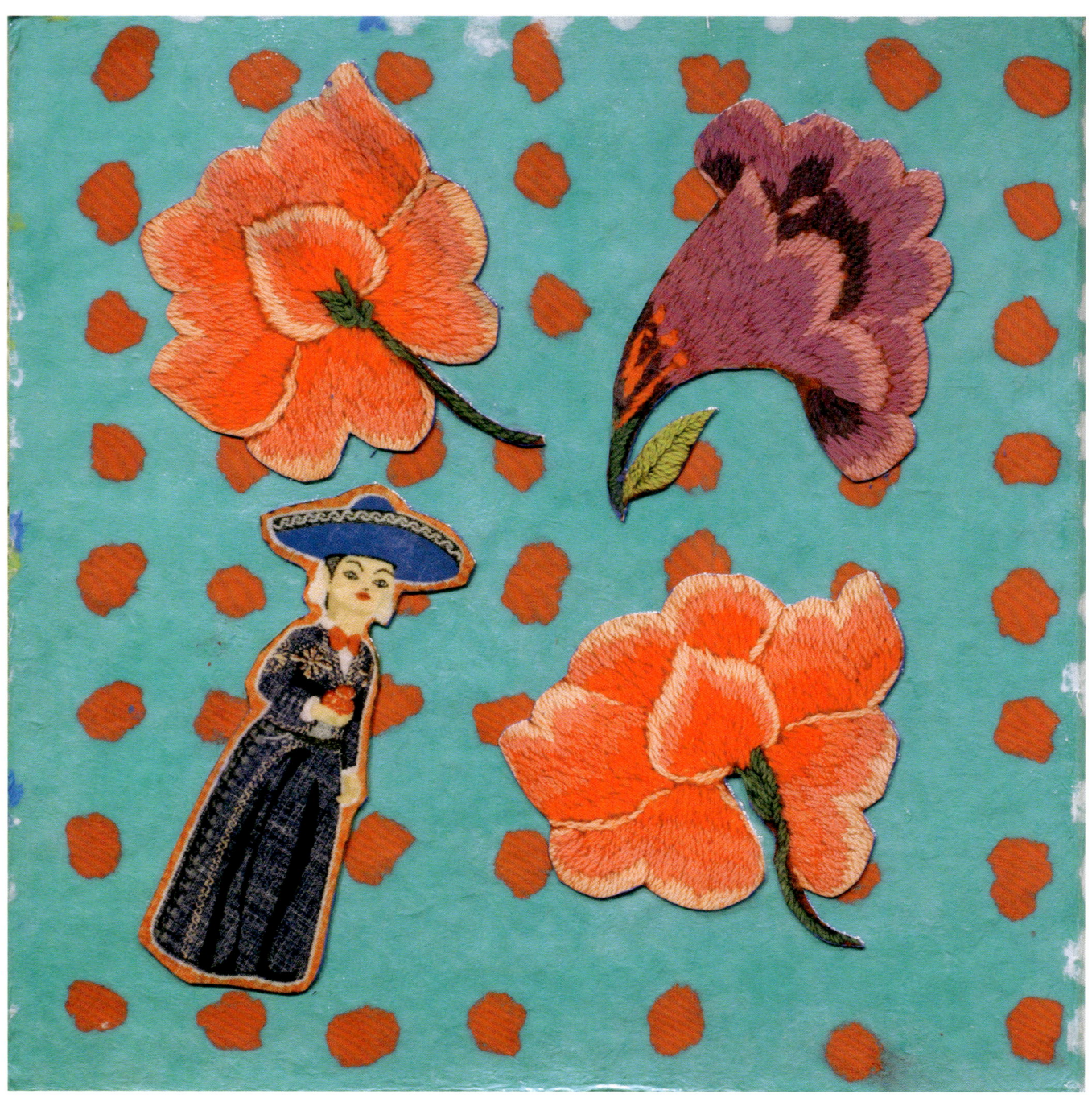

Mariachi de las Flores No. 2
2014
Mixed media on
handmade paper
12 x 12 in.

Pink Confection
2014
Mixed media on
handmade paper
6 x 6 in.

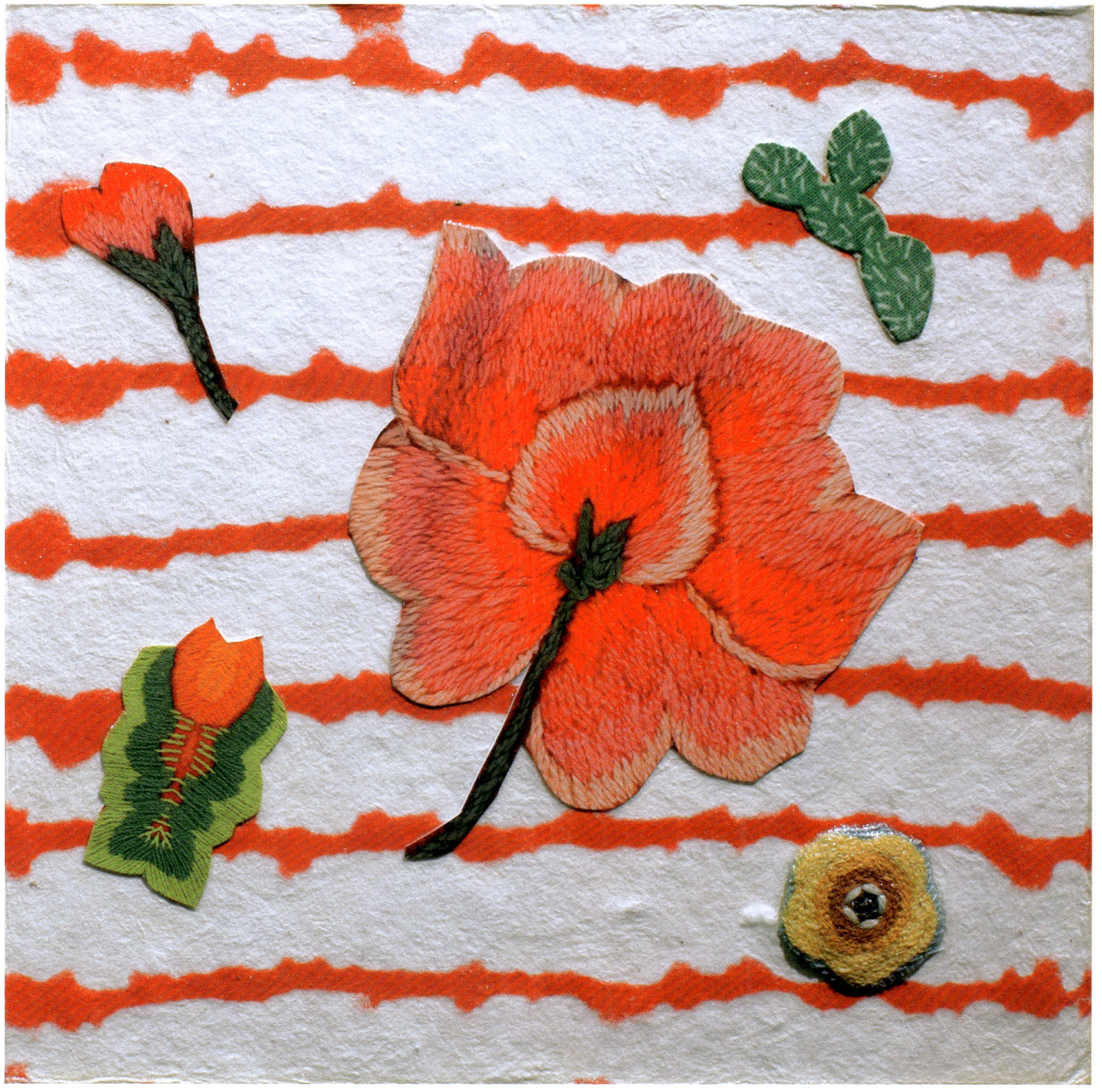

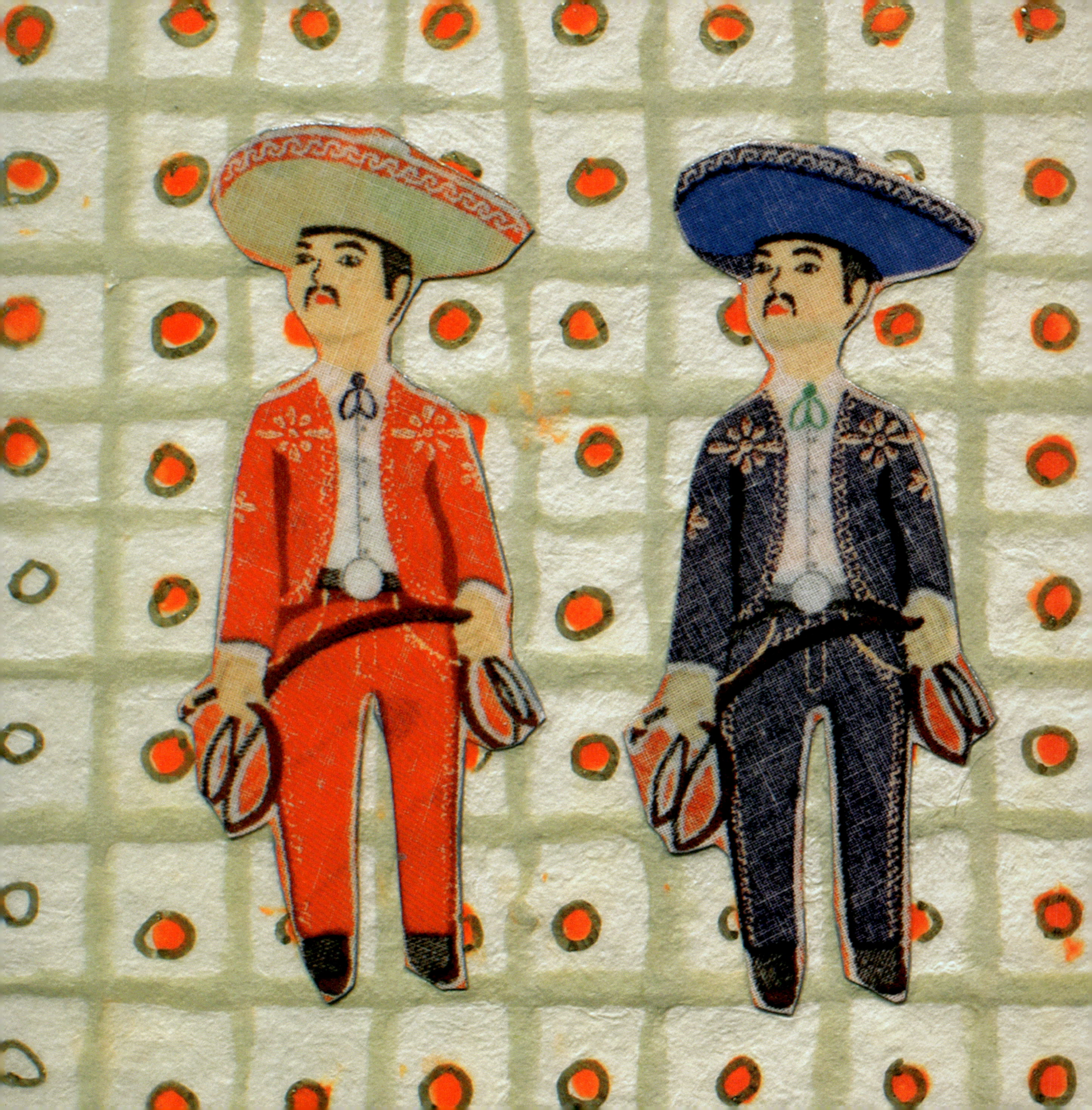

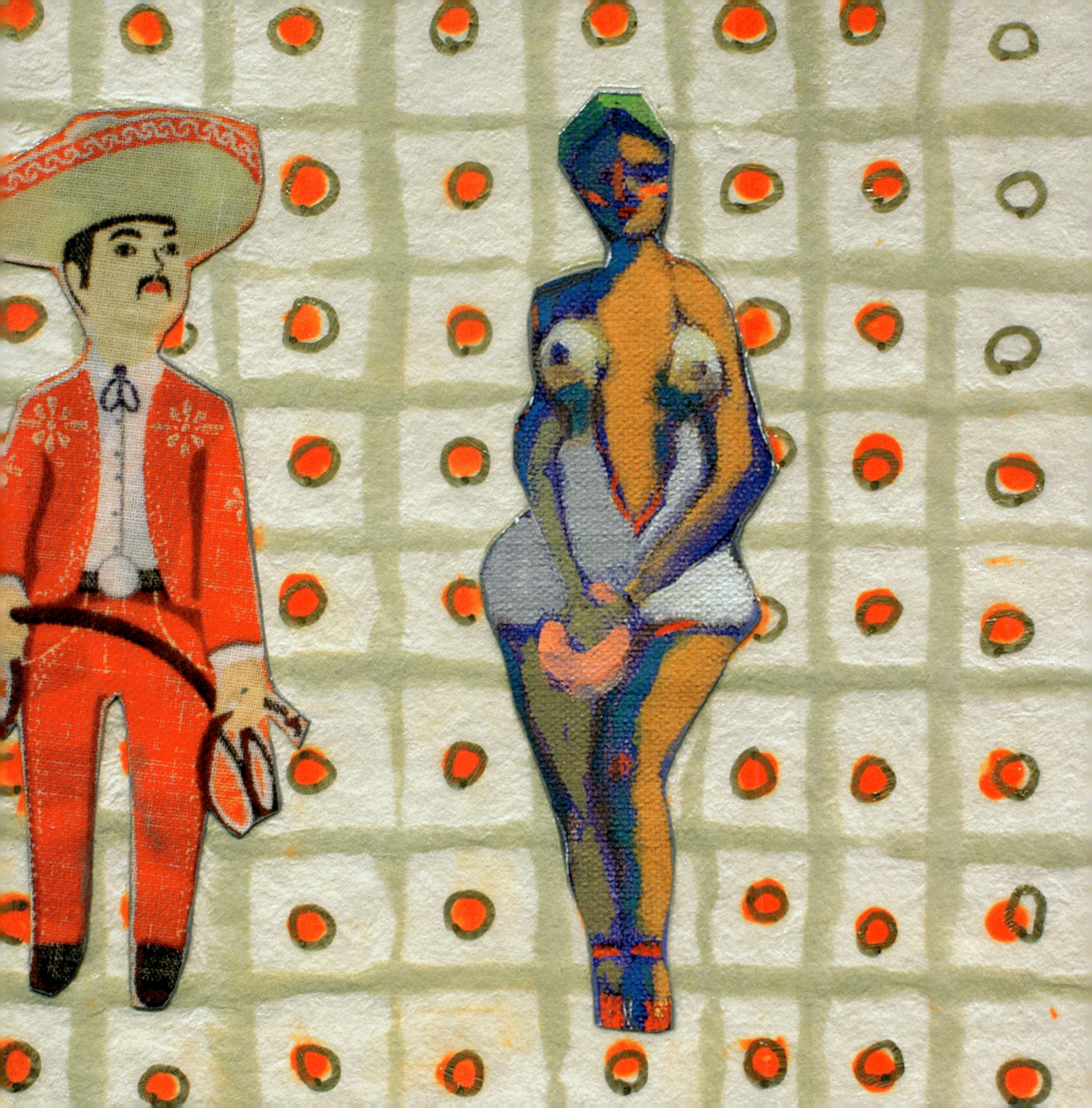

One of These Things
Is Not Like the Other
2014
Mixed media on
handmade paper
8 x 16 in.

Taste of Success
2014
Mixed media on
handmade paper
12 x 12 in.

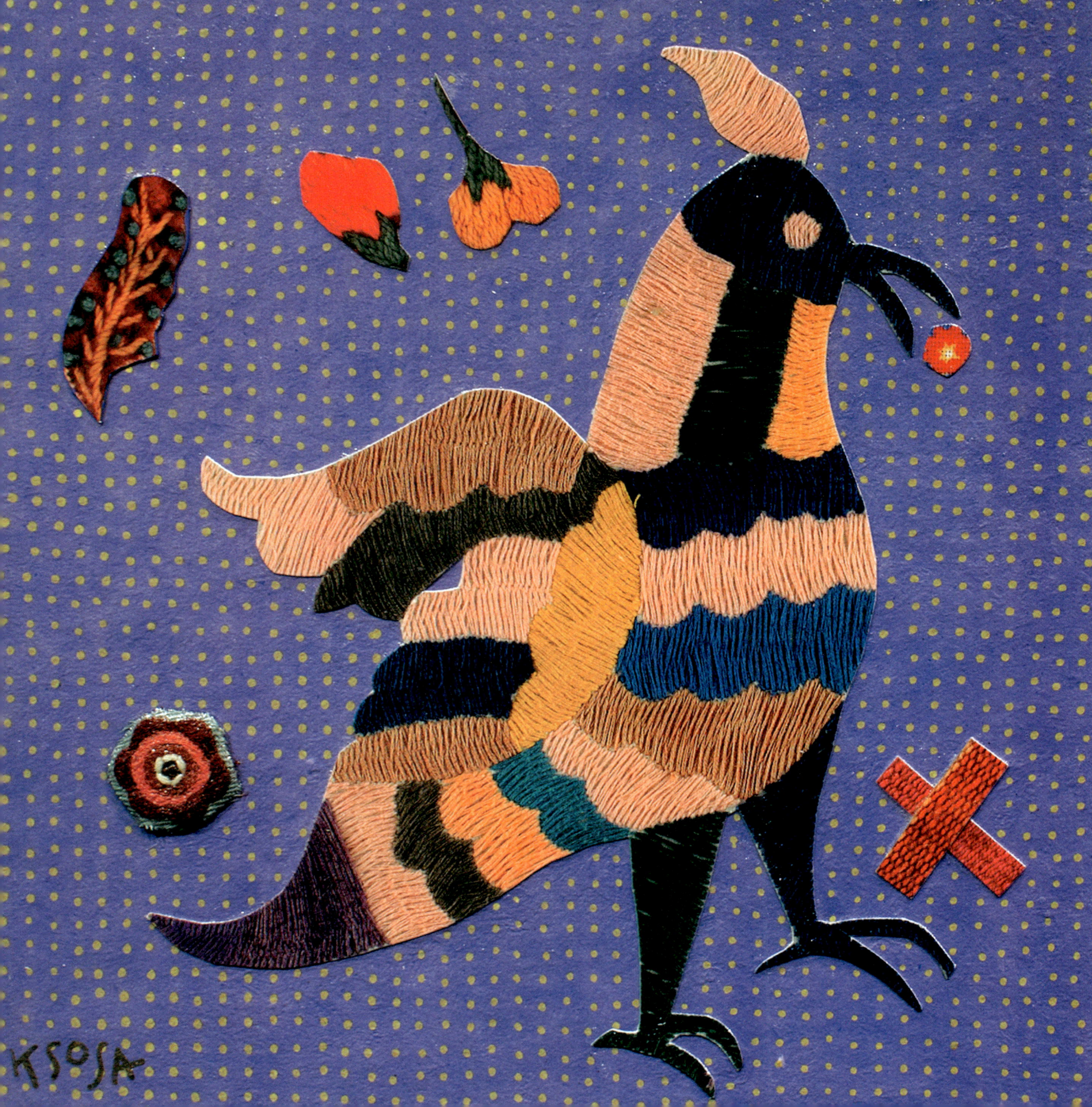

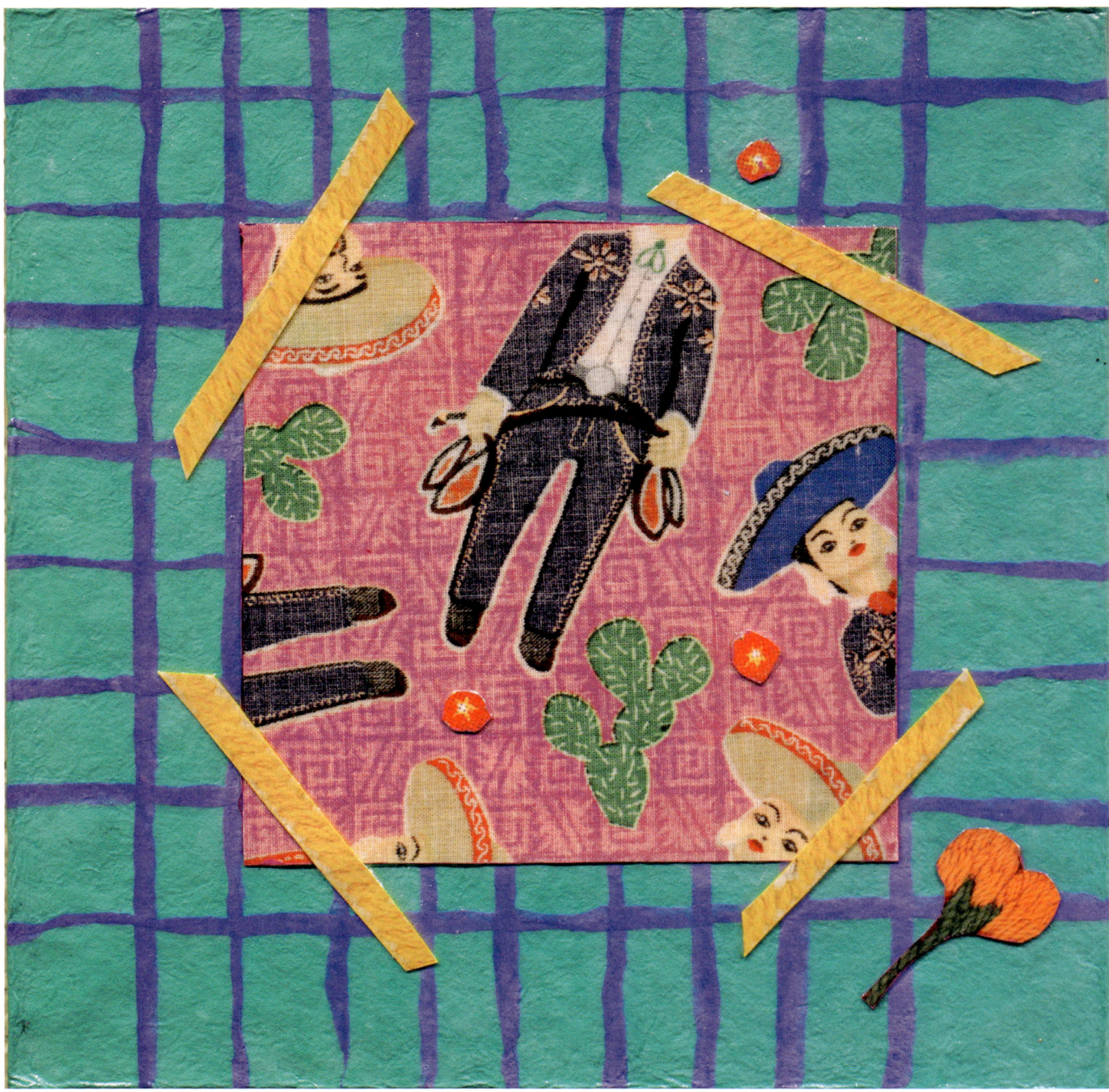

Lost My Head
2014
Mixed media on
handmade paper
10 x 10 in.

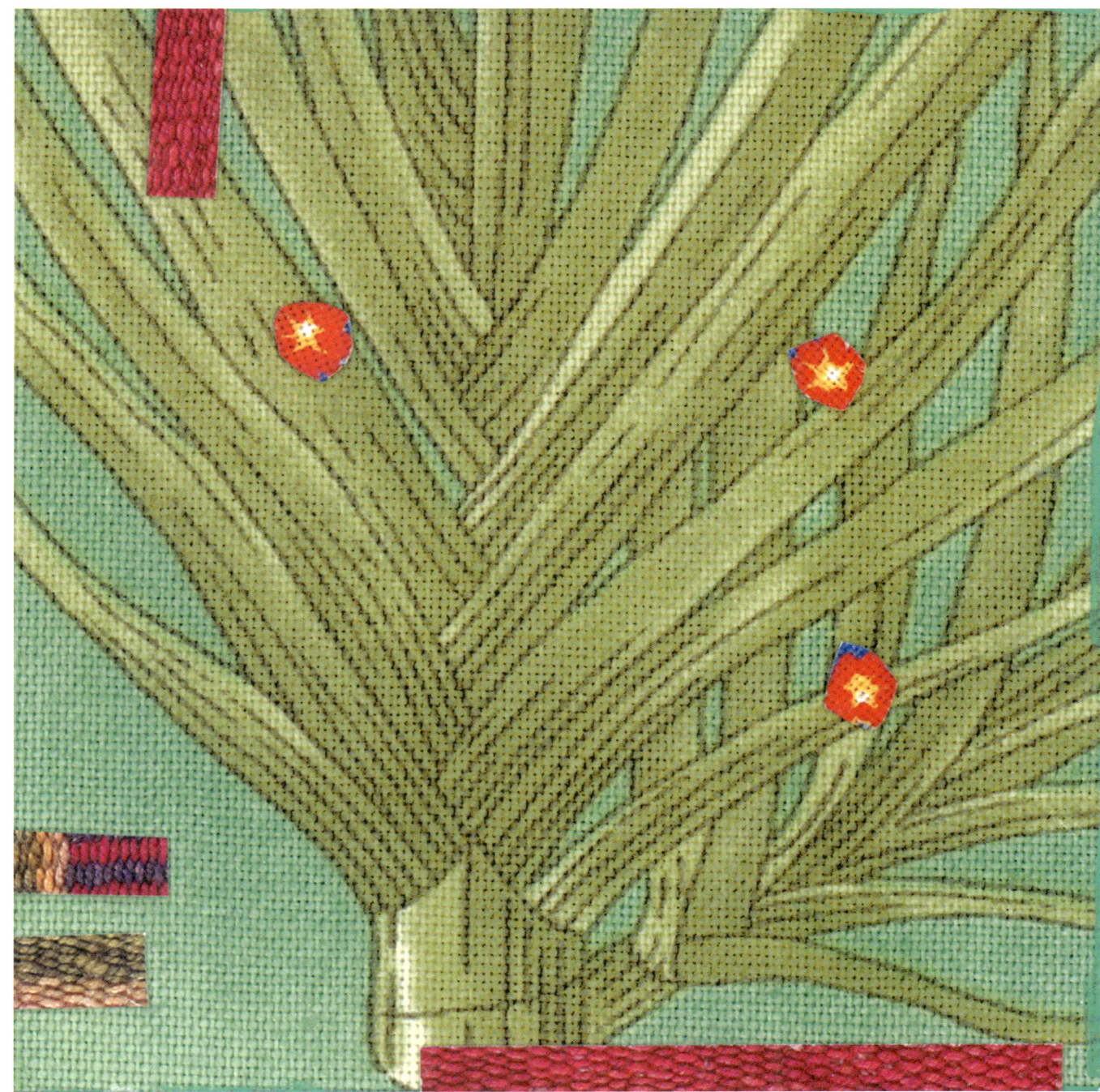

Planta de Flores Rojas
2014
Mixed media
6 x 6 in.

Found Objects

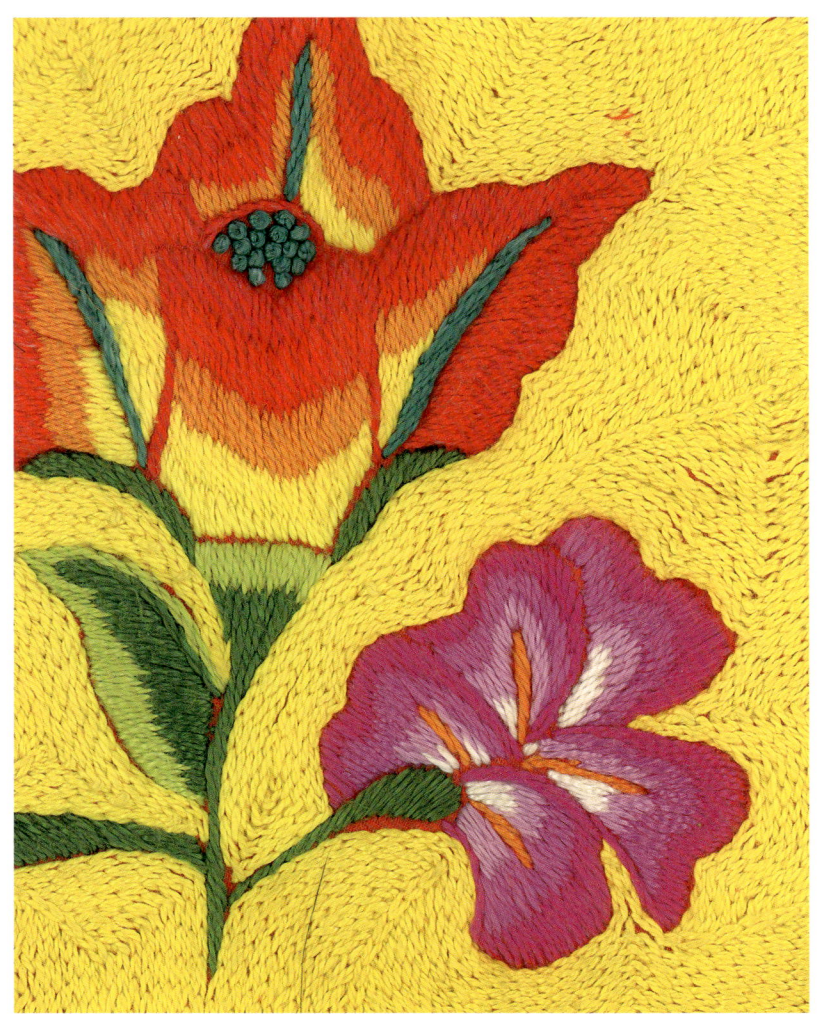

VPrida Huipil No. 3 (detail)
2011
Digital textile manipulation
20 x 20 in.

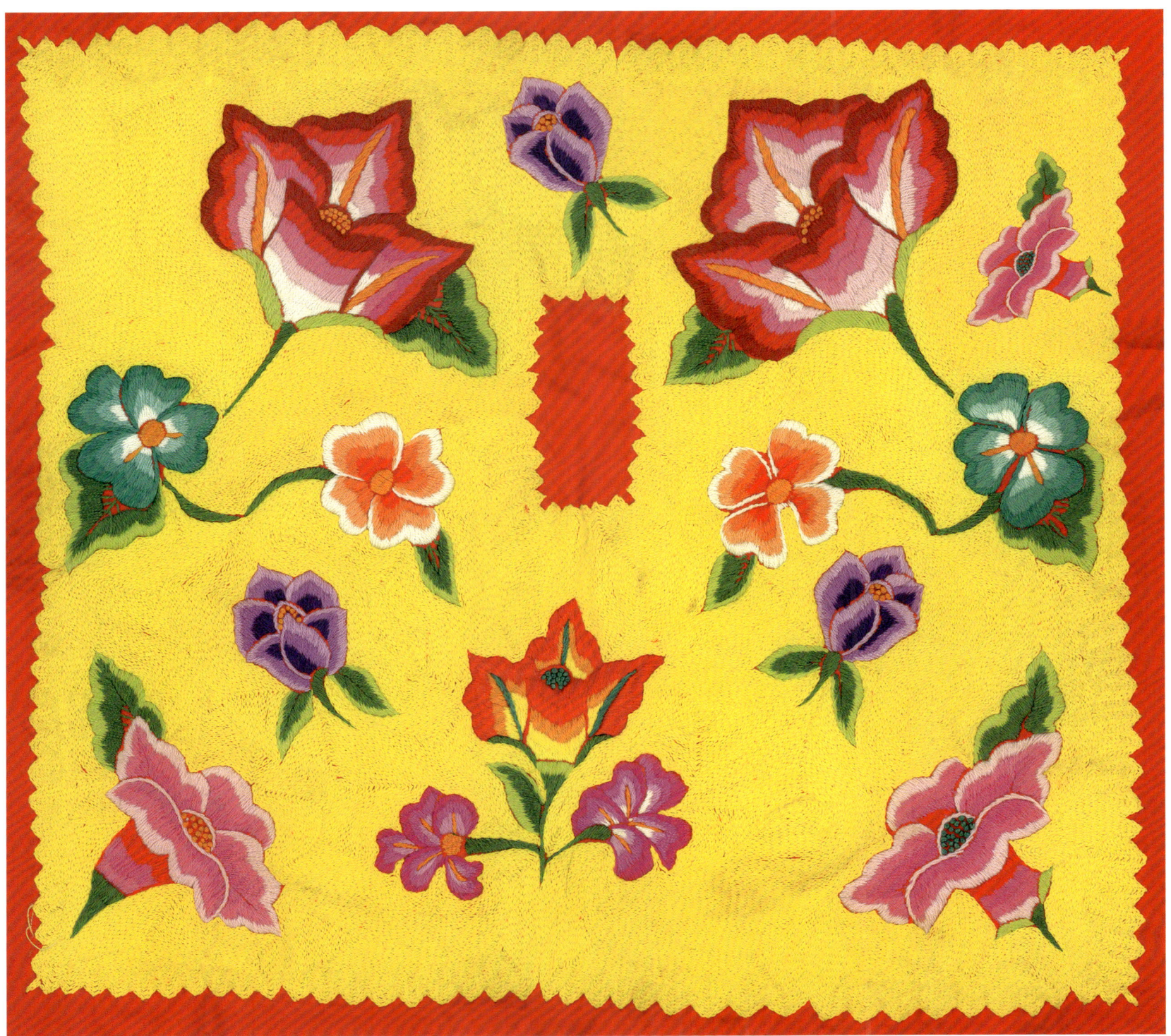

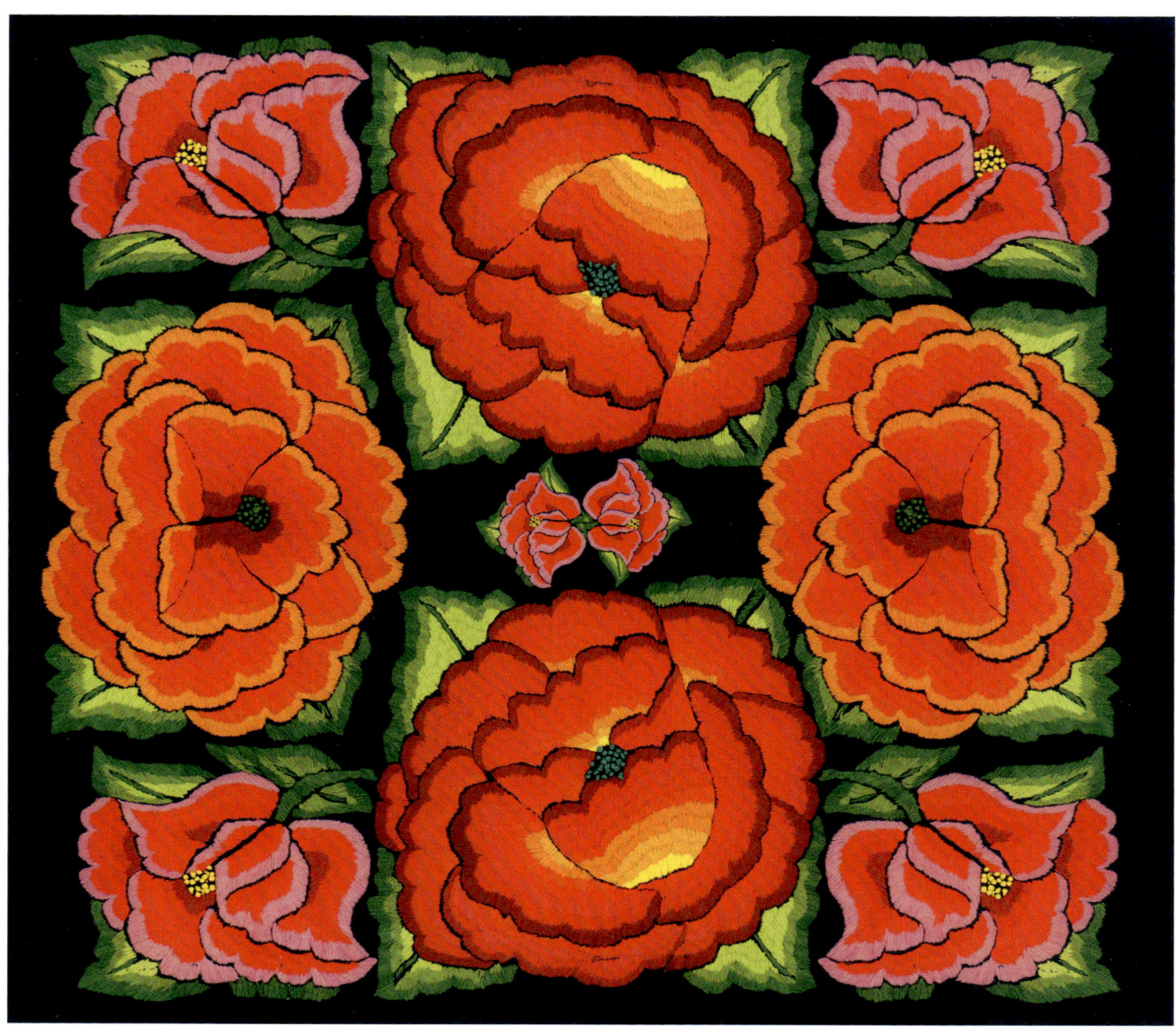

San Miguel Huipil No. 2
2011
Digital textile manipulation
16 x 16 in.

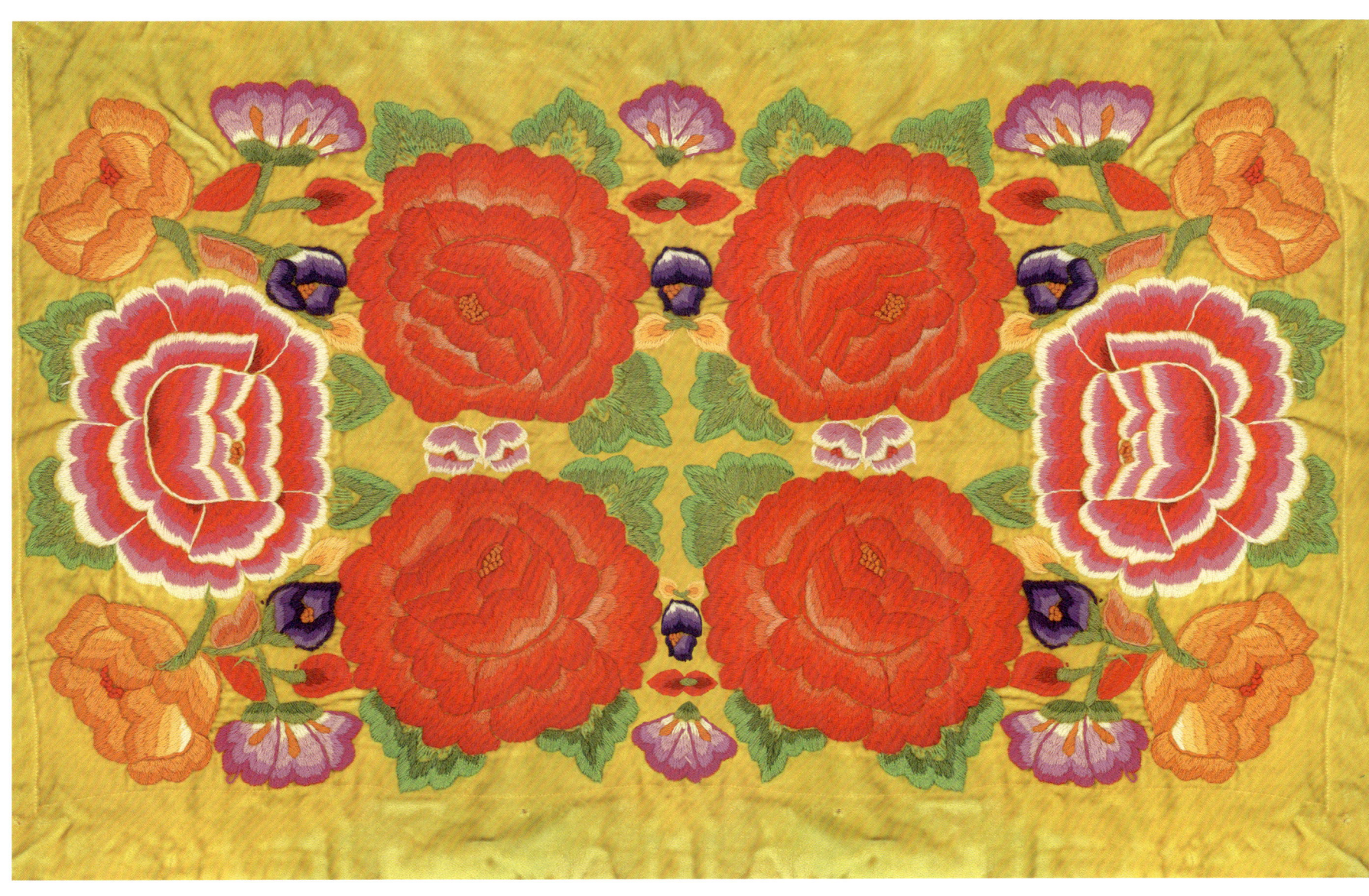

VPrida Huipil No. 1
2011
Digital textile manipulation
24 x 45 in.

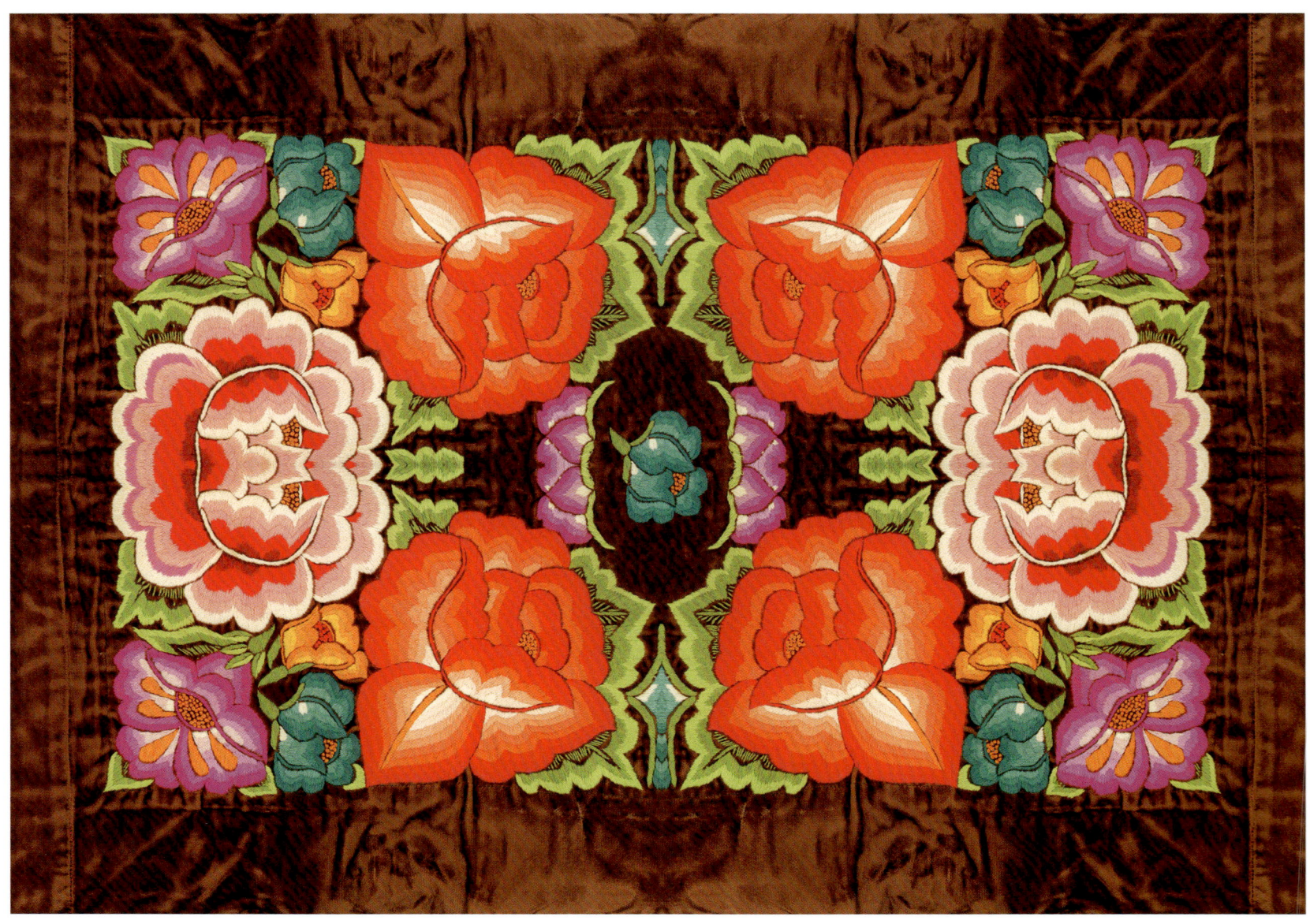

Milagro Huipil No. 3
2012
Digital textile manipulation
24 x 42 in.

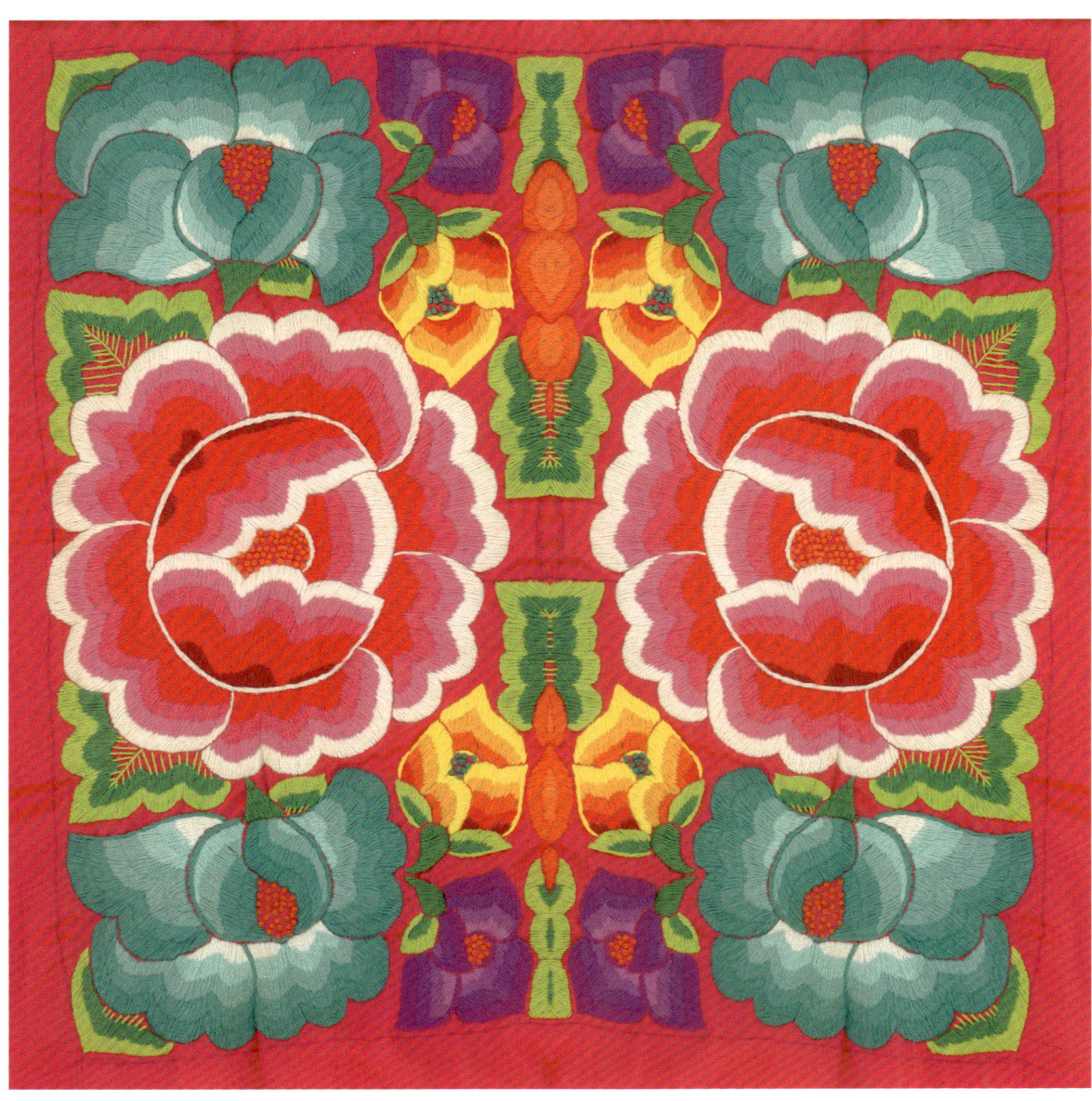

Tepoz Huipil No. 1
2011
Digital textile manipulation
16 x 16 in.

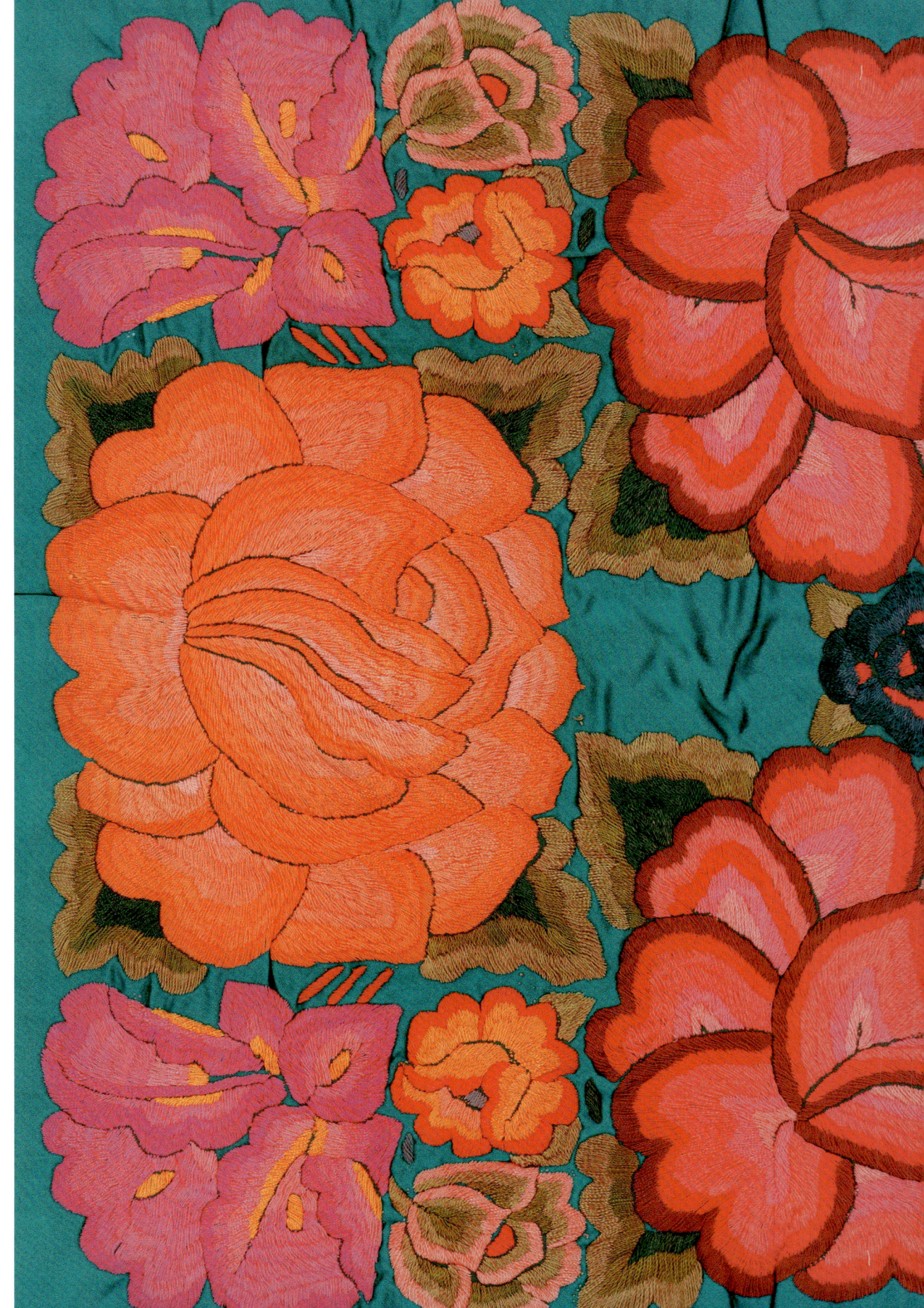

San Miguel Huipil No. 1
2010
Digital textile manipulation
27 x 45 in.

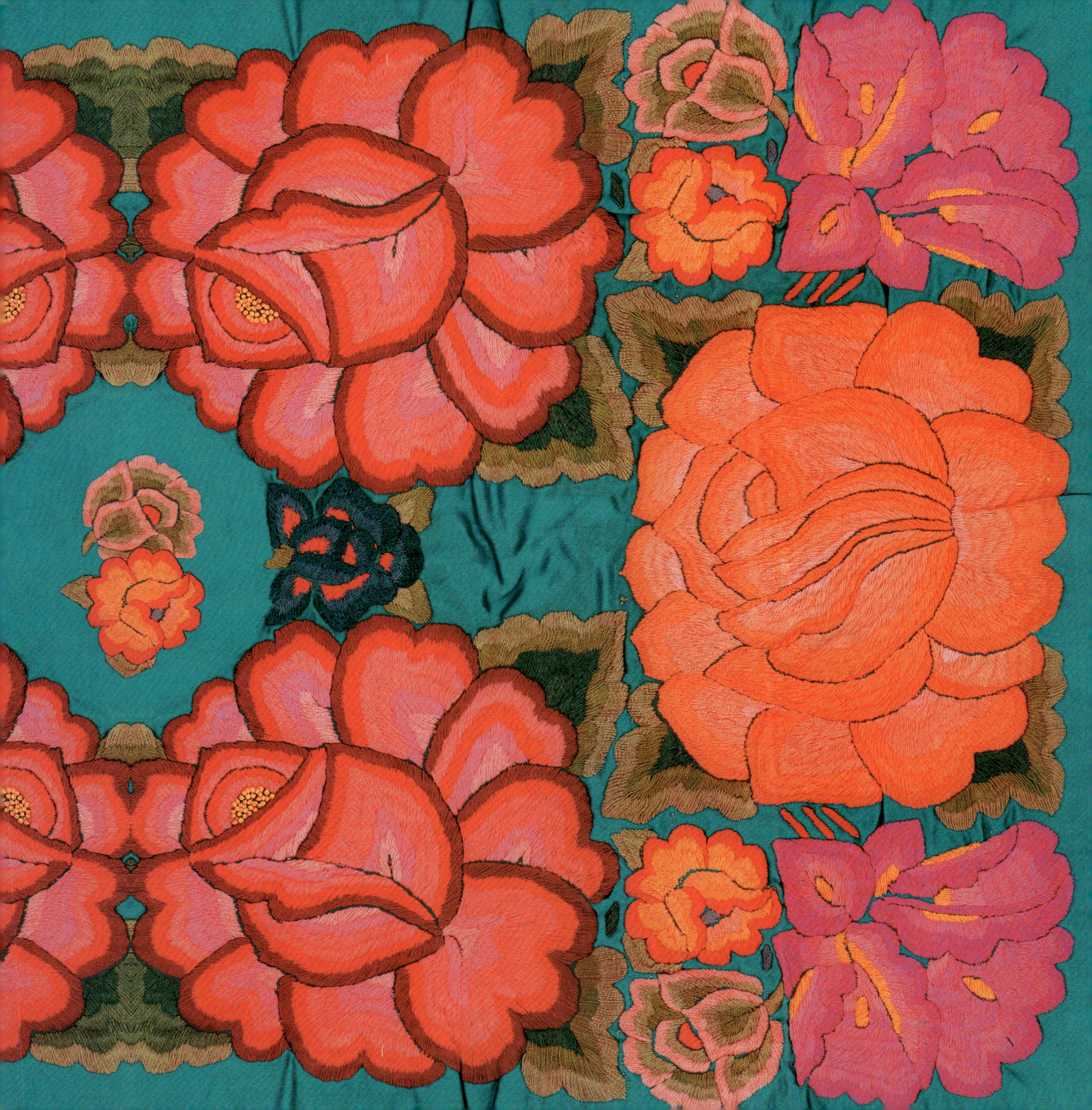

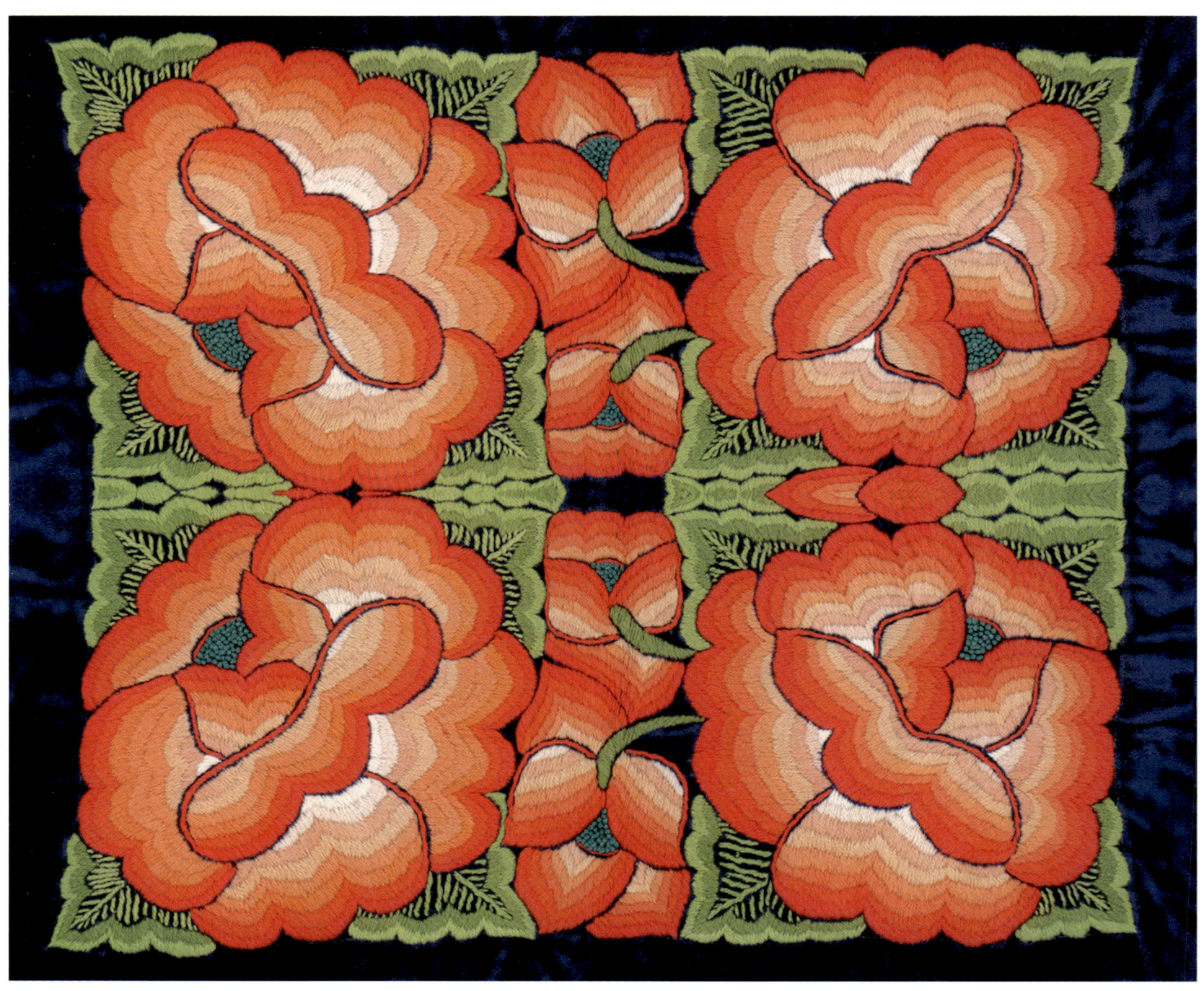

Blue Velvet Huipil
2010
Digital textile manipulation
30 x 36 in.

Huipiles

MESTIZAJE

Nopalitos
2007
Oil portrait collage
48 x 36 in.

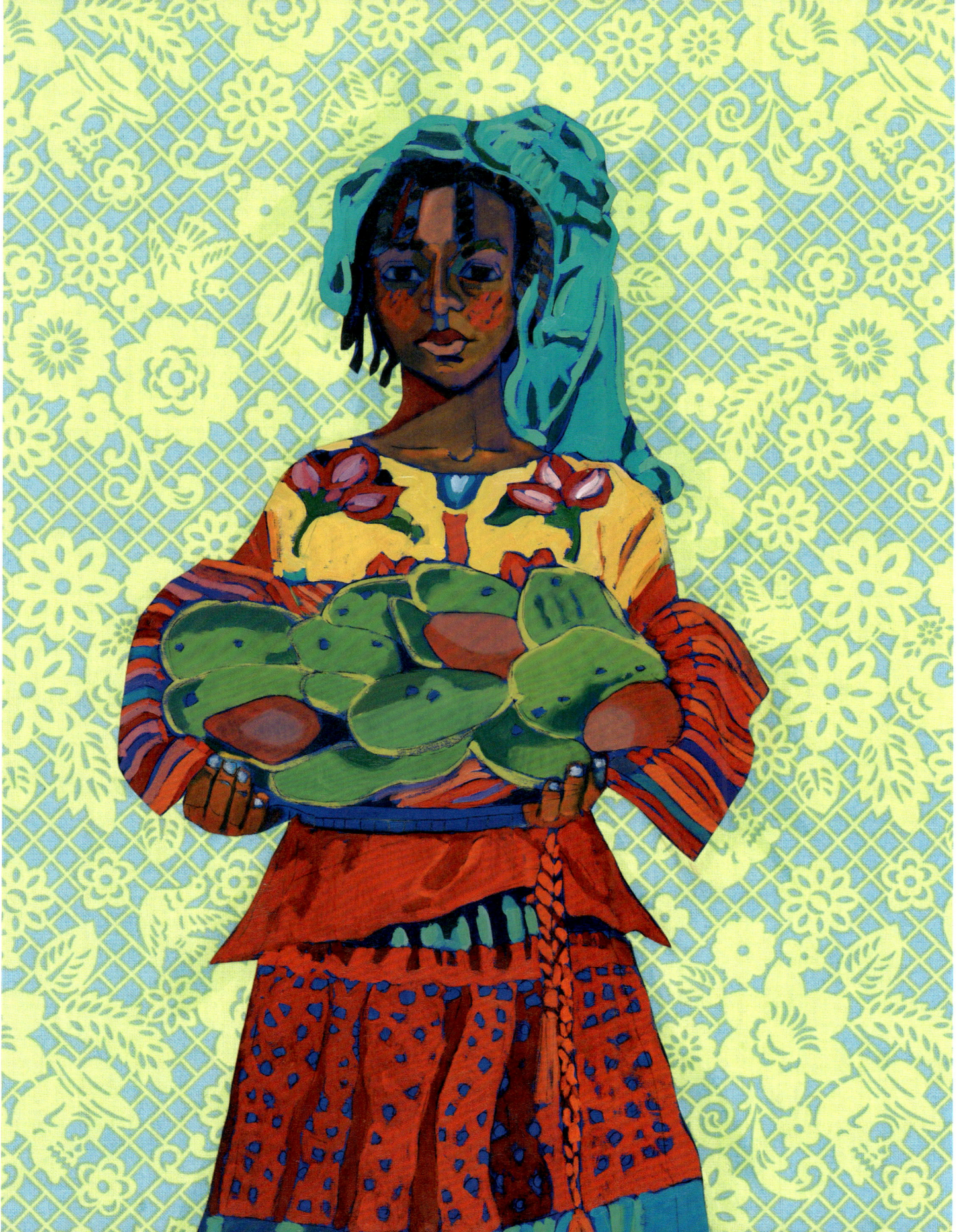

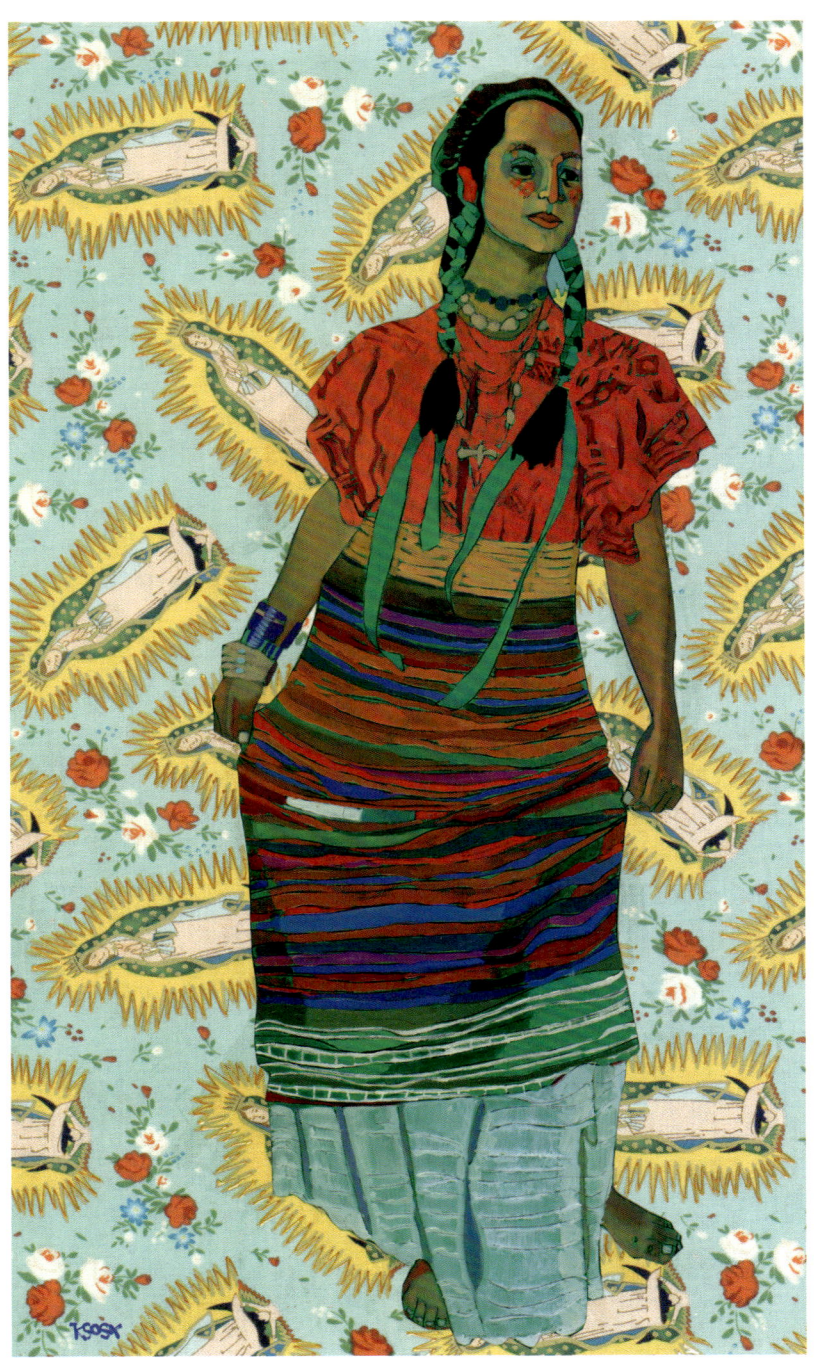

Our Lady of Grace
2007
Oil portrait collage
48 x 30 in.

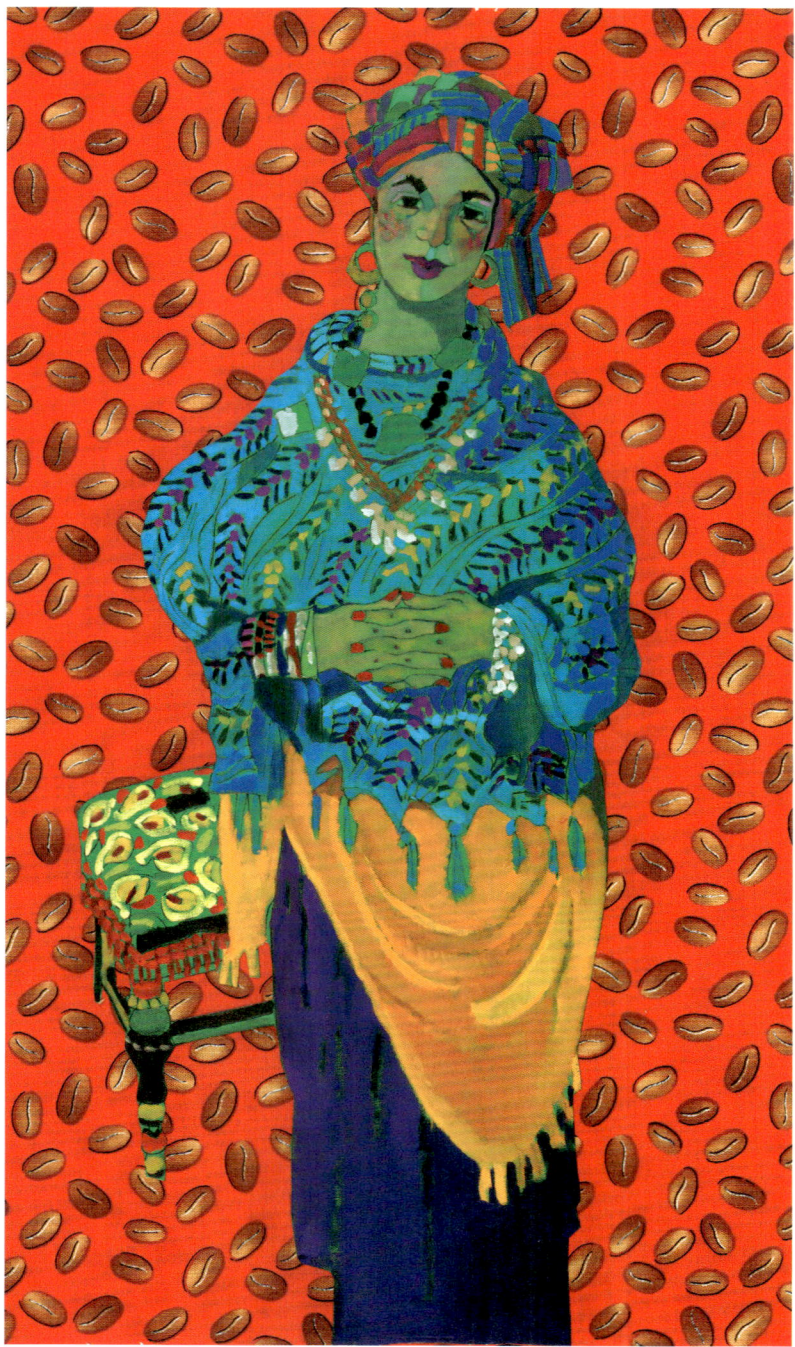

Choquito la Chicana
2006
Oil portrait collage
40 x 30 in.

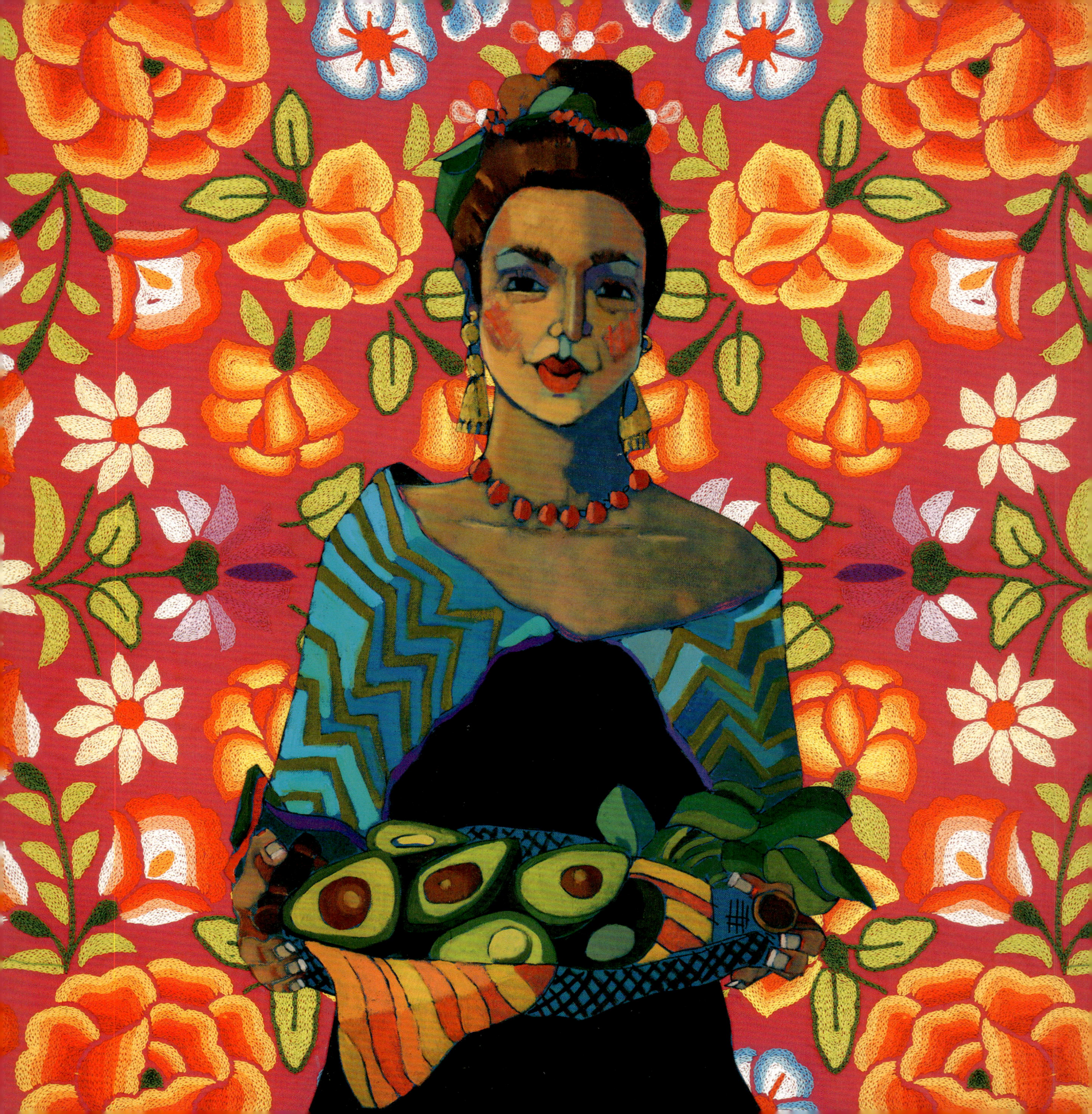

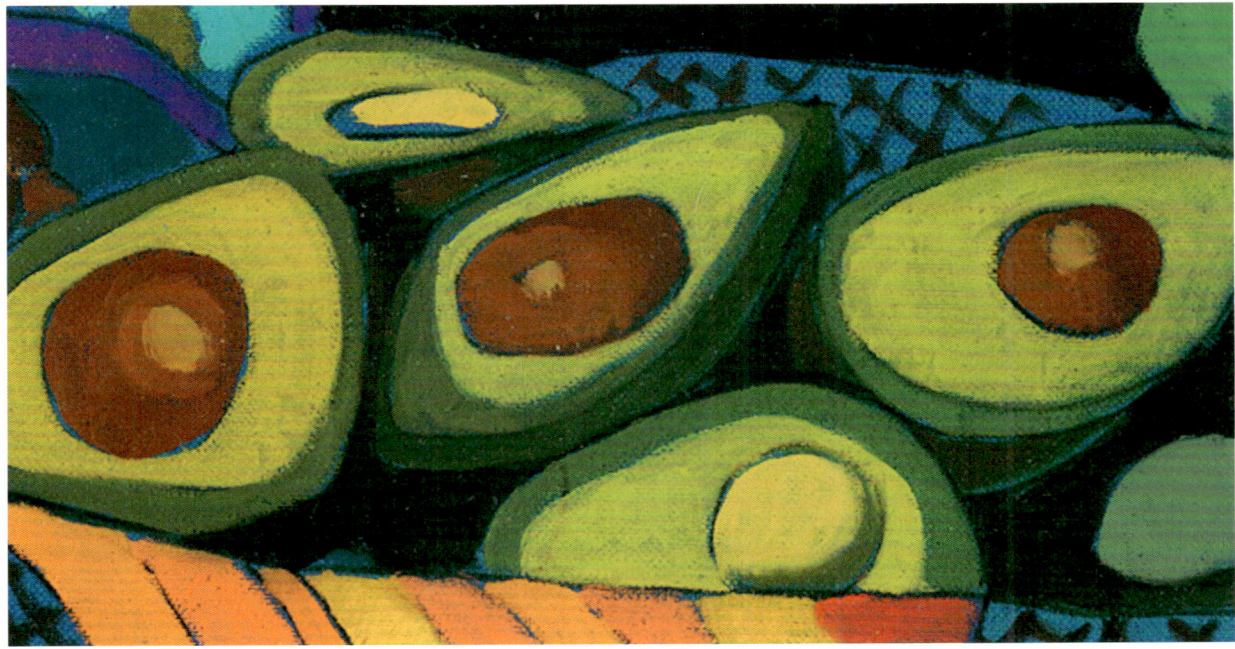

Olivia's Offering
2017
Oil portrait collage
30 x 30 in.

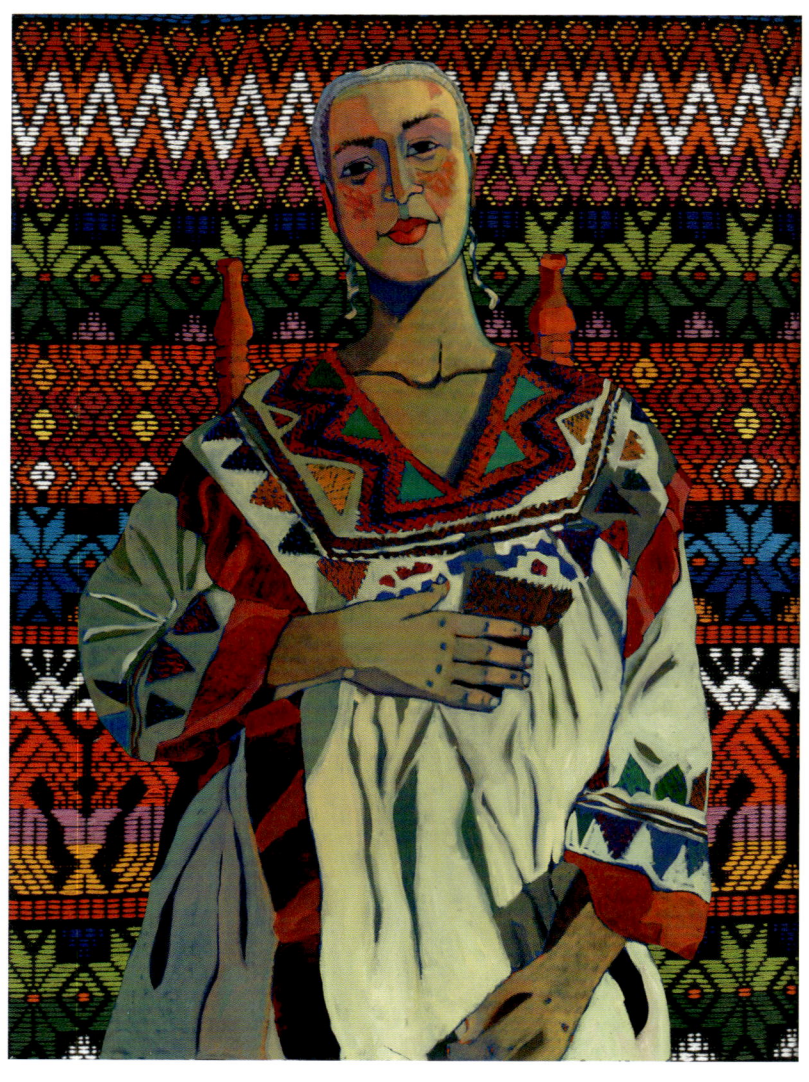

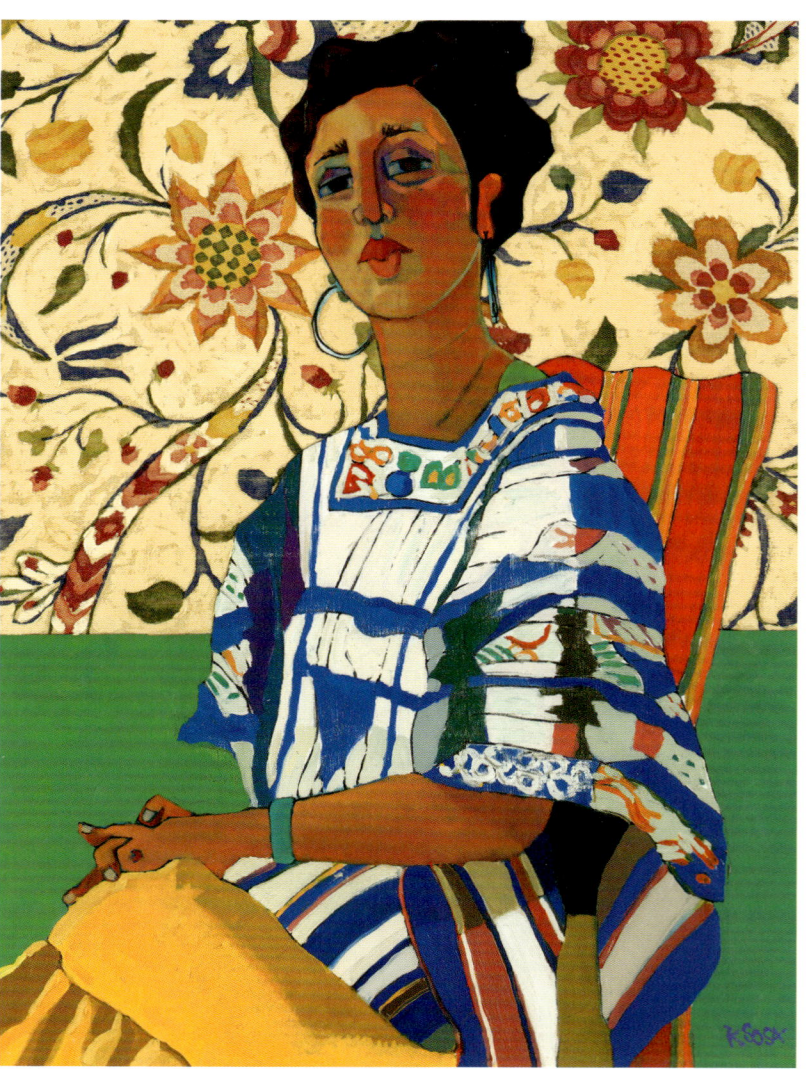

Señora López
2007
Oil portrait collage
48 x 36 in.

La Reina Huipilista
2006
Oil portrait collage
36 x 30 in.

Huipilista Poderosa (in progress)
2009
Oil on canvas
20 x 28 in.

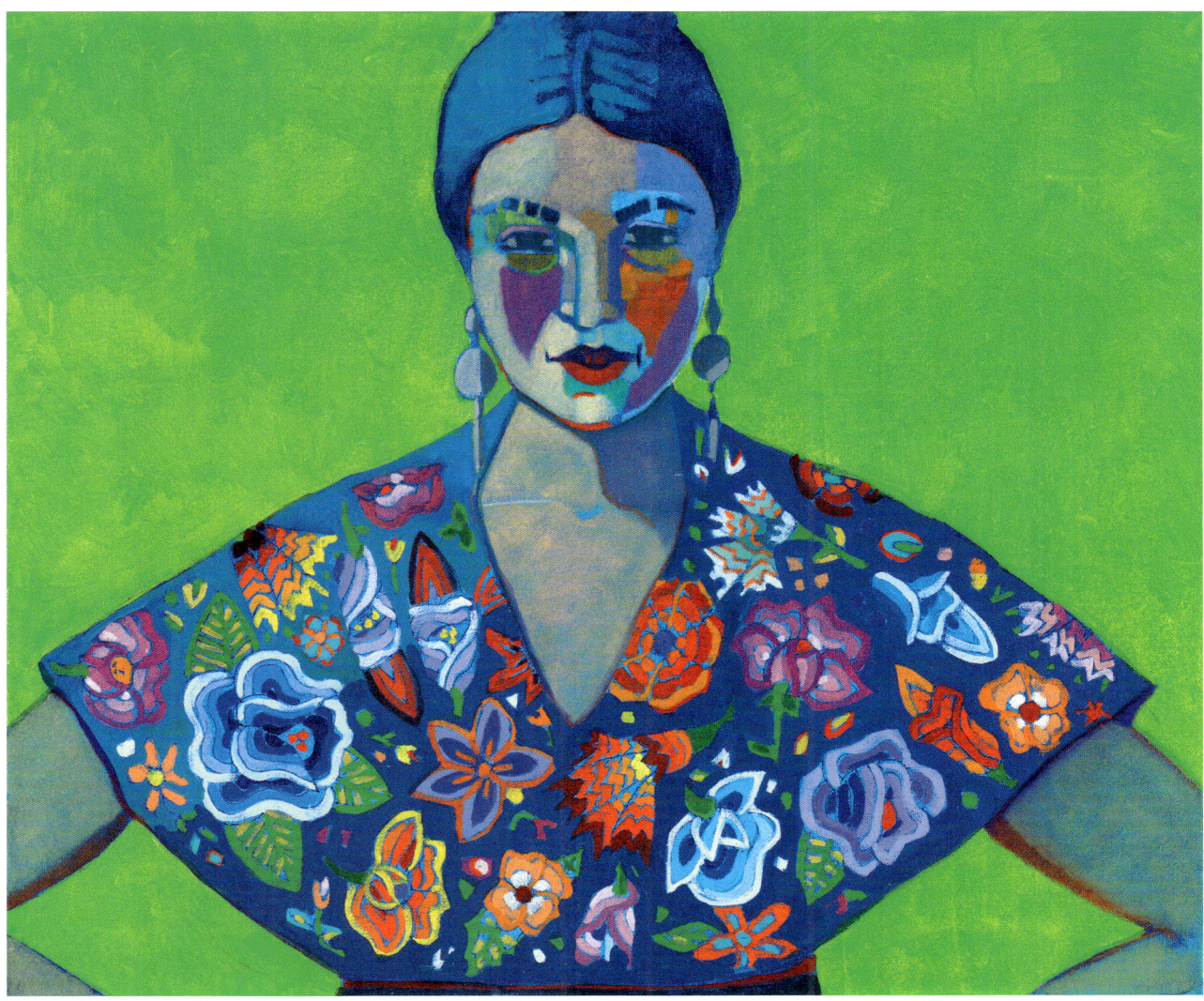

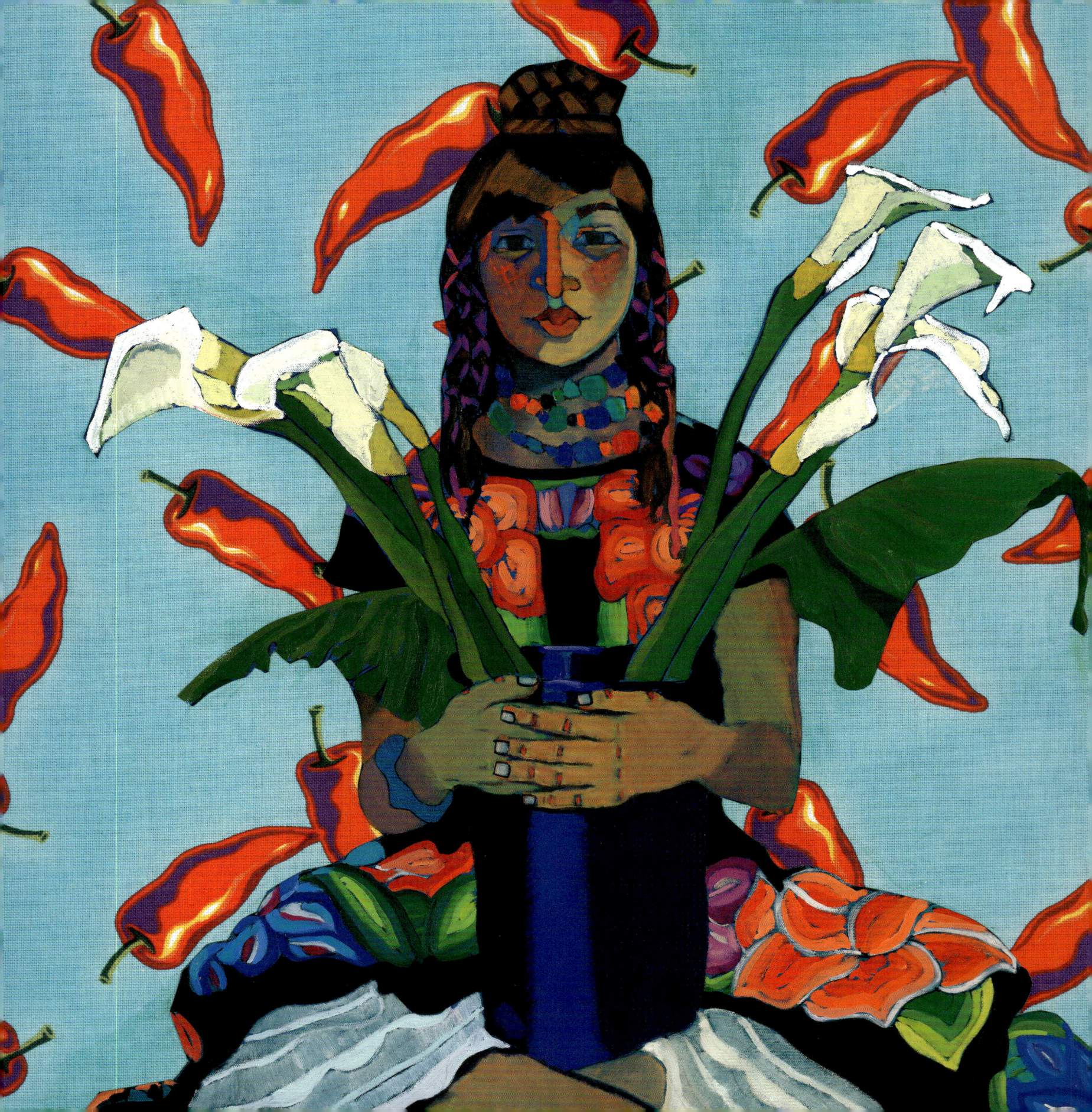

Chile Lilies
2006
Oil portrait collage
36 x 48 in.

Cactus Garden Huipilista
2008
Oil on canvas
30 x 30 in.

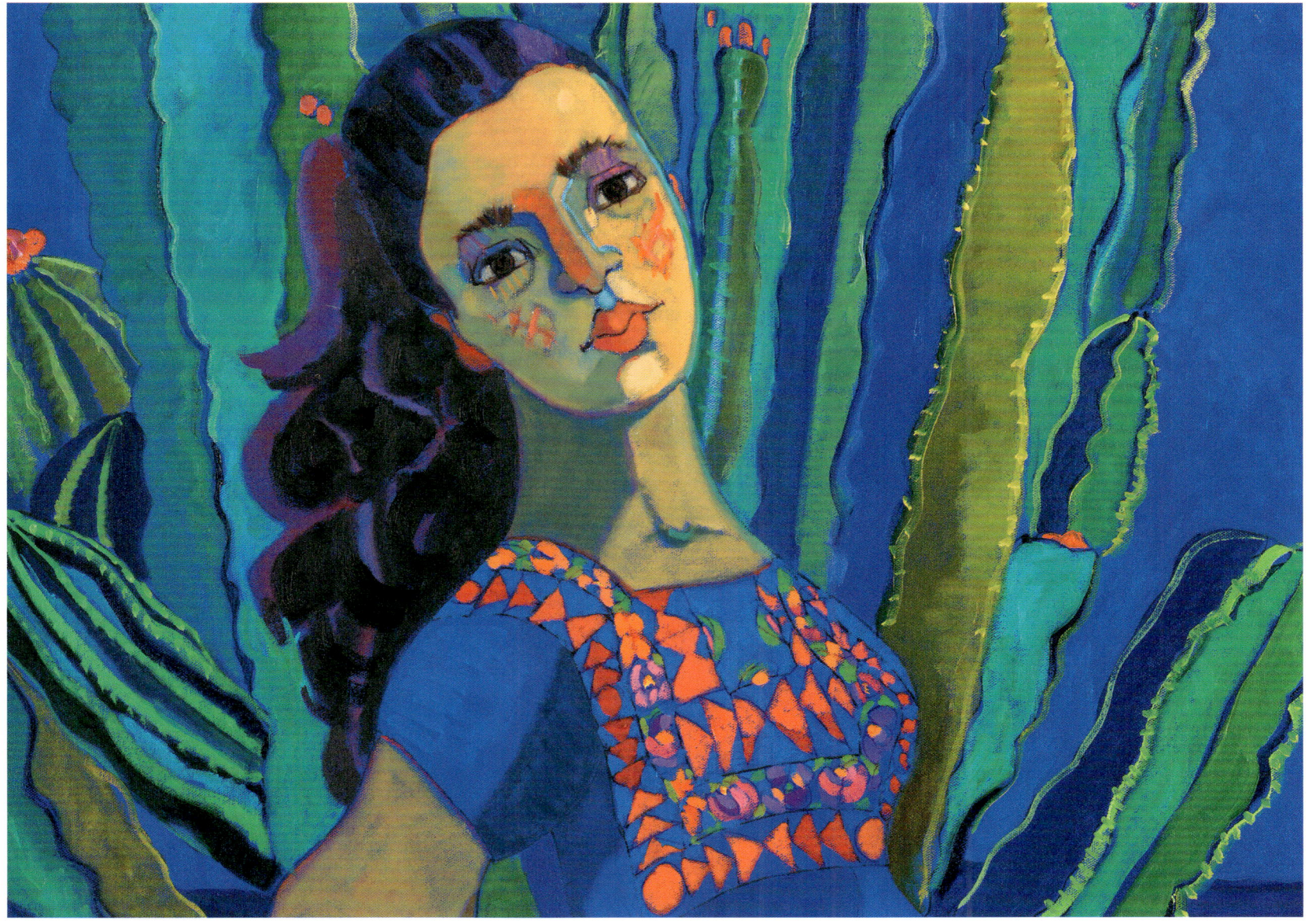

Artivism, Installations, and
Public Art

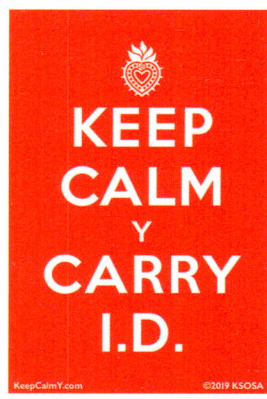

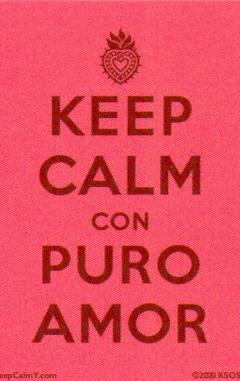

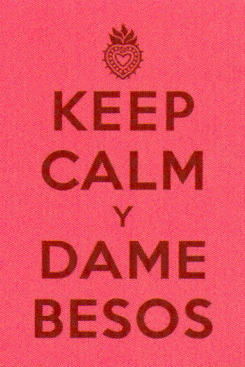

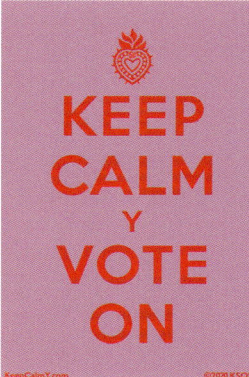

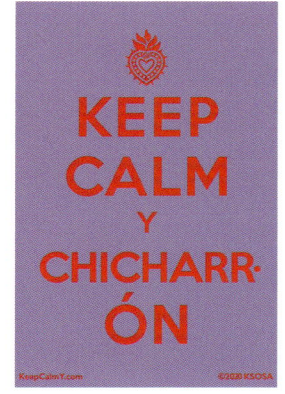

Assortment of
individual works
2020
Ink on plexiglass
31 x 22 in. each

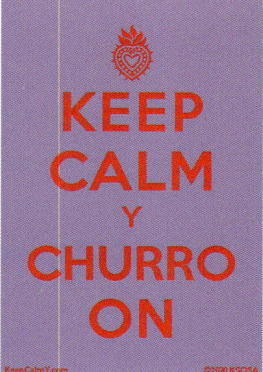

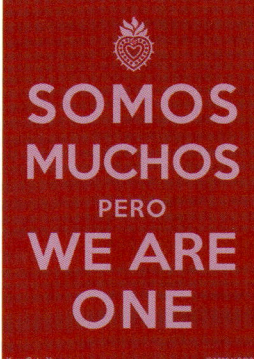

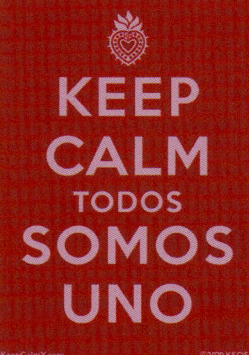

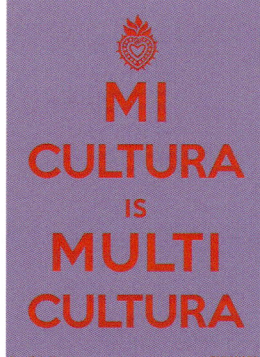

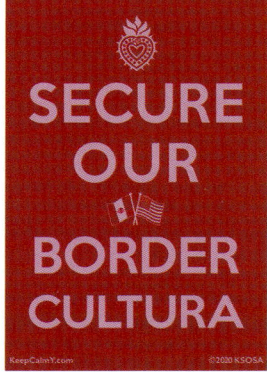

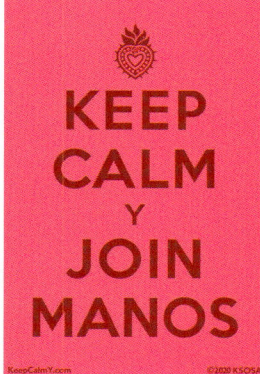

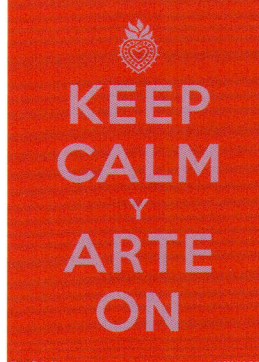

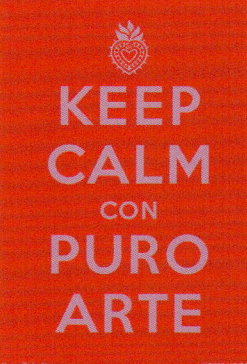

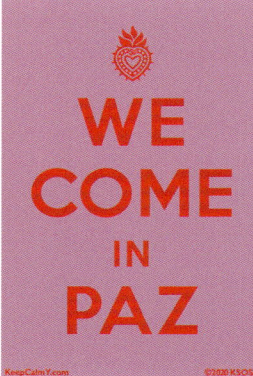

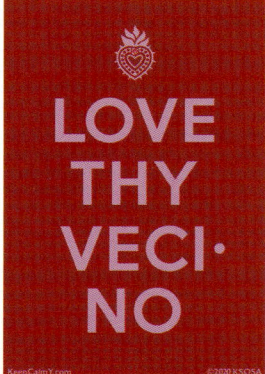

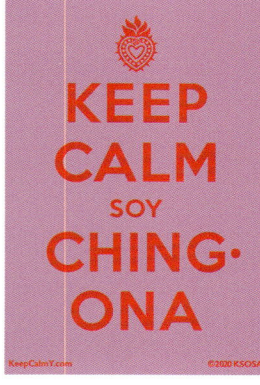

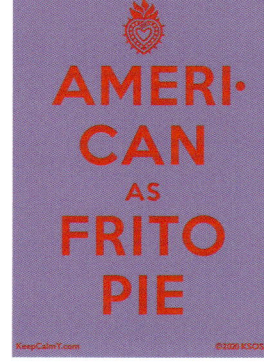

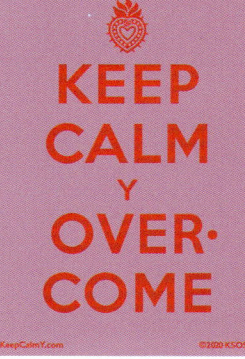

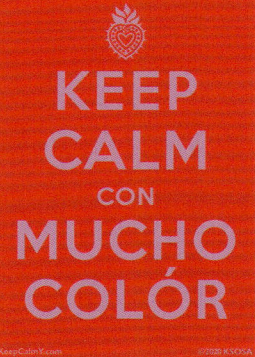

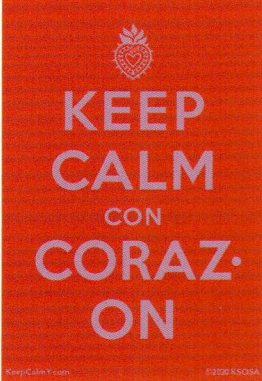

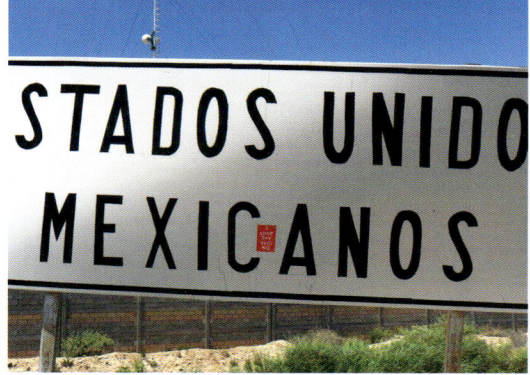
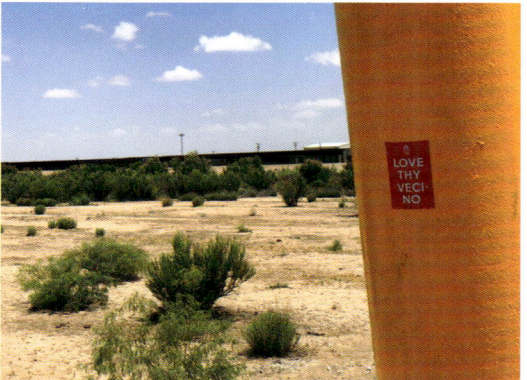

Fort Hancock–El Porvenir Bridge,
Texas and Mexico

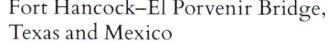

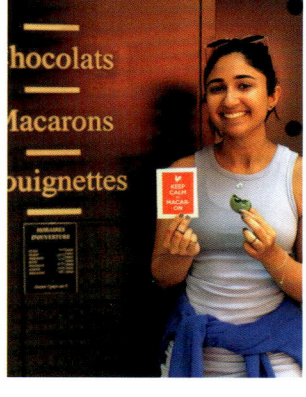
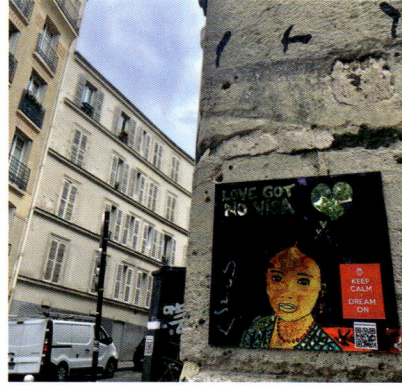
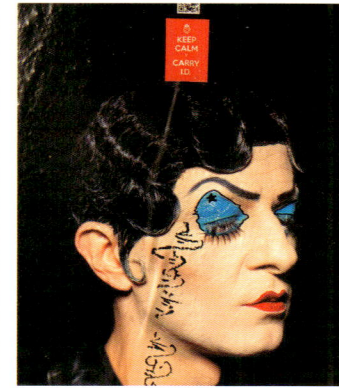

Paris, France

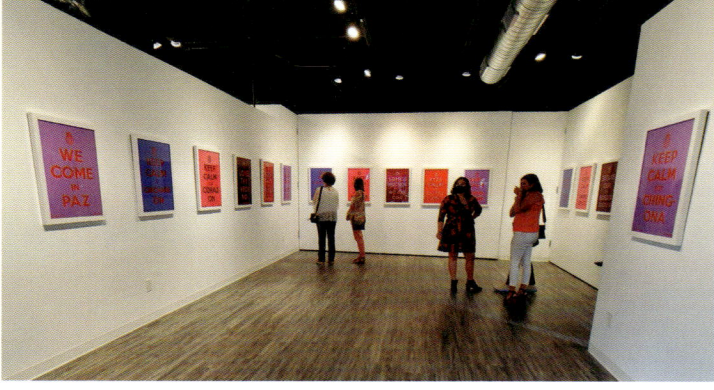
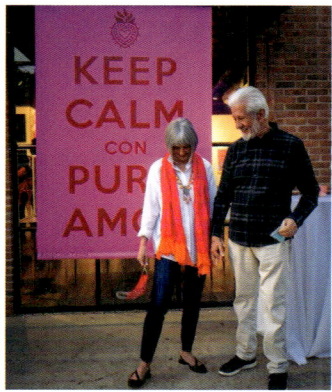

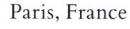

Keep Calm Show, AnArte Gallery,
San Antonio, Texas

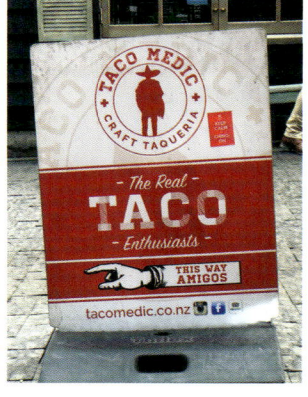
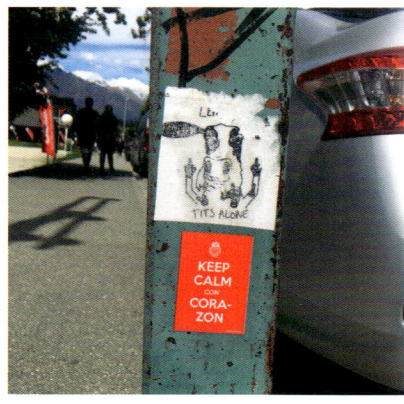
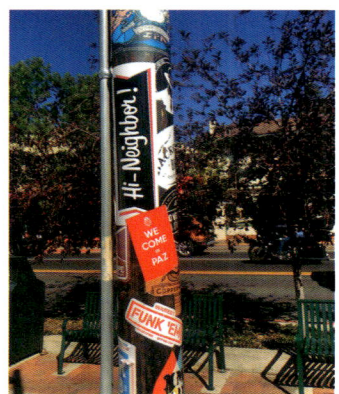

Queenstown, New Zealand,
and Estes Park, Colorado

Public Art

La Gloriosa Historia de San Pedro Creek on My Mind: A Story in Five Episodes. Designs for five tile murals on San Pedro Creek, Bexar County, San Antonio, Texas. Cocreated with Lionel Sosa. Photo and graphics by Nick Bailey and Tanner Freeman.

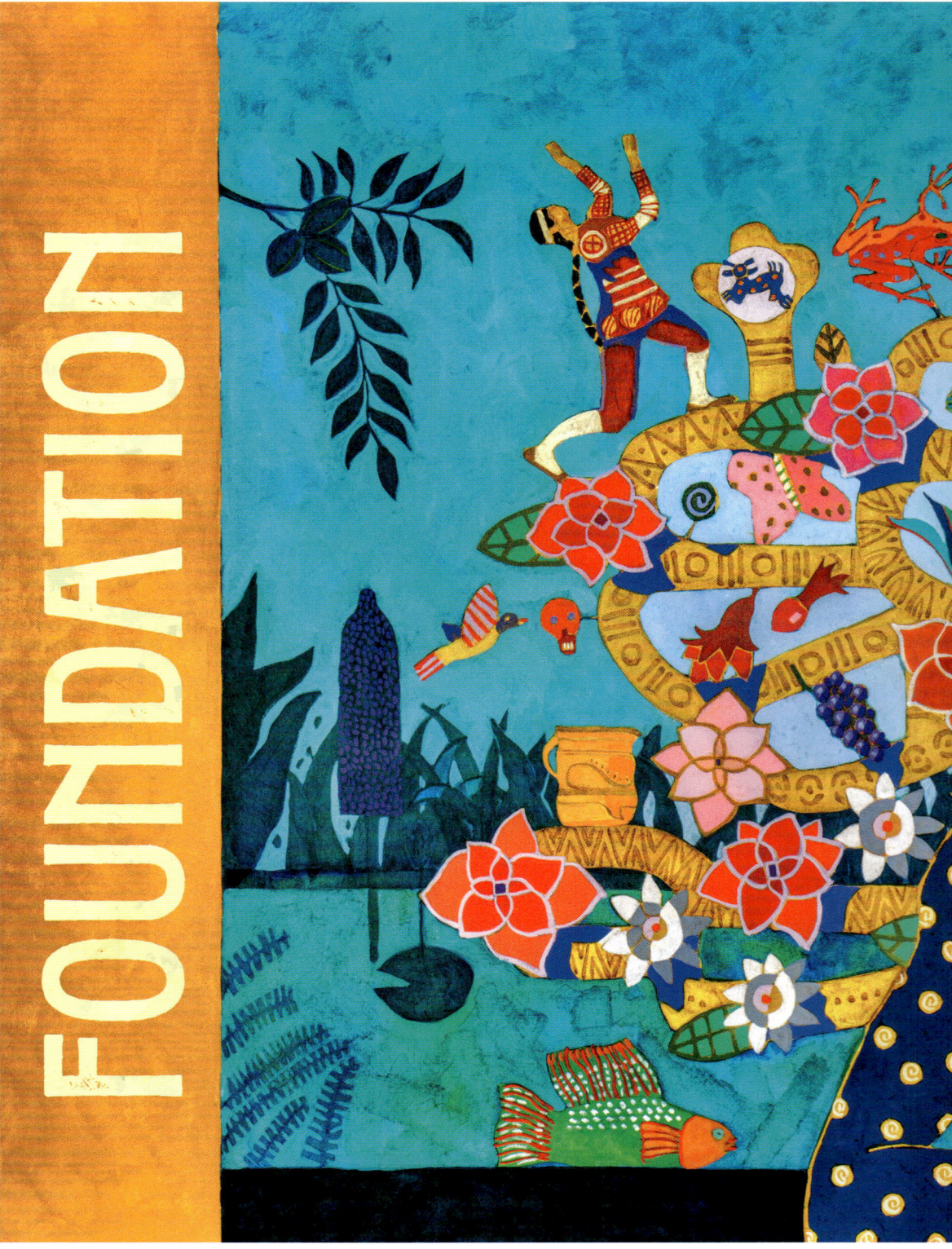

La Gloriosa Historia de San Pedro Creek
on My Mind: A Story in Five Episodes
Episode 1: Foundation / Fundación
2022
Oil on canvas
48 x 96 in.

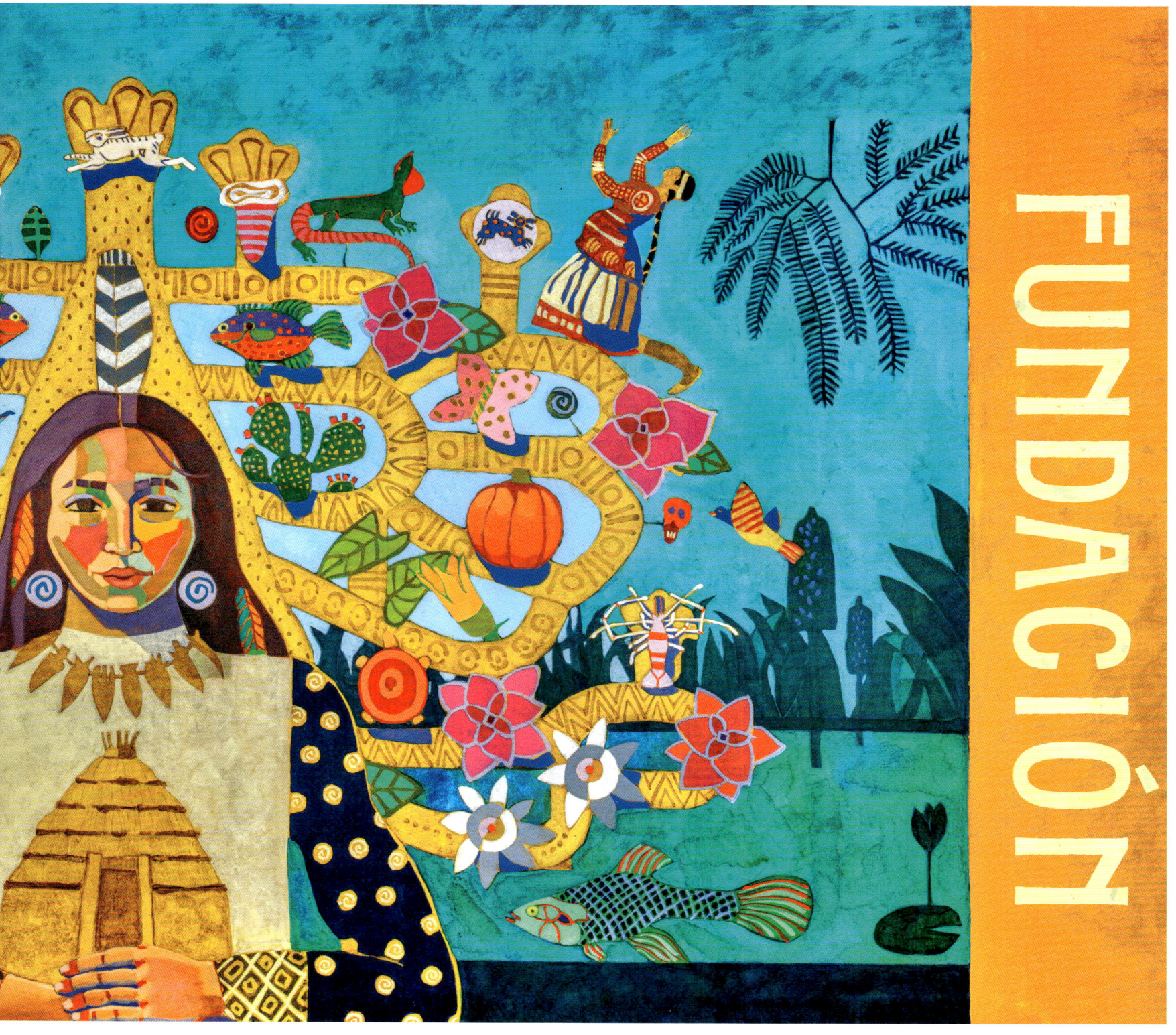

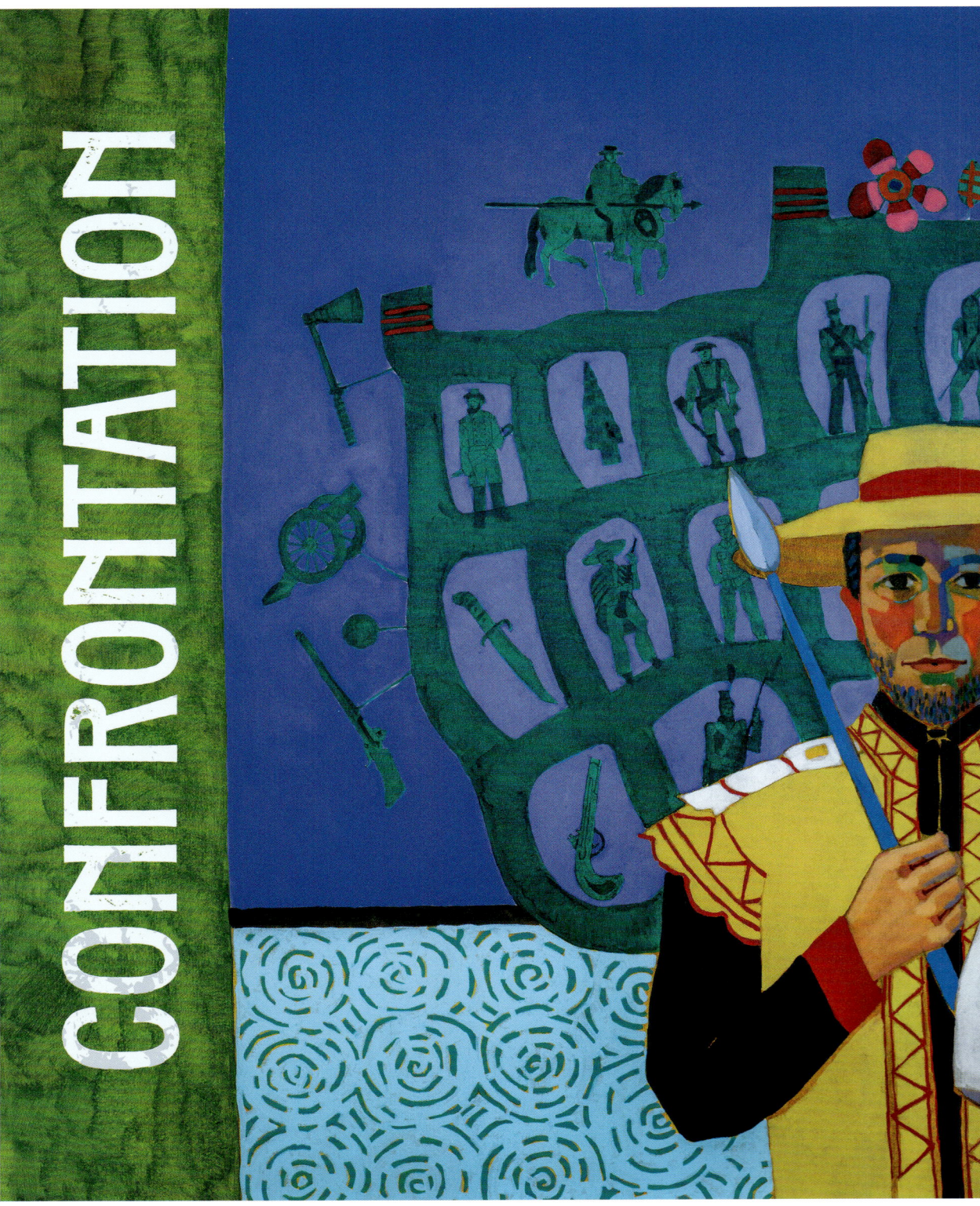

*La Gloriosa Historia de San Pedro Creek
on My Mind: A Story in Five Episodes
Episode 2: Confrontation y Colaboración*
2022
Oil on canvas
48 x 96 in.

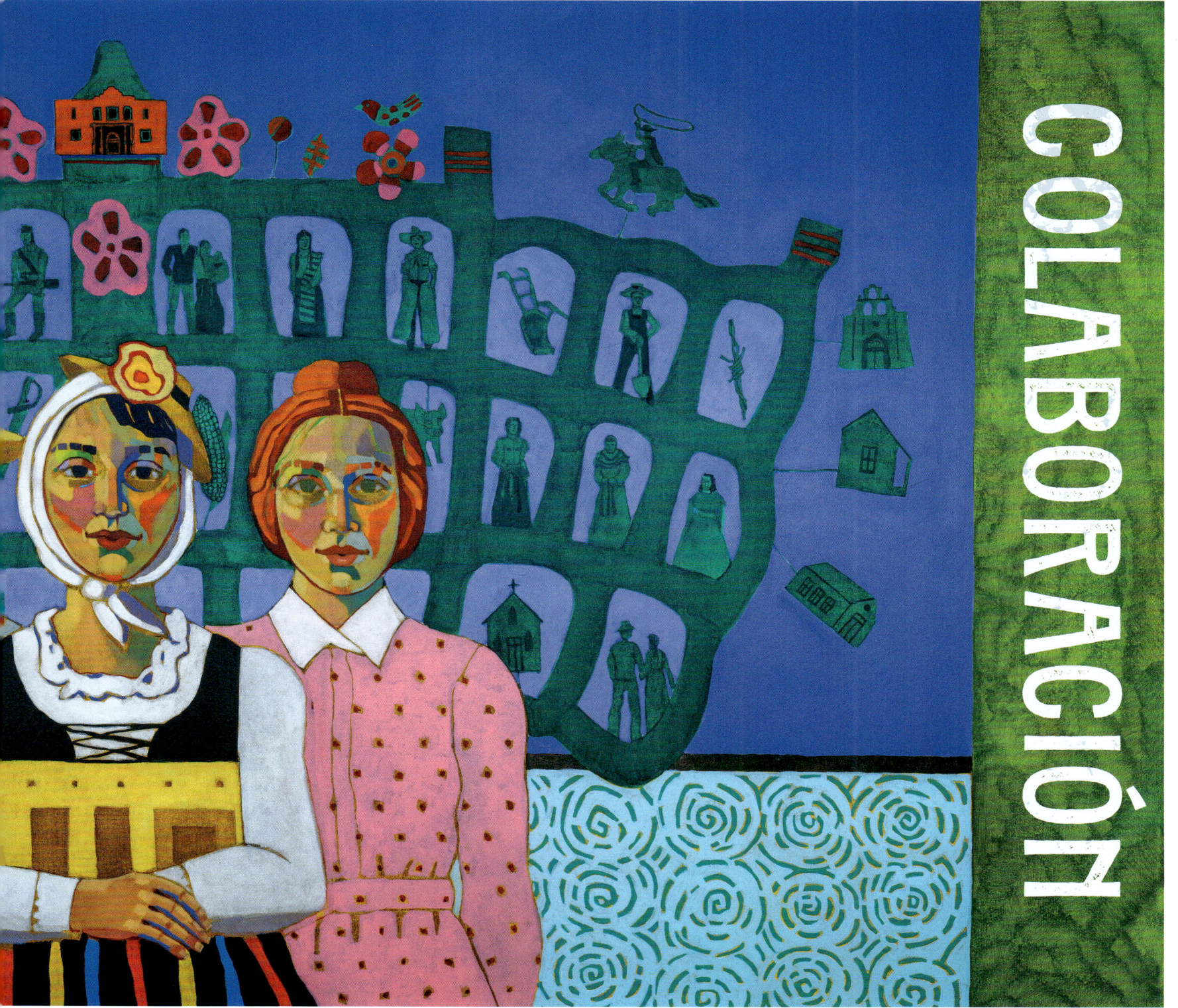

COLABORACIÓN

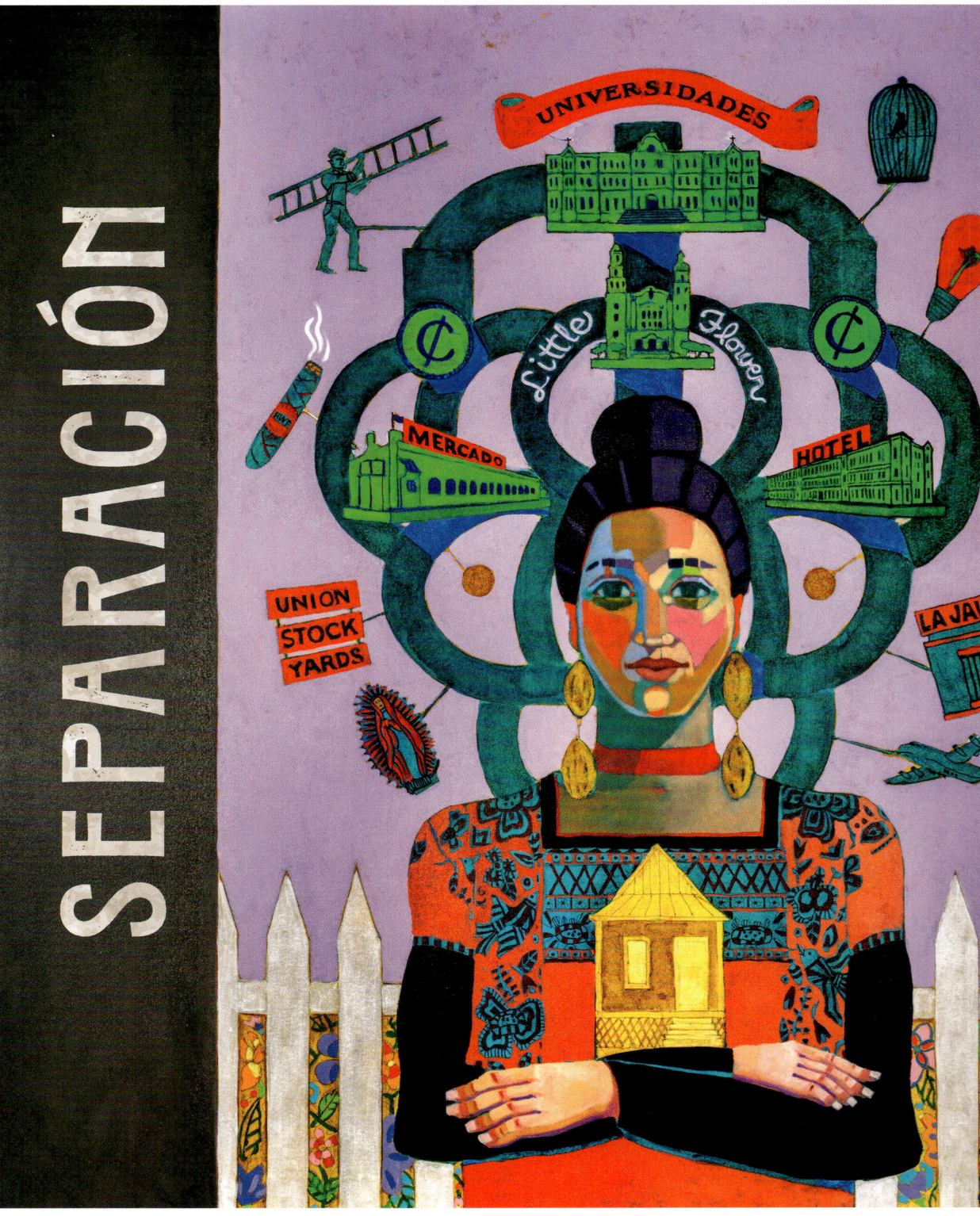

La Gloriosa Historia de San Pedro Creek
on My Mind: A Story in Five Episodes
Episode 3: Separación / Separation
2022
Oil on canvas
48 x 96 in.

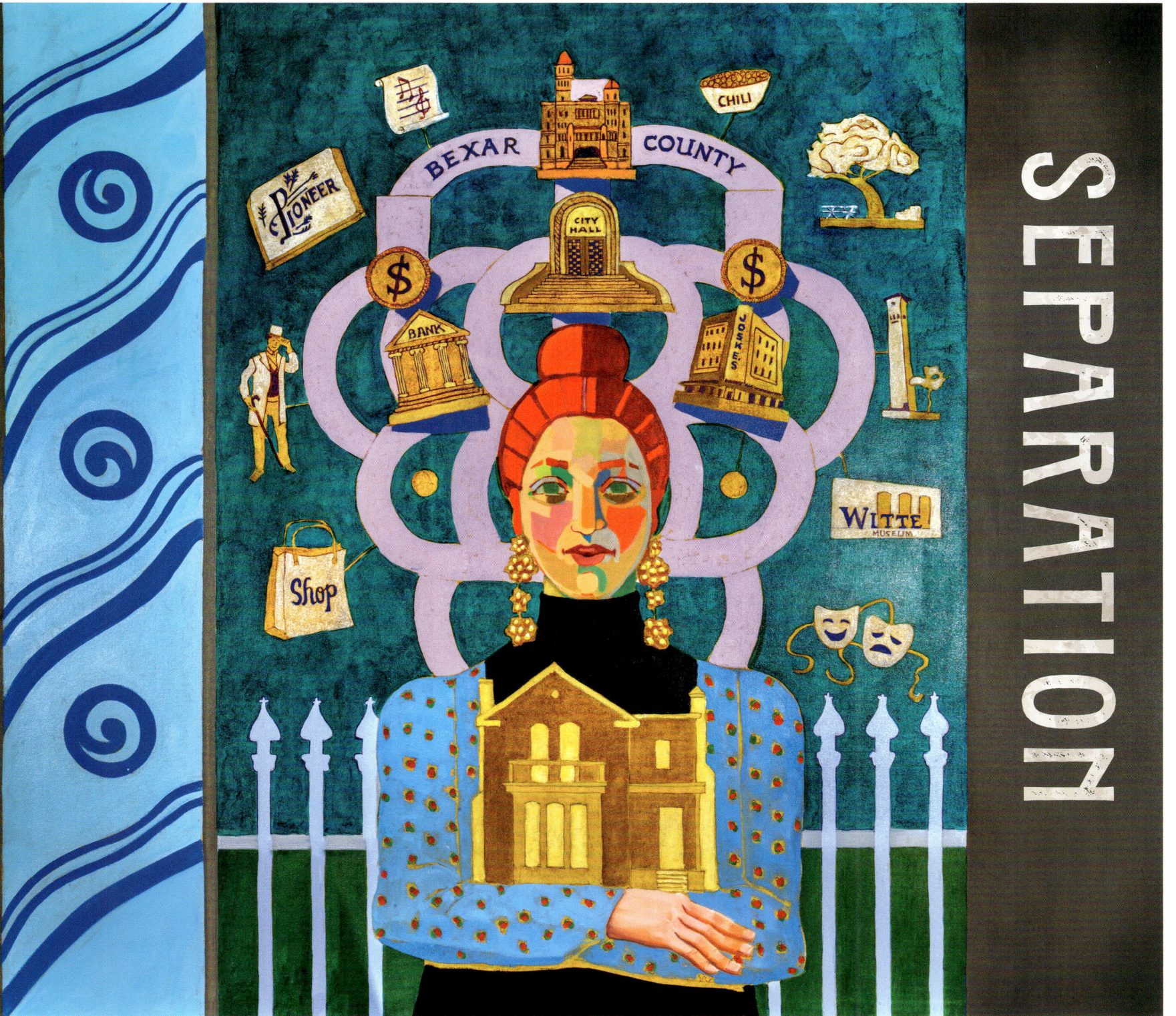

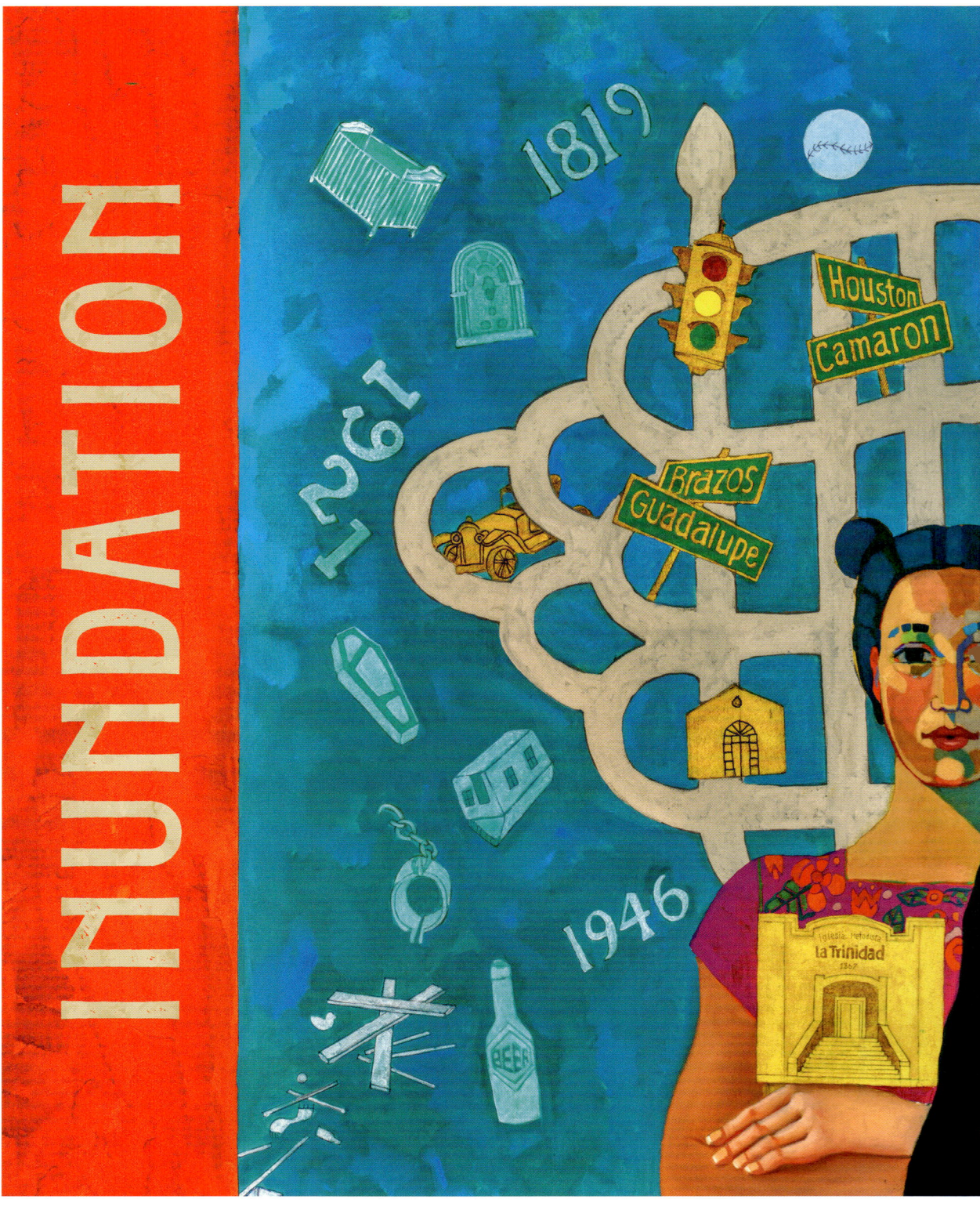

La Gloriosa Historia de San Pedro Creek on My Mind: A Story in Five Episodes Episode 4: Inundation y Constricción
2022
Oil on canvas
48 x 96 in.

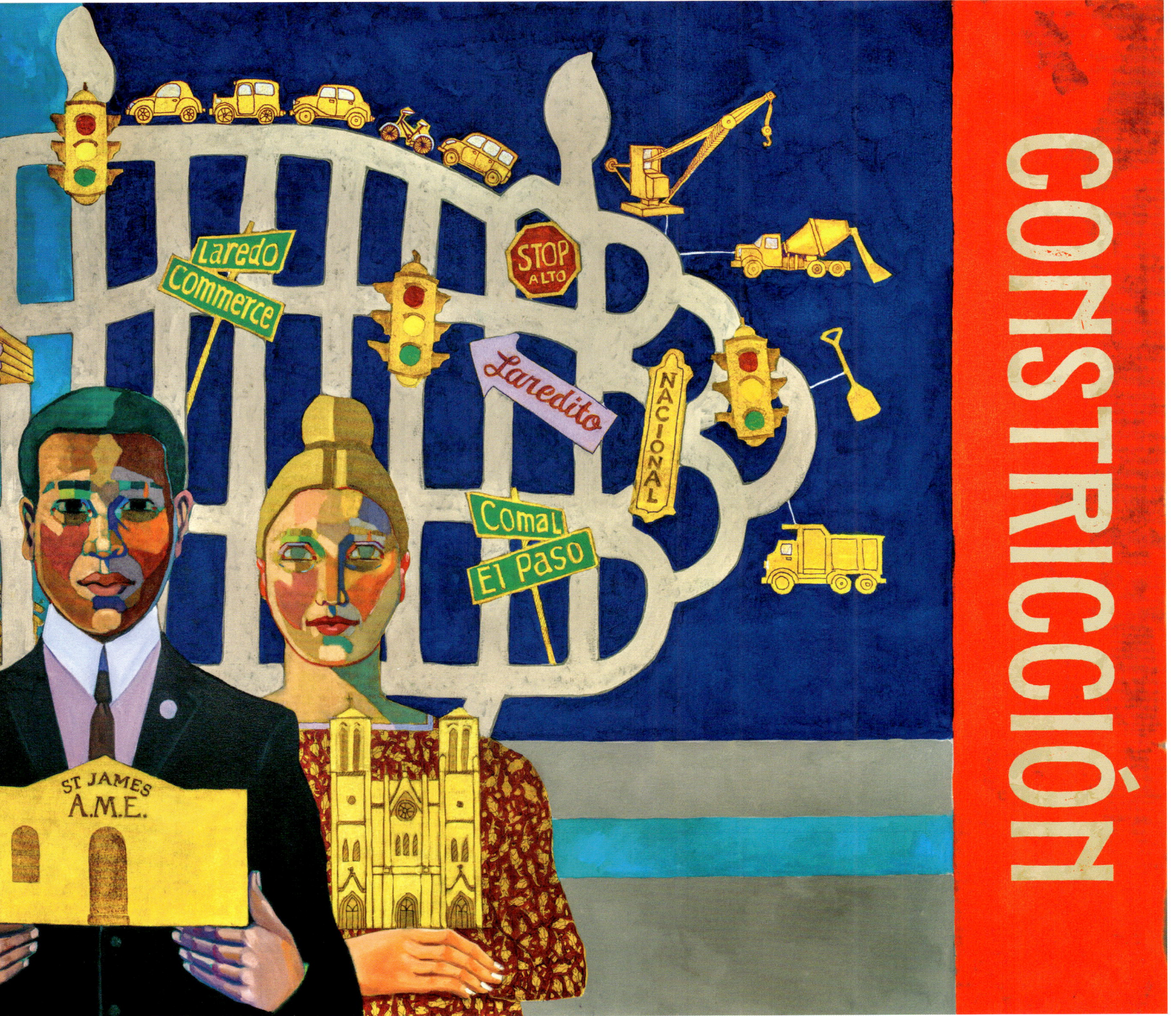

CONSTRICCIÓN

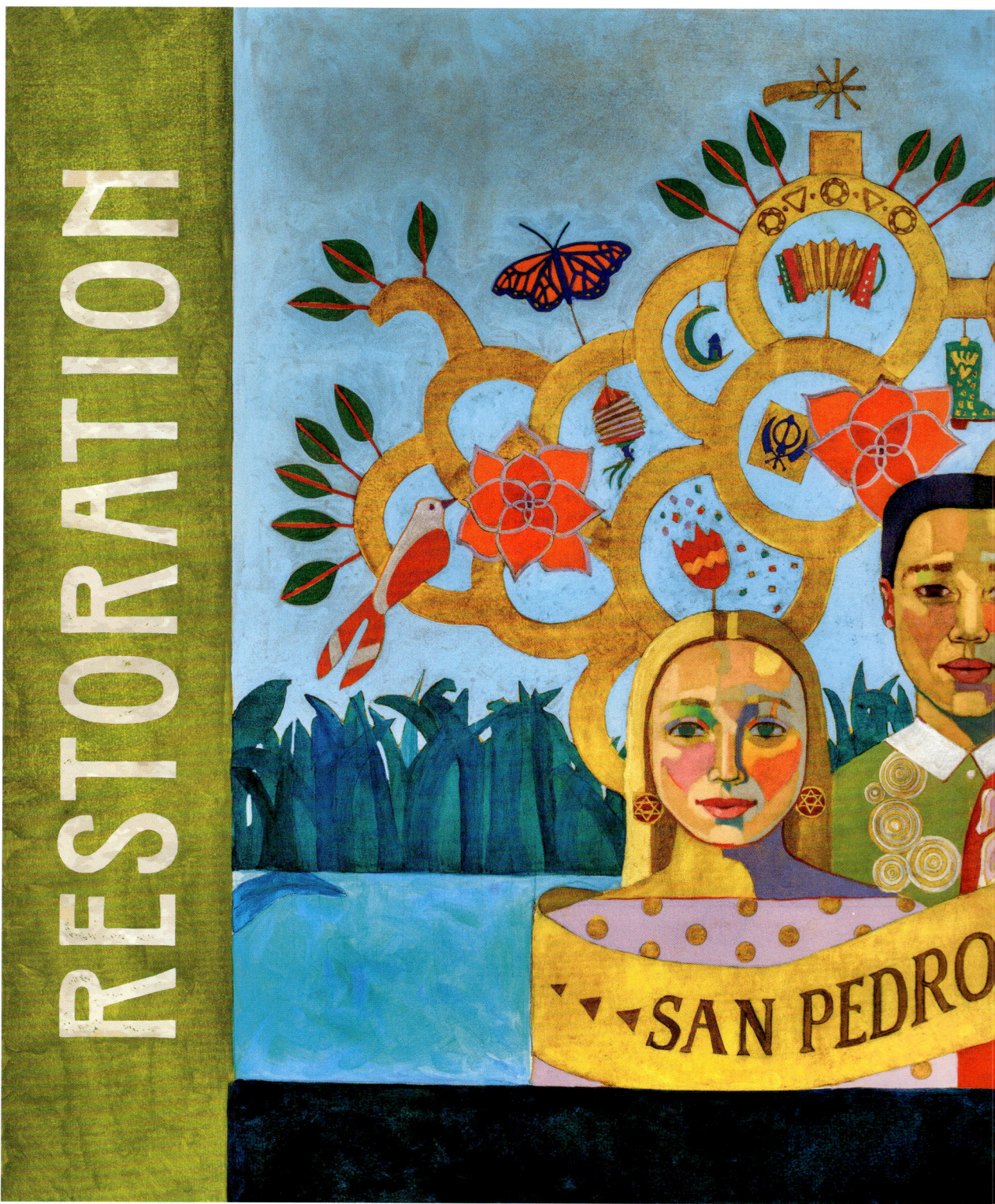

RESTORATION

La Gloriosa Historia de San Pedro Creek on My Mind: A Story in Five Episodes Episode 5: Restoration / Restauración
2022
Oil on canvas
48 x 96 in.

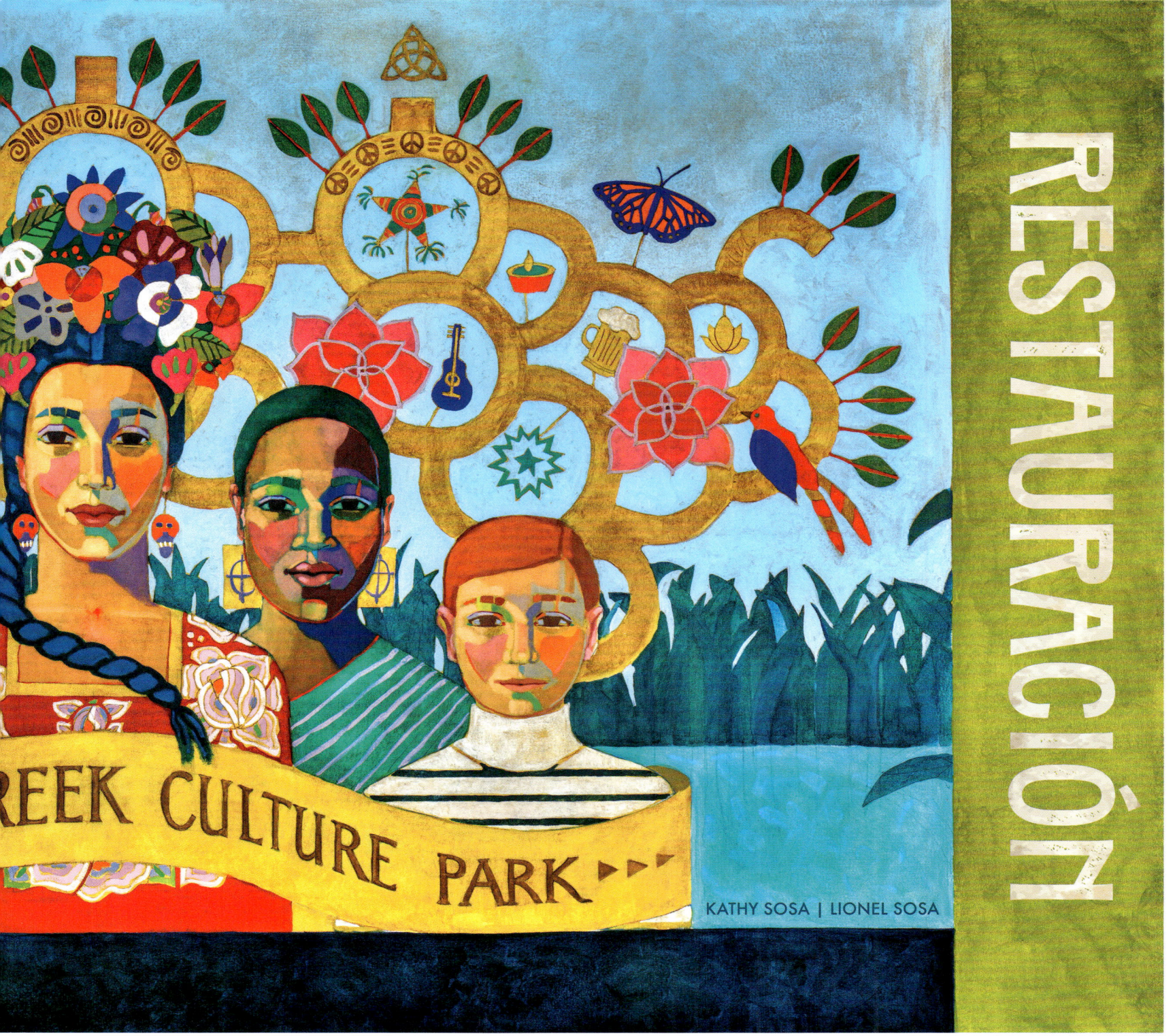

REEK CULTURE PARK ▶▶▶

KATHY SOSA | LIONEL SOSA

From the Beginning: San Antonio
Roses, Corazones Sagrados,
Chili Queens, and Canary Islands
Mural for Texas Public Radio,
San Antonio
Archival ink on watercolor paper
4 x 20 ft.

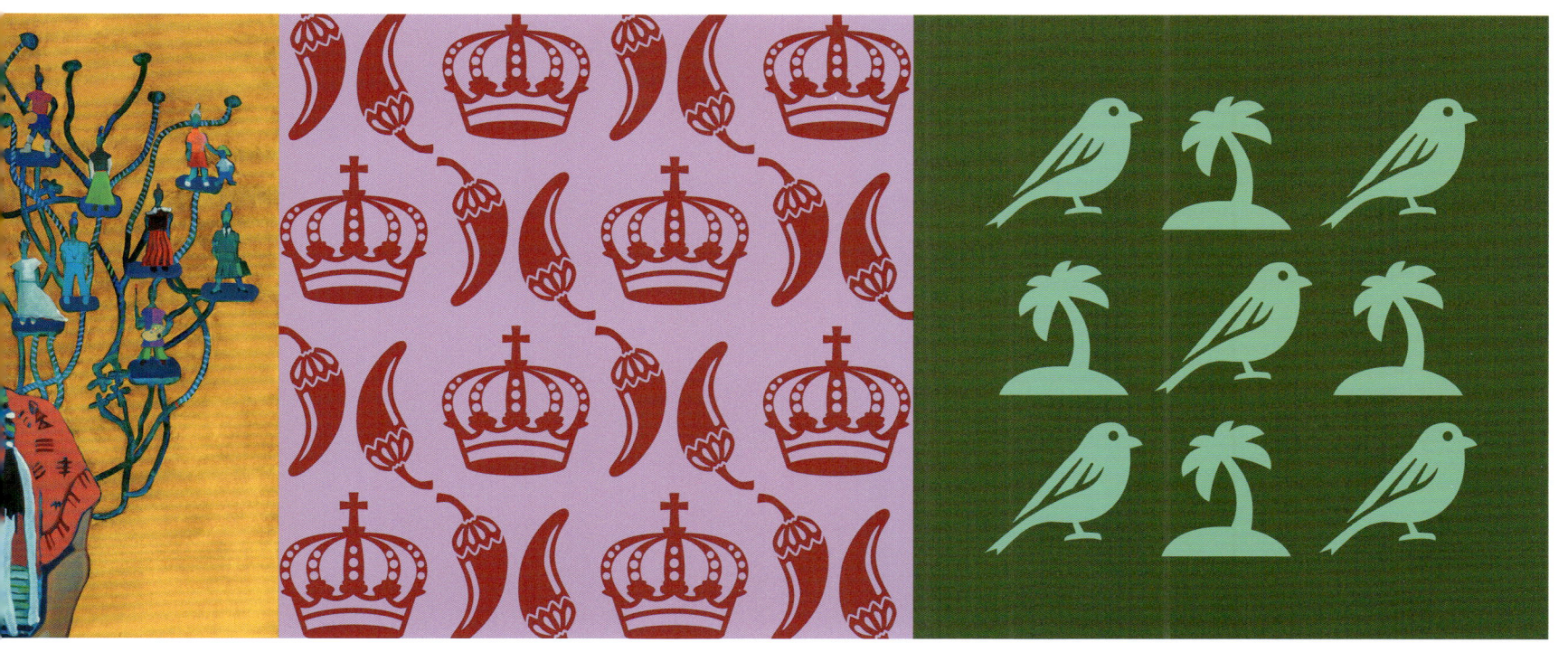

*Santa Gastronomía: Origins of Tex-Mex
Cuisine on My Mind*
Design for mural, La Villita's Maverick
Plaza, San Antonio, Texas
2024
Oil on canvas
30 x 30 in.

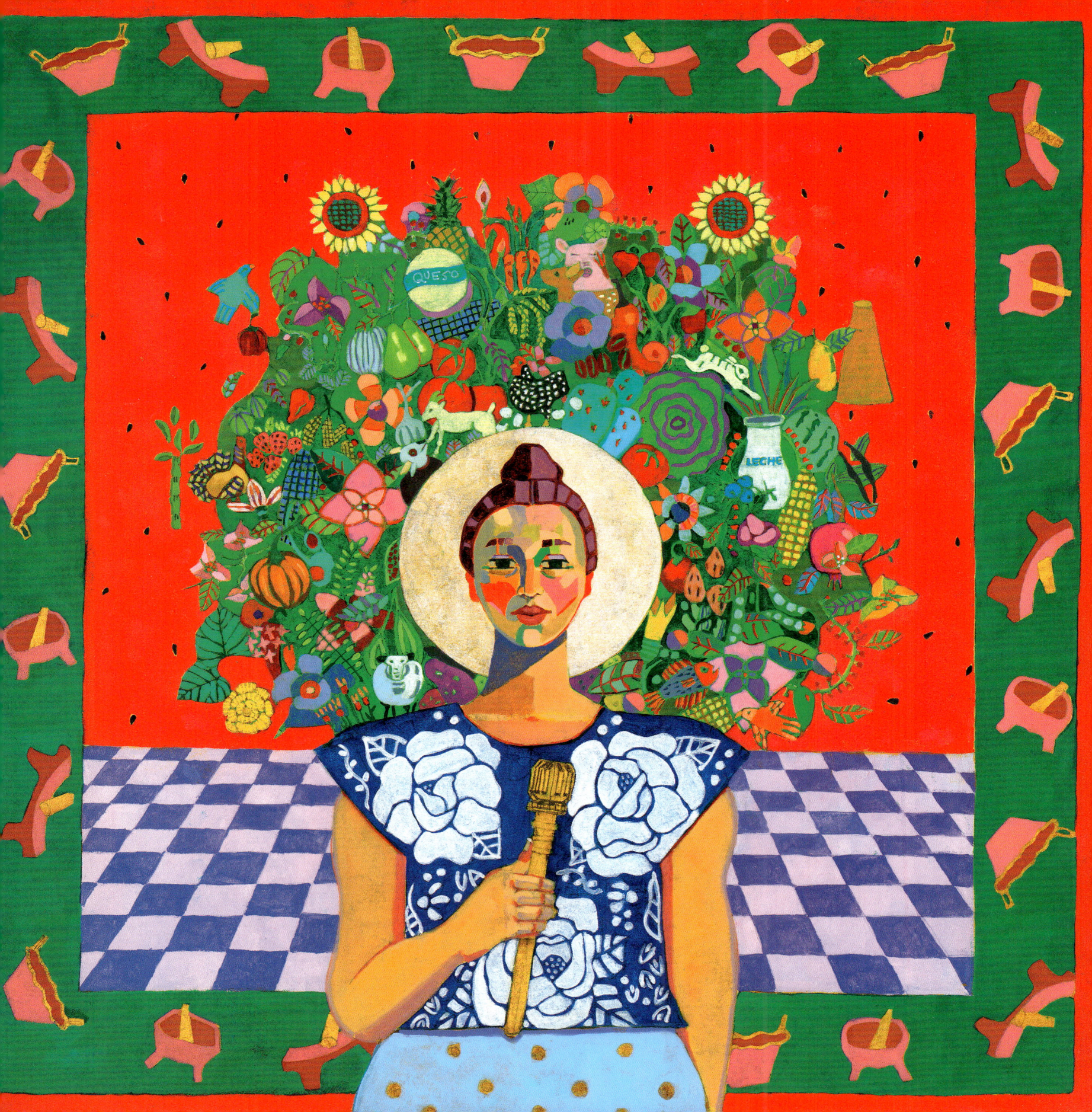

Altar Installations

Built to honor the dead and welcome them back to the land of the living each year, altars are displayed in homes, schools, businesses, churches, and the public square during the annual celebration in November.

Reliquary altarpiece from *Ofrenda for Women We've Lost*
Altar for Main Plaza (detail)
City of San Antonio Día de los Muertos celebration
2019
Cofabricators: Carlos Jimenez, Dina Wooten
Photograph: Ansen Seale

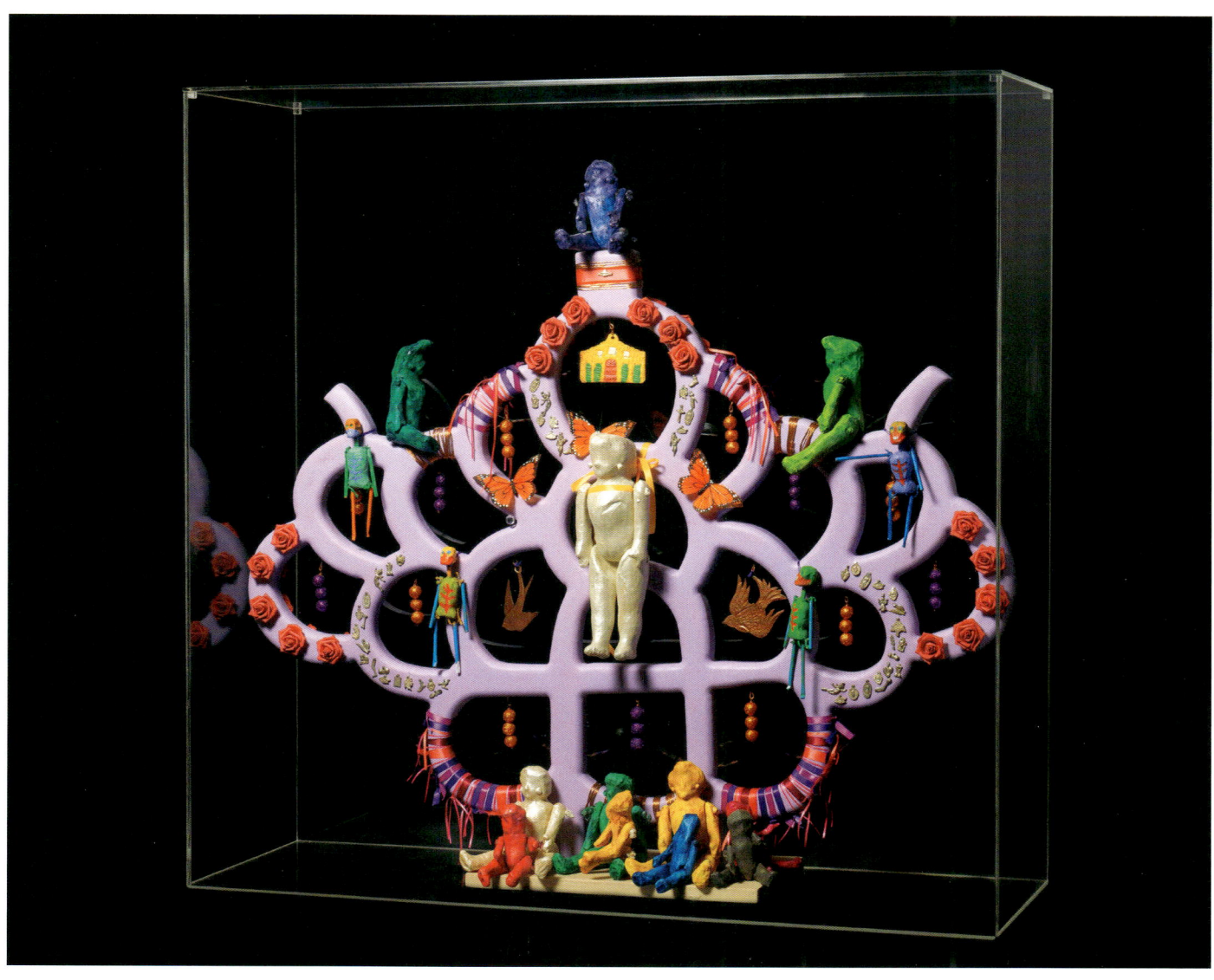

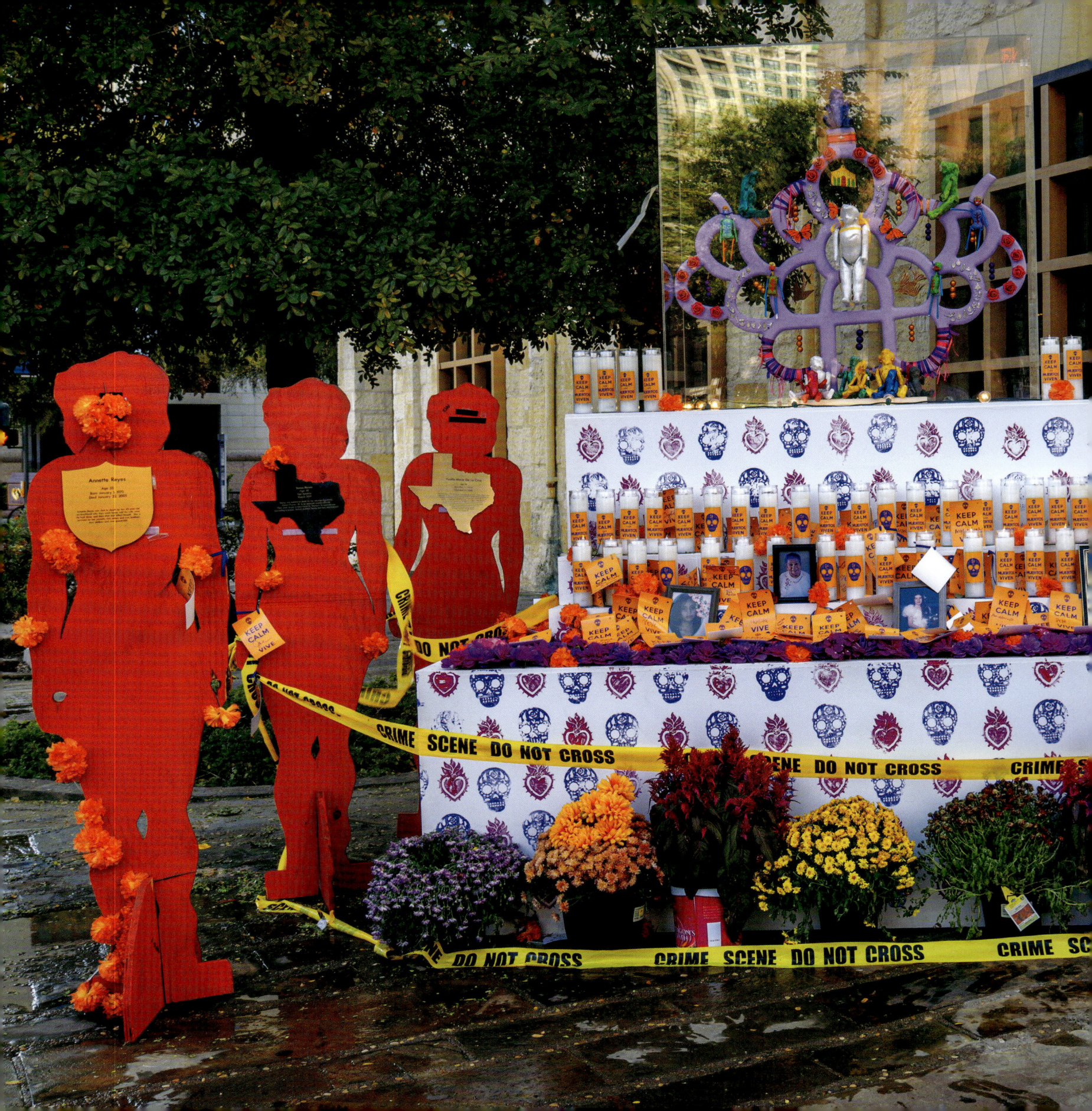

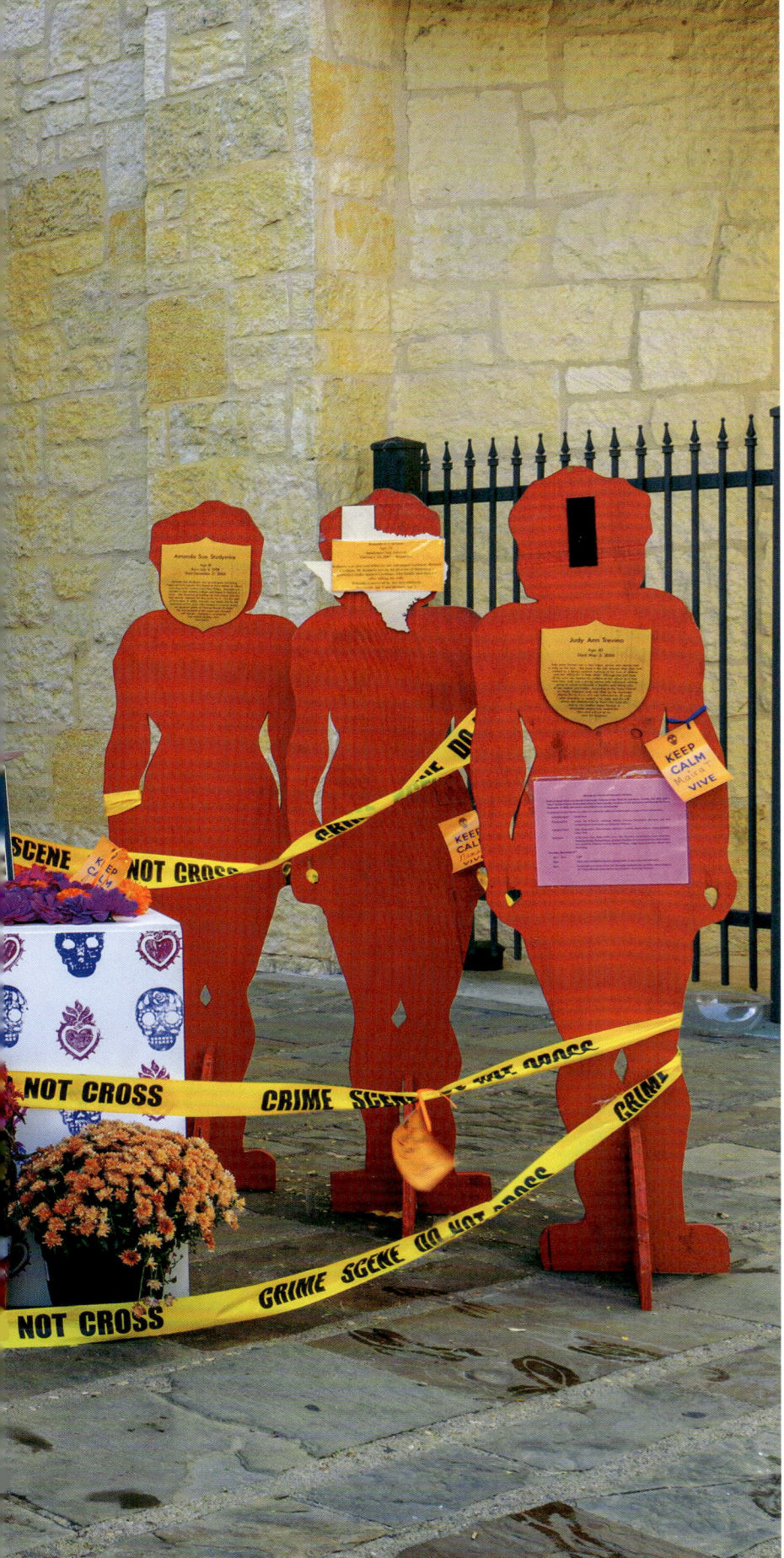

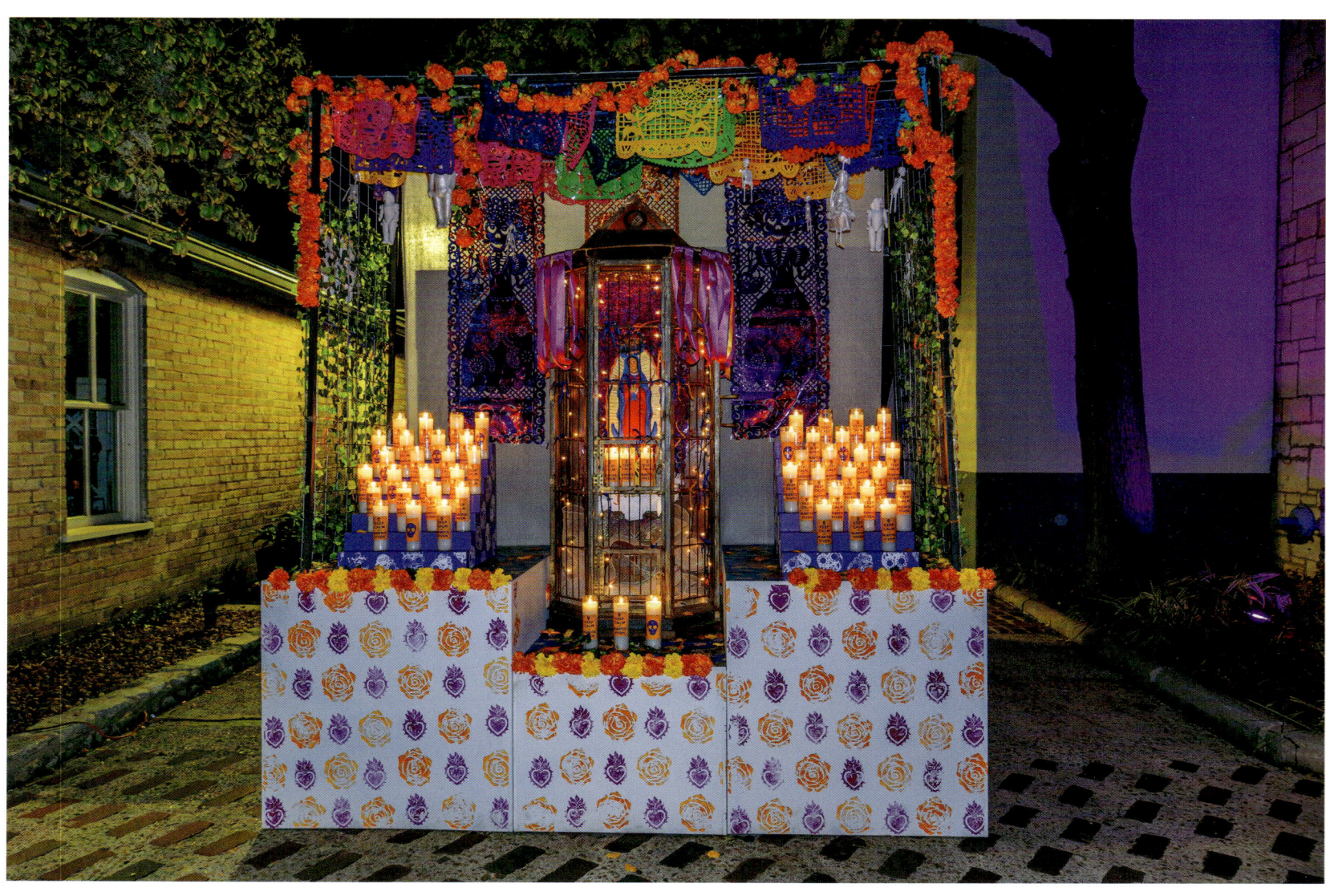

Where Have All the Women Gone?
Altar for La Villita
City of San Antonio Día de los Muertos celebration
2019
Cofabricator: Carlos Jimenez
Photographs: Al Rendon

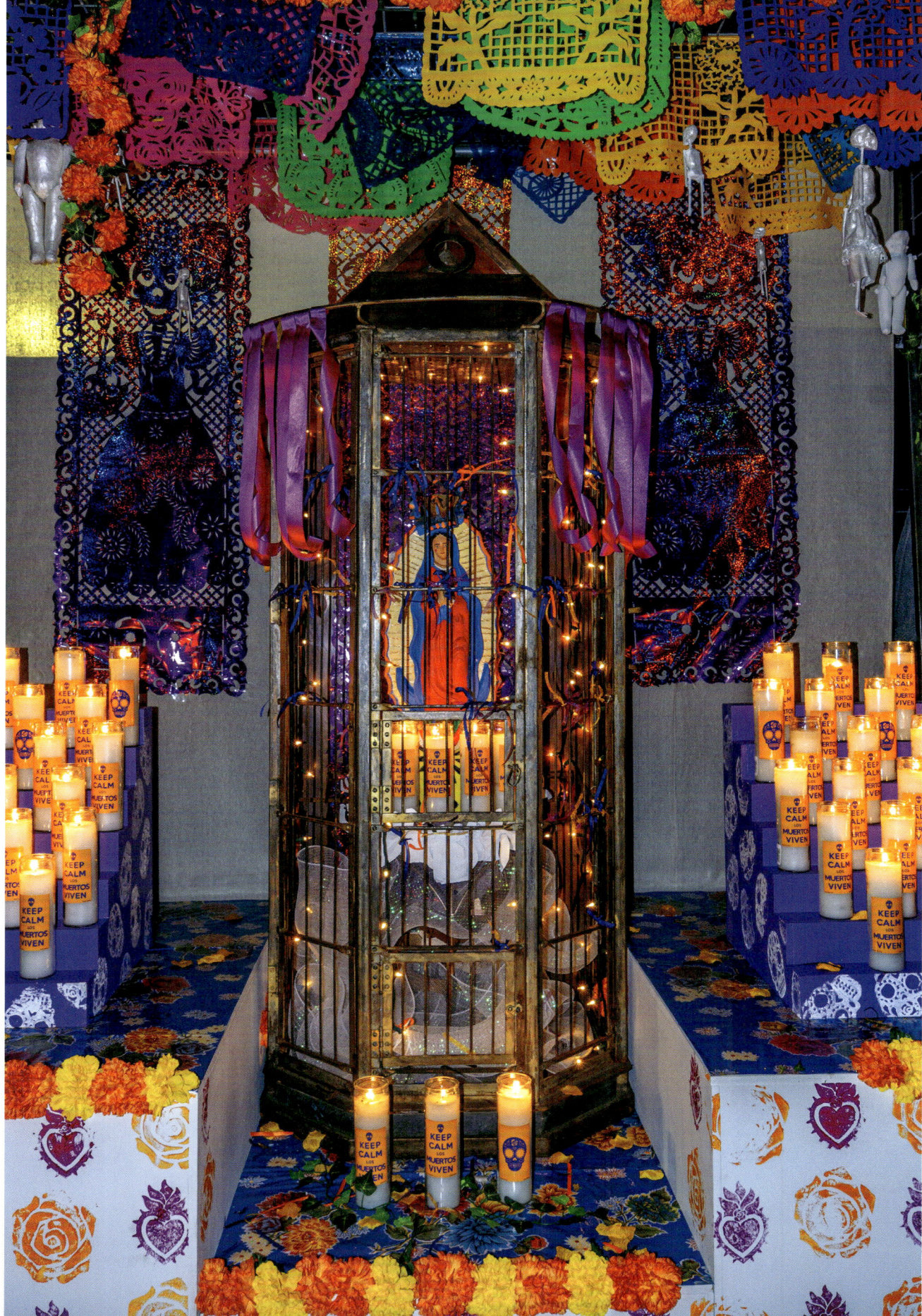

Revolutionary Women

Revolutionary Women of Texas and Mexico: Portraits of Soldaderas, Saints, and Subversives is an anthology of essays published in 2020. Sosa served as coeditor and coillustrator and created the cover illustration. She is now reinterpreting the illustrations as oil portraits. Series completion projected for 2025.

Illustrations for *Revolutionary Women of Texas and Mexico*
2020
Pen and ink
Cocreated with Lionel Sosa

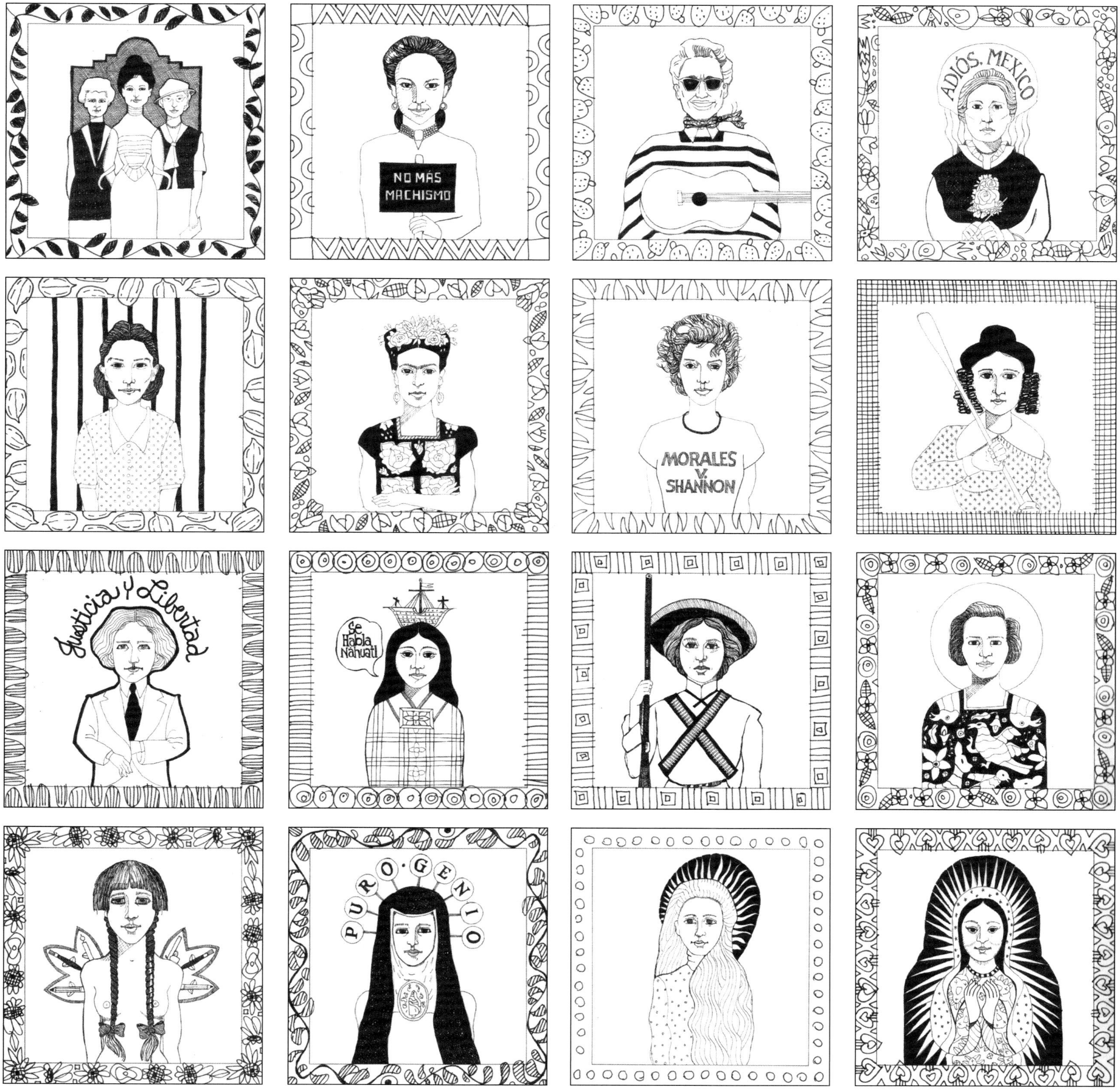

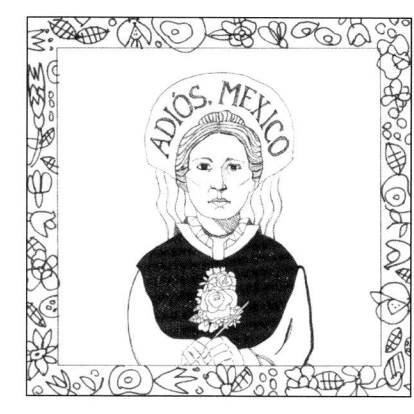
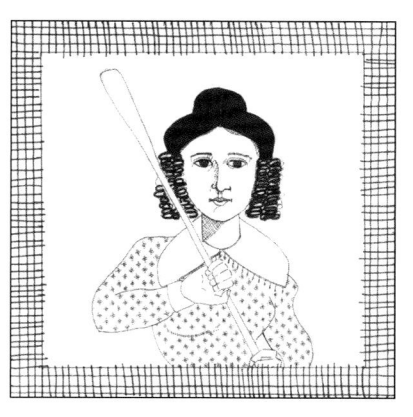
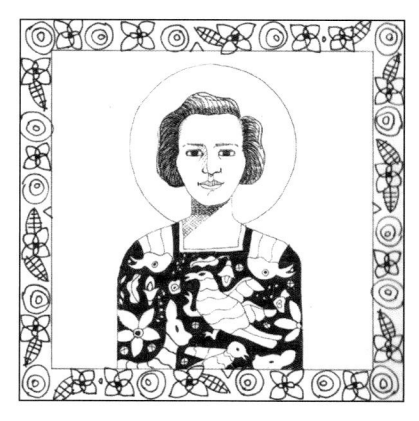
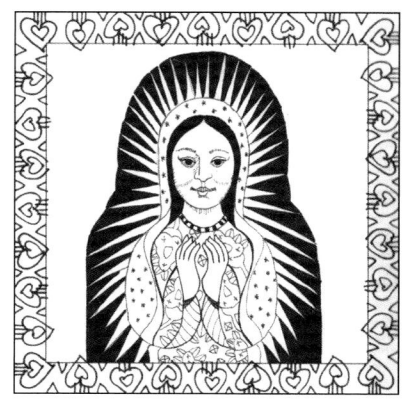
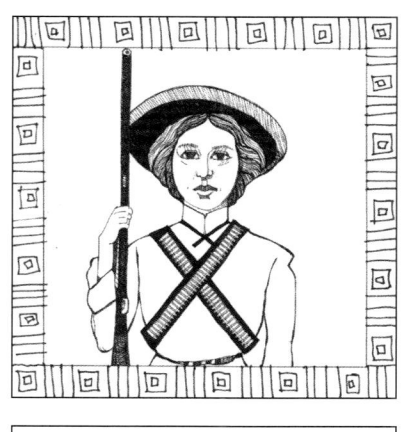
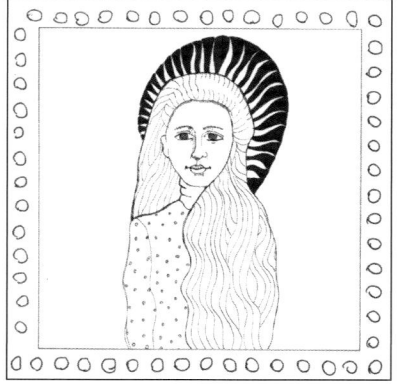
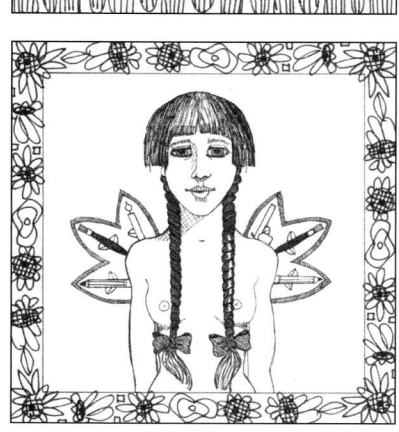
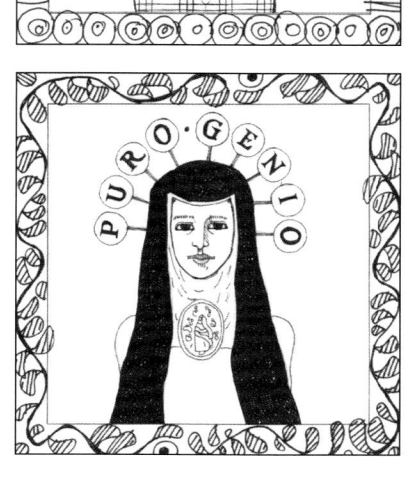

MESTIZAJE

Zapatista
2021
Oil on board
30 x 30 in.

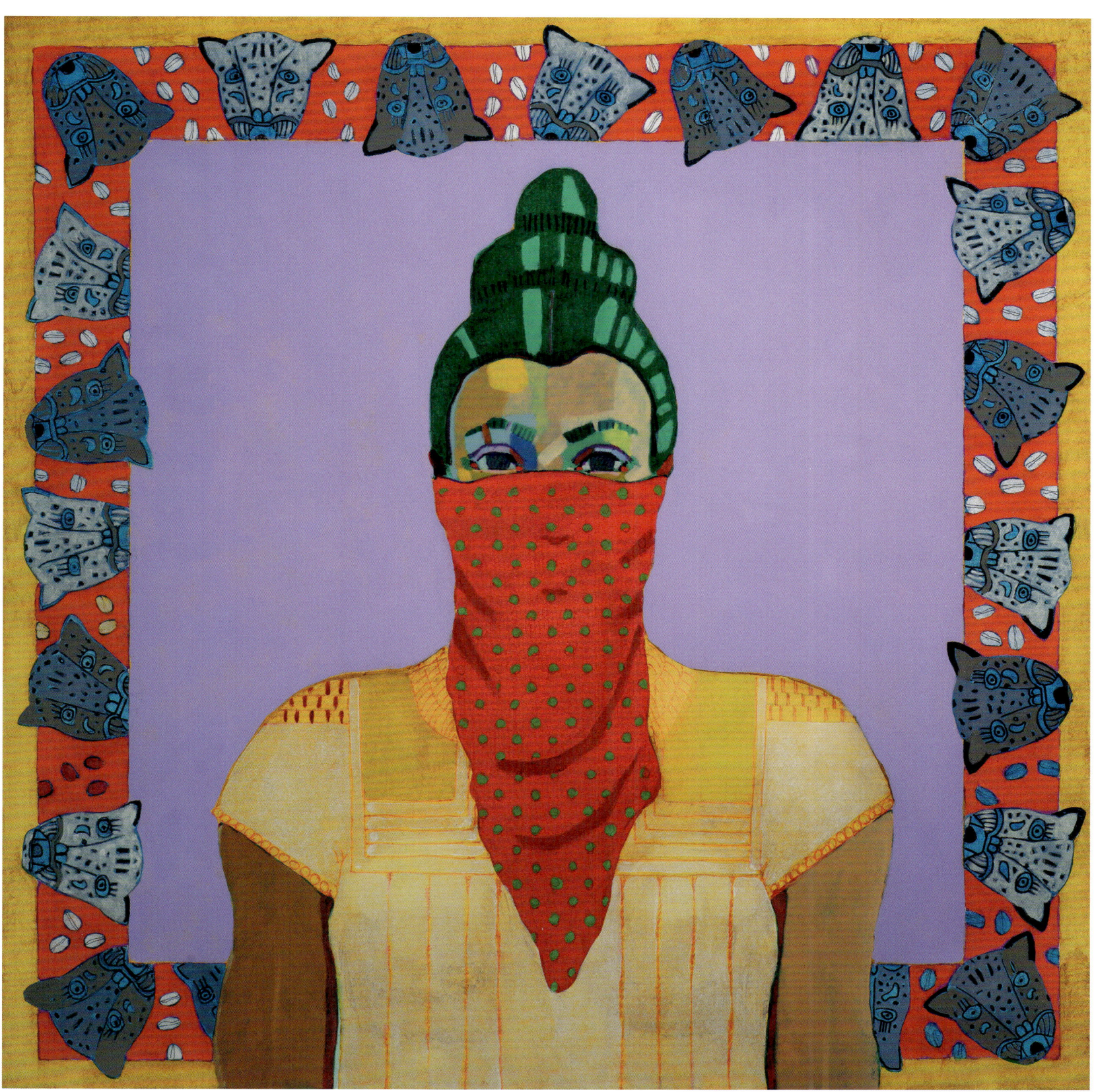

About the Artist

Artist Statement

These pieces, bold of palette and boldly feminine, are *puro mestizaje*, a total mix. They are a product of a borderland, where people have mixed and merged for centuries and formed a blended culture that has become uniquely our own. The artist is participant, observer, and celebrant in an emerging culture, with a particular vantage point. Dive in and meet family, friends, neighbors, acquaintances, real and imagined—all of whom rejoice in their *mexicanidad*, though very few were born in Mexico. Encounter the fibers, symbols, and icons of a thriving blended culture.

Declaración de la artista

Traducción por Tony Beckwith y Gabriela Gámez

Estas piezas, de paleta atrevida y audacia femenina, son puro mestizaje, una mezcla total. Fueron producidas en la región fronteriza donde los pueblos se han mezclado y fusionado durante siglos para formar una cultura mezclada que se define como totalmente nuestra. La artista es participante, observadora y celebrante en una cultura emergente con una perspectiva particular. Aquí se encontrará con familia, amigos, vecinos, conocidos —orgullosos todos ellos de su mexicanidad, aunque muy pocos nacieron en México—. Aquí conocerá las fibras, símbolos e íconos de una floreciente cultura mezclada.

On Becoming an Artist and the Mestizaje That Inspires Me

Kathy Sosa

As a child I was transplanted from the small-town segregated culture of the American Deep South into the blended culture of the Texas-Mexico borderland. There was a sudden feeling of finding home with the food, with the people, in a place where the music, the language, the cuisine, the colors, patterns, and rhythms exist in a form like that of no other place on planet Earth. To a child landing here in 1968, this environment seemed at once exotic and familiar. After almost sixty years, the fascination has never waned.

       In my part of the world . . .

       We speak Spanglish.

       We eat Tex-Mex.

       We sing and dance to Willie Nelson and Flaco Jiménez . . . sometimes at the same time.

       We have ancestral and cultural ties to both sides of the political divide known as the US-Mexico border, which of course has not always existed. Starting in 1521 and for three hundred years we were Nueva España. In 1821 we became the Mexican region of Coahuila y Tejas; that lasted fifteen years, until Texas achieved independence in 1836. The independence and later statehood of Texas established the current border, but by then the deed was done and, as they say, "What nature hath joined together no government can put asunder."

In Mexico, this blend of blood and culture is called *mestizaje*, and it is said to have begun with Hernán Cortés and his Indigenous translator Malinalli, known to many as La Malinche. Together they gave rise to what José Vasconcelos has dubbed *la raza cósmica*, "the cosmic race." This mestizaje continues to this day all around me in San Antonio. It sucked me in almost as soon as I arrived. I fell in love with it. I married it, twice. And I gave birth to two of its children. I have spent the last twenty-one years attempting to tell its stories on canvas, on paper, in public art, and with altar installations.

A self-taught artist, I began painting at age forty-eight after several careers, the longest of which was in Hispanic advertising. Hispanic advertising is the art of convincing US Latino consumers and voters to prefer the brands, services, and candidates that you are selling. The first job at an ad agency was to organize what turned out to be one of the country's first major traveling exhibitions of the works of Hispanic artists. This was an introduction to museum exhibitions and to the images, themes, and symbols of Hispanic culture as it is lived in the United States. Immediately moved, thunderstruck, and smitten, I've never gotten over it. To think that twenty years later I would walk back into this world as an artist myself was far beyond imagining.

After a run in the ad agency's public relations department, a job opened up where the magic happens: the creative department, the Holy Grail, heart and soul of any self-respecting ad agency, first as a copywriter and later as creative director. Here I discovered an appetite for conceptual frameworks that could support storytelling. In advertising parlance, these are called campaigns; later in my artistic life this became an itch to paint in series.

Participation in workshops with some notable figurative, realist teachers has been helpful along the way. Even though I don't trade in realism, their tutelage and advice have advanced my understanding of the craft. Having dabbled in printmaking, my intention is to someday master the tiny press in my studio. Papermaking has become a passion and has led to using handmade papers as a launchpad for mixed media storytelling.

Más o menos twenty-five years ago, on our first trip to the Mexican state of Oaxaca, I encountered and acquired my first huipil, the handwoven Mesoamerican garment made and worn by the Indigenous women of the region. This first one was soft with age and redolent with the stories of the women who had woven and worn it. It spoke to me as few things have. I covet, and when I can afford it, collect them obsessively to this day.

But it was on a visit to the Metropolitan Museum of Art in New York for the *Matisse: The Fabric of Dreams—His Art and His Textiles* exhibit, which was described as "the first exhibition to explore Henri Matisse's lifelong fascination with textiles and its profound impact on his art," that I began to imagine the integration of Mesoamerican textiles into art. Encountering his series of paintings of women in Romanian peasant blouses ignited a desire to paint women in huipiles (which, no offense to Monsieur Matisse or the Romanians, are much more colorful and richer with patterns than Romanian peasant blouses). Throughout Mesoamerica, huipiles are integral to culture, place, and identity. And so it was a joyful, though not altogether surprising, discovery that many women in my borderland hometown of San Antonio appreciated, studied, collected, and wore the huipil, some to celebrate their roots in Indigenous Mexico; others as a treasured symbol of our blended borderland culture; others because it was the most natural choice in the world; and still others for the sheer sake of their great beauty. This discovery led to some deep and abiding friendships along with a series of paintings of women of various colors and ethnicities donning huipiles, and a group show with the Smithsonian Latino Center.

Árboles de la vida, Trees of Life, are found in many cultures, but the most common and breathtaking are the ceramic árboles made by the masters of Mexican *arte popular*. The forms of the three-dimensional sculptures, when flattened to two dimensions, seemed the perfect platforms for communicating the lives and stories of the women around me. The sculptures and the women are endlessly inspiring, and together they tell us what real and imagined women are thinking, caring, or obsessing about at the imagined moment.

Sobre convertirme en artista y el mestizaje que me inspira

Kathy Sosa
Traducción por Tony Beckwith y Gabriela Gámez

Cuando era niña, fui reubicada de la cultura segregada de un pequeño pueblo del sur de Estados Unidos a la mezcla cultural de la zona fronteriza entre Texas y México. Hubo una repentina sensación de encontrar un hogar con la comida y con la gente; en un lugar donde la música, el idioma, la cocina, los colores, patrones y ritmos no existen de forma similar en ningún otro lugar del planeta Tierra. A una niña que aterrizó aquí en 1968, este lugar le parecía exótico y familiar al mismo tiempo. Después de casi sesenta años, la fascinación no ha disminuido jamás.

En mi parte del mundo…
Hablamos Spanglish.
Comemos comida Tex-Mex.
Cantamos y bailamos con Willie Nelson y el "Flaco" Jiménez… a veces, a la par.

Tenemos vínculos ancestrales y culturales con ambos lados de la división política conocida como la frontera entre Estados Unidos y México, que por supuesto no siempre ha existido. A partir de 1521 y durante trescientos años fuimos Nueva España. En 1821 nos convertimos en la región mexicana de Coahuila y Tejas, que duró quince años, hasta 1836, en que Texas logró su independencia. La independencia y posterior condición de Estado de Texas establecieron la frontera actual, pero para entonces la acción se había perpetrado y, como dice el dicho,

"Lo que la naturaleza ha unido ningún gobierno lo separe".

En México, a esta mezcla de sangre y cultura se le llama mestizaje y se dice que comenzó con Hernán Cortés y su traductora indígena Malinalli, conocida por muchos como La Malinche. Juntos dieron origen a lo que José Vasconcelos ha denominado "la raza cósmica". Este mestizaje continúa rodeándome hasta el día de hoy en San Antonio. Me absorbió casi tan pronto como llegué. Me enamoré de él. Me casé con él dos veces. Y di a luz a dos de sus hijos. He pasado los últimos veintiún años intentando contar sus historias en lienzo, papel, arte público e instalaciones de ofrendas y altares.

Una artista autodidacta, comencé a pintar a los cuarenta y ocho años después de varias carreras, la más larga de las cuales fue en publicidad hispana. La publicidad hispana es el arte de convencer a los consumidores y votantes latinos de Estados Unidos de que prefieran las marcas, los servicios y los candidatos que uno vende. El primer trabajo en la agencia de publicidad fue organizar lo que resultó ser una de las primeras exposiciones itinerantes importantes de obras de artistas hispanos en Estados Unidos. Esta fue una introducción a las exposiciones de los museos, así como a las imágenes, temas y símbolos de la cultura hispana tal como se vive en los Estados

Unidos. Inmediatamente conmovida, atónita y enamorada, nunca he logrado superarlo. Pensar que veinte años después volvería a este mundo como artista era mucho más allá de lo imaginable.

Después de trabajar en el departamento de relaciones públicas de la agencia de publicidad, se abrió un trabajo donde ocurre la magia: el departamento creativo, el Santo Grial, corazón y alma de cualquier agencia de publicidad que se precie de serlo —primero como redactora publicitaria y posteriormente como directora creativa—. Aquí descubrí un apetito por marcos conceptuales que pudieran apoyar la narración de historias. En el lenguaje publicitario, esto se llama "campañas", pero más adelante en mi vida artística esto se convirtió en un deseo de pintar en series.

La participación en talleres con algunos maestros figurativos y realistas notables ha sido útil en el camino. Aunque no oficio el realismo, su tutela y asesoramiento han avanzado mi comprensión del oficio. Habiendo incursionado en el grabado, mi intención es algún día dominar la pequeña prensa en mi estudio. La fabricación de papel se ha convertido en una pasión y ha llevado al uso de papeles hechos a mano como plataforma de lanzamiento para la narración en medios mixtos.

Hace más o menos veinticinco años, en nuestro primer viaje al Estado de Oaxaca, México, encontré y adquirí mi primer huipil, la prenda mesoamericana tejida a mano que confeccionan y usan las mujeres indígenas de la región. El primero era suave por el paso del tiempo y olía a las historias de las mujeres que lo habían tejido y usado. Me habló como pocas cosas. Hasta el día de hoy los codicio, y cuando puedo permitírmelo, los colecciono obsesivamente.

Pero fue en una visita al Museo Metropolitano de Arte de Nueva York para ver una exposición llamada *Matisse: The Fabric of Dreams—His Art and His Textiles*, descrita como "la primera exposición que explora la fascinación de toda la vida de Henri Matisse por los textiles y su profundo impacto en su obra", que por primera vez imaginé la integración de los textiles mesoamericanos en el arte. El encuentro con su serie de pinturas de mujeres con blusas campesinas rumanas encendió el deseo de pintar mujeres con huipiles (que, sin ofender al Monsieur Matisse ni a los rumanos, son mucho más coloridos y ricos en estampados que las blusas campesinas rumanas). En toda Mesoamérica, los huipiles son parte integral de la cultura, el lugar y la identidad. Así que fue un descubrimiento gozoso, aunque no del todo sorprendente, que hubiera muchas mujeres en mi ciudad fronteriza de San Antonio que apreciaban, estudiaban, coleccionaban y usaban el huipil, algunas para celebrar las raíces del México indígena, otras como un símbolo preciado de nuestra mezcla cultural fronteriza, otras porque era la elección más natural del mundo y otras simplemente por su gran belleza. Este descubrimiento condujo a algunas amistades profundas y duraderas, y a una serie de pinturas de mujeres de diversos colores y etnias vistiendo huipiles, así como a una exposición grupal en el Smithsonian Latino Center.

Los árboles de la vida se encuentran en muchas culturas, pero los más comunes e impresionantes son los árboles de cerámica hechos por los maestros del arte popular mexicano. Las formas de las esculturas tridimensionales, cuando se aplanaban a dos dimensiones, parecían la plataforma perfecta para comunicar las vidas y las historias de las mujeres a mi alrededor. Las esculturas y las mujeres son infinitamente inspiradoras; juntas nos dicen qué piensan, de qué se preocupan o se obsesionan estas mujeres, reales e imaginarias, en el momento imaginado.

Career Highlights

In 2007 Sosa began to explore the artistic expression of *mestizaje*, the blending of peoples, races, ethnicities, languages, ideas, habits, and cultures characterizing the Texas-Mexico border region that has been her home since childhood. She received national recognition for the result of that passion with the traveling exhibition *Huipiles: A Celebration*, which debuted at the Mexican Cultural Institute in Washington, DC, as part of the Smithsonian Latino Center's 2007 summer season, "Mexico at the Smithsonian," before traveling to the Museo Alameda in San Antonio in 2008. The year 2009 saw Sosa's one-woman show at San Antonio's Contemporary at Blue Star art space. Her work has since traveled the country and been featured on CNN and in *FiberArts, skirt!, San Antonio Woman*, the *San Antonio Express-News, Country Lifestyle*, and *Destinations*. It is available in San Antonio through AnArte Gallery.

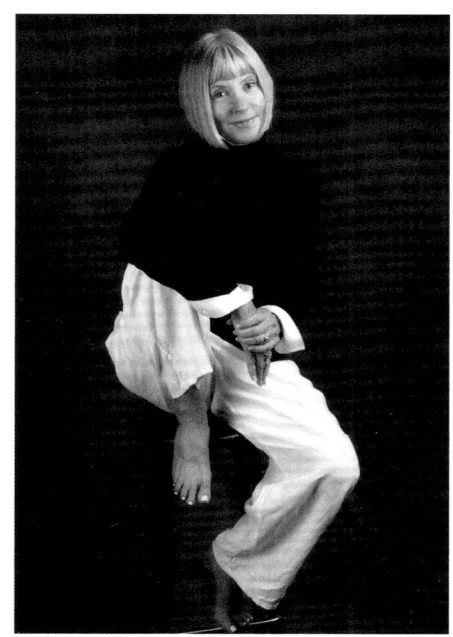

Photo by Ramin Samandari

2006, Texas Conference for Women, commissioned portrait, Martha Stewart, San Antonio, Texas

2007, "Mexico at the Smithsonian"/Mexican Cultural Institute, artist and curator, *Huipiles: A Celebration*, Washington, DC

2007–08, Museo Alameda, artist and curator, *Huipiles: A Celebration*, San Antonio, Texas

2008, Galeria Ortiz Contemporary, two-woman show, *Sosa/Prida Otra Vez*, San Antonio, Texas

2008, Shain Gallery, one-woman show, *Huipiles*, Charlotte, North Carolina

2008, Contemporary at Blue Star, Día de los Muertos altar exhibition, *Pan de anillo*, San Antonio, Texas

2008, Girl Scouts of Greater South Texas, commissioned painting for headquarters, *Retrato de Sally Cheever*, San Antonio, Texas

2009, Kchisos Gallery, one-woman show, Santa Fe, New Mexico

2009, Contemporary at Blue Star, one-woman show, *Trees of Life*, San Antonio, Texas

2009, UTSA Art Collection, multiple pieces, University of Texas at San Antonio, San Antonio, Texas

2010, SAY Sí, Día de los Muertos festival exhibition, San Antonio, Texas

2010, AnArte Gallery, *Kathy Sosa: Trees of Life*, San Antonio, Texas

2011, Contemporary at Blue Star, group exhibition, *Models and Mannequins*, San Antonio, Texas

2011, Palo Alto College Cultural Arts Gallery, two-person show, *Sosa y Sosa*, San Antonio, Texas

2011, AVANCE San Antonio, commissioned painting for headquarters boardroom, *Los Niños on My Mind*, San Antonio, Texas

2011, ArtPace Chalk It Up, showcase artist, outdoor arts festival, San Antonio, Texas

2011, KLRU-TV (Austin PBS), featured artist, *The Art of Día de los Muertos*, documentary produced and directed by Ed Fuentes

2012, Wichita Falls Museum of Art, *Kathy Sosa: Prints and Paintings*, Midwestern State University, Wichita Falls, Texas

2012, Texas A&M University–San Antonio, public collection, multiple paintings, San Antonio, Texas

2012, Voice for International Development and Adoption (VIDA), exhibition and fundraiser, Hudson, New York

2012–13, Robert and Frances Fullerton Museum of Art, *Kathy Sosa: Adornment and Identity*, California State University, San Bernardino, California

2013, James R. Reynolds Art Gallery, *Kathy Sosa: Prints and Paintings*, Texas A&M University, College Station, Texas

2013, Texas A&M University, artist in residence, College Station, Texas

2013, Arts SA, commissioned painting, *Tree of Life and Death: Rite of Spring on My Mind*, exhibited at McNay Art Museum, San Antonio, Texas

2013, Northwest Vista College, two-woman show, *Women's History Month Exhibition*, San Antonio, Texas

2013, Waterworks Visual Arts Center, one-woman show, *Adornment and Identity*, Salisbury, North Carolina

2013, NAO at the Pearl Brewery, one-woman show, *Latin American Flavors*, San Antonio, Texas

2014, Southwest School of Art, featured artist installation, Día de los Muertos, San Antonio, Texas

2014, Museum of the Southwest, one-woman show, *Identidad*, Midland, Texas

2014, Charles H. MacNider Art Museum, one-woman show, *Adornment and Identity*, Mason City, Iowa

2014, Anderson Center for the Arts, *Kathy Sosa*, Anderson, Indiana

2014, Texas A&M University–San Antonio, large-scale public art commission, *Jaguar on My Shoulder—Texas A&M San Antonio on My Mind*, San Antonio, Texas

2015, Polk Museum of Art, *Her Ethereal Self: Portraits by Kathy Sosa*, Florida Southern College, Lakeland, Florida

2015, Paul and Lulu Hilliard University Art Museum, one-woman show, *Her Self*, University of Louisiana at Lafayette, Lafayette, Louisiana

2015, Georgetown Art Center, group show, *Women Painting Women*, Georgetown, Texas

2015–16, Centro de Artes, two-woman show, *Sosa+Castillo: Trees of Life: Cultura, tradición e innovación*, San Antonio, Texas

2015–16, Goddard Center, one-woman show, Ardmore, Oklahoma

2016, Dock Space Gallery, two-person show, *Sosa+Sosa*, San Antonio, Texas

2016, Hotel Contessa, corporate commission for lobby, *La Contessa de San Antonio*, San Antonio, Texas

2016–17, Carver Community Cultural Center, group exhibition, *La entrada del espejo* [Entrance to the Mirror], San Antonio, Texas

2018, Plaza Club, two-person show, *Kathy & Lionel Sosa Show*, San Antonio, Texas

2018–present, *Keep Calm y Join Manos*, ongoing artivism project

2019, AnArte Gallery, *Kathy Sosa: 52*, San Antonio, Texas

2019, Galeria EVA, *Kathy Sosa: Árboles 2.0*, San Antonio, Texas

2019, City of San Antonio, Día de los Muertos celebration, featured artist, commissioned altars for Main Plaza and La Villita, San Antonio, Texas

2020, Texas Public Radio, large-scale art commission for headquarters on San Pedro Creek, San Antonio, Texas

2020, AnArte Gallery, *Keep Calm y Dream On—Artivism*, San Antonio, Texas

2020, Trinity University Press, *Revolutionary Women of Texas and Mexico: Portraits of Soldaderas, Saints, and Subversives*, cover design, coillustrator, and coeditor

2021, Centro San Antonio, Art Everywhere Project, selected artist, *Keep Calm et Macar-On*, San Antonio, Texas

2021, Bexar County and San Antonio River Authority, selected artist (with Lionel Sosa), five-panel tile mural for San Pedro Creek Culture Park, *La Gloriosa Historia de San Pedro Creek on My Mind*, San Antonio, Texas

2021, City of San Antonio Department of Arts and Cultural Affairs, selected artist, public mural for Maverick Plaza at La Villita, *La Santa Gastronomía de San Antonio*, San Antonio, Texas

2021–22, University of Texas at Rio Grande Valley, commission for permanent art collection, painting donated by Sandra Cisneros, *Gloria Anzaldúa*, Edinburg, Texas

2024, Trinity University Press, *Mestizaje: The Feminist Art of Kathy Sosa*, with a foreword by Sandra Cisneros and essays by Kathy Sosa, Ricardo Romo, Carla Stellweg, and Jennifer Speed

2024, *El otro lado del espejo*, coproducer, four-part documentary series

2024, Instituto Cultural Mexicano, group exhibition, *Las muñecas del calle Guadalupe*, San Antonio, Texas

2024–25, Museo de Arte de Querétaro, *El otro lado del espejo: San Antonio Artists in Querétaro*, Querétaro, Mexico

About the Essayists

Sandra Cisneros

Sandra Cisneros is internationally acclaimed for her poetry and fiction, which have been translated into twenty-five languages. She is the recipient of numerous awards, including National Endowment for the Arts Literature Fellowships in poetry and fiction, a MacArthur Fellowship, the Texas Medal of Arts Award, the PEN/Nabokov Award for Achievement in International Literature, and the National Medal of Arts. She lives in San Miguel de Allende.

Sandra Cisneros es internacionalmente aclamada por su poesía y su ficción, que han sido traducidas a veinticinco idiomas. Ha recibido numerosos premios, como becas en poesía y ficción del National Endowment for the Arts, una beca de la Fundación MacArthur, la Medalla de Artes de Texas, el PEN/Nabokov Award for Achievement in International Literature y la Medalla Nacional de las Artes de Estados Unidos. Actualmente reside en San Miguel de Allende.

Ricardo Romo

Ricardo Romo is an urban historian and the author of *East Los Angeles: History of a Barrio*. He writes a weekly column for *La Prensa Texas* and blogs for *Latinopia*, and he is the publisher of *Latinos in America*, a Substack newsletter. He served as the president of the University of Texas at San Antonio from 1999 to 2017 and lives in San Antonio.

Ricardo Romo es un historiador urbano y el autor de *East Los Angeles: History of a Barrio*. Escribe una columna semanal para *La Prensa Texas* y un blog para *Latinopia*, y es el editor de *Latinos in America*, un boletín de Substack. Sirvió como presidente de la Universidad de Texas en San Antonio de 1999 a 2017, y vive en San Antonio.

Jennifer Speed

Jennifer Speed is a research development strategist at Princeton University and has taught undergraduate history and theology courses for more than twenty years. Her work has been supported by the American Historical Association, the Spanish government, the National Endowment for the Humanities, and the Andrew W. Mellon Foundation. She is a native of San Antonio.

Jennifer Speed es una estratega de desarrollo de investigación en la Universidad de Princeton y ha enseñado clases en historia y teología a nivel universitaria durante más de veinte años. Su trabajo ha sido apoyado por la American Historical Association, el gobierno español, la Fundación Nacional para las Humanidades y la Fundación Andrew W. Mellon. Ella es nativa de San Antonio.

Carla Stellweg

Carla Stellweg is an independent consultant specializing in Latin American and Latinx art and a professor of art history at the School of Visual Arts in New York City. She has worked as a director of museums and nonprofit organizations, writer, editor, and curator, and she is an occasional visiting professor at the National Autonomous University of Mexico and the Monterrey Institute of Technology and Higher Learning.

Carla Stellweg es una especialista independiente en el ámbito del arte y los artistas latinoamericanos y Latinx, y es profesora de historia del arte en la Escuela de Artes Visuales en Nueva York. A lo largo de su carrera ha ejercido como directora de museos y entidades sin fines de lucro, escritora, editora y curadora, y a veces se desempeña como profesora visitante en la Universidad Nacional Autónoma de México y en el Instituto Tecnológico y de Estudios Superiores de Monterrey, México.

Acknowledgments

The artist wishes to acknowledge the friends, colleagues, collectors, and patrons whose encouragement has brought to light the works featured in this book. First among them: my partner and love of my life, Lionel, who supports me in every way and without whom I would not be an artist. Special thanks to teachers Nelson Shanks and Kerry Dunn, as well as Colaboradora Creativa charter members Sandra Cisneros and Ellen Riojas Clark, fellow *huipilistas* de San Antonio, and shameless early supporter Betty Gaddis Yndo. I greatly appreciate institutional collectors, including Maria Ferrier, Texas A&M University–San Antonio, University of Texas at San Antonio, Our Lady of the Lake University, Texas Public Radio, the City of San Antonio, and the County of Bexar.

Thanks to Chuck Maurer for his invaluable technical genius and Edgar Ortiz for his immense design talents. I appreciate early collectors Patricia Diaz Dennis, Joe Hoang, and Margaret Kanyusik, as well as career advisers Ana Montoya, Sandra Higgins, Gabriela Gámez, and Katherine C. Carter.

Special thanks to Pilar O'Leary who, during her tenure as director of the Smithsonian Latino Center, chose to present our exhibition *Huipiles: A Celebration*. I owe a debt to all the women and families who design, weave, embroider, and fabricate intricate and breathtaking Mesoamerican textiles and who have created magnificent *árboles de la vida* for generations.

My immense gratitude is due to those of particular importance to the success of this book: the Tobin Endowment, Carolyn and Hal Adams, Kelley and Pat Frost, Frosted Home, Robert K. Brown and Dennis Karbach, Rocio and Ron Heller, Karen Lee Zachry, and the Tiny Finch.

*Good Girl, Bad Girl: Portrait
of Margaret Kanyusik* (detail)
2009
Oil on canvas
30 x 30 in.

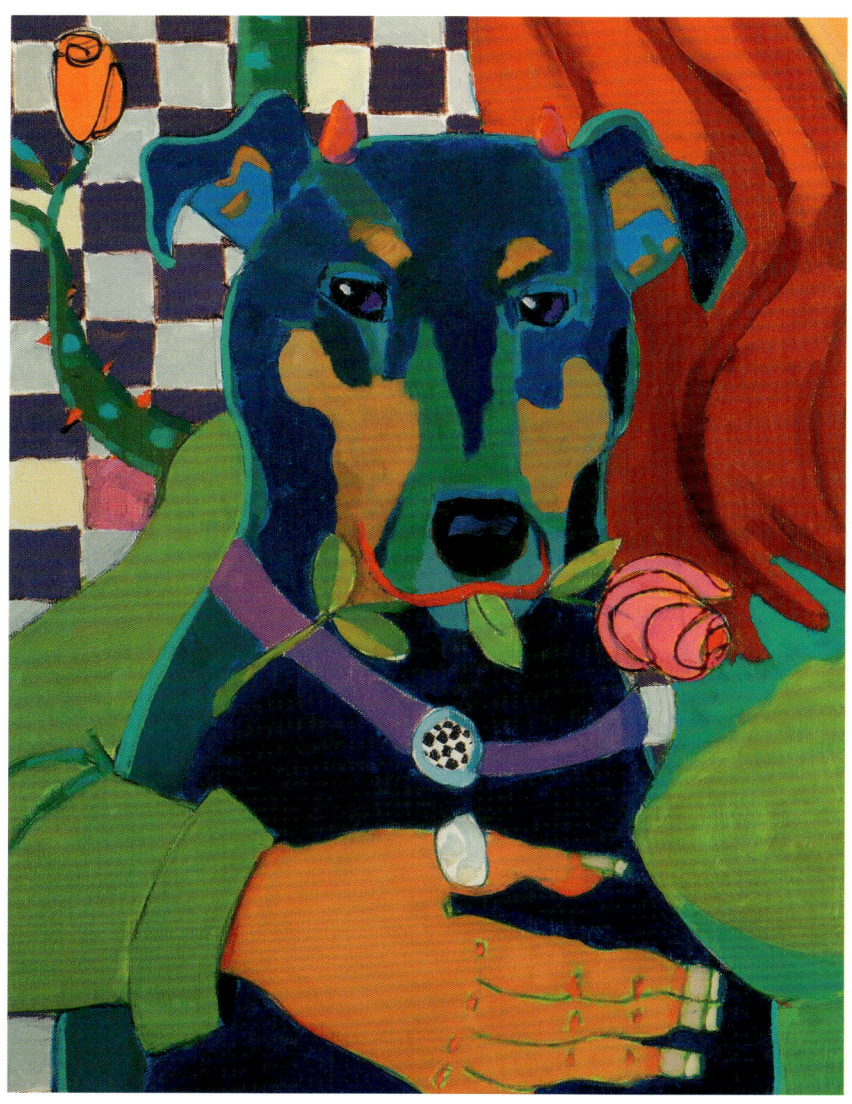

Morning Coffee (detail)
2003
Oil portrait collage
24 x 24 in.

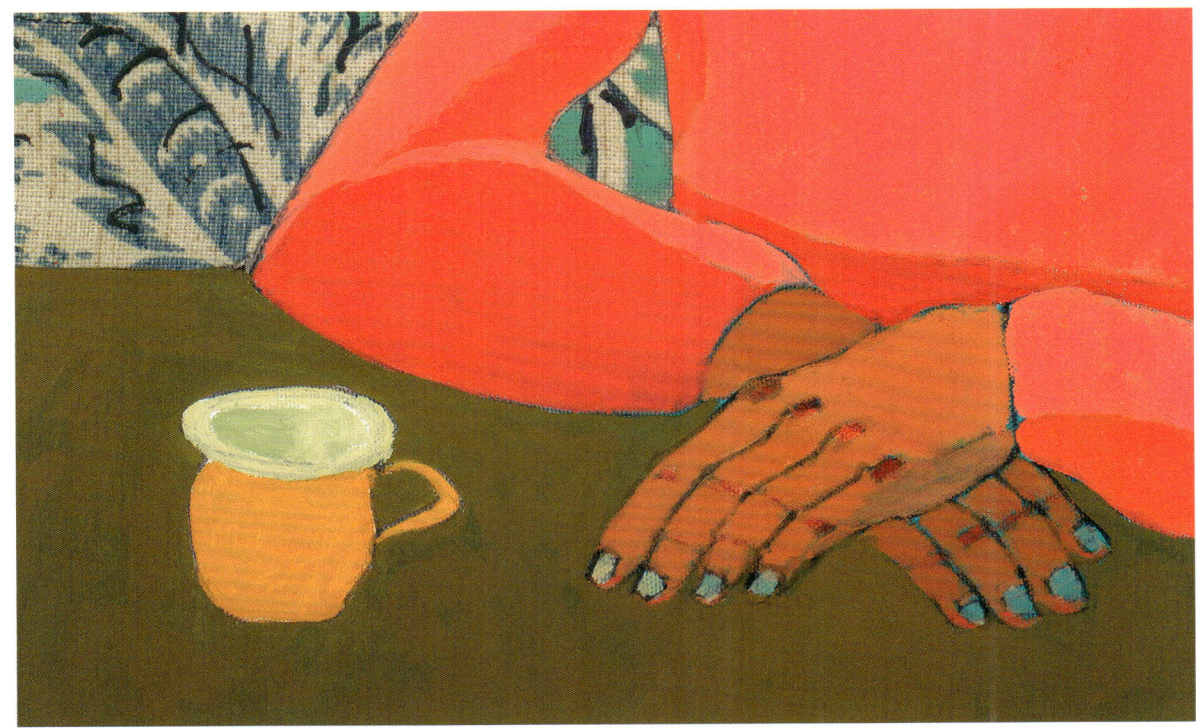

The Celllist
2006
Oil on canvas
30 x 30 in.

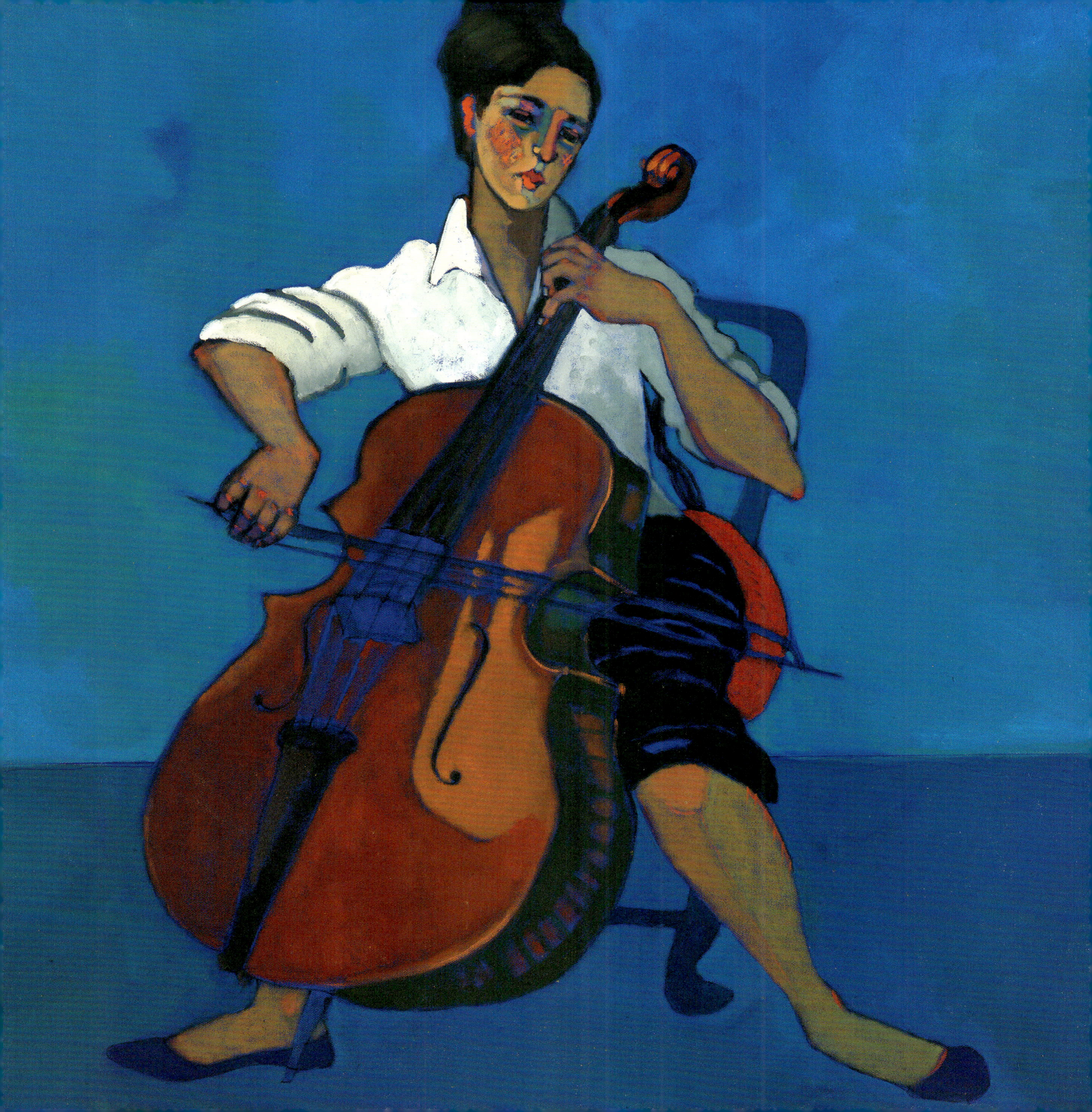